The New Cycle and New Finance in China

Shusong Ba

The New Cycle and New Finance in China

厦门大学出版社 XIAMEN UNIVERSITY PRESS 国家一级出版社 全国百佳图书出版单位

Springer

Shusong Ba
Hong Kong, People's Republic of China

Translated by
Feng Yue
College of Foreign Languages
Fujian Normal University
Fuzhou, China

Yongzhong Qiu
College of Foreign Languages
Fujian Normal University
Fuzhou, China

Zhongwu Luo
Department of English and International Studies
China Foreign Affairs University
Beijing, China

Xiujuan Xie
College of Foreign Languages
Fujian Normal University
Fuzhou, China

ISBN 978-981-16-8208-7 ISBN 978-981-16-8209-4 (eBook)
https://doi.org/10.1007/978-981-16-8209-4

Jointly published with Xiamen University Press
The print edition is not for sale in China (Mainland). Customers from China (Mainland) please order the print book from: Xiamen University Press.

This Springer imprint is published by the registered company Springer Nature Singapore Pte Ltd.
The registered company address is: 152 Beach Road, #21-01/04 Gateway East, Singapore 189721, Singapore

Preface

In recent years, I have worked in different cities such as Beijing, New York and Hong Kong and engaged in different jobs, such as being a visiting scholar at a university, a researcher at a government think tank, being engaged in the specific operation and management of financial institutions, as well as conducting the research work of trade associations and societies. However, from the nature of work, it is consistent, that is, I have been involved in some specific financial policies and market activities with the mentality of researchers, observers and thinkers and have tried to identify problems worthy of consideration for follow-up analysis. It is my original intention of compiling this book to sort out these analyses and experiences from time to time and share them with readers.

In the financial market, one of the key reasons why experience is important is that the market is often driven by various forces, showing periodic reciprocating fluctuations, with the experience of the previous cycle often providing some reference for the next new cycle. At the same time, each cycle is different, that is to say, each economic cycle can be said to be a new cycle in a specific sense. As an observer and researcher of financial market, it is natural to think more about the new changes in the financial industry under different economic cycles. This is why the book is entitled *The New Cycle and New Finance*.

At present, China's economic development is entering a new era, when in the financial system supported by high-speed growth since the reform and opening up, with the decline of economic growth from high-speed to medium-high-speed growth, and the monetization process gradually coming to an end, the original financial growth model is bound to face adjustment and may show a trend of gradual release of risks under the new growth environment. In particular, when the macrogrowth gradually stabilizes, the economic structure is greatly divided. The risks of some enterprises with overcapacity have not been cleared, high-quality enterprises are still in the process of cultivation, and the rise of emerging financial institutions has brought increasingly fierce competition. It is difficult for the traditional financial system to find quality customers and assets. In order to pursue profit growth, financial institutions may choose to let some funds circulate within the financial system, resulting in various financial chaos. From the perspective of the development law of the financial system itself, finance has certain procyclicality, that is, in the upward cycle of economic operation, with the strong financing demands and rising asset prices, the financial system will also move toward an upward channel, and the prosperity of the financial system will further promote economic prosperity and asset prices. However, in the downward cycle of economic operation, asset prices have shrunk, business conditions of enterprises have deteriorated, financing needs have been shrinking, and the financial system will also enter the downward cycle, which will lead to further economic downturn. Although the transformation of economic development modes does not mean that the economy will inevitably enter a downward cycle, in order to reduce the pain and continue to maintain a high profit level in the adjustment process of economic development mode transformation, the financial industry may move toward a high-risk self-leverage stage.

In this context, macrofinancial policies pay more and more attention to risk prevention. Under such a new market environment and policy tone, the financial industry may face a reshuffle or a comprehensive test of the original business model. After a high-risk stage of chaos, under the external constraints of strong supervision, the financial industry will also undergo tremendous development mode and structural adjustment and then gradually realize the high-quality development of the financial industry. Since the 19th National Congress of the Communist Party of China has taken prevention and resolution of major risks as a decisive battle in the three major ones of building a moderately prosperous society in all respects, financial risk is naturally considered as one of the most prominent major risks. According to the *Plan for Deepening the Reform of Party and State Institutions,* recently issued by the Central Committee of the Communist Party of China, the traditional financial management system of "one bank, three commissions" (People's Bank of China, China Banking Regulatory Commission, China Securities Regulatory Commission and China Insurance Regulatory Commission) has been broken. The CBRC and the CIRC will merge to form the China Banking and Insurance Regulatory Commission, and the responsibility of drafting important laws and regulations on banking and insurance and the basic system of prudent supervision will be assigned to the People's Bank of China. As can be expected, under the new financial management system, attention will be paid to the shadow banking business that is outside the scope of supervision under the original supervision system, financial institutions and businesses with unclear regulatory responsibilities, unclear regulatory subjects and overlapped or repeated supervision, cross-financial fields that are constrained by their respective regulatory authorities and cannot be effectively supervised, and financial businesses that are engaged in the same type of business but have inconsistent regulatory standards and are prone to regulatory arbitrage, which are the main manifestations of financial chaos at present. Against the background of risk prevention, strong supervision and chaos control, the financial industry will gradually step into a new stage of re-establishment and improvement of rules, gradual release and exposure of risks, reshuffle and transformation of the industry from the early stage of high risk and leverage.

In the reshuffle of the industry, if we can gain insight into the transformation of economic development modes, the financial system can find new development opportunities. Deleveraging can be said to be the driving force for reshuffling the financial industry. How to take the initiative in the industry reshuffle is the key for financial institutions to reconstruct the market structure in the next step. At present, macropolicies pay more and more attention to the shift of the main contradiction in Chinese society into the one between the people's ever-growing needs for a better life and the unbalanced and inadequate development. From a macroeconomic point of view, the unbalanced and insufficient part in China's economy can be said to be the focus of future economic transformation, also be the most likely to form a new economic growth point in the future, and at the same time, and have the greatest potential to become the main object of financial services. On the one hand, residents' consumption is accelerating and upgrading, and how to strengthen financial services in the field of consumer finance will become an important direction for financial institutions' business expansion in the near future; on the other hand, scientific and technological innovation has entered an active period, and scientific and technological innovations such as blockchain and big data have gradually changed our lifestyles and financial services. It can be predicted that the development of these financial technologies will become the main factors to promote financial innovation for a long time to come.

How to conform to the law of economic development and find a new direction of financial development in the new economic cycle is the main content of this book. This book mainly presents some of my papers, reports, essays and speeches as a financial practitioner, with some of the papers completed by my students and me, and much content a result of our discussions. Thanks to Xiamen University Press and Editor-in-Chief Song Wenyan, for it was their supervision that gave me the motivation to assemble these articles into a book. I would also like to express my gratitude to many leaders, experts and scholars in the financial industry who have provided me with a lot of valuable information and suggestions in the process of writing and compiling this book, whose names will not be listed one by one here. Although a great deal of energy has been put into the writing of this book, due to the limited professional level, mistakes and deficiencies are inevitable. Experts are welcome to correct them in order for me to make continuous improvement in the future follow-up research.

Hong Kong, People's Republic of China
March 2018

Shusong Ba

Contents

Part I
Macro Economy and Financial System

Chapter 1
Has China's Economy Reached a Turning Point?

China's economic data have been moderately positive since the beginning of 2017. Its economic growth has been slightly better than expected. Exports and domestic consumption have improved, and gains have been made in other areas as well. As a result of this short-term upturn, there has been considerable debate about whether China's economy is entering a "new growth cycle". But from a structural perspective, the economy does not really possess factors contributing to a significant rise in economic growth in the longer term. At the same time, the recovery of the global economy remains weak, and anti-globalization sentiment is spreading. China's current economic situation should be seen as something closer to renewed volatility rather than the beginning of a new and more robust economic cycle.

1.1 China's Economy Itself is Still Clearing up

A new cycle requires a reshaping of the demand and supply side of the economic growth picture. At present, China's financial system and economy as a whole are undergoing fluctuations in the process of shedding inventories. This is not the start of a new cycle.

Economic cycle marks the change in the rhythm of the macroeconomic system. Therefore, we need to broaden our horizon and analyze the factors that affect economic growth in order to judge whether a new cycle begins. Domestic and international business economic cycles show that the start of a new cycle often requires low factor prices, low capital costs and new growth points. Among them, low factor prices mainly depend on the long-term impact of population growth, the improvement of labor productivity, the promotion of one-time decline in the cost of production and a relative revaluation of human capital as a result of new technological breakthroughs. Low capital prices are reflected in the reforms that produce financial deleveraging and expand new financing channels in addition to cuts in interest rates and the bank deposit ratio. What is more noteworthy is that the start of a new cycle requires

S. Ba, *The New Cycle and New Finance in China*,
https://doi.org/10.1007/978-981-16-8209-4_1

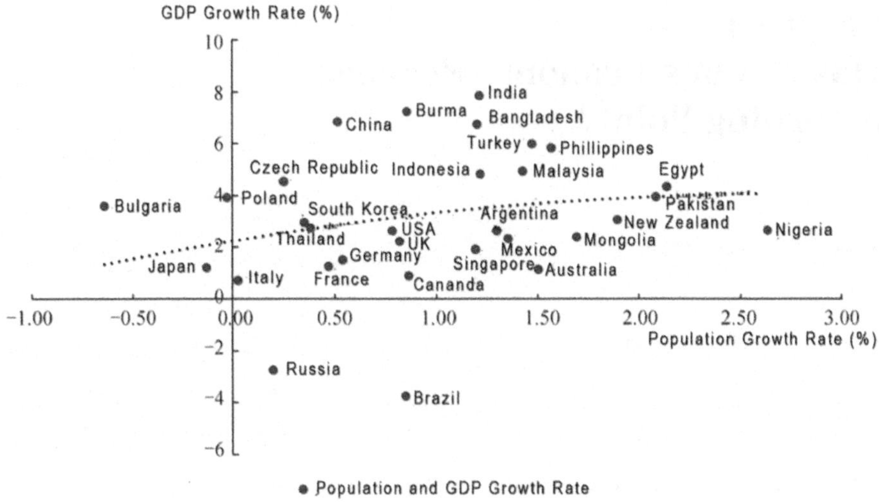

Fig. 1.1 Population and growth across the globe. *Source* Wind Information

the exploration of new growth points to stimulate demand and form a long-term sustainable economic growth momentum.

Firstly, one of the channels influencing domestic factor prices is the long-term population growth, while the decline in the labor supply caused by China's aging population has exerted a direct impact on the potential output of the economy (see Fig. 1.1). In 2010, China saw a turning point in demographic dividend: The growth of the working age population (individuals from 15 to 64 years of age) continued to decline, indicating an aging population. This has a direct impact on the marginal changes of the demand and supply of the labor force. On the supply side, the marginal decline of the labor force will affect the stock of human capital and further affect the price of labor; on the demand side, the marginal reduction of the total population will have a structural impact on the demand for housing in the medium and long term.

Solution to the problem of an aging population affecting economic growth lies in the improvement of the quality of human capital through structural reform. Take Japan, which has the most serious problem of an aging population, as an example. Although the decline in the size of the labor force has had a negative impact on Japan's economic growth, the improvement in the quality of human capital is also making a positive contribution to its economic growth momentum (see Fig. 1.2). At present, it has been confirmed that China's population is already aging. The irreversibility of aging will make the labor costs relatively high over the longer term. Therefore, the factor prices do not support the start of a new cycle before the introduction of major reforms to further improve the labor supply structure.

Secondly, from the perspective of capital, the current domestic financing costs are still at a relatively higher level compared with the historical levels. One of the reasons for the rise in financing costs is the complexity of financing channels. Therefore, before substantial progress is made in deleveraging the economic and financial

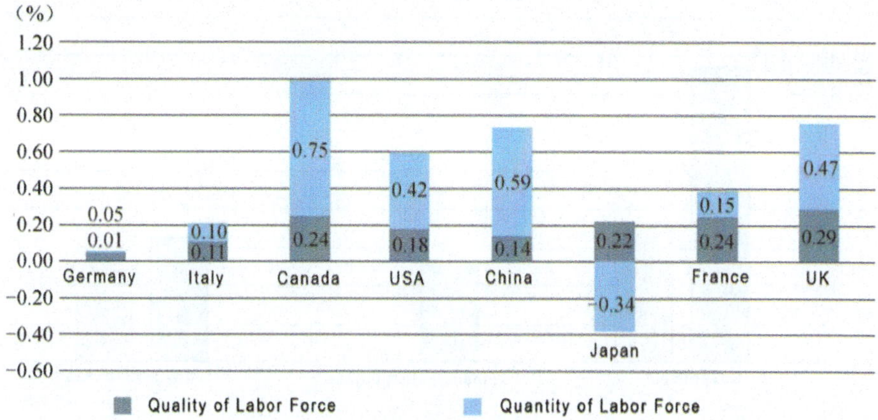

Fig. 1.2 Contribution of labor force to economic growth. *Source* The Conference Board Total Economy Database

systems, the financial environment may promote short-term economic recovery, but not enough to create a new economic cycle. In recent years, China has seen rapid development of the financial sector with numerous types of financial institutions gaining footholds. The problem brought about by the excessive prosperity of the financial industry is the lag time from the activities of the financial sector to affect the real economy. After more links and institutions sharing the funds, the financing costs of the real economy will also rise (see Fig. 1.3). The essence of financial deleveraging is to dismantle this elongated link and promote the transparency of the

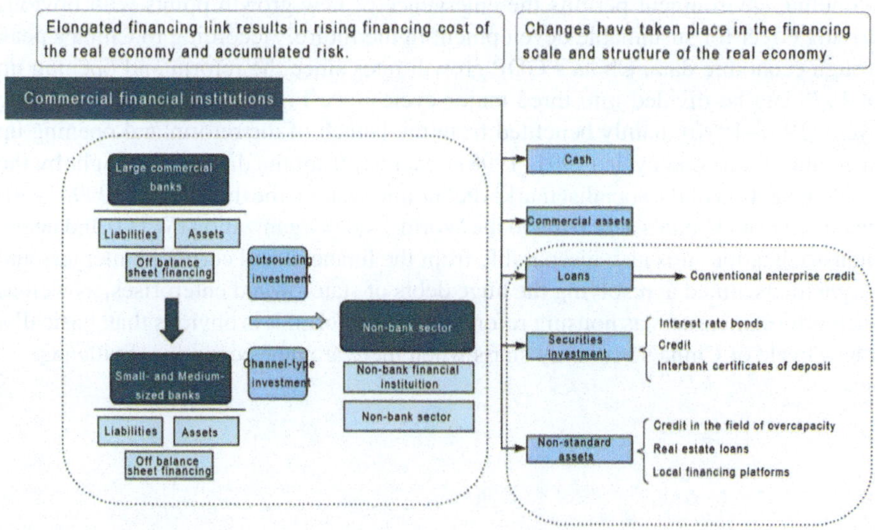

Fig. 1.3 Elongated link of finance and the necessity of deleveraging

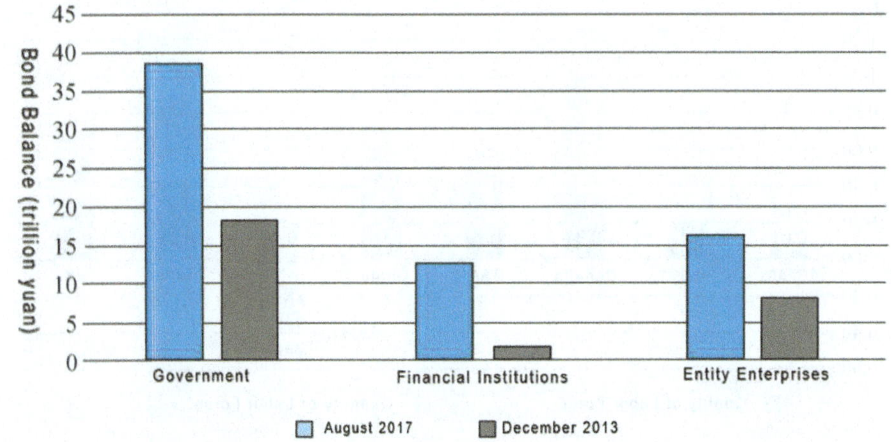

Fig. 1.4 Capital flows during the period of bond market leverage. *Source* Wind Information

whole transaction process; however, due to the cross cutting between the leverages of the financial sector and that of the real sector (see Fig. 1.4), excessive financial deleveraging could cause corresponding upward pressure on corporate financing.

Under the current dual goals set by policymakers of achieving steady growth and controlling risks, there is great need for controlling leveraging and easing pressure on corporate financing. It is clear that funding costs cannot be reduced overnight. In this sense, only when financing channels are broadened and further deleveraging has been achieved can it be said that a new cycle is about to begin.

Finally, the emergence of a new cycle depends on whether the internal and external economic environment permits the emergence of new growth points with obvious driving effect for sustainable development in the future. According to China's peak trough economic data, China's GDP growth rates since the reform and opening up in 1978 can be divided into three major cycles (see Fig. 1.5). The first economic cycle (1981–1990) mainly benefited from the launch of the reform and opening up program; the second cycle (1991–1998) benefited from the dividend brought by the implementation of the socialist market economic system; the third cycle (1999–1990) benefited from China's accession to the World Trade Organization (WTO) and heavy industrialization. It is also inseparable from the financial and corporate mergers and acquisitions aimed at resolving the huge debts of state-owned enterprises, as well as such reform measures as housing reform and tax reform. It is obvious that, basically, a new cycle of China's economy starts when there are new economic dividends.

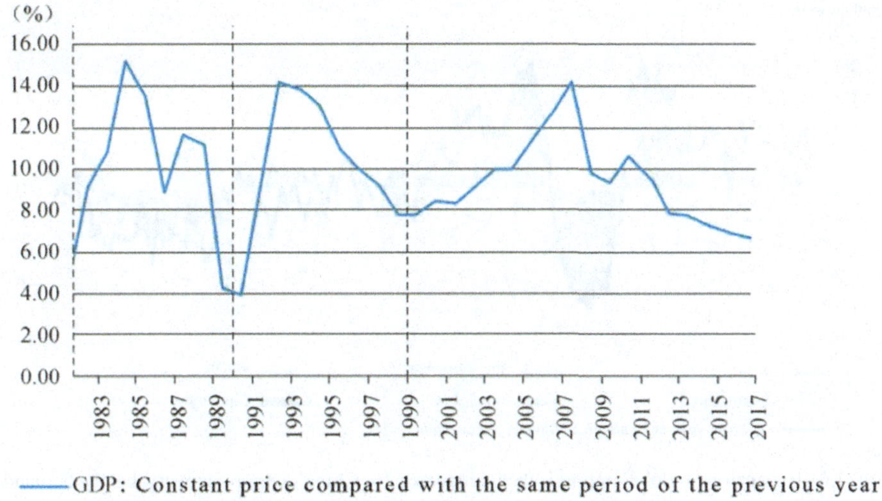

Fig. 1.5 Data of China's economic growth. *Source* Wind Information

1.2 Unclear Global Economic Cycle

The world is witnessing slow economic recovery, and there is no evidence of a new cycle of the global economy. This will inject volatility into China's economy.

China's economic development and the transformation of world economic growth through globalization are intertwined. Economic and financial globalization has increased interdependence, increasing the likelihood of a global impact from shocks to any major component of the global system. Even the current trend against further globalization has not reversed this trend of deeper economic integration. China's economic growth is an important contributor to global growth, but it is subject to a continuing global economic rotation. Over the longer term, macroeconomic growth of countries around the world will display a considerable amount of synchronization and mutual influence.

The health of the export sector contributed to China's recent economic recovery. The United States took the lead in the global economic recovery, and the European Union has also regained its economic footing. A stable global economy formed the basis of a recovery in China's domestic trade. But the outlook for long-term stability of the global economy is not all that reassuring. At present, the global recovery is mainly attributed to the super loose monetary policies of the developed economies. The economy of the United States and the European Union is still not entirely at pre-crisis levels, while Japan and emerging market countries are still undergoing weak recovery. In view of the increasing synchronization of the global economy, the weak recovery of the global economy is a significant obstacle to a new cycle for China's economy (Figs. 1.6 and 1.7).

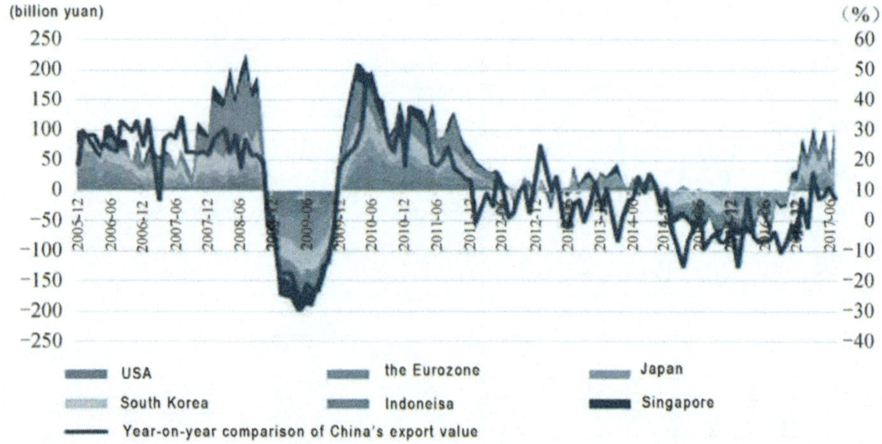

Fig. 1.6 Expansion of global import is the main reason for China's export recovery, but the demand of major economies is still weaker than the pre-crisis level. *Source* Wind Information

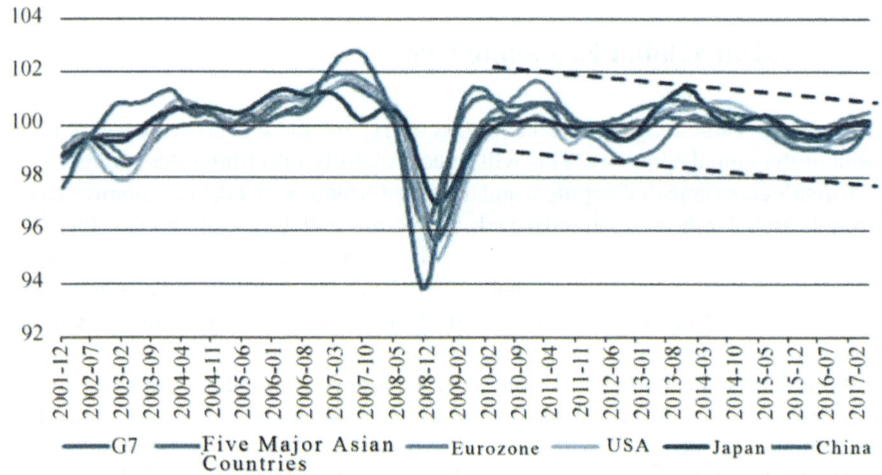

Fig. 1.7 Comprehensive leading indicators of major OECD countries have not reached the pre-crisis level. *Source* Wind Information

From the perspective of longer-term supply factors, only limited progress has been made in adjusting the global economic structure. The world is facing labor productivity bottlenecks brought about by an aging population. Moreover, there is a need to deal with problems stemming from the accumulation of state debt under an outdated economic model and low interest rates, coupled with low levels of investment. In addition, research shows that in periods of sluggish economy, structural reforms and monetary or fiscal stimulus will have an effect on the economic performance, but it is difficult to determine the time required. The policies may achieve results after they have been implemented for years, and it is unclear when there will be new growth points to create an impetus for a new global economic cycle.

1.3 New Cycle and the Third Path Beyond Hard Landing

Judging from China's economy and the external environment, we can see that the economy has not started a new cycle, and it is not likely to have a hard landing, either. The current Chinese economy is more likely to follow a third path, that is, the growth continues to show relative weakness and fluctuates within a narrow band.

From a historical point of view, the start of a new cycle often calls for major structural reforms which tend to be a drag on economic growth in the short term. This suggests that the prerequisites for the economy to start a new cycle are not an absolute increase in growth in the short term, but rather the enhancement of the economy's ability to prevent risks and recession.

Since 2016, significant progress has been made in reversing deflation as a result of the efforts to reduce industrial overcapacity and the need to protect the environment from some types of production. In 2017, strengthened environmental regulations have helped improve corporate earnings and repaired balance sheets. This has set the stage for structural reforms. But China is still facing industrial overcapacity and distortions in capital allocation, while it is also facing the problems of unreasonable income and industrial structures. The economy remains too heavily dependent on the real estate and infrastructure. Sustainable and efficient investment driven by new demand or new technology has not yet emerged in sufficient quantities. Support for economic growth is still relatively fragile. Therefore, the current form of China's economy is more likely to maintain a steady growth within a narrow range. Bankruptcies and government assistance are likely to resolve some of the economic distortions as well as the mismatch between the real economy and financial markets. Further efforts should be made to repair the national balance sheet and optimize the nation's economic structure if China is to build a healthier economic and financial environment.

Changes in the driving forces of an economy are closely linked to the state of a nation's economic development. A shift of economic drivers will inevitably lead to a change in the economic growth rate. China's economic policymakers should focus on stabilizing macroeconomic growth at current levels, upgrading the economic structure and finding ways to optimize economic drivers. Since 2015, there have been significant improvements in a number of areas, noticeably in corporate profitability and the reduction of corporate debt (Fig. 1.8).

The structural adjustment of China's economy and changes to the pattern of domestic consumption require greater attention. The spending on the demand side exceeds investment, and this has been one of the key contributors to economic growth, but the economy is now excessively dependent on this spending. As the increase in total social consumption is not significant, we cannot argue that the economy

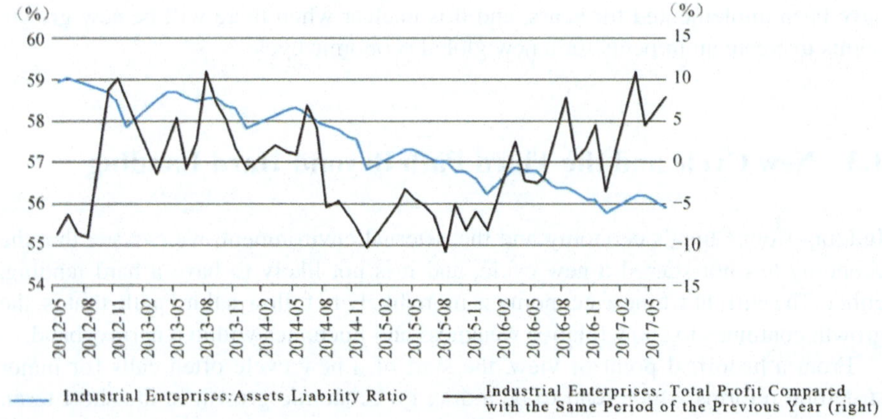

Fig. 1.8 Industrial enterprises witness growth amid the trend decline in the growth rate of total economic output. *Source* Wind Information

has reached the beginning of a new growth cycle. Structural changes in domestic consumption need to be achieved before this can be determined conclusively.

The long-term driving force for consumption is related to income levels and the age of the population, and these are long-term factors affecting economic growth. In theory, a country's per capita income development level and consumption structure have a stable relationship. When per capita gross domestic product (GDP) reaches US$10,000, we can say that per capita income will reach a level of relative affluence. At present, China's per capita GDP has reached more than US$8100, equivalent to that of Japan in the 1970s. In the 1950s, when the per capita income of the United States reached this level, the structure of US consumption showed significant changes. In recent years, consumer spending by China's urban and rural residents showed a decline in the proportion of spending on food and clothing, while there were significant increases in spending on health care, entertainment, education and other services. It can be inferred that, although the new cycle of economic growth has not yet started, the internal structure of the economy is changing the effects of asset prices on economic growth. Understanding these structural changes in the economy will help our understanding of longer-term economic patterns and the required direction of policy regulation (Figs. 1.9 and 1.10).

The deepening of supply-side reforms coupled with a gradual trend toward financial deleveraging and a reduction of industrial overcapacity will result in short- and medium-term price fluctuations. Naturally, this may lead to fluctuations in the near term economic performance and could create changes in market expectations. As risks to the economy and financial system are addressed, studying China's economic structure and the occurrence of dynamic optimization will be more conducive to understanding the economic direction. In the future, if the problems accumulated under the old growth model are addressed and removed and major structural reforms such as replacing state-owned enterprises with companies of mixed ownership, it is

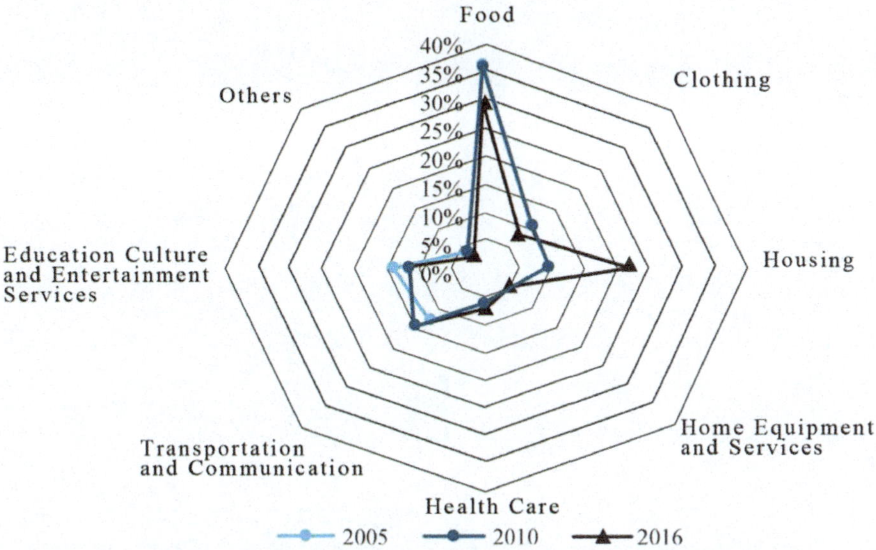

Fig. 1.9 After 2005, the structure of personal consumption in the United States began to change along with the periodic changes of per capita income. *Source* Wind Information

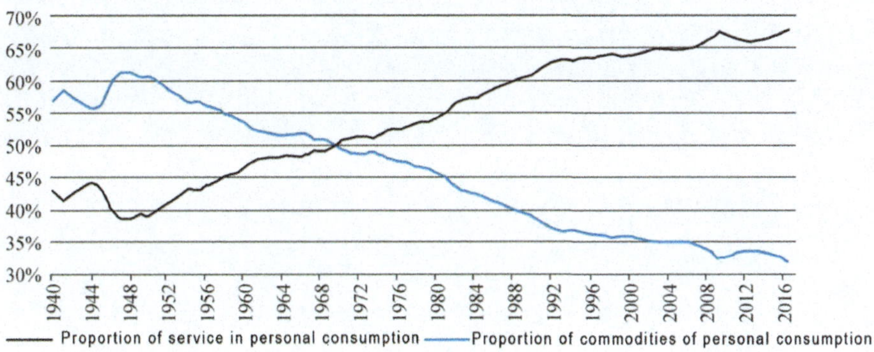

Fig. 1.10 Consumption structure of Chinese residents is undergoing a trend change

expected that the economy will enter a new cycle where there is greater productivity. At this point in China's economic development, it can only be said that the economy is exhibiting new characteristics. China has not started a new economic cycle.

Chapter 2
On China's Economy and Financial Industry

2.1 A New Stage: New Features in Economic Cycle and Structure

1. Economic Trend in 2016 under China's Economic New Normal

The insurance industry has attracted high attention as a more and more important and active market subject in the financial market. Meanwhile, the operation of insurance institutions and the development of insurance market are more and more closely related to the macroeconomy. Therefore, it is necessary to consider the development of the insurance industry from the macroeconomic level.

We can evaluate the current economic performance through diachronic analysis. During the Asian financial crisis, China's economy witnessed a periodic low point before China took a series of reform and opening-up measures, such as accession to the WTO, reform of state-owned enterprises, divestiture of non-performing assets and listing of state-owned banks as well as cultivation of the real estate market, which stimulated the most sustained growth cycle since China's reform and opening up to 2007. It reached a cyclical high point in 2008, followed by a steep decline due to the US subprime mortgage crisis in 2008, and reached a periodic low point in 2009. After 2009, driven by a package of economic stimulus policies represented by RMB 4 trillion, China's economy experienced a V-shaped reversal. To be more accurate, the economic growth reached its peak during the first quarter of 2010, and then it gradually fell with weakened stimulus. I think it is still declining and has not reached the bottom yet. The recovery in the first quarter of 2016 was mainly attributed to the periodic recovery of the real estate market and the fiscal expenditure supported by the rising land revenue. With the real estate market gradually entering the adjustment stage, China's economy again entered the stage of decline.

The most important feature of the new normal period is that China's economy has entered the period of structural transformation, facing the formation of the new drivers and the gradual weakening of the old ones of economic growth. It is of great importance to understand the trend of industrial change in this period of economic

S. Ba, *The New Cycle and New Finance in China*,
https://doi.org/10.1007/978-981-16-8209-4_2

transformation. The 13th Five-Year Plan for Economic and Social Development of the People's Republic of China (The 13th Five-Year Plan) summarizes the features of the economic operation in this stage as an improved economic structure, a shift in the drivers of growth and faster transformation of the growth model. The slowdown of China's economic growth contributes to a more balanced economic structure. Meanwhile, a series of changes in China and across the globe will inevitably prompt China to find new impetus for its economic growth because the dividends, including demographic, investment, trade, resources and savings dividends, which have supported China's rapid economic growth for the past 30 years, are gradually weakening. The so-called transformation is to find new drivers for China's economic growth.

2. Focus of Economic Policy: Supply Side Reform

From a different perspective, we can describe the supply side reform as the transformation from the growth of primary expansion to the second stage of after benchmarking growth and finally to the growth of breakthrough innovations. In other words, economic transformation means the transformation from the growth of primary expansion to after benchmarking growth and finally to the growth of frontier expansion.

China's policymakers had a gradually deepened understanding of the changing internal and external environment and proposed corresponding policy ideas. In May 2014, the policymakers first decided that "China's economy has entered a new normal" and also gave the definition of the new normal; the five concepts for development were put forward at the Fifth Plenary Session of the 18th CPC Central Committee in October 2015, calling for "development that is innovative, coordinated, green, open, and inclusive." The five new concepts can be understood as a new response to the new internal and external economic environment. At the 11th meeting of the central finance and economy leading group in November 2015, the policymakers proposed "supply side reform," which further clarifies the focus of recent policies.

After the supply side reform was put forward, some changes have taken place in the focus of policymakers on economic policies at different stages. We can see this from three authoritative articles published in *People's Daily*. The policy focus of the third article has changed significantly compared with that of the first two, which emphasize the need to stimulate consumption and investment to some extent when recession strikes, so as to avoid excessive economic downturn in a very short time. The third article, Authoritative Personage on Current Chinese Economy was issued on May 9, 2016, stressing that the supply side is the focus of the next stage and that the stimulation on the demand side should not be too emphasized to hinder the supply side reform. This shift in policy focus is directly related to changes in the internal and external economic situation.

3. Flexible Renminbi Exchange Rates Increase the Leeway for Economic Policies to Cope with External Fluctuations

At present, the global economy is still in a complex and changeable state in the short term, with cyclical differentiation. Many developed economies have stepped into the era of negative interest rates, a very good development stage for financial institutions such as insurance companies. These companies are facing different economies of different economic cycles, so they can make use of the global economic differentiation to match assets and liabilities in different markets.

The interest rates in some developed countries are at historical low levels, and it is very unlikely for them to rise because the global economic growth is slowing down and the return on investment is declining. The bonds with negative interest rates in the world amount to RMB10 trillion, posing a huge challenge to insurance funds. More and more developed countries begin to step into the era of negative interest rates. In the short term, the economic situation is not optimistic, but actually there are also some new opportunities. In the longer term, the world is actually at a new starting point of the new Kondratieff wave.

We have observed that the flexibility of renminbi exchange rate has been significantly improved so as to cope with the impact of external economy in the turbulent international environment. Now the market has gradually accepted the flexible renminbi exchange rates, which provides a good buffer for dealing with external shocks. Since August 2015, the People's Bank of China (PBOC) has been adjusting the renminbi exchange rates in line with the supply and demand of the market. After experiencing short-term fluctuations, the exchange rate of renminbi against US dollar has remained stable in the first quarter of 2016. Due to the uncertainties brought by Britain's vote to leave the European Union, renminbi has been under pressure for a short time since the second quarter. The gap between onshore and offshore markets once widened. From the fundamental point of view, Brexit will help alleviate the short-term pressure of renminbi devaluation. It is noteworthy that PBOC has begun to pay attention to adjusting the onshore and offshore exchange rates so as to maintain a relatively stable exchange rate spread, reduce arbitrage opportunities and help stabilize market expectations.

4. New Progress of China's Macroeconomic Policies

Progress has been made in the following policies of great concern since the beginning of 2016:

The first is over-capacity reduction. The plan encountered repeated setbacks and was promoted amid great difficulties, but it has now entered the middle to late stage, and the progress of over-capacity reduction determines the recovery of enterprise profits. Poor progress in the plan will most likely cause both the best and the worst enterprises in the industry to lose money. Therefore, when evaluating current economic policies, we should not simply emphasize economic growth rate, but we should pay more attention to the improvement of enterprise profits.

The second is de-leveraging. China is now witnessing the coexistence of reducing leverage and stabilizing leverage. In fact, the government departments have been continuously increasing leverage, and there is still a certain gap between the leverage of Chinese government departments and that of developed countries. The residential sector is also continuously increasing leverage, which is also at a low level compared with that of the developed countries. This is attributed to China's high savings rate and short-term recovery in the real estate industry. It is the non-financial enterprise sector that is really reducing leverage. But the real estate industry with good sales status, some competitive service industries and emerging industries are constantly increasing leverage. However, industries with high inventories, high leverage and overcapacity are generally undergoing the process of deleveraging. It can be expected that the enterprise sector will continue to reduce leverage in the next few years. It is very unlikely for us to see a sharp increase in leverage in the short term.

The last is inventory shedding. According to the PMI value and the statistics of listed companies, the inventory of finished products in the manufacturing industry and PMI of the whole manufacturing industry have been on the decline ever since 2012 when China began to carry out large-scale inventory shedding.

A trend change took place in China's foreign investment in 2016 when the scale of its outbound investment began to surpass foreign investment in China. Chinese enterprises only focused on resources at the early stage of their overseas investment, but now they are paying more and more attention to industrial innovation, integration and grafting so as to promote China's industrial upgrading. The real estate industry has become a very important factor among others to affect China's investment and overall economic performance. The economic recovery in the first quarter of 2016 is largely attributed to the periodic recovery of the real estate industry, which has boosted the real estate market itself and led to the recovery of the land market, thereby supporting the government's investment in infrastructure. The gradual economic decline after the second quarter can also be said to be a result of the sluggish real estate market. In the short term, due to its adjustment, the real estate industry is declining gradually and, as a result, China's economy at the macrolevel is also witnessing a recession. China began to tighten its monetary policy while keeping it relatively loose, and, as a result, China began to reduce the leverage and tighten real estate policies in some cities, which is also the direct reason for inventory shedding.

2.2 Transformation of the Financial Industry

Economic transformation will inevitably lead to the transformation of the financial industry. The financial system in China, including the insurance industry, is best at serving the growing and mature enterprises. However, in the period of economic transformation, there are not only a large number of start-up enterprises, but also a great many transforming enterprises and distressed enterprises to be restructured. Therefore, the economic transformation brings a very realistic challenge to the transformation of the financial industry; that is, the financial industry can no longer provide financial service only to growing and mature enterprises, but should also provide service to enterprises during their whole life cycle. In fact, the start-up enterprises and those in transformation and adjustment are still getting insufficient financial support from the financial industry. The banking, securities and insurance industries have to take this into consideration in their own transformation.

Several new trends in the banking industry are worthy of notice. The number of newly added banks is increasing, and more private banks are entering the banking industry. The rural credit cooperatives, the banking institutions in rural areas, have been restructured into rural commercial banks, the number of which reached 1000. These rural commercial banks, together with village banks, constitute a multi-level rural financial system. The Commercial Banking Law of the People's Republic of China will soon be amended. After its amendment, commercial banks are expected to expand its business scope and gradually realize comprehensive operation, and some financial institutions similar to banks are expected to obtain restricted qualifications of licensed banks. Financial supervision, which is insufficient and poorly coordinated, may be improved. The interest rate liberalization is gradually coming to an end. The central bank will see progress in its main tasks, such as controlling interest rates, accelerating the disposal of non-performing assets of banks and promoting the securitization of non-performing assets.

The insurance industry across the globe has gradually entered the stage of implementing the risk-oriented solvency system, and the regulatory rules of the solvency of insurance companies have been constantly improved. The EU began to implement Solvency II in 2016 and adopted the implementation decisions of IFRSs 9 and 10. The United States has also started the first year of self-risk and solvency assessment, and China has carried out the assessment since January 2016. According to the data available, the actual capital increase under the new regulatory rules is higher than the minimum capital and the solvency adequacy ratio is higher than that of Solvency I, especially for property insurance companies. The high growth of the insurance liability side has witnessed a turning point. In 2015, the high rate of return on investment, together with the downward movement of the capital price center, contributed to high-speed growth of insurance premium and income in 2016, which, in turn, led to the expansion of the scale of insurance funds. However, in 2016, the return on investment became lower, and the supervision of medium and short-term wealth management products was strengthened. Therefore, the growth of premium is expected to slow down in the future. At present, the insurance investment is faced with pressure, and the improvement of long-term asset allocation calls for further improvement of the domestic bond market. In the short term, non-standard assets are still worthy of investment. Due to the competition and premium rates marketization, the debt cost of insurance companies is on the rise. In addition, in a market of low interest rates, the yield curve of bonds is moving down. Therefore, diversified investment channels have to be sought for insurance funds, and this poses a huge challenge to the insurance industry. Under this backdrop, it is an important option to allocate assets in markets such as Hong Kong, where there is relatively reasonable valuation.

China's investment banking industry is undergoing drastic adjustment and change in line with the market structure. If we compare the market value of listed investment banks around the world, 15 of the top 20 are Chinese investment banks. While the market value is rising, the change of the industry pattern deserves more attention. By comparing the development of American investment industry, we can find that the liberalization of commission in the US investment market and the change of registration system from separate operation to mixed operation have exerted a profound impact on the development of American investment banking business, which can be used as a reference for analyzing and evaluating the development of China's investment industry.

The relevant systems show that China's securities companies are roughly in the development stage of those in the United States in the 1980s. The commission rates are fluctuating; the whole industry is undergoing differentiation and reform; the construction of the registration system is exerting a far-reaching impact on the whole industry. The securities industry is a very important carrier for the development of direct financing. However, securities business lacks depth at the present stage and involves homogeneous competition in channel-type and asset-light business. The new asset-heavy business is facing the difficulties of insufficient market space and tightened policies. Therefore, we judge that, in the near future, the securities industry should strive for the expansion of each business line so as to achieve comprehensive development. But this homogeneous competition may persist for a period of time.

From the history of the investment industry in the United States and the development of Chinese securities companies in recent years, we can see that the development of the new innovative industries such as asset management industry, credit industry and direct investment industry will support the further development of the whole industry. Therefore, it is an inevitable trend for innovative industries to be conventional and asset heavy. Securities companies should focus on the new third board business, fixed income, currency and commodities (FICC) business, prime broker, wealth management and other emerging businesses and seize the new opportunities to promote the reshuffle of the industry.

The development of the global leasing business is highly correlated with the economic cycle. The United States is well ahead of other countries in terms of leasing business volume, while China's leasing business volume ranks second in the world. The top 10 countries with the largest business volume in the world occupy more than 80% of the global market share. Since 2007, with the establishment of banking financial leasing companies, capital from all walks of life has been rushing in, and enterprises and registered capital have been increasing significantly, resulting in the exponential growth of the leasing industry. The total business volume increased more than 500 times from an average of RMB 8 billion in 2006 to RMB 4440 billion in 2015. The major shareholders of the financial industry, domestic capital and foreign capital take 40, 30 and 30% of the financial leasing market share. In this stage of industrial transformation, financial leasing plays an increasingly important role in broadening the financing channels for small- and medium-sized enterprises, spurring the development of producer services, promoting industrial innovation and upgrading and serving the development of the real economy.

Internet finance is seeking new growth points in the process of adjustment. Financial technology has received extensive attention after the adjustment of Internet finance, and small- and medium-sized enterprises and the retail sector are the main force of financial technology investment. Payment and financing are still the main directions of investment. At present, on the one hand, Internet finance is witnessing significant adjustments with many problems propping up in the process; on the other hand, a number of excellent enterprises with global competitiveness have emerged in the field of Internet finance in China. The scale of the entire Internet financial market and the number of users of Internet finance in China rank top in the world. Personal application and mobile finance are still the main targets of mobile payment. The intelligent wealth management has also seen significant growth, and the digitization of currency has attracted increasingly great attention. The blockchain technology is most likely to be applied in payment, transaction banks and capital markets.

2.3 New Driving Force of China's Economic Growth

In 2016, the newly added loans are mainly the residents' medium- and long-term loans, which account for 45% of the total. In 2017, with the tightened policies on the real estate industry, loans were invested in infrastructure and emerging industries. The transition from investment in real economy to that in virtual economy has become one of the hot topics at present. Can finance really thrive alone when the funds simply circulate in the financial sector for the sake of arbitrage? Behind the expansion of bank balance sheet is the expansion of local government debts, the financing of the real estate industry and the financing of industries with high pollution, high energy consumption and overcapacity. The newly added loans brought by debt swaps are estimated to be about RMB 4.5 trillion.

China's economy witnessed short-term recovery in 2017, and it peaked before declining after the first and second quarters when the inflection point of real estate investment in short term has appeared. Infrastructure investment will grow in the first half of the year and see moderate decline in the second half. Investment in the manufacturing industry will remain stable, but there is still industry differentiation in terms of the driving forces of development. There is a narrowing space for the decline of industries with overcapacity such as the steel industry. Emerging industries such as Technology, Media and Telecom (TMT) and emerging investment in driving force will maintain a high growth rate. This marks the gradual transformation of the old and new driving forces of China's economy.

China's export is bottoming out thanks to the sustained recovery of global trade since the third quarter of 2016. However, China's rising labor costs and the declining global trade restrict the space for further recovery. In terms of consumption, the restriction of income, the fission of structure and the slowdown of automobile production and sales will lead to the differentiation of China's consumption, and the growth rate will slow down steadily. Among them, consumption degradation in first-tier cities coexists with consumption upgrading in third and fourth-tier cities. Automobile consumption accounts for nearly 40% of China's durable goods consumption, which is the core factor determining the trend of China's consumption. The sales growth of all kinds of automobiles and passenger cars turned negative in April 2017, while the retail growth of passenger cars in May remained negative in May.

The demand driven by China's new investment is helping the transformation of old investment and financial deleveraging is an important variable affecting the financial market and China's macroeconomy in 2017. The volume and price of interbank negotiable certificates of deposit (NCDs) have risen simultaneously, which has become a new way to increase leverage. Off balance sheet financing, especially interbank financing, has become the main tool for off balance sheet expansion. The asset side, through various carriers, forms a three-tier asset management structure of capital acquisition, investment management and channel business, through which the capital finally flows to all kinds of standard and non-standard financial assets. The outsourcing market was formed due to the lack of professional investment research team, strict local supervision and limited investment, which involves bank's balance sheet expansion and releverage by means of pledge and maturity mismatch. Increase of leverage, in essence, is regulatory arbitrage and fund arbitrage. Regulatory authorities should promote coordination by establishing a unified regulatory framework for asset management, and improve the regulatory framework combining prudent macro- and micromanagement.

Chapter 3
On Monetary Stimulus and China Economy's Deep Structural Contradiction

3.1 Reasons and Future Trend of Renminbi Exchange Rate Fluctuation

Since 2016, the renminbi exchange rate, influenced by both external and internal factors, has undergone violent fluctuations.

Externally, the impact of spillover effect caused by the differentiation of economic cycles and economic policies among developed economies such as Europe, the United States and Japan is an important reason for the fluctuation of renminbi exchange rate. Renminbi middle price is decided by taking the closing exchange rate and a basket of currency exchange rates into consideration, which shows that the trend of renminbi exchange rate is more related to a basket of currencies. Since 2016, the exchange rates of the above countries and regions have shown obvious fluctuations. The highest dollar index is close to 100, while the lowest is less than 92. The exchange rate market has also been volatile as a result of the fluctuating US economy and the brexit referendum.

Internally, the fluctuation and improved flexibility of renminbi exchange rates show that the exchange rate is largely driven by the market factors. With the deepened reform of exchange rate formation mechanism, the participants in foreign exchange markets are more diversified and the market expectation is also more diversified and scattered. Diversified participants and their changing behavior may aggravate the fluctuation of renminbi exchange rate in the short term. Since 2016, due to the factors such as the deleveraging of foreign currency liabilities of enterprises and the increasing willingness of overseas merger and acquisition, the supply of foreign currencies in China's foreign exchange market has failed to satisfy the demand, and the closing exchange rate of renminbi against the US dollar has been devalued against central parity rate.

An analysis of the fluctuation of renminbi exchange rates shows that, from January to early February 2016, the fluctuation range of renminbi exchange rate increased, which can be regarded as a result of the exchange rate reform on August 11, 2015. The market needs time to get adapted to the change of exchange rate formation

S. Ba, *The New Cycle and New Finance in China*,
https://doi.org/10.1007/978-981-16-8209-4_3

mechanism, and it also takes time to gradually solve the problem of large difference between offshore and onshore exchange rates. With strengthened communication with the central bank, the market had an increasingly good understanding and acceptance of the exchange rate formation mechanism. Since the end of February, the fluctuation range of renminbi exchange rate has increased, which is also the purpose of the exchange rate reform. As the renminbi exchange rate is largely determined by the market, both the fluctuation of renminbi and that of other major currencies in the market will increase. Take the exchange rate against the US dollar as an example. In March and April, the US dollar index continued to fall to around 92 due to the low expectation of Fed's interest rate increase, while it continued to rebound in May and June because of rising expectation of interest rate increase. During this period, the renminbi appreciated first and then depreciated against the US dollar. It should be noted that under the current exchange rate formation mechanism based on the closing exchange rate and a basket of currency exchange rates, the fluctuation range of renminbi against a basket of currencies is usually lower than that of renminbi against US dollar. From the beginning of March to the end of June, the annualized volatility of the reference rate for the renminbi against the dollar is 4.28% while the annualized volatility of the CFETS renminbi exchange rate index is only 2.31%. The exchange rate of renminbi against the US dollar becomes more flexible, and the bilateral fluctuation is normalized; in addition, flexibility of the exchange rate of renminbi against a basket of currencies is also steadily improving on the basis of relative stability, thus enhancing the degree of market-oriented fluctuation of renminbi exchange rate.

What will happen to the renminbi exchange rate next? From the beginning of 2016 to October of the same year, the fluctuation of renminbi exchange rate generally presents a trend of asymmetric and strategic depreciation, that is, when the US dollar becomes stronger, renminbi will be pegged to a basket of currencies; therefore, while the renminbi depreciates against the US dollar, it remains stable and even appreciates against a basket of currencies; when the US dollar weakens, renminbi will be pegged to the US dollar, and it will weaken with the US dollar and depreciate against a basket of currencies. Renminbi exchange rate is closely related to the trend of the US dollar. Stronger US dollar put greater pressure on renminbi's asymmetric and strategic depreciation.

Under the new renminbi exchange rate formation mechanism, the exchange rate of US dollar is still the most important factor affecting renminbi exchange rate in the second half of the year. Domestically, since the exchange rate reform on August 11, 2015, the pressure of capital outflow and devaluation caused by the expectation of devaluation has been greatly reduced, and there is relatively limited space for enterprises to further eliminate foreign currency liabilities. However, residents and enterprises actively seek overseas asset allocation and this will continue to affect renminbi exchange rates in the medium and long terms. Successful solution of the problems of high financial leverage and asset bubbles will also be a key variable affecting the trend of renminbi exchange rate. At the same time, China's economic transformation, as a more fundamental variable, determines the improvement of labor productivity in China, which, in turn, exerts a direct impact on the trend of the

RMB exchange rate in the medium and long terms. In addition, the relative trend of renminbi and US dollar interest rates also has a great impact.

3.2 Regulatory Authorities' Attitude Toward the Trend of Renminbi Exchange Rate

Judging from the current market policies and the central bank's statement, the central bank may be inclined to focus on fundamental indicators such as the current account surplus and maintain the basic stability of the renminbi exchange rate. The recent slowdown of capital outflow also confirms from a particular perspective that the renminbi exchange rate may have been relatively balanced. In the turbulent international environment, the central bank may expect the new renminbi exchange rate formation mechanism to play the dual role of realizing the market-oriented exchange rate fluctuations and stabilizing the exchange rates.

The central bank has accumulated experience in dealing with volatile foreign exchange markets in the process of handling exchange rate fluctuations. The strategies include: first, combine the handling of short-term market exchange rate fluctuations with flexible adjustment of exchange rates. Renminbi has suffered great pressure of depreciation several times as its exchange rate against the US dollar rose from 6.0 at the beginning of 2014 to 6.2 before the exchange rate reform on August 11, 2015, and then to close to 6.7 in early July 2016. The reduced capital outflow, flexible exchange rate adjustment and increased volatility play an important role in stabilizing exchange rates. Second, adjust the spread between offshore and onshore markets. A relatively stable exchange rate spread and reduced arbitrage opportunities between offshore and onshore markets will also help to stabilize market expectations. This also requires that the central bank should cultivate the offshore renminbi market and enrich the central bank's regulatory tools in the offshore market so as to avoid causing huge fluctuations when carrying out the regulations. Finally, combine the handling of the fluctuation of foreign exchange market with the liberalization of capital account. We should keep capital account opening relatively stable, and, at the same time, adhere to the asymmetric promotion policy of capital account opening, that is, we should continue to introduce measures to encourage capital inflow while remaining prudent when introducing measures that may lead to capital outflow. On the whole, we should maintain the continuity of capital control policies so as to avoid market panic caused by rash capital control measures.

The term of "currency war" is often used to discuss the operation of the regulators. I believe that "currency war" is a too general and somewhat dramatic and entertaining term for the discussion of exchange rate policies, and it fails to define the specific contents of these policies. However, from the perspective of the global economy, major global monetary authorities have reached the consensus that the deep-seated structural contradictions of the economy cannot be solved through monetary policy stimulus alone. Therefore, competitive currency devaluation will not be a consistent long-term option for major economies. Despite deglobalization and protectionism in international trade, these economies have exercised considerable restraint in exchange rates and are more active in exchange rate coordination. Since the beginning of 2016, many G20 sessions have repeatedly reiterated their position of avoiding competitive currency devaluation.

Various countries have been supporting this common position through their actions: After Japan entered the era of negative interest rates, the yen remained strong, which is against Prime Minister Shinzo Abe's desire to devalue the yen so as to boost exports and inflation. The Japanese government has repeatedly given verbal warnings, but so far, no intervention has been carried out. After brexit, a new round of global monetary easing was expected to take place, but even the UK did not cut interest rates at the BOE interest rate meeting in July. Instead, it did so in August only after confirming the impact of brexit on economic fundamentals.

3.3 Impact of Renminbi's Inclusion into SDR on Renminbi Exchange Rates and Related Products

According to the plan, the inclusion of renminbi into the special drawing rights (SDR) basket took effect on October 1, 2016, after which the renminbi exchange rate is expected to gradually stay out of the trend of market-oriented exchange rates, and the central bank will gradually withdraw from the intervention of daily transactions. With the deepening of renminbi internationalization, more and more countries and regions begin to use and hold renminbi, and more and more supply and demand parties will participate in game of the renminbi exchange rate market, which will inevitably lead to improved flexibility of renminbi exchange rate.

In the short term, the inclusion of renminbi into the SDR basket exerted little influence on the trend of renminbi exchange rate which is mainly affected by domestic and foreign economic environment. In the medium and long terms, after being included in SDR basket, renminbi will play a more important role in supplementing and gradually replacing the existing international reserve currencies in emerging markets and neighboring countries. Therefore, renminbi exchange rate policies should be designed with the purpose of maintaining a relatively stable exchange rate against emerging market currencies while showing flexibility in the exchange rate against the US dollar in an appropriate range, so as to gradually get rid of the synchronous rhythm of the exchange rate as "quasi-US dollar" formed due to small exchange rate fluctuations, thereby enhancing the influence of renminbi among international currencies.

In addition, China's central bank is also faced with the balance and option of internal and external policy priorities. With renminbi becoming an international reserve currency, the international coordination of monetary policies becomes more important. The effect of the central bank's independent monetary policies will be weakened, and the problem of economic growth in the Chinese mainland is the problem of global economic development to a certain extent. At present, the economy in the Chinese mainland is faced with the pressure of structural transformation. With deepened financial reform, China will face the trade-off between the goal of internal economic growth (or internal balance goal) and the goal of external stability of renminbi exchange rate, just as the monetary authorities of Latin American countries and Asian countries did in the 1980s and 1990s. As an economy with a large domestic demand market, China should give priority to ensuring the space for independent decision making in its monetary policies. The renminbi exchange rate is relatively flexible: It remains stable and strong against most currencies of emerging markets, but the exchange rate against the US dollar can fluctuate in a larger range.

Chapter 4
Origin and Trend of Financial Deleveraging

Financial deleveraging is the reduction of practices without capital support or out of regulation. The level of financial leverage should be compatible with economic growth, capital adequacy and regulatory requirements. Once it exceeds the speed of economic development or fails to get the support of capital, financial bubbles will be formed.

The increase of money market interest rate and the tightening of liquidity have broken the foundation of increasing leverage, raising the cost of financing and narrowing the spread of interest. This is the necessary condition for financial deleveraging and will exist during the whole process of reducing leverage.

In the early stage of deleveraging, the amount of financing of enterprises may be reduced, but in the long run, the financing structure of enterprises will be optimized and the cost will be reduced, which provides more effective support for the development of the real economy.

The five priorities of the supply side structural reform, namely cutting overcapacity, destocking, deleveraging, reducing costs and improving weak links, have become the starting point of China's economic reform. Among them, deleveraging mainly involves the reduction of the leverage of government departments, non-financial enterprises and household sectors. However, there is no clear definition and measurement index for financial deleveraging. The financial industry, as a market entity of high-leverage operation, has a low self-owned capital ratio. Therefore, one of the important contents of its supervision is to ensure the support of sufficient capital for its asset expansion, while the process of excessive leverage is the process of asset expansion without sufficient capital support. Since 2016, the deleveraging of China's financial system has gradually attracted the attention of the market. The asset expansion of financial institutions with banks as the main body began to step out of the monitoring scope of traditional regulatory indicators, causing local impact on the money and bond markets within a certain period of time.

S. Ba, *The New Cycle and New Finance in China*,
https://doi.org/10.1007/978-981-16-8209-4_4

4.1 Background of Financial Leverage

1. Basis for Leverage: Loose Monetary Environment

Since the financial crisis in 2008, various countries have launched quantitative loose monetary policies to stimulate the economy. Under this backdrop, China's monetary environment has been relaxed as a whole since 2015. The central bank had cut the benchmark interest rates five times in one year, and interbank market interest rates represented by Shibor had remained low. By 2016, the one-year deposit interest rate of 10-year treasury bonds had also dropped below 3%. Low interest rate leads to reduction of the financing costs and provides a market basis for financial leverage.

It is noteworthy that since 2015, changes have taken place in currency derivation, with decreased proportion of traditional currency derivation driven by bank credit expansion and enhanced currency derivative ability of the shadow banking system. From the data of money supply, it can be seen that since 2015, the growth of the base currency balance has slowed down year on year, but the money multiplier has increased significantly, and the year-on-year growth rate of M2 had witnessed fluctuations, remaining relatively high in 2015. Since 2016, the scissors gap between M1 and M2 has expanded for a time, showing that the volatility of money supply has increased and the level of currency liquidity is relatively high.

Relaxed monetary environment and low interest rates provide the basis for financial leverage. Financial institutions obtain liquidity from the central bank through lower financing costs, and achieve arbitrage through pledge and maturity mismatch. However, this arbitrage based on liquidity needs to be supported by a higher rate of return of the real economy. From a macroperspective, since 2014, China's return on capital has been lower than the cost of financing, which determines the unsustainability of liquidity arbitrage.

2. Manifestations of Leverage

The expansion of bank balance sheet is the most direct source of leverage. However, there are different forms of bank balance sheet expansion. The expansion through the deposit and loan business will not lead to funds simply circulating within the financial sector for arbitrage thanks to relatively perfect and strict supervision. However, this round of leverage has shown new characteristics in the adjustment of asset liability structure. The liability side relies on the interbank liabilities that can be rapidly expanded, while the asset side directly or indirectly invests in bonds, non-standard assets, equity, etc. Both, to a certain extent, have stayed away from supervision, resulting in the deviation between asset expansion and capital support. Both the expansion of on balance sheet assets and that of off balance sheet assets show two important characteristics: First, the asset expansion takes on different forms; second, small and medium-sized institutions become the main force of asset expansion.

In terms of on balance sheet assets expansion, interbank business has become the main means of financing and the growth rate of broad credit far exceeds that of loans. Bank capital mainly comes from deposits, which leads to the passive liabilities of banks. Driven by leverage, banks actively develop their own active liability business, mainly including interbank borrowing (lending), matched sale of repo, issurance of bonds, etc. Almost all the activities of active liabilities occur between banks. In recent years, the number and price of interbank certificates of deposit have risen simultaneously, which has become one of the new ways of financial leverage.

The obvious change in the on balance sheet assets is that the proportion of loans decreases and that of investment increases gradually. Among the investment assets, the investment in standardized bonds decreased, while the proportion of non-standard and equity assets increased. The growth rate of broad credit under the framework of MPA is much higher than that of loans, and the forms of asset expansion are more diversified. Small- and medium-sized banks have become the main force of asset expansion. In 2016, the growth rate of on balance sheet assets of non-listed small- and medium-sized banks was 23.5%, far higher than the average 10.8% of listed banks.

Off balance sheet financial management, especially interbank financial management, has become the main tool for off balance sheet expansion.

By the end of 2016, the scale of financial management has reached RMB 29.1 trillion. Although the year-on-year growth rate has decreased, it still maintains at 24%, which is higher than the growth rate of on balance sheet assets. The proportion of off balance sheet financial management in on balance sheet assets increased from 6.5% at the end of 2014 to 16.5% at the end of 2016. In May 2015, the scale of interbank financial management exceeded that of private customers for the first time and showed a trend of rapid growth. As of the first half of 2016, it accounted for more than 15%. Interbank financial management rapidly expanded the scale of asset management and became the main force of off balance sheet expansion.

3. Driving Force of Leverage: Regulatory and Capital Arbitrage

Diversified forms of asset expansion make it increasingly difficult to track the flow of capital. Under the current regulatory framework, the fundamental driving force of leverage is to achieve regulatory arbitrage and capital arbitrage. The non-standard assets on the balance sheet and their off balance sheet operation can help avoid the risk capital provision and other regulatory indicators, and remove the restrictions on the credit scale and industry through embedded channels. In the initial stage, capital arbitrage has a huge interest margin, but with tightened liquidity, it becomes increasingly passive. After the adjustment of the bond market, the cost and return are inversely linked. Faced with long-term maturity mismatch, banks have to maintain high-cost active liabilities so as to avoid asset recovery and maintain the interbank chain.

One form of regulatory arbitrage is the extension of interbank chain, behind which two problems exist.

Different regulatory requirements on different asset management institutions in terms of investment scope and leverage ratio call for cooperation between different types of financial institutions. One of the business cooperation modes is channel service. The existence of such business has led to the rapid expansion of asset management scale of securities and fund subsidiaries, from RMB 8 trillion in 2014 to RMB 33 trillion at the end of the third quarter of 2016. The transfer of assets between financial subindustries can achieve regulatory arbitrage, but it is not conducive to supporting the real economy. The extension of interbank chain not only increases the financing costs and operational risks, but also distorts the allocation of resources. The mosaic of multi-layer products and the extension of interbank chain bring two problems into the limelight: One is the problem of customer risk adaptability. For the end customers as ultimate risk takers, is there a mismatch between low-risk tolerance and high-risk assets? The other problem is the compliance of final asset investment. For the product as final asset, does it conform to the regulatory provisions of asset management and has its risk been properly assessed?

Regulatory arbitrage also contributed to the development of the outsourcing market, which involves two levels of leverage.

The outsourcing market resulted from the contradiction between the rapid expansion of the asset management scale of small- and medium-sized banks and their relative lack of investment and research capacity. However, with the pursuit of interest spread in the outsourcing market, the main body of the outsourcing business has expanded from small- and medium-sized banks to all kinds of banks. During the peak period in 2016, the outsourcing scale of financial management funds of the four major banks (Industrial and Commercial Bank of China, Agricultural Bank of China, Bank of China and China Construction Bank) ranged from RMB 2.5 trillion to3 trillion, and that of the whole industry may reach RMB5 trillion to 6 trillion. The extension of the outsourcing market creates larger room for leverage, which involves two types of leverage and arbitrage. The first is the leverage through expansion of bank balance sheet when banks raise funds from the interbank market through issuing interbank deposit certificates or interbank financial management before investing in the asset side; the second is the releverage by means of pledge and maturity mismatch when the asset management outsourcing investment managers invest in such assets as bonds.

This expansion of banks' balance sheet shows that the capital flow is unregulated. In on balance sheet investment, the proportion of bonds decreased, while the proportion of non-standard assets increased due to the non-standard return to the statement. Most of the non-standard assets were held in various asset management and trust plans, which made it difficult to track the capital flow. As for the flow of financial management funds, influenced by the Circular of China Banking Regulatory Commission on Regulating Investment and Operation of Financial Management Business of Commercial Banks, the proportion of non-standard assets gradually decreased, while the proportion of bonds and money market increased. The proportion of investment interest rate securities and credit bonds increased in 2016. The leverage in the debt market and simple circulation of funds in the financial sector became increasingly obvious. The risk of rapid expansion of nominal scale, that is, the risk of so-called simple circulation of funds and bubbles, was still accumulating in the financial sector. The excessive pursuit of return by funds makes the liquidity reserves with surplus inventory as the main part become thin, which aggravates the tension of liquidity and brings challenges to the liquidity and position management of banks.

4.2 Changes in Market Operation After Financial Deleveraging

1. Reverse the Expectations of Leverage

To achieve the reduction of financial leverage, the first thing is to get rid of the relaxed liquidity environment necessary for increasing leverage. Since 2016, the central bank has been firm in its policy guidance for deleveraging in the financial market. In order to prevent the funds from simply circulating in the financial sector for arbitrage, a series of measures have been adopted to squeeze asset bubbles and reduce the leverage ratio of the financial system. These measures include: releasing long-term liquidity and reducing operation frequency in the open market, increasing costs and maintaining a tight balance of liquidity. Since August 2016, the central bank has restarted 14-day and 28-day reverse repurchase, indirectly increasing the costs of capital by extending the term. Tight balance of liquidity is maintained with the continuous withdrawal of funds through operation in the open market.

We should maintain a stable and neutral monetary policy, and raise the interest rate center of money market. The monetary policy report of the third quarter of fiscal year 2016 clearly put forward "active adjustment of structure", "active reduction of leverage" and "active removal of bubbles". The monetary policy report of the fourth quarter clearly stated that "the monetary policy should remain stable and neutral" and "funds should not flow from the real economy to the virtual economy, and unreasonable leverage should be avoided". Around the Spring Festival of 2017, the central bank followed the trend, raising MLF and open market interest rates twice. The interest rate hike cycle in the money market started, and the regulatory plan of financial deleveraging was advanced steadily.

The increase of interest rate and the tightening of liquidity in the money market have broken the foundation of increasing leverage, raising the cost of financing and reducing the spread of interest. This is the necessary condition for financial deleveraging and will exist in the whole process of deleveraging.

2. Macroprudent Regulation and Microprudent Regulation

The new features of balance sheet expansion of leveraged banks show that the traditional consensus credit cannot accurately capture the trend of capital operation of financial institutions. Therefore, since 2016, the central bank has established a macroprudential assessment (MPA) system to conduct framework regulatory assessment on financial institutions, and the system has been constantly improved. Since the first quarter of 2017, the central bank has explicitly included the off balance sheet financial assets into the broad credit after deducting cash and deposits, linking its growth rate with that of M2 money supply and controlling the disorderly balance sheet expansion of small and medium-sized banks. The calculation of macroprudential capital adequacy ratio according to broad credit has become an important factor in deciding the assessment results of banks. Through the constant improvement of MPA system, we can carry out systematic and dynamic macroprudential regulation from the dimensions of scale, growth rate and proportion.

The constraints on small and medium-sized banks are weaker because these banks have higher return on investment but are less sensitive to the increase of capital costs. In addition, the existing incentive and punishment mechanism of MPA system is relatively single, and the differential interest rate is applied only to the statutory deposit reserve. Therefore, we can strengthen the regulatory constraints by strengthening the punitive measures, such as issuing the standing loan facility (SLF) interest rate plus 100 basis points to the local legal person financial institutions failing to meet the macroprudential requirements, and linking the MPA assessment results with the market access and qualifications.

Besides macroprudential regulation, microprudential regulation, as a supplement and foothold of macroprudential regulation, also needs to be refined and updated. Macroprudent regulation and microprudent regulation should be combined to break the trading structure of arbitrage between banks and non-bank institutions, and make up for regulatory failure.

The microprudential regulation of China Banking Regulatory Commission (CBRC) on single financial institutions is conducted on the basis of the CAMELS rating system, and in the process of regulation, penetration regulation of assets is particularly important. In the new regulatory submission requirements in 2017, detailed requirements on asset penetration list have been made for both on balance sheet investment and off balance sheet financial management. By improving the transparency of statistical information, shadow banking can be put under regulation and the underlying assets can be checked.

Another manifestation of microprudential regulation is the establishment of a unified regulatory framework for asset management business. China has been implementing a separate regulation system. With increased cooperation among different types of financial institutions, the limitations of regulation on one type of institutions are increasingly prominent. A unified framework of regulation on asset management business contributes to the combination of institutional regulation and functional regulation, which is conducive to achieving the regulatory objectives of deleveraging, eliminating non-standard assets, reducing channel business, breaking rigid repayment and prohibiting cash pooling. The policy recommendations of the Financial Stability Board (FSB) on strengthening the regulation of asset management business mainly focus on three aspects: liquidity mismatch risk, leverage risk and securities and lending business risk. Liquidity management under normal and stress conditions should be strengthened; requirements on stress testing and information disclosure should be stricter; the measurement methods of leverage level of asset management products should be improved and the monitoring and prevention of leverage risk should be strengthened; the reinvestment of cash pledge should be standardized, and the regulation of discount coefficient should be improved. In our regulatory reform, we should also reduce the regulatory blind areas and achieve penetration through the reform of statistical reporting system, prohibition of multi-layer product nesting, monitoring of capital flow by third-party custody and establishment of positive list system of interbank business. We should strengthen internal capital constraints and risk control by prohibiting capital pooling, unifying leverage requirements, controlling risk concentration, unifying capital constraint and carrying out risk reserve management.

4.3 Financial Deleveraging: Impact and Countermeasures

Financial deleveraging has started with the adjustment of the bond market since the fourth quarter of 2016. Has the financial leverage decreased a little bit after the regulatory authorities took measures from the liquidity and macro- and microprudential levels? The growth rate of the scale of fund subsidiaries has gradually decreased to 33% in the fourth quarter of 2016, and the growth rate of the scale of securities companies' asset management is relatively low; however, as of February 2017, the single-month interbank certificates of deposit have reached RMB 1.9 trillion, and the net financing amount excluding repayment due was more than RMB 800 billion, both of which reached a record high. From this data, we can see that there is still a long way to go if we want to reduce leverage. Results cannot be achieved in financial deleveraging in a short period of time. When the market interest rate increases, the asset end with shorter duration is adjusted rapidly, and the short-term deleveraging effect is obvious; once the central bank relaxes control, with the decrease of interest rate, the chain of investment bonds will work again and the leverage reduced in the early stage will be revived after interbank certificates of deposit are issued and interbank financing are conducted. And it takes the asset end sometime to replace the maturity mismatch in the early stage. Deleveraging is the result of multi-party game in the market, and it is a recurrent phenomenon.

But it is undeniable that with the end of liquidity easing in 2017, deleveraging will persist, which will exert an impact on banks, the asset management industry and the real economy.

In the early stage, deleveraging will exert such negative effects as interest rate inversion on the banking industry, and the balance sheet expansion will not continue during this process, but it will witness contraction. With strengthened regulation, the diversified forms of asset expansion have been brought under the regulatory framework, which requires the support of sufficient capital. In the long run, it has a positive impact on the asset quality and risk mitigation of the banking industry, and it also forces the banking industry to stay away from fund arbitrage and return to the right track of indirect financing.

For the asset management industry, this round of deleveraging will lead to the reshuffle of outsourcing managers, the loss of foundation for simple channel business and the upgraded cooperation between institutions from simple channel service to that of complementary advantages; the outsourcing investment has been differentiated, and investment ability has become an important criterion for the selection of outsourcing managers; measures are taken to guide the industry to return to the nature of asset management and will have a profound impact on the asset management industry. These measures include improving the management mechanism of outsourcing investment, establishing a white list mechanism, strengthening regular reporting and communication, implementing an elimination system, stipulating the proportion of co-investment by outsourcing managers and deferring payment of excess earnings.

As for the real economy, it is undeniable that in the process of this round of leverage, due to the increase of capital supply, the total amount of enterprise financing has increased, but the multi-layer chain and channel have also increased the transaction cost and operational risk. Moreover, due to the multi-layer capital transfer, the final direction of capital flow may deviate from the direction of policy guidance, thus weakening the regulation and control of capital allocation, which will have a negative impact on the real economy in the long run. Therefore, in the early stage of deleveraging, the amount of enterprise financing may be reduced, but in the long run, the financing structure will be improved and the cost will be reduced, which will enable finance to provide more effective support for the development of the real economy.

Financial deleveraging is the removal of the leverage that is without capital support and out of regulation. The level of financial leverage should be compatible with economic growth, capital adequacy and regulatory requirements. Once it exceeds the speed of economic development, lacks capital support or evades regulation, financial bubbles will be formed. Deleveraging is a test to financial institutions. The financial industry has to adjust and optimize its business structure and improve the ability of liquidity management first. The banking industry should focus on light development so as to get adapted to the process of deleveraging.

Chapter 5
A More Realistic Policy Orientation: Stabilizing the Slope of Rising Leverage Ratio

The macropolicy and economic performance in the past few years were closely related to deleveraging. The huge debt expansion since 2009 has brought China's economy into the vortex of debt; inflation in 2010 turned into debt deflation in 2012; China faced Minsky Moment in 2013, trying to deleverage by tightened monetary policies and market clearance; from 2014 to 2015, China decided that tightened monetary policies were not sufficient for deleveraging, and that we should implement relaxed policies and develop equity financing for that purpose. Leverage should move between different sectors in a loose liquidity environment and through such policies as deleveraging by increasing equity and shedding inventories of the real estate industry. The policy keynote in 2016 was readjusted, and excessive easing is not conducive to deleveraging, which means that returning to real neutral monetary interest rate will be the choice under the keynote of deleveraging. At the same time, speeding up the clearance of "zombie enterprises" and controlling the debt of local governments should be included in the process of deleveraging.

5.1 Characteristics of China's Macroleverage Ratio

Since Chinese government's economic stimulus of RMB 4 trillion in 2009, China's macroleverage ratio has risen rapidly from 141% at the end of 2008 to 254% at the end of 2016, with an average annual increase of 14%. The leverage ratio decreased slightly in 2011, but continued to increase at an average annual rate of 15.6% after 2012. In 2016, China's macroleverage showed signs of slowing down. The leverage of the enterprise sector slowed down significantly, mainly because the profits of enterprises improved and the residential sector became the main force of increasing leverage. Specifically, since 2008, the leverage ratio of the enterprise sector has increased by 8.8% annually, which is second only to the offshore financial centers such as Ireland, Luxemburg and Hong Kong of China, and far higher than those of developed countries such as the United States, Japan and the UK; the leverage ratio

S. Ba, *The New Cycle and New Finance in China*,
https://doi.org/10.1007/978-981-16-8209-4_5

of the residential sector, with an absolute increase of 44.4% and an average annual growth rate of 3.3%, also ranks high in emerging economies; the leverage ratio of government departments is the most moderate, which was 46.4% at the end of 2016, with an average annual growth rate of 2.4%. However, we should guard against the implicit debt expansion of local governments, which is not included in the statistics, and the rapid expansion of state-owned enterprises can largely be attributed to the support from these local governments.

After the international financial crisis, the rise of the leverage ratio of enterprises was mainly caused by state-owned enterprises. The asset liability ratio of these enterprises gradually increased from 57.4% in 2008 to 61.3% in 2016, while the leverage ratio of private enterprises decreased from 57% to 51.9% in the same period. Thanks to the introduction of financial resources by local governments, the average annual growth rate of the total liabilities of local state-owned enterprises was 21%, while that of central enterprises was 18% from 2008 to 2015. In other words, the local governments played an irreplaceable role in the rapid debt expansion of state-owned enterprises, and the financing right obtained by local governments after the financial crisis is an important driving force for local state-owned enterprises to increase leverage.

5.2 Deleveraging or Stabilizing Leverage

Deleveraging means clearance. Studies have also shown that it is the leverage ratio but not the level of leverage that is more directly related to risks; therefore, the speed of debt inflation should be controlled. Nomura Securities once proposed the "5-30 rule", that is, the rise of the ratio of credit to GDP by more than 30% within five years is often the precursor of crisis. The rise of leverage ratio, with an average annual growth rate of 6% from 2000 to 2007, was a significant warning signal before the financial crisis in the United States. In fact, the overall leverage ratio of the United States has not really been reduced after the crisis, but it was basically stabilized at around 248% through internal leverage.

In the European Union, only countries like Spain and Germany see a small decline in leverage, while France and Italy have basically maintained a stable leverage ratio. In the difficult process of deleveraging, the unemployment rate and inflation rate in Spain have seen sharp rise, the financial market has plummeted, and economic recession and even political turmoil have appeared. The German government has learned the lessons from the European debt crisis, taking the initiative to reduce the debt ratio of the government and promoting the balance of budget. Besides, the reform of the labor market aimed at reducing welfare and promoting employment has been carried out for a decade and begins to achieve initial results. As a result, in 2014, Germany achieved its budget balance for the first time in 45 years. For China, the more realistic goal in the short term is to reduce the annual rising rate of leverage ratio of about 15% to less than 10%. In the long run, effective deleveraging calls for active structural reform.

The positive thing is that, in 2016, China's macroleverage ratio showed signs of becoming stable. It is noteworthy that the leverage ratio of non-financial enterprises, which has been climbing rapidly at an average annual rate of 7% since 2011, slowed down in 2016 and increased by about 2% in the whole year. The marginal slowdown is partly due to the positive change of GDP deflator index and partly due to the slower growth of financing of the enterprise sector. Private enterprises continued to reduce leverage in 2012, but the deleveraging of state-owned enterprises has not really started. Profit improvement brought by PPI rise gave rise to slowdown of leverage ratio, but sustained slowdown calls for the improvement of the enterprises' real competitiveness through the internalization of the exogenous profitability under the rising price. For this purpose, we should cut overcapacity and handle "zombie enterprises".

The elimination of deflation and the improvement of exports create a better time window to stabilize the macroleverage ratio. The end industrial deflation in November 2015 was of great financial significance because it enabled China to successfully avoid the trap of debt deflation. Meanwhile, the profitability of upstream enterprises has been improved comprehensively, and the probability of systemic credit risk in upstream enterprises has been greatly reduced. Although the current PPI and corporate profits are declining, the PPI and industrial enterprise profit centers are expected to stay at around 5% and 16% respectively, both new highs since 2012. The completion of European and American balance sheet repair and the slow rise of external interest rates created favorable external conditions for deleveraging. After the international financial crisis, the balance sheet repair of European countries once lagged far behind that of the United States, but now the gap is narrowing: the US residential sector started to increase leverage from the third quarter of 2016, the rapidly rising debt ratio of European government departments has also slowed down, and the deficit ratio has been reduced to the level before the crisis. The end of balance sheet repair in Europe and the United States has two implications for China: China's exports benefit from revived global trade and the narrowing output gap of Europe and the United States; in addition, the slow rise of external interest rates gave rise to moderate domestic deleveraging. Both internal and external factors contributed to the higher profitability of microenterprises, which have basically carried through the most difficult moment. The year 2014 witnessed deep deflation in the industrial sector and low level of export. Things have changed as the policies today are obviously more stable, and it is unlikely for there to be a comprehensive policy shift in 2017.

5.3 Measures to Stabilize Leverage Ratio

Maintain stable and neutral interest rates. From 2013 to 2016, interest rates dropped dramatically, but it turns out that tightened financial policies are not conducive to deleveraging, and neither are relaxed policies. Too high interest rate will increase the interest payment cost of enterprises, which will lead to passive leverage; too low interest rate makes it easier to obtain loans, and enterprises will actively increase leverage. Therefore, the stable and neutral interest rates can create the most favorable monetary environment for the decrease of the leverage ratio.

Speed up the elimination of "zombie enterprises" and restrain local government debts through reform. Financial deleveraging aims to restrict the rise of debt ratio from the asset side, which is only a link to stabilize leverage, and the core is to handle the problems of the debt side. At the end of 2016, the State Council issued the Emergency Mechanism for Local Government Debt Risks to carry out classified and graded emergency treatment of local government debts, strengthen the accountability of debt risks, and prevent regional systemic risks. In addition, in the first half of 2017, the Ministry of Finance frequently warned local governments of their expansion of implicit debts, aiming to control the disorderly expansion of implicit debts of local governments and promote the elimination of "zombie state-owned enterprises". At present, the most urgent thing should be to speed up the reconstruction of the relationship between central and local financial power and administrative power, and it is also necessary to carry out the reform of state-owned enterprises, which is an effective mechanism to restrain debt expansion and stabilize leverage ratio in the medium and long term.

Use easy credit to offset the damage caused by financial deleveraging and high interest rates to the SMEs. Since the second quarter of 2017, due to high interest rates, 239 companies have canceled the issurance of bonds, the amount reaching RMB 229 billion. At present, the median ROA (return on assets) of the CSI 300 index is 6.5%, while the average weighted loan interest rate has risen to more than 5.5%. As is mentioned above, improving the profitability of microenterprises is also an important and more sustainable way to stabilize leverage ratio. High interest rates will weaken the profitability of enterprises and are not conducive to deleveraging. The previous adjustments show that it is often the small- and medium-sized private enterprises that bear the cost of credit crunch.

Chapter 6
On Financial Reform and the New Normal

China's economy is steadily entering the new normal thanks to a series of policies and internal and external economic factors. In the process, the transformation of the financial system is of great significance because the economic new normal itself includes the new normal for the financial system to get adapted to the transformation of the economic system. Besides, the transformation of the financial system or its entering the new normal will play a positive role in pushing the whole economic system toward the new normal.

We can interpret the relationship between the economic new normal and the financial new normal mentioned in the central economic work conference from this perspective. The year 2015 is a key year for China to comprehensively deepen reform. Financial reform, like other reforms in other fields, should also be in line with the transformation requirements of the economic new normal and follow the great logic of the transformation and reform of China's economy.

6.1 Economic New Normal and Financial New Normal

The central economic work conference defined the new normal from three dimensions and nine aspects, directly putting forward new requirements for the transformation of the financial system.

In terms of long-term growth, the economic growth center will move downward from high-speed growth to medium–high-speed growth. China's economic development is gradually changing into that of high quality and efficiency, and from factor driven to innovation driven. The advantage of low-cost labor is gradually weakening, and economic development will rely more on the quality of such factors as quality human capital and technological progress. In the process, the financial system dominated by commercial banks must get adapted to the change of growth rate and growth driving force, transform the longstanding business mode relying on large-scale credit expansion and begin to focus on promoting the transformation of economic system

S. Ba, *The New Cycle and New Finance in China*,
https://doi.org/10.1007/978-981-16-8209-4_6

through the reform of the financial system. At the same time, the financial system also needs to face the test of the steady decline of economic growth. In this process, it is necessary for us to prevent local regional financial risks from growing into systemic and global ones.

Short-term fluctuations show that various parts of demand are also changing, emphasizing personalized and diversified consumption, investment in new technologies and new products, and large-scale "going-out" strategy. The economic structure is also gradually optimized. These changes in growth driving force and demand also put forward new demands on the financial system. Many new demands cannot be satisfied by the traditional financial system. Therefore, it is necessary to promote the transformation of the system and duly relax financial regulation and financial access so as to attract new financial institutions and create new financial service models.

The macrocontrol policies should aim to promote transformation and resolve risks through reforms. The year of 2015 is a crucial year for comprehensively deepening the reform carried out in nine major areas, including administrative examination and approval, investment and price, etc., so as to accelerate the cultivation of new economic growth points, explore the direction of industrial transformation and development and remove the risk of overcapacity.

In 2015, China, adhering to the principle of seeking progress while maintaining stability, will maintain the continuity and stability of macropolicies and continue to implement active fiscal policies and prudent monetary policies. Moderate monetary policies help to resolve the risks of high leverage and economic bubbles, and strong fiscal policies also make it possible to realize the primary goal of "stable growth" in 2015. Correspondingly, such a new macropolicy environment is also needed to maintain a relatively stable financial environment through stable and moderate monetary policies, so as to serve the transformation of the entire economic system. At the same time, the macrofinancial control system should shift from direct control of interest rates, loan scale and other quantitative indicators to relying on market-oriented control tools such as interest rates and exchange rates.

6.2 New Trend of Financial Reform Under the New Normal

China's financial reform needs to take current economic development into consideration and adapt to the new normal of economic development.

First, there is an urgent need for the commercial banks to transform themselves under the new normal when China's economy will shift from high-speed growth to medium–high-speed growth. When the economy goes down, some hidden risks will appear, and commercial banks will face greater pressure brought by these risks. After the continuous credit expansion, some enterprises in China have an excessively high leverage ratio, and some industries with overcapacity will continue to undergo adjustment. The Opinions of the State Council on Strengthening the Management of Local Government Debts urges to settle the debts of all kinds of financing platforms.

The financing platforms providing loans are faced with greater risks, and the ratio of non-performing loans of commercial banks will continue to rise.

At the same time, with the deepened reform of market-oriented interest rates, the traditional business mode of commercial banks is challenged. The easier access to the license of private banks further intensifies the competition in the banking industry. The exposure draft of Deposit Insurance Ordinance of China was released, which will provide institutional guarantee for preventing moral hazards and handling bankrupt banks. Profound changes have taken place in the internal and external environment of the banking industry, making the transformation of commercial banks an urgent task.

Under the new normal, commercial banks should actively seek changes, adapt to the pace of interest rate liberalization, accelerate the adjustment of their own business mode and strengthen internal cost control and risk management in response to the challenges brought by market changes.

Second, new opportunities should be provided for the development of capital market under the new normal. The meeting required that the reform of state-owned enterprises should aim at solving problems, focusing on improving the vitality and efficiency of enterprises. The separate operation of state-owned enterprises, state-owned capital and state-owned assets regulation is expected to become a new form of state-owned assets management, and it is also the top priority of the new round reform of state-owned enterprises. The reform, including merger and acquisition, equity transfer, asset divestiture, share sale and asset replacement, provides new development opportunities for the investment banking business and the capital market.

In 2014, new breakthroughs were made in the reform of China's fiscal and taxation systems. After the promulgation of the new budget law, a series of documents, such as the Opinions on Strengthening the Management of Local Government Debts (hereinafter referred to as Document No. 43), Provisions on Deepening the Reform of Budget Management System, and Measures for Including the Local Government's Stock Debts into Budget Management have outlined a new framework for financing, management and operation of local government debts. According to the provisions of Document No. 43, social capital is encouraged to participate in the form of "franchise" in the investment and operation of "public welfare undertakings with certain return" such as urban infrastructure. The governments enable private–public partnership (PPP) projects to yield long-term stable income by means of franchise rights, reasonable pricing and financial subsidies. However, PPP projects usually have a long term, and the return cycle of PPP mode may not be able to cater to the risk preference of social capital at this stage. Because PPP projects enjoy a clear franchise transfer, stable cash flow and necessary government subsidies, such projects should involve asset securitization products, to remove the liquidity and term barriers for social capital entering PPP projects. At the same time, compared with the project income bonds and project income notes, asset securitization can be more effective in risk isolation. With the promotion of PPP mode, there will be new opportunities for the development of asset securitization.

Third, new requirements are put forward for financial support of new industries under the new normal. The meeting called for active seeking and cultivation of new growth points. Under the new normal, investment should still play the key role in economic development. Although traditional industries are relatively saturated, there are still many investment opportunities in infrastructure interconnection and some new technologies, products, business forms and models. The emerging industries, service industries and small and microenterprises are becoming more important in the process of industrial upgrading. However, it is difficult for the traditional asset-heavy risk assessment model of commercial banks to adapt to the asset-light direction of economic transformation under the new normal, and new requirements have been put forward for investment and financing services of new industries. The financial market needs a new tool for reasonable allocation of risk income. This kind of new tool, such as mezzanine financing between low-risk senior debt and high-risk equity investment, should not only consider the financing needs of different types of enterprises, but also consider the risk characteristics of enterprises in different industries.

Fourth, new requirements have been put forward for renminbi internationalization under the new normal. The meeting called for accelerating the reform of foreign investment, striving to improve the efficiency and quality of foreign investment, promoting the going out of advantageous industries and steadily promoting renminbi internationalization. Renminbi internationalization began with the pilot project of renminbi settlement for cross-border trade, and the currency has become the seventh largest payment and settlement currency and the ninth largest foreign exchange transaction currency in the world. Under the new normal, the pattern of China's foreign investment has changed. The direct overseas investment of China's non-financial enterprises is expected to exceed that of direct foreign investment in 2016, when foreign direct investment may become an export channel of net capital. Under the Belt and Road initiative, Chinese enterprises are actively seeking efficient and quality foreign investment. Export of renminbi and promotion of renminbi internationalization only through current account surplus can no longer meet the needs of China's economic development. We should actively seek to export renminbi through capital account and create a new pattern of renminbi internationalization. In the process of enterprises' going out, efforts should be made to promote the use of renminbi in transactions of resources and bulk commodities, so as to enhance the pricing power of renminbi in global supply; the going out of enterprises and the export of renminbi need financial support and renminbi payment and settlement businesses abroad need reliable financial supporting services.

Part II
Financial Institutions

Chapter 7
On the Development Prospect of China's Banking Industry

Recently, Moody's and Standard and Poor's successively lowered China's sovereign credit rating outlook and the rating outlook of several financial institutions, including commercial banks and policy banks, from stable to negative mainly because they believe that China's sustained and strong credit growth leads to continuous accumulation of risks in the banking system and poorer quality of the banking industry's assets. International financial institutions need to deepen their understanding of the reality of China's economy and the development and actual operation of China's banking industry. It also shows that China's banking industry needs to actively integrate into the international financial market and strengthen in-depth interaction and exchange with international institutions.

7.1 Generally Healthy Fundamentals of China's Banking Industry

First, China's banking industry still yield huge profits; both the asset profit rate and capital profit rate are excellent compared with those of other countries, and it has strong endogenous capital supplement ability. By the end of the fourth quarter of 2015, China's commercial banks had realized a net profit of RBM 159.26 billion, with an average return on assets of 1.10% and an average return on capital of 14.98%. US commercial banks had realized a net profit of US $152.1 billion in 2015, with an average return on assets of 1.03% and an average return on capital of 9.23%. Besides, the main regulatory indicators of China's banking industry remained at a good level. By the fourth quarter of 2015, the core tier-one capital adequacy ratio of China's commercial banks was 10.91%, the tier-one capital adequacy ratio was 11.31%, the capital adequacy ratio was 13.45%, the liquidity ratio was 48.01%, and the provision coverage rate was 181.18%. This shows that China's commercial banks have a strong capability of offsetting risks. They have enough capability of bearing losses with their own capital even if their assets are lost.

S. Ba, *The New Cycle and New Finance in China*,
https://doi.org/10.1007/978-981-16-8209-4_7

Second, China's banking industry has a lower proportion of non-performing loans. According to the international standard, it is normal if the non-performing loan ratio is kept below 5%. The non-performing loan ratio in developed countries in Europe and America is usually around 3%. As of the fourth quarter of 2015, the non-performing loans of China's commercial banks reached RMB 1274.4 billion, with a non-performing loan ratio of 1.67%. It can be seen that although the non-performing loan rate of China's banking industry has slightly increased due to the impact of the economic downturn, the proportion of non-performing loans is still low compared with that of their international counterparts.

Third, China's banking industry has been optimizing its income structure, and its ability of risk dispersion has been improved. The industry is actively engaged in business transformation, actively responding to the challenges of interest rate liberalization, vigorously developing intermediary business such as bank card, custody, agency, investment banking, consulting, etc., so as to reduce the dependence on interest income. Besides, the strategies such as the Belt and Road Initiative and the free trade zone have led to the expansion of international investment, financing and settlement business. It will also boost the demand for business involving bank fees and commission. Data shows that non-interest income is becoming an important factor contributing to the growth of the net profit of China's banking industry, with the proportion increasing year by year, from 17.5% at the end of 2010 to 23.73% at the end of 2015. As the acquisition of non-interest income requires less capital and involves a wider range of business, commercial banks can disperse risks while achieving higher financial leverage.

7.2 Credit Structure and Non-Performing Loans of China's Banking Industry

In recent years, China's banking industry has been actively carrying out the adjustment of its credit structure and has achieved remarkable results. As of 2015, the non-performing loans were mainly concentrated in the manufacturing industry (RMB 392.14 billion, accounting for 37.1%) and the commerce (RMB 368.96 billion, accounting for 34.9%), which together accounted for more than 70% of all non-performing loans. In response to the increase of these two types of credit risks, the banking industry has carried out prompt and effective measures to adjust its credit structure. According to the data in the annual reports of 11 listed banks (5 major state-owned banks and 6 joint-stock banks, the same below), the loans of the manufacturing industry and the commerce totaled RMB 13.92 trillion, down RMB 3.05 trillion compared with 2013, and their proportion in loans decreased from 26% in 2013 to 21%. The proportion of the industries with non-performing loans is decreasing. However, retail (personal) loans, education, finance, culture and other tertiary industry loans are thriving. The total retail loans of the above 11 listed banks amounted to RMB 20.82 trillion, accounting for 32% of the total loans, an increase of 3% compared with 2013. Retail loans consist mainly of low-risk mortgage loans, business loans with relatively high risks and credit card loans. Judging from the data, we can see that the rate of non-performing retail loans has increased, but it is mainly due to the rise in the non-performing rate of personal business loans. Compared with corporate loans of the manufacturing industry, retail loans have the characteristics of smaller amount per loan, earlier risk exposure and higher interest rate, and pose no serious risks to the banks. The rates of non-performing loans of education, finance, culture, sports and entertainment industries are all below 0.5%. With the growth of China's national revenue, the leverage ratio of the residential sector is on the rise, and with the continuous and rapid development of the tertiary industry, the proportion of high-quality assets in bank assets will continue to increase.

The banking industry is adjusting the asset structure and strictly controlling the new risks, and it has also strengthened measures to write off non-performing assets. In 2015, the above 11 listed banks have written off loans of RMB 305.6 billion, an increase of 283% compared with 2013. Thanks to this, risk assets are not accumulated in the banking system.

In the future, with economic development, the quality of the cyclical industries' assets will remain stable, the proportion of new low-risk assets will continue to increase, and the banking industry will step up its efforts to write off non-performing loans. It is expected that the banking industry will be able to keep the lowering non-performing loan rate under control.

7.3 Risk Control Capability and Disposal Tools of China's Banking Industry

Compared with the end of 1990s, China's banking industry has seen significant improvement in its risk control capability. The risk management system has changed from single credit risk management to comprehensive risk management; the risk control procedure has changed from post-event control to prior control; the risk management has been changed from passive management to active management; and the concept of risk management has changed from the pursuit of risk minimization to the optimization of risk and return.

The introduction of Basel Accord in China's regulation contributed to the improvement of risk management of the banking industry and the perfection of the capital regulation system in recent years. At present, the five state-owned and some joint-stock commercial banks have applied the advanced approaches of Basel Accord. According to the report of the Basel Committee in April 2016, China has applied the capital definition, capital retention buffer, countercyclical capital buffer, liquidity coverage and its disclosure requirements, leverage ratio and its disclosure requirements, regulatory requirements of global systemically important financial institutions and regulatory requirements of domestic systemically important financial institutions. The work of drafting other regulatory measures has also begun. This indicates that historic progress has been made in the construction of capital regulation system of commercial banks meeting international standards and reflecting China's national conditions. The implementation of IRB has changed the current risk management system of China's banking industry from the levels and dimensions of risk governance, policy process, measurement model and data IT. In particular, China's banks will change from the qualitative and expert experience-based risk management mode to the mode combining qualitative and quantitative approaches, and huge changes will also take place in loan procedure, business system and specific operation mode. This makes China's banking industry more calm and confident in the face of diversified risks.

Recently, the Chinese government has tried out a series of policies such as the securitization of non-performing loans, the usufruct transfer of non-performing assets, and the "debt to equity swap", actively guiding the banking industry to adopt market-oriented, diversified and comprehensive approaches to handle non-performing assets. These policies will effectively curb the expansion of non-performing assets. On February 1, 2016, the People's Bank of China restarted the pilot work of securitization of non-performing loans of the six banks including Industrial and Commercial Bank of China (ICBC), China Construction Bank (CCB), Bank of China (BOC), Agricultural Bank of China (ABC), Bank of Communications (BOCOM) and China Merchants Bank (CMB), with a total amount of RMB 50 billion. It enables the banks to recover the loan principal of assets without increasing liabilities and convert a large number of non-performing loans into bonds in the hands of investors through securitization, thereby increasing the liquidity of assets and dispersing the financial risks of the banking industry as a whole.

7.4 Financial Services Provided by Banks

Banks should change its role from serving the enterprises that have positive cash flow to serving the enterprises during their whole life cycle.

In the process of economic transformation, many entrepreneurs regard participation in the financial industry as one of the alternatives of transformation. It is not totally unreasonable because the existing financial service system cannot support economic and industrial transformation, which forces some enterprises to actively participate in the financial industry.

Therefore, the current financial services should change from supporting asset-heavy enterprises in the traditional economic growth mode to supporting innovative enterprises of asset-light operation, and from mainly serving the enterprises that have positive cash flow to serving the enterprises during their whole life cycle. For example, in the process of cutting overcapacity, shedding inventories and deleveraging, a large number of enterprises are shut down or shift to other lines of production, and there are also mergers and acquisitions. This is exactly the stage when a large number of financial services are needed. However, many commercial banks often avoid providing financial services most needed due to the maladjustment of their business models and poor management capabilities.

Objectively, the banks have been very competitive in providing sufficient services for enterprises with heavy assets and profits, and the banks have also accumulated sufficient experience in serving these customers. However, an evaluation at this specific stage of economic transformation shows that if the service mode of banks in this period of economic transformation is still driven by the traditional mortgage guarantee, then the traditional industries with large amount of assets for mortgage guarantee are generally the traditional industries with heavy assets, while many of these industries such as the steel and cement industries, are precisely the ones with overcapacity in this round of economic adjustment. If the banking industry sticks to the traditional asset-heavy management mode, precious financial resources will continue to flow to some industries with overcapacity, which will objectively hinder the development of emerging industries.

In the period of economic transformation, a large number of enterprises are innovative enterprises in need of adjustment, merger and reshuffle. These enterprises need various financial services such as consulting and financing at this very stage. If commercial banks are still providing the traditional financial services such as deposits, loans and foreign exchange, it is often difficult for these enterprises to find corresponding services and products provided by the banks when they encounter difficulties in business. The commercial banks' risk preference of credit business will naturally drive them to withdraw from such services and products.

I want to stress that in the period of economic transformation, the financial industry should also be transformed. If commercial banks fail to do so, its importance will gradually decline in this round of transformation. Financial institutions that can meet these new financial needs will undergo rapid development. The good thing is that the operation of China's macroeconomy is gradually stabilizing, and structural reform will improve the macroenvironment for the long-term healthy development of China's banking industry.

In the short term, the operation of China's macroeconomy is gradually stabilizing. China's economy grew by 6.7% in the first quarter of 2016, which was slightly lower than that in the first and fourth quarters of 2015, but it still operated in a reasonable range between 6.5% and 7%. This growth rate is higher than that of developed countries and emerging economies. Especially, the main economic indicators have shown positive improvement since March 2016. Some international institutions have also raised their expectations for China's economic growth to be above 6.6% for the whole year. On April 12, 2016, the report released by the International Monetary Fund (IMF) lowered the global economic growth forecast by 0.2 percentage point, but increased the forecast of China's annual economic growth by 0.2 percentage point. At the same time, the reform of local government budget system and the replacement of existing debts have been continuously promoted, and the overall risk situation is stable and controllable. According to the budget report deliberated and passed by the NPC and CPPCC, the scale of newly increased local governments' debts in 2016 reached RMB1.18 trillion, nearly double that of 2015. With the issuance of over

RMB3.2 trillion of replacement bonds, the financial burden of local governments has been reduced and the debt sustainability has been improved.

In the medium and long term, structural reform has laid a solid foundation for the long-term healthy development of China's banking industry. In 2016, the central working conference proposed the five major tasks of "reducing overcapacity, shedding excess inventory, deleveraging, reducing cost reduction, and strengthening points of weakness" so as to promote structural reform. Supply side reform will result in the shutdown of some enterprises in the short term, which inevitably leads to the continuous exposure of the risks of "old assets". But in the long run, the promotion of supply side reform is conducive to the recovery of profitability of traditional industries and the creation of new high-quality assets. It is of great significance to improve the structure of customers, optimize the structure of loans, improve the quality of assets and reduce the overall credit risks of China's banks.

Besides the supply side reform, such structural arrangements as leverage replacement and direct financing can achieve good effects on the mitigation of debt risks. Currently, leverage replacement mainly involves leverage reduction among enterprises and leverage increase in the government and residential sectors. Traditional industries reduce leverage while the emerging industries increase leverage. The leverage ratio of Chinese government is not high compared with that of developed countries, and there is a lot of room for fiscal policies. The leverage ratio of China's residential sector has shown an obvious increase in recent years, reaching nearly 40% at the end of 2015, but it is still at a low level compared with that of other major economies, and there is still a certain room for further increase in the future. The leverage ratio of traditional industries and upstream industrial enterprises is higher, while such emerging industries as medicine, computer, media and downstream consumer service enterprises have a low leverage ratio. Preferential policies are provided for emerging industries, encouraging them to increase leverage ratio and speed up the generation of new assets. Traditional industries with overcapacity and a large number of zombie enterprises are encouraged to promote the debt restructuring and cut overcapacity so as to restore the balance of supply and demand and improve the profitability of these industries.

Structural reform not only curbs rising asset risks of banks due to result disorderly expansion and quantitative growth, but also resolves the real risks of the banking industry through improving the quality of stock assets and creating high-quality new assets. It solves the deep-seated problems of investment-debt cycle, and consolidates the foundation for long-term healthy development of the banking industry. Therefore, when evaluating the risks of China's banking industry, we should not only pay attention to the increase of short-term non-performing loans, but we should also pay attention to its adjustment of business structure and the support of economic structural reform to remove risks and promote long-term sustainable growth.

Chapter 8
On Commercial Banks and Economic Transformation

I would like to offer some insights concerning commercial banks. First, we can see the macroeconomic fluctuations from the operation of commercial banks.

I have witnessed the expansion of banks like the Industrial Bank Co., Ltd. and China Minsheng Banking Co., Ltd (CMBC) from local small banks to regional banks, and then to nationwide ones before they were organized and got listed on the stock market. When the decision makers of a bank with assets of only RMB10 billion or RMB 100 billion read any good or bad news, they will first judge whether the news has anything to do with the bank, and then assign relevant work to relevant business departments as soon as possible. However, according to my experience, when a bank has assets of more than RMB500 billion, it is related to almost every piece of news. Therefore, banks with large assets have participated in the whole process of macroeconomic fluctuations through assets, liabilities and other businesses. This is true in China, and it is also the case in European and American countries.

I was particularly impressed by one thing mentioned during my exchange with people from the financial sector in New York. They said that in October of a certain year, the Federal Reserve spotted a sharp decline in the volume of settlement business. In the past, such large fluctuations were often signs of major problems in the financial system. In the end, after repeated research, they found out the reason behind it: China observed the first seven-day National Day holidays in that year. Until now, I can never forget how shocked I was. In fact, there were not many direct economic exchanges between China and the USA at that time. However, through direct or indirect financial business exchanges, China's policy of observing long holidays could affect the business settlement volume of the Federal Reserve. This shows the influence of globalization.

Similarly, after the continuous expansion of banking business to different industries and regions, we can basically grasp the trend of macroeconomy through the changes of banking business coverage in different industries. We decided to invite these bank decision makers to share with you because we can see traces of China's macroeconomic fluctuations from their speeches.

S. Ba, *The New Cycle and New Finance in China*,
https://doi.org/10.1007/978-981-16-8209-4_8

Recently, people are very concerned about the non-performing assets of banks. From the evolution of the banks' non-performing assets in different industries and regions, we can clearly see the challenges of this round of economic transformation in China and the corresponding countermeasures. In this round of economic restructuring, most of the banks with the earliest and fastest growth of non-performing assets are located in the Yangtze River Delta, like Jiangsu Province and Zhejiang Province. The non-performing assets of these national banks accounted for 70–80% of the annual new non-performing assets. This shows that in this round of China's economic restructuring, the export-oriented and labor-intensive enterprises with low added value and little brand effect were the first ones to be impacted. With the continuous economic adjustment, the impact has gradually spread to the central and western regions and extended to small and microenterprises with single financing channels.

We can see the change of financial structure from the operation of commercial banks. Shao Ping, former president of Ping An Bank Co., Ltd., mentioned in his handout that in recent years, a saying in the banking sector goes like this: when the banking industry is faced with multiple challenges, it the time for real bankers to give full play to their professional knowledge and capabilities. In the past, the business models of banks were relatively simple, and different banks had similar business models. The first step was to increase deposits. After that, the amount of loans can be calculated according to such indicators as the deposit loan ratio and asset liability management. Under the regulation of interest rates, the real interest rates of the market were often higher than the official loan interest rates of the banks, so the allocation of the loans became a problem. At that time, the banks could earn considerable profits thanks to the large spread between deposit and loan interest rates. It wasn't a time for real professional bankers to give full play to their professional knowledge, because there was no big difference in the depth of their knowledge about banking. But now, things are different. The control of interest rate, exchange rate and license plate is being relaxed, and new competitors are swarming into the banking industry. After the deregulation of interest rates, people are discussing how to evaluate banks. In the past, we took 15, 20, 30% profit growth for granted. Now, after repeated discussions, we believe that it is a good bank that maintains profit growth faster than GDP growth. Of course, Ping An Bank is probably still enjoying a double-digit profit growth rate.

Now, commercial banks are faced with many new challenges because they are facing new customers such as small and microcustomers as well as asset-light, service-oriented and technology-based customers. Banks are not familiar with these customers as they did not provide services for these customers in the past. Banks have to learn how to manage the risks of these customers and meet their needs for financial services. In recent years, banks have introduced more new products than before. In the past few years, banks basically had three types of business: deposits, loans and foreign exchange. At that time, the business managers in banks were very proud because they thought they knew how to do business. Now, many new banks ask me to recommend people to be their high officials like a vice president or head of department. When I asked about the qualifications of the candidates, they replied that it would be better if the candidates had never worked in banks before, because if they were restricted by the old ideas of traditional banking industry and would not take the initiative to update their knowledge, it would be difficult for them to understand many new products.

We can also see the close interaction between the transformation of commercial banks and the economic transformation through the operation of commercial banks. Many business models gradually become mature through practices. Recently, Mr. Wang from the private banking department of CMB explained how the bank succeeded in becoming a leader in private banking business. He mentioned in the lecture that CMB found that urban white-collar workers with higher education have higher requirements for payment and settlement, and they are more skilled in using the Internet. Therefore, CMB took the lead in launching the all-in-one-card service, attracting some of the white-collar workers in the cities. Then, these white-collar workers put forward new requirements, forcing CMB to launch hierarchical customer services, giving rise to the Golden Sunflower debit cards. Therefore, I put forward a very important standard when I participated in the discussion on the issue of new banking licenses: banks with newly approved banking licenses should have new business models.

Banks have the capability of allocating resources. They can play a very important role in promoting economic transformation, and the financial industry can contribute to the merger and reshuffle of industries with overcapacity and high leverage. At present, both people at home and abroad are very concerned about the high leverage of Chinese enterprises. The leverage ratio is rising with the decline of economic growth. One of the most important reasons is that the financial sector may have allocated resources to industries and departments with long-term low efficiency. Of course, higher growth rate and larger loans do not necessarily result in the rising leverage ratio because the leverage ratio will remain low or even decline in the period of rapid growth if the benefits generated by the investment are good enough. Therefore, high leverage is directly related to the continued allocation of valuable financial resources by the financial system to underperforming sectors.

In order to promote economic transformation, the banking industry must transform itself accordingly. For example, the new driving forces of economic growth we want to foster are often new customers to traditional commercial banks. From my own experience, there is such a dilemma even now, that is, loans must be secured by mortgage, because once there is a problem, at least there is a mortgage guarantee. But few customers have enough assets as collateral. These customers are precisely those assets-heavy enterprises with overcapacity and high leverage ratio. The enterprises in need of financial support are often asset-light enterprises, such as service and high-tech enterprises, which are unfamiliar to traditional banks. Banks ask for collateral, but these asset-light enterprises are not able to meet the banks' requirement. Many banks used to grant loans to film projects, but even the directors didn't know how much the film company could mortgage, so they asked the banks to make an assessment. If the film failed to be successful, the directors would give the copy of the film as collateral. As a result, the banks were faced with relatively high risks. Therefore, banks must look for new business models, so as to find new methods to evaluate the credit and repayment ability of enterprises.

So, how about the transformation of commercial banks? Judging the transformation and evolution of commercial banks from the three realms of Zen, we can draw many enlightening conclusions. Zen masters describe the different stages of Zen meditation this way: at the beginning of meditation, a meditator sees a mountain as mountain, and sees the water as water; when the meditator is somewhat enlightened, he sees a mountain more than just a mountain, and sees the water more than just water; when the meditator comes to a thorough understanding, he will again see a mountain as mountain, and sees the water as water. I would like to use the stages of Zen to illustrate the different stages of the transformation of commercial banks under the new normal.

The first stage is the traditional business model of the banking industry when banks have their own business models. Banks are banks, and the roles of different banks were very clear, with ABC, BOC, ICBC and CCB performing their respective duties.

After the deregulation of financial regulations, the banks are now entering the second stage when the structure and mode of the market are not stable, and the framework of market is also changing. In the new business environment, the bankers keep thinking actively, constantly adding other elements to the traditional banking business model. Therefore, people will think that this is not the bank we are familiar with. Banks are no longer banks only.

The third stage refers to the shuffling period after the confusion and differentiation periods. The differentiation leads to different positioning and strategies among banks to be tested by the market. A clearer market pattern is likely to appear gradually in this stage. However, this new pattern is different from the one we are familiar with. I have studied the possible changes in banks after the emergence of interest rate liberalization. Nordic countries once experienced such changes: the large state-owned banks with an absolute monopoly position in the market and a market share of more than 50% have become insignificant regional ones after interest rate liberalization while those banks with sound business model, sufficient capital, and successful integration and merger through skillful use of capital market are likely to stand out and become the new "mountain" and "water" in the third stage.

At this stage, there are many new problems to be studied. In the future, we will invite financiers to communicate with you from different perspectives. Dr. Chen Dong used to be the research director of Galaxy Securities and then worked in the headquarters of China Life Asset Management Company Ltd. (CLAMCL). Later, he was sent to Hong Kong as CEO of CLAMCL. Now he is CEO of Taiping Financial Holdings Co., Ltd. Is he a buyer's investment manager or an executive of a financial holdings company? He is both, and he is neither. This may be one of the characteristics of the financial shuffle period, which is both a big challenge to and a test of financiers.

Chapter 9
China's Banking Industry in Globalization 3.0

CBRC Chairman Guo Shuqing said recently that Banking 3.0 era has come. The banking industry should make use of financial technologies such as big data, cloud computing, blockchain, artificial intelligence and other new technologies to innovate service methods and processes, integrate traditional service resources, link online and offline advantages and improve the efficiency of resource allocation of the whole banking industry so as to satisfy customer and social needs in a more advanced, flexible and efficient manner.

How should the banking industry cope with the all-around competition inside and outside the industry and smoothly realize its transformation and upgrading when faced with the changes and new challenges in the Banking 3.0 era?

9.1 Financial Technology Forces Banking Industry to Make Changes

According to statistics, the number of active mobile devices in China has exceeded 1 billion, 95% of China's enterprises have invested in mobile devices and applications, and the total number of app store applications is close to 150,000.

More than 60% of mobile applications will be integrated with data analysis. Big data technology has reduced the research and development cost of products by 50% for the manufacturing industry across the globe. Nearly 50% of CIOs plan to give priority to the development of data projects.

According to statistics, China's online banking transaction scale has exceeded RMB 600 trillion in recent years, and the growth rate of transaction scale has remained at a high level. The number of users of online banking and payment has increased rapidly, reaching 350 million and 450 million respectively by the end of 2016.

Financial technology is forcing the banking industry to make changes. Under this backdrop, China's banking industry begins to attach greater importance to the development of new business models such as Internet finance, and most of the bankers

S. Ba, *The New Cycle and New Finance in China*,
https://doi.org/10.1007/978-981-16-8209-4_9

regard it as a development priority. Among the various forms of Internet finance, China's banking industry attaches the greatest importance to Internet banking, mobile payment and direct banking.

9.2 Transformation of Profit Models

With the interest rate liberalization, the income structure of banks tends to be diversified amid competitions, and the net interest margin continues to narrow. With the completion of interest rate liberalization, the net interest margin of the banking industry has continued to decline. In the third quarter of 2016, the overall interest margin of commercial banks declined by 30 basis points. The decline of interest margin means that banks transfer income to enterprises and residents, which also forces the banking industry to improve its risk pricing ability and adjust its business structure. The continuous decline of deposit and loan interest rates has intensified the competition among commercial banks, stimulated the expansion of business scope, put forward higher requirements for the financial innovation ability of banks, improved the efficiency of financial intermediaries and optimized the income structure of banks, but it has also caused greater fluctuations of the financial market.

The trend of financial disintermediation is remarkable, and the proportion of direct financing is increasing. With the continuous improvement of the multi-level capital market in the Chinese mainland, the financing channels of high-quality enterprises are increasingly diversified. The proportion of direct financing such as stocks and bonds in social financing is increasing. This poses challenges to banks and intensifies the competition among banks. In the era of Internet finance and broad asset management, the investment channels of bank customers have been expanded. With the rapid development of shadow banking, deposit diversion has exerted impact on customer deposits of commercial banks, and their ability to take deposits has also been weakened.

The leverage ratio of non-financial sectors remains high, and the non-performing asset rate of banks is also rising. In recent years, the leverage ratio of non-financial sectors (enterprises) in the Chinese mainland remains high, resulting in increasing financial costs of enterprises and the accumulation of systematic risks. Therefore, deleveraging has become an important task in the China's economic transformation. In the 2016 survey, 73.2% of the bankers thought that the risk of loans granted to industries with overcapacity was the most serious credit risk of China's banking industry, which was much more serious than other factors. Their attitude shows that the banking industry is worried about the industries with overcapacity.

The process of renminbi internationalization has been accelerated, and the opening of capital account has been steadily promoted. The renminbi's inclusion in the SDR basket increases the demand for renminbi assets, which has a profound impact on the process of renminbi internationalization. In the 2016 survey, 75.8% of the bankers believed that renminbi's inclusion in the SDR basket would accelerate renminbi internationalization, and 53.9% of bankers believed that allocation of renminbi assets would be increased. The acceleration of renminbi internationalization provides a rare new growth point for China's banking industry, which is being tested by multiple factors, such as the downward pressure of domestic economy, the slowdown of profits and the reduction of interest rate spread due to interest rate liberalization. It has also put forward higher requirements on risk management.

Especially since the exchange rate reform on August 11, 2015, the fluctuation of renminbi exchange rates has increased, and the fluctuation of offshore and onshore renminbi price spread has intensified. The fluctuation of exchange rates and the ensuing uncertainties have brought new challenges to the renminbi business of commercial banks. In recent years, the opening of capital account in the Chinese mainland has been steadily promoted. On December 5, 2016, Hong Kong Stock Market Trading Interconnection Mechanism was established to strengthen the interconnection between the markets of the Chinese mainland and Hong Kong. Thanks to the mechanism, the interaction between domestic and foreign capital markets is becoming more frequent, and the banking industry will face new opportunities and challenges in risk management.

9.3 Three Development Trends

1. Intelligent Banking: A Technologically Advanced Business System

The emergence of intelligent banks will provide convenience to consumers who have not received sufficient banking financial services, and bring richer financial services to small- and medium-sized enterprises. Different from the traditional banks, intelligent banks will be supported by data analysis and IT technology in its development. The performance of an intelligent bank will mainly depend on its technological strength rather than its financial products.

Retail consumers will be able to obtain more comprehensive overall customized service, receive point-to-point digital service based on paperless application and certification, use domestic and international mobile electronic payment, embrace biometric technology with higher security and use electronic credit cards based on big data consumption habit model.

Investors will be able to use digital system that supports mobile and online payment, receive digital wallet service based on digital trade and ecosystem, conduct digital sales of bank products such as deposits, loans and mortgages, carry out artificial intelligence asset management and investment consulting and establish credit rating system based on big data credit model. Banks will be able to enjoy advanced and flexible IT infrastructure, develop database design capability based on new network technology and analysis methods. They will also be able to have data analysis ability based on big data consumption model, acquire more dynamic user information through artificial intelligence technology, carry out network security system construction and provide customer information protection.

In the construction of the information system, the Chinese bankers will focus on the construction of the core trading system, credit management system and risk management system. Among various information technologies, the Chinese bankers are most concerned about mobile Internet technology, big data technology, and secure and controllable information technology.

According to the statistics of *Chinese Bankers Survey*, among the main application fields of information technology, the fields based on big data technology, such as management refinement and customer marketing, attract the most attention. In the application of information technology, the most serious problems faced by China's banking industry arise from insufficient internal data integration, poor availability of external data, and lack of data mining and processing technology, which highlights the importance of the construction of database and the analysis ability of big data models.

2. Light Banking: Flexible and Efficient Business Model

The scale growth is decoupled from the profit growth. The development mode of China's traditional banking industry is: financing (replenishing capital)—lending (expanding asset scale)—income growth (realizing income growth)—refinancing. However, since 2015, the scale growth of China's banking industry has begun to decouple from the profit growth. The proportion of risk-weighted assets in total assets of such banks as China Merchants Bank has been declining, and the transformation into banks with light assets has achieved initial results.

Lighter assets lead to lighter income. The growth rate of off balance sheet assets (mainly financial assets) is higher than that of balance sheet assets. Meanwhile, the proportion of retail business with low capital consumption is increasing. The proportion of non-interest income of China's banking industry is still relatively low, but it has shown a growing trend in recent years.

Diversified forms of business are being conducted. Broad asset management and broad investment banking business have become the key development direction. At the end of June 2016, the scale of asset management business in the Chinese mainland was about RMB 60 trillion, of which the scale of wealth management products was RMB26.28 trillion. We can see that wealth management has become the largest subindustry. According to *Chinese Bankers Survey* on the sources of income from intermediary business, commercial banks' income from investment banking and the income from financial management rank top two. Banks will strive to improve the ability of asset allocation during their development of asset management business. The investment banking business mainly focuses on innovative equity financing products such as industrial funds and PPP projects. The basic investment banking business such as bond underwriting, investment and financing consulting, and syndicated loans will be promoted.

Assets are securitized. The idle assets are being tapped, the issuance scale has been expanded, and the pricing mechanism is being explored. In 2016, the securitization of non-performing assets was restarted, and a total of 14 non-performing ABS orders were issued, with a total amount of BRM15.61 billion. Non-performing ABS has become a new way to deal with non-performing assets. In addition, asset securitization can effectively adjust the banks' asset structure and revitalize the idle assets. At the same time, the issuance scale of credit asset securitization has been on the rise. In 2016, a total of 108 orders were issued, with a total amount of RMB390.853 billion. The underlying assets are mainly personal housing mortgage loans and enterprise loans, accounting for more than 70% of the total. China Development Bank (CDB) has a high market share of more than 25%. However, due to the poor mobility in the secondary market, we mainly use the market inquiry pricing mechanism, and the market pricing mechanism is still under exploration.

Transaction banks are developed. There is a new trend in business transformation. With the accelerated development of interest rate liberalization, renminbi internationalization, cross-border transactions and Internet finance, the transaction banking business has become the key to transforming and developing traditional commercial banks, expanding their income channels and enhancing their competitiveness. Transaction banks focus on payment and settlement, cash management, supply chain finance and trade finance. The purpose of developing transaction banks is to develop new business growth points, expand the source of low-cost liabilities, improve customer service, yield stable income, reduce business risks, change business service mode and expand cross business. At present, the factors impacting the development of the transaction business mainly include the ability of product research and development, the coordination of cross-regional transit, cross-departments and cross-product lines, the ability of risk control, the collaborative ability of the head office and branches and infrastructure construction.

3. International Banks: A Global Perspective

In recent years, although there is still a gap between Chinese banks and big foreign banks, the internationalization of China's banking industry is deepening. Generally speaking, China's banking industry is still at the early stage of internationalization, with blind expansion, vicious competition and blind pursuit of quantity and scale.

In 2015, the combined bank internationalization index (BII) of the five major banks was 8.9, and that of the five joint-stock commercial banks was 2.7, indicating a relatively low degree of internationalization. Among them, the BII of Bank of China was the highest (21.57), followed by industrial and Commercial Bank of China (8.94), Bank of Communications (7.15), China Construction Bank (4.33) and Agricultural Bank of China (3.41)。

Different types of banks show great differences in terms of overseas distribution. The five major banks have a wider scope of overseas distribution. The joint-stock commercial banks are still in their infancy, and the branches are mainly distributed in Hong Kong and Southeast Asia. As of 2015, the overseas branches of the five major banks in Central Asia and Europe accounted for 71.4%, and the branches in Asia alone accounted for 44.4%. Bank of China still leads in terms of the number of overseas branches, accounting for more than 50%.

9.4 Development Prospect of the Banking Industry in 2017

Regulation will be tightened, the monetary policies will remain stable and neutral, and macroprudential management is constantly improving. In 2017, the domestic monetary policies will be tightened, the interest rate center of the money market will be improved, and financial deleveraging will continue. At the same time, MPA will be put into practice and continue to improve, and broad credit will lead to the return of rational bank asset expansion.

In terms of credit risks, the accumulation of non-performing assets will slow down, different approaches will be adopted to handle non-performing assets, and importance will be attached to the profitability of enterprises. Since 2016, the accumulation of non-performing assets in China has slowed down significantly. Recently, the non-performing asset ratio in Shanghai (0.68%) and Zhejiang (2.17%) has declined, and the national NPA rate is basically stable at 1.74%. At the same time, multiple approaches have been adopted to handle non-performing assets in various regions, and market-oriented debt-to-equity swaps can be seen everywhere. In 2017, it is necessary to pay close attention to the short cycle of inventory replenishment and corporate profitability.

Infrastructure and emerging industries will be the focus during the credit structure adjustment. In 2017, under the overall tight liquidity environment in China, the credit growth rate will witness a return and become stable, and the monthly volatility will be reduced. The modes of PPP and industrial funds will become important channels for banks to invest in infrastructure.

In terms of profit forecast, the net interest spread is expected to become stable, the scale of profit will grow steadily, and the profit growth rate will bottom out. In 2017, due to weakened asset repricing factors, the reduced impact of replacing business tax with value-added tax (VAT) and the tightening liquidity, the market interest rate will rise, and the net interest spread of domestic banking industry will witness a moderate decrease before becoming stable. The profitability of the banking industry saw weak recovery in 2016, with a net profit increase of 3.54%, and the growth rate is expected to continue to be on the rise in 2017.

Chapter 10
Upgrade of China's Outsourcing Business

Banks vied to participate in asset management business in their transformation and innovation in the past few years, but now, it has become an area of much concern that involves tightened regulation and risk management. This is because the leverage of the financial system has been increasing in the past several years while many of these asset management products were carriers of leverage. Under the backdrop of deleveraging, there are some new changes and trends in regulatory policies and industry development.

We will approach the phenomenon from the following three perspectives: the environment formed in this round of financial leverage, our moves in deleveraging financial markets, and the future trend of regulation and its possible impact on the asset management industry.

A relatively loose and low interest rate monetary environment is the realistic basis for this round of leverage. Since 2015, Shibor interest rate has been maintained at a low level, and it remained so even in 2016, which can be said to be the international phenomenon. However, China's interest rate has always been maintained at a low level until the fourth quarter of 2016 when bond market interest rates began to rise.

There is a relatively relaxed policy of money supply in the environment of low interest rate, and the whole derivation of money is undergoing a significant change. Since 2015, the growth rate of the balance of the basic currency has decreased year on year, but the multiplier of the whole currency has increased significantly, which directly leads to the relatively high year-on-year growth rate of M2. After the reform of renminbi exchange rate in 1994 and the unification of exchange rates, a large number of double surpluses of current account and capital account led to a large amount of foreign exchange to be purchased by the central bank in the foreign exchange market, forming the money supply of foreign exchange funds. Now, we can see that the currency derivative function of the shadow banks is obviously enhanced.

Commercial banks, as the main body of financial institutions, are facing the pressure of expansion and structural adjustment of on balance sheet and off balance sheet assets. The proportion of asset side investment on the balance sheet increased, and the proportion of standard bond investment, non-standard and equity assets also

S. Ba, *The New Cycle and New Finance in China*,
https://doi.org/10.1007/978-981-16-8209-4_10

increased. The proportion of off balance sheet assets dominated by financial management to balance sheet assets increased from 6.5% at the end of 2014 to 16.5% at the end of 2016. The past two years saw the expansion through the use of this as leverage. At present, we are going through the reverse process of expansion, and we should reduce the increased leverage. Under the MPA macroprudential framework launched by the central bank, the growth rate of broad credit is far higher than that of loans. It means that only loans are controlled within a limited scope, and the forms of asset expansion will be more diversified.

In the era of great development of the asset management industry, the growth rate of broad credit was obviously higher than that of loans. Among the expanded products, interbank certificates of deposit saw an increase in both volume and price and have become an important new way to increase leverage. There were about 10 issuers of interbank certificates of deposit in 2013, and only a small number of institutions were doing the business. At the end of 2016, there were 489 issuers, and interbank certificates of deposit became a business attracting wide involvement. By May 2017, the business scale was RMB 6.56 trillion, and the main participants were also expanding. In August 2015, fund companies were granted qualifications to allocate funds, and insurance companies were granted qualifications to invest in November 2016. From the fourth quarter of 2016, the issuing interest rate began to rise. The interbank certificates of deposit have become the main tool to connect the whole interbank business chain. Off balance sheet financial management, especially the interbank financial management, has become the main tool for off balance sheet expansion. By the end of 2016, the scale of financial management was RMB29.05 trillion, accounting for 16.5% of the on balance sheet, with an increase of approximately 10% in the past two years. The scale of interbank financial management exceeded that of private customers for the first time in May 2015 and became the main force of off balance sheet expansion. By the end of 2016, the scale of interbank financial management was RMB 5.99 trillion, accounting for 20.61%. The scale has doubled compared with the beginning of 2016, accounting for more than half of the newly added scale.

From the categories of financial institutions, small and medium-sized banks have become the main force to accelerate the expansion of on balance sheet and off balance sheet. In 2016, the growth rate of on balance sheet assets of non-listed banks was 26.8%, far higher than the average growth rate of 13% of listed banks. The growth rate of the financial management of rural financial institutions remained above 100%, and the average growth rate of urban commercial banks was 65%, both of which were far higher than that of large commercial and joint-stock banks. The proportion of financial management of rural financial institutions and urban commercial banks increased from 14.5% at the beginning of 2014 to 20.8% at the end of 2016.

Under certain pressure from competition, small and medium-sized banks can remove the restrictions of business areas and outlets through financial management and avoid the capital regulation. The small and medium-sized banks are competition driven. In specific external environment, we should pay close attention to the risks of these banks, especially the liquidity risk, in the process of deleveraging. Through various carriers, the asset side has formed a three-layer structure of asset management: capital acquisition, investment management and channel, finally making the funds flow to all kinds of standard and non-standard financial assets. In this process, securities companies and fund subsidiaries have witnessed rapid expansion, with their assets increasing from RMB8 trillion in 2014 to RMB 34.5 trillion at the end of 2016, and the proportion of channel-type assets is very high.

Different asset management institutions will participate in such an asset management business in different ways according to their ability to obtain funds. A popular word in this respect is asset shortage. At that time, as long as one can get good assets, it will not be a difficult thing to match the source of funds in the market. Under this background, the outsourcing market came into being. In fact, there are two levels of deleveraging in outsourcing. When deleveraging, we should analyze the deleveraging in recent years and act accordingly.

The direct cause of outsourcing was that small and medium-sized banks lacked professional capabilities, so they needed to rely on external forces, such as those having influence on customers and outlets in the local market. In terms of national financial asset investment, the outsourcing business of small and medium-sized banks has developed rapidly, and then all kinds of banks joined. According to the survey, the outsourcing scale of financial management funds of the four major banks was between RMB 2.5 trillion and RMB 3 trillion when the business was most thriving in 2016. The outsourcing scale of the whole industry was roughly estimated to be RBM5.6 trillion. How did the banks increase leverage in outsourcing? There are mainly two levels:

The first level is that banks raise funds from the interbank market by issuing interbank certificates of deposit or carrying out interbank financial management and then invest in the asset side. This process is the leverage of bank's statement expansion.

At the second level, asset management, outsourcing investors' investment in bonds and other assets are releveraged by means of pledge and maturity mismatch. If the real outsourcing business needs to be deleveraged, it is actually the reverse process of these two levels of leverage. This is also the reason why many outsourcing redemptions have formed market pressure recently, because too much leverage was increased in the past.

With so many structures and channels built behind the leverage, where are the funds? In on balance sheet investment, the proportion of bonds decreased, and the proportion of non-standard assets increased due to the non-standard return to the statement. Most of the non-standard assets were held in various asset management and trust plans, which made it difficult to track the capital flow. In fact, due to certain restrictions on normal financing in the existing loan financing system, such as the restrictions on projects in the real estate industry and local platforms with high debt pressure, the outflow of funds from banks to nonbank entities is in the form of continuous increase of funds provided to other financial institutions. Affected by the Circular No.8, the proportion of non-standard assets has gradually decreased, and the proportion of bonds and money markets is increasing.

Regulatory arbitrage and capital arbitrage are very important motivations of leverage. Regulatory arbitrage is to reduce the loan loss provision and registered capital, and break through the industrial and regional restrictions through the off balance sheet operation and framework design. With the adjustment of the bond market, the cost–benefit has been inverted. The financial institutions and commercial banks, which always think they are smart in calculating, are subsidizing the market. In order to avoid asset recovery and maintain the interbank chain, they may passively maintain the high cost of active liabilities. Commercial banks were faced with the pressure of absorbing deposits as they were 20 years ago. At that time, everyone had to fulfill the quota, so the families of the bank clerks were mobilized. After 20 years, the commercial banks are in a similar situation. The risk of credit scale is still accumulated inside the financial system.

Why do multilayer products and the extension of the interbank chain become the focus of the regulatory policy? There are two main reasons.

One is the adaptability of customer risk. Have the right risk products been sold to the right customers or have the high-risk assets been sold to the low-risk customers through the structural arrangement? Protection must be provided through the structure. The second is the compliance of underlying asset investment. As for the product of underlying assets, does it conform to the regulatory provisions of asset management, and has its risk been properly assessed? These two reasons deserve our attention.

Of course, this round of leverage is quite different from that in 2013. The investment of the base currency has changed from low-cost foreign exchange funds to high-cost open market operation. In 2013, the interbank chain entered the market of non-standard assets mainly through buying back the sale. I have been a director of Industrial Bank Co., Ltd. for six years, exploring the interbank financial management market. But generally speaking, I was very concerned about mismatch and maturity matching. Later, the regulatory authorities issued regulations to limit the areas of bank mismatch. In 2016, the interbank chain has changed, and it entered the bond market mainly through interbank certificates of deposit and the leverage of financial management, and the regulation has restricted the arbitrage from the very beginning.

Leverage aims to stimulate the market, and deleveraging will also lead to the adjustment of the market. Since the fourth quarter of 2016, the bond market began to undergo adjustment. At that time, the market was facing relatively great pressure. However, some institutions began to take the initiative to redeem their products, resulting in constant tension in the market. At present, the signs of reducing leverage are not so obvious. Therefore, the first step is to keep the leverage ratio stable. More efforts must be made for substantial reduction of the leverage ratio.

What are happening in the financial markets when we are deleveraging? Banks are operating in the dynamic market; the surplus short-term liquidity is recovered through positive repurchase, and the long-term liquidity is released through different channels; costs are being raised, and a tight balance of liquidity is maintained. It is unrealistic to expect that sufficient and vigorous liquidity can lead to deleverage. In August 2016, banks restarted 14-day and 28-day reverse repurchase, which indirectly increased the costs of capital by lengthening maturity. Generally speaking, they have been trying to maintaining the tight balance of liquidity in the market and have created many new liquidity tools to maintain this balance.

The investment and recovery in the whole market are in a tight balance. Monetary policies remain stable and neutral, and the center of interest rate in the money market is steadily moving upward. In the past, people were used to adjusting deposit and loan interest rates. Now, the central bank does not want to exert a greater impact on the market, so it ensures the slow increase of interest rates and conveys the policy message of tight liquidity balance through active reduction of leverage and prevention of unreasonable leverage increase.

At the same time, macroprudential assessment (MPA) system is applied. The world has been paying close attention to macroprudential assessment since the financial crisis. It is found that the MPA system of the central bank has made a very important exploration, sending the signal that from the first quarter of 2017, after deducting cash and deposits, off balance sheet financial assets would be incorporated into the broad credit scope to curb regulatory arbitrage. As a result, some small banks had but a small scale of credit in the first quarter. The core of MPA assessment is to restrict the growth of bank assets through restricting the growth rate of broad credit and restrain the disorderly expansion of small and medium-sized banks through the coupling of the growth rate of M2 and that of the broad credit included in off balance sheet financing.

China Banking Regulatory Commission (CBRC), China Insurance Regulatory Commission (CIRC) and China Securities Regulatory Commission (CSRC) issued several industry regulations within a short time, sending such a policy signal from the beginning of 2016 that the CBRC will strengthen its regulation in 2017. This discussion will center on bank asset management. The key to deleveraging lies in bank asset management, because it decides whether the society has great influence on the capital network customers. Regulation mainly aims to prevent the banking industry from violating financial laws, regulatory rules and internal rules. It also involves the regulatory arbitrage, arbitrage from the funds simply circulating in the financial sector and arbitrage through illegally granting credit, transferring assets or providing other services to related parties. Improper innovation, trading, incentive and charging are also under regulation.

It is difficult to see where the funds flow through the previous statistical system, so how to improve the transparency of statistical information and how to realize the transparency of shadow banking and penetrate its underlying assets? Under such policy guidance, what are the colleagues in the financial industry doing? At this time, the fund subsidiaries reacted very quickly, and the growth rate of fund subsidiaries and asset management of securities companies decreased significantly. Fund subsidiaries are very sensitive to the policies, and they are quick in adjusting their business models.

In March 2017, the issuance of interbank certificates of deposit exceeded RMB2 trillion and showed signs of speeding up again. According to the data, the bank statements are actually expanding. Financial deleveraging is actually a repeated process. This has also led to the following question to be discussed in the industry: how much room is there for deleveraging the financial sector when we do not reduce inventory and deleverage in the real economy? The high leverage results from the high leverage ratio and inefficient capital possession in the non-financial sector. Everyone is criticizing that the financial sector has moved from the real economy to the virtual economy. It would not happen if there had been a large number of projects with high returns for financial institutions in the real economy.

According to very rough statistics, the enterprise sector now has liabilities of over RMB 100 trillion, and, calculated by the interest rate of 4–5%, the liabilities may be the same as our GDP in a year. If the rate of return of the real economy does not improve and no progress is made in cutting overcapacity and shedding inventory, then deleveraging is likely to be repeated in the financial industry.

May and June of the year 2017 witnessed the peak of maturity of interbank certificates of deposit. The quantity and price of interbank certificates of deposit are very good reference indices to measure the effect of deleveraging.

The last is the direction of supervision and its impact on the asset management industry. Macroprudential assessment system is used to restrict the pro economic cycle in the financial system and carry out macroprudential regulation. The existing incentive and punishment mechanism of MPA is relatively single, mainly relying on the differentiated legal deposit reserve ratio. The research in future should focus on how to link the assessment results of MPA with the qualifications, licenses and business scope so as to strengthen the constraints of regulation. With the microprudential regulation, we should break the structure of arbitrage trading between banks and nonbank institutions, and make up for the shortcomings of macroprudential regulation in the tools of incentive and punishment mechanism.

The abnormal fluctuation of the stock market in 2015 and the rapid expansion of the scale of leveraged asset management products in 2015 and 2016 reflect a common problem, namely the segmentation and low efficiency of regulation. How to improve the coordination of regulation? Starting from the unified framework of asset management, we should reduce the blind area of regulation, achieve its penetration and impose internal capital constraints. The goal is to reduce leverage, remove non-standard and channel-type assets, break rigid repayment and forbid cash pooling.

In this process, small and medium-sized banks' financial statements witnessed rapid expansion in 2016, but it is not sustainable. Therefore, we should caution against the risks of financial products of small and medium-sized banks, especially the risks of liquidity and maturity mismatch. If the cost of active liabilities is significantly higher than the cost of capital, it will be impossible for interbank liabilities to expand continuously. The issuance cost of liabilities will rise, while the income of assets will decline. The continuous contraction of income space will soon lead to the risks of financial products of small and medium-sized banks.

There is a certain degree of outsourcing redemption, but in fact, in this process, there is still space for outsourcing business. Different financial institutions do have their own core competitiveness, so the outsourcing redemption will lead to the reshuffle of managers and reshape the business form of bank asset management. At present, the regulatory policies in this aspect are still under consideration and in the process of gradual clarification. The outsourcing business is making very slow progress. In the long run, there is still a lot of space for cooperation between different financial institutions. It does not mean that we should not carry out outsourcing business. Instead, there should be an upgrade from the simple channel-type business to that of complementary advantages. Small and medium-sized banks need the help of securities and fund companies in asset allocation, that is, they need problem-solving asset allocation schemes, not just channel-type asset allocation scheme. With complementary advantages and strengthened asset allocation capabilities, the outsourcing business is expected to witness market differentiation and has the ability to turn its asset allocation channel to multi-strategy cross-border asset allocation and trading. This is another very important policy impact on the market brought by regulation.

Chapter 11
Net Interest Margin of Commercial Banks at Home and Abroad

The People's Bank of China started the reform of interest rate liberalization at the end of the twentieth century. After more than 20 years of development, macro regulation relies more heavily on market-oriented monetary policy tools and transmission mechanism, and interest rates play an increasingly important role in optimizing resource allocation. As the interest rate liberalization has entered a new stage, net interest margin, as an important indicator to measure the operational efficiency of Chinese commercial banks, has attracted more and more attention from different fields.

As the main intermediary service institutions in China's financial market, commercial banks play an important role in the financial market as the bridge and media between the supply and demand of funds. According to CBRC statistics, the non-interest income of China's banking industry accounted for 23.80% in 2016, a year-on-year increase of about 0.07%. Nearly, 80% of the income came from the traditional interest spread. It can be seen that although the share of non-interest income is expanding year by year, the net interest spread, as the basis and main contributor of the profits of Chinese traditional commercial banks, still plays an important role in business income. In 2016, the average net interest spread of China's banking industry was 2.22%, with a year-on-year decrease of about 0.32%. With deepened adjustment of China's macroeconomic structure, accelerated interest rate liberalization and tightened benchmark interest rate, China's commercial banks are faced with the urgent problem of improving net interest spread.

Asset liability business is the main body of the traditional business of China's commercial banks, and net interest spread is an important target variable of bank assets and liability management. The analysis of the relationship between net interest spread and various factors and its influence can provide reference for banks to optimize the structure of assets and liabilities. As there is fierce competition at home and abroad, it is of great practical significance for China's commercial banks to understand the overall operating efficiency and net interest spread of the banking industry so as to determine the level of net interest spread reasonably and gradually improve their independent pricing ability.

S. Ba, *The New Cycle and New Finance in China*,
https://doi.org/10.1007/978-981-16-8209-4_11

In recent years, China's banking industry witnessed narrowed interest spread, concentrated risk release and slower profit growth. By studying the factors influencing the net interest spread, we can promote development of China's banking industry in the new environment, constantly adjust its structure while steadily developing traditional business and explore ways to advance its strategic transformation.

At the macrolevel, the research on the influencing factors of net interest spread can provide sound policy basis for the government's macro regulation. In China, the interest rate is an important tool for the government to carry out macroregulation. At present, the interest rate has not been fully liberalized, and the benchmark interest rate spread between deposits and loans has a great impact on interest rate fluctuation of commercial banks. Benchmark interest rate spread is the boundary of the range of net interest spread in China's banking industry. Generally speaking, the net interest spread is positively correlated with the change of benchmark interest spread. The larger the benchmark interest spread is, the larger the net interest spread will be. We should understand the change in net interest spread of China's banking industry and the influence of various factors at different levels, and this will help the government adjust the benchmark interest rate of deposits and loans, and formulate reasonable, timely and effective monetary and economic policies to keep the situation under control.

Some foreign countries have realized the liberalization of interest rates earlier within a shorter time. Therefore, there are more researches on net interest spread in other countries. In recent years, the research on bank interest spread is increasing at home and abroad, most of which are conducted by using qualitative and quantitative approaches. In order to provide a theoretical basis for commercial banks to increase profits and improve market competitiveness, the author systematically summarizes the research on net interest spread from the following four aspects: definition, models and influencing factors of interest rate spread as well as regression methods.

11.1 Interest Spread Between Deposits and Loans and Net Interest Spread

The researchers home and abroad have not reached a consensus on the definition of interest rate spread of commercial banks. But generally speaking, interest rate spread can be divided into interest rate spread between deposit and loan and net interest rate spread, and it can also be divided into nominal interest rate spread and actual interest rate spread. Net interest rate spread often refers to the interest rate spread mentioned in daily life, in the actual operation of commercial banks, or in theoretical research. The interest rate spread between deposits and loans can be understood as the difference between deposit interest rate and loan interest rate. It can more truly reflect the efficiency, operation and management of commercial banks. By analyzing the net interest spread, we can find the factors directly affecting the interest rate spread of commercial banks.

There are many definitions and calculation methods of the net interest rate spread, but two of them are often used in practice. In the annual reports of most listed commercial banks, the net interest rate spread is equal to the bank's net interest income (interest income minus interest expense) divided by interest assets. But in most academic researches, it is equal to net interest income divided by total bank assets. This is due to the fact that the variable of net interest rate spread is directly provided in BankScope, the database used in most literature studies. BankScope database is a common database for research on interest rate spread, a professional and authoritative tool jointly produced by Fitch Rating, an international institution, and Bureau van Dijk, a European financial information database provider. BankScope uses the total assets of the bank in defining net interest rate spread. In order to facilitate statistics and comparison, most theoretical researches adopt the definition of net interest rate spread given by BankScope. There are generally two theoretical models about the determinants of net interest rate spread: one is the dealership model, which has become the mainstream model in this field after continuous improvement and expansion; the other is the micromodel of the banking firms. Most of the researches on the determinants of net interest rate spread are based on these two models.

The idea of dealership model is to regard the banks as a risk-aversion intermediary or dynamic leaders, constantly promoting coordination between the borrower and the lender and at the same time report the interest rates of deposit and loan acceptable to both sides. The banks also change the interest rates of deposits and loans according to the supply of deposits and the demand of loans, so as to achieve dynamic balance. The theoretical framework of the dealership model, which was first proposed in 1981, empirically analyzed the determinants of net interest rate spread of commercial banks. The model has been constantly revised, based on the cognition that the interest rate spread is mainly determined by the average interest rate of the money market rather than the deposit and loan interest rates. On this basis, a rich theoretical model has been formed by dividing loans and deposits into different categories, considering both credit risks and the interest rate risks, and including operating costs as a factor affecting the interest rate spread. Some scholars subdivide the business of commercial banks into two categories: traditional type and innovative type, and creatively introduce the dynamic into the model. A new model is established, which also involves nontraditional business and operating costs.

Different from the dealership model, the core idea of micromodel of the banking firm is to consider banks in a static environment. The function of the banks is to set the interest rates of deposits and loans, so that the supply of deposits and the demand of loans can achieve market clearing at the same time. This model takes into account the credit risks of banks due to non-performing loans and the interest risks due to the mismatch of assets and liabilities.

11.2 Factors Influencing Interest Rate Spread

Microfactors. Many studies have been carried out from different perspectives on the microfactors that affect interest rate spread. One theory holds that risk preference, transaction size and interest rate volatility of commercial banks have a strong positive correlation effect on interest rate spread. The second theory believes that the volatility of core capital and deposits will affect the net interest spread of commercial banks and that core capital and net interest spread are positively correlated. It also holds that deposit insurance system, capital scale and default risk affect the stability of commercial banks' operation, and that default risk is negatively correlated with net interest spread. The third theory believes that average operating cost, risk aversion, interest rate risks of money market, credit risks, covariance between interest rate risks and credit risks, and transaction scale will affect net interest spread.

Researchers in China have carried out more extensive studies in this respect, believing that, besides the above factors, the internal financing structure of each bank is one of the important factors affecting its net interest spread. Tax, loan losses, expenses, development of intermediary business, asset scale and return on total assets have a direct impact on net interest spread. Researchers have also carried out studies on loan default rate, capital buffer, liquidity premium, loss rate, risk-free benchmark interest rate and credit asset ratio, thinking that these factors are closely related to the net interest spread of commercial banks.

Industry factors. It is believed both at home and abroad that the structure of market competition structure is an important industry factor affecting commercial banks' interest rate spread, and that the size of market share will also affect the net interest spread of commercial banks. It is believed that the stronger the monopoly power is, the higher the corresponding interest spread will be. Besides, in the competition of the banking industry, the substitutability of financial products is negatively correlated with net interest spread.

Macrofactors. Foreign scholars have found that there is a significant positive correlation between inflation and net interest spread. However, this obviously does not apply to all countries. All studies on the banking industry in Western Europe, Southeast Europe, Latin America and Tunisia have arrived at the opposite conclusion, that is, inflation is negatively correlated to net interest soread. Some scholars believe that the correlation between inflation and net interest spread depends on whether inflation is predictable. If the market can predict inflation, banks will raise interest rates accordingly, and, as a result, net interest spread will increase. If inflation happens against the prediction, the rising inflation rate will lead to the banks' delayed adjustment of interest rates. The rise of net interest rate will raise the costs of the banks and have a negative impact on net interest spread.

Analysis shows that there is a negative correlation between economic growth rate and net interest spread. Too high economic growth rate will lead to the increase of loan default risks, which will in turn reduce the net interest spread of banks. On the contrary, some think that the low economic growth rate will increase the credit risk of borrowers and the risk premium, thus increasing the net interest spread of banks. In addition, the reduction of the government's fiscal deficit will reduce the net interest spread. Researchers in China also believe that the macrofactors are the main factors affecting the net interest spread of China's commercial banks. The fluctuation of business cycle will also affect the net interest spread of banks.

11.3 Four Regression Methods for the Study of Factors Affecting Interest Spread

The researchers at home and abroad use four different regression methods for empirical research on the factors affecting interest rate spread.

The first is one-step regression. That is to say, all the factors that may affect the net interest spread of banks, whether they are microfactors, industry factors or macrofactors, are put into an equation. Due to its simplicity and strong operability, one-step regression method is widely used at home and abroad. However, this method fails to consider the serial correlation among inter-bank competition, information opacity and macroeconomic shocks. Both the net interest spread of banks and the independent variables will change continuously with the passage of time.

The second is a simple two-step regression method. It divides the factors affecting net interest spread into microfactors (including industries) and macrofactors. In the first step, the data of net interest spread is regressed by microfactors (including industries), and the second step is to regress the net interest spread by macrofactors.

The third is a complex two-step regression method. Similar to the second regression method, it also divides the factors affecting net interest spread into two levels: microfactors (including industry) and macrofactors. In the first step, the data of net interest spread are regressed by microfactors (including industry). In this step, the part of interest spread that can be explained is called "pure spread." In the second step, macrofactors are used to analyze the constants in the first step. This method is widely used in foreign countries, but it is seldom used by Chinese scholars.

The fourth regression method is also called dynamic linear model. It considers the influence of time and includes the variable of time lag in the regression model. However, this dynamic regression method may lead to biased estimation and fail to take into account the endogenous problems among explanatory variables. Of course, this problem can be solved by using the generalized method of moments (GMM) and selecting appropriate tools in the dynamic panel.

Generally speaking, deeper and broader researches have been carried out in other countries. Most of the researches in China are based on the research results abroad, and there are few innovations in theoretical models and research methods. Most of the Chinese scholars' research on net interest spread of China's commercial banks is limited to theoretical analysis. Empirical research has not lead to systematic models, and the conclusions vary, which affects its guiding effect on the operation of commercial banks. The world is now facing complex and changeable economic and financial situations, and China's commercial banks are also facing new changes and challenges in their business environment. In the period of economic downturn, commercial banks are facing much pressure and many challenges in their development: the quality of assets is yet to improve, and the credit cost remains high; the impact of interest rate liberalization persists, and the interest spread of the banking industry continues to narrow; the economic activities becomes less dynamic, and it is increasingly difficult for the intermediate business to increase income; the cost investment is insufficient, and the efficiency still needs to be improved; the capital regulation has been strengthened continuously, and the profit model of scale expansion is challenged; the international business environment is complex, and overseas and holdings institutions grow rather slowly; new financial business forms come into being, and there is an obvious trend of payment and financial disintermediation, etc. Under this backdrop, we must accelerate the research of net interest spread of commercial banks in China. But in the process of research, we should pay more attention to the relationship between the evolution of net interest spread and interest rates liberalization, and we should also pay close attention to the specific connotations of net interest spread in the special institutional environment of China.

Chapter 12
Transformation of Commercial Banks Under the New Normal

As China's economy entered the new normal, the business environment of China's banking industry has undergone great changes, and at the same time, it is facing new opportunities and challenges. Asset quality is yet to improve, and interest rate and exchange rate liberalization has been constantly promoted. New financial formats such as Internet finance are growing rapidly, and regulation has been strengthened. All has attracted much attention.

Besides, the reduced net interest spread and the slower profit growth calls for the transformation of the traditional business models. It is necessary to transform commercial banks by adjusting the customer and business structures so as to improve the commercial banks' competitiveness. In the years of economic cyclical decline, China's banking industry has withstood the severe test of economic downturn. They have also been actively adapting themselves to the new economic environment, promoting economic transformation, and have significantly enhanced their ability to provide financial support for the sustained and steady growth of China's economy in the new growth platform for a period of time in the future.

12.1 Changing External Environment of China's Banking Industry

1. ROE of China's Banking Industry

The change in ROE of China's banking industry shows that, with economic transformation and intensified competition, the narrowed net interest spread of China's listed banks and the pressure of asset quality has resulted in gradual slowdown in profit growth, making the ROE of China's banking industry quickly approach the global average level. Since 2013, the ROE of China's banking industry has declined at an average annual rate of 1–2% points, from nearly 20% in 2013 to 13.4% in 2016 (see Fig. 12.1).

S. Ba, *The New Cycle and New Finance in China*,
https://doi.org/10.1007/978-981-16-8209-4_12

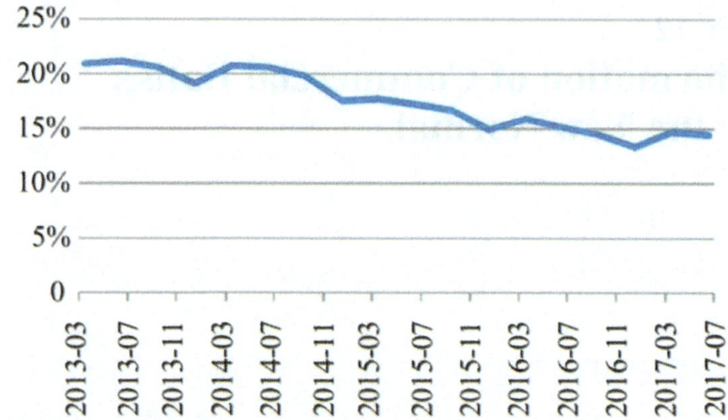

Fig. 12.1 Trend of average ROE of China's banking industry

2. Profit Growth Rate of China's Commercial Banks

From the statistical data analysis, the profit growth rate of China's banking industry is gradually close to that of non-financial listed companies, and obvious differentiation begins to appear among different banks, so it is necessary to find new profit growth points. In the past, the profit of China's banking industry grew quickly, thanks to the policy dividends brought about by capital injection and divestiture of non-performing assets, the expansion of market and the advantages of license plates. However, in recent years, the profit growth of China's banking industry has continued to decline and is returning to normal, gradually approaching that of non-financial listed companies. Obvious differentiation begins to appear among different banks in the decline. In the expansion period, the expansion of scale and high-speed growth caught the most attention. In the period of decline, we can observe whether the asset layout in the expansion period can withstand the test of cyclical decline. For example, in the debt side, is there sufficient market-oriented innovation ability to deal with the crisis of savings loss when new products and sales channels appear? Is there sufficient ability of asset liability risk management to cope with market risks amid relatively great fluctuations in interest and exchange rates? Therefore, it may be difficult to see the difference in the competitiveness of different banks in the period of industry expansion because the structures of large and small banks are very similar. However, banks are different in their competitiveness in the stage of industry decline.

The net interest spread in the second quarter of 2017 was slightly higher than that in the first quarter, but, on the whole, the net interest spread of China's banking industry will continue to narrow due to the development of direct financing and the intensified market competition. This trend can also be seen by comparing the net interest spread of commercial banks in the Hong Kong market. In the increasingly competitive environment, it is particularly important to improve competitiveness and seek new profit growth points.

12.2 Transformation of Commercial Banks with Declining Profits

From the current trend of the market, in the period of economic transformation, commercial banks are facing the pressure of transforming their traditional business models. When the profit growth rate drops, different banks are also actively exploring new directions of transformation.

1. Banks Exploring New Growth Points in the New Market Environment
(1) Light banks and transaction banks: starting point of improving competitiveness in the new environment

From the information disclosed in the semi-annual report of listed banks in 2017, it can be seen that in the current period of industry decline, different banks begin to adopt different business strategies. Some banks are still taking the path of expansion and continue to expand the scale of their assets and liabilities; some banks take the initiative to reduce their balance sheets and carry out the transformation of income structure, that is, they choose to be light banks. After a round of reshuffle, there will be different business models and strategies. Besides, banks in different regions are also differentiated, because the formation, rise and transmission of non-performing asset rate in this economic cycle is closely related to the location of different regions. At first, the newly added non-performing assets of Jiangsu, Zhejiang provinces and other places in the region with high leverage ratio accounted for nearly half of the total, and they were gradually transferred to the central, western and northeast regions. The places in the Yangtze River Delta were the first to suffer from risks, but, after several years of adjustment and handling, the situation in these regions is improving. In this case, banks need to take the asset portfolio, and regional and industry layout into consideration, rather than just follow the crowd.

Since 2015, the scale growth of the banking industry has begun to decouple from the growth of profits, and some banks have been striving to be light ones. From the perspective of asset structure, the growth rate of off balance sheet assets dominated by financial management is higher than that of balance sheet, and the proportion of retail business with low capital consumption continues to increase; from the perspective of income structure, the proportion of non-interest income of international advanced banks is about 40%, and that of Chinese banks is relatively low, but it shows a growing trend in recent years (see Fig. 12.2). It can be said that it is a major trend for the banks to be light ones. But at the same time, we should also see that there must be the support of real business for the banks to be light. Therefore, banks should attach great importance to ensure enough customers and traditional business so as to provide a basis for the banks to be light.

Investment banking and asset management business have become active areas to drive the transformation of banks. Broad asset management and investment banking business are the key development directions for listed banks to promote strategic transformation and form core competitiveness. The so-called broad asset management and investment banking require that banks should not only serve as a sales

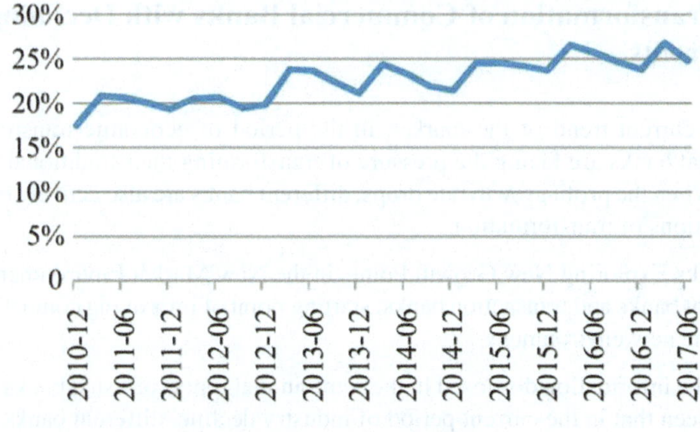

Fig. 12.2 Proportion of non-interest income of Chinese banks

channel for fund, securities and trust companies but should also meet the new needs of asset allocation, improve their capabilities of product design and strengthen the coordinated service of financial institutions in the upper, middle and lower reaches of the asset management industry. This is a big development trend, and the banking industry must adjust itself amid the rapid development of direct financing.

For example, since 2017, the decline in the scale of deposits in China's banking industry and the growth in the scale of monetary funds are basically the same in level. We can roughly see the trend of monetary funds eating into bank deposits. This trend may not appear quickly in the near future, but in the medium and long term, the impact will become more and more obvious if banks do not take active measures. According to international experience, the current deposit ratio of American banks has decreased from 60 to 10% due to the rise of monetary funds. Judging from the operation of monetary funds in recent years, the return of monetary funds continues to be higher than that of bank financial products and deposit income. With the continuous customer penetration of fund products, it is likely to see the substitution process of the US market repeat in the Chinese market if China's banking industry does not carry out broad asset management and investment banking, and the market-oriented financing channels will continue to erode the bank's debt base.

As for its position on the value chain of asset management, investment banking business has actually become the product design department of commercial banks' asset management departments. The linkage of investment banking and asset management business help commercial banks to provide more targeted customer services. According to statistics of income sources of intermediary business in *Chinese Banker Survey*, the income from investment banking and that from financial management rank top two among all the sources of income of commercial banks. The main development direction of asset management business is to guide the industry to return to the nature of asset management and improve the ability of asset allocation. The investment banking business mainly involves innovative equity financing products such as industrial funds and PPP projects, and it also involves the basic business such as bond underwriting, investment and financing consulting, and syndicated loans.

New value chain has been formed with the rise of transaction banks. Transaction banking is becoming a new trend of corporate business transformation. Interest rate liberalization has been accelerated, renminbi internationalization is being promoted and cross-border transactions and Internet finance are thriving. Under this backdrop, the development of transaction banking business has increasingly become the key for traditional commercial banks to transform and develop themselves, expand their income channels and enhance their competitiveness. Transaction banking mainly involves payment and settlement, cash management, supply chain finance and trade finance.

Another purpose of developing transaction banks is to serve small and medium-sized enterprises. By providing transaction and payment system services for small and medium-sized enterprises, banks can collect a large amount of information about enterprises, so as to get the credit information of small and medium-sized enterprises that lack credit support in the banking system. Then, banks can act accordingly when dealing with these enterprises. Therefore, the development of transaction banking can help banks to explore new business growth points, expand low-cost sources of debt and improve customer loyalty. At the same time, it can also help expand cross business and income channels, which also provides support for the real economy.

The transaction banking business is restricted by poor cross regional and departmental coordination. The main factors restricting the development of transaction banks are poor product research and development capabilities, poor coordination between regions, departments and product lines, poor risk control capabilities, poor coordination between head offices and their branches, and poor infrastructure construction.

(2) Asset Quality and Banks' Competitiveness

According to *Chinese Banker Survey 2016*, up to 81.3% of bankers believe that credit risk is the main risk that the banking industry will face. Although the asset quality of the banking industry has improved in the first half of 2017 due to the economic recovery, there is still great downward pressure on the macroeconomy, and operational difficulties of the real economy are being transmitted to the financial sector. This is also a test of the asset portfolio of commercial banks in their expansion period. The survey shows that 58.7% of the bankers believe that the rise in non-performing loans is mainly caused by factors at the macrolevel. We are now in the period of changing pace in economic growth, the period of painful structural adjustment and the digestion period of early policy stimulus when the real enterprises generally have cyclical overcapacity. The cash flow of some industries has shrunk and their profits have declined. Fundamentally, it reflects the banks' cross-cycle competitiveness.

One of the challenges faced by the banking industry in the period of economic expansion is that the short-term assessment mechanism might lead to delayed release of credit risks. Therefore, asset quality is a very important factor to test the cross-cycle operation ability of banks. From the data of the semi-annual report, the proportion of non-performing assets of some banks began to decline. There are regional factors behind this, and it is also the result of increased write-offs and adjustment of asset structure. At present, we are in a period of economic transformation, and the complexity of economic operation is increasing. We should not only strengthen the management based on the quality of individual assets but also strengthen the management based on asset portfolio. After judging the macrofactors, regions and industry, we should actively adjust the asset portfolio. Compared with the capability of post-event handling of bad assets, the capability of making strategic layout in advance is of greater importance. For example, when the economy is in transition, the non-performing rate of defensive sector such as clothing, food, housing and transportation is relatively low, while the cyclical industries will undergo great fluctuations. With this knowledge, we can make strategic layout in advance. This is the management based on asset portfolio. When we realize the risks of different regions, we should put resources in those with minimized risks.

At present, most of the banks still rely on the traditional disposal methods such as collection of non-performing loans, write-offs and restructuring. Only a few banks begin to employ the new disposal methods such as the transfer or securitization of non-performing assets and debt-to-equity swaps. In the future, with the deregulation and support of regulatory authorities, listed banks should not only improve the traditional methods but should also actively make innovations to improve the efficiency of collection. We should cultivate the market-oriented non-performing assets disposal ability, get feedback and make improvement in the whole process, and take appropriate non-performing assets disposal methods and scheme designs, so as to cultivate the core competitiveness of listed banks in the disposal of non-performing assets.

(3) Financing Structure Adjustment

The 2017 national financial work conference clearly proposed to develop direct financing, improve the structure of indirect financing, and reduce the operating costs of financial institutions. Therefore, the banking industry needs to learn how to use the capital market and expand relevant business, such as investment banking, asset management, merger and acquisition. At present, more than 60% of mergers and acquisitions in China are conducted with the listed companies as the main body. If the banking industry fails to understand the operation, investment and financing of listed companies, it will be difficult for the industry to get involved in these mergers and acquisitions.

2. External Regulation: Adjustment of Business Model

The framework combining macroprudential regulation and microprudential regulation has been constantly improved. The regulatory measures have been constantly improved through the MPA system, and we have achieved systematic, dynamic macroprudential regulation, and regulation on the scale, growth rate, proportion and other dimensions has been carried out. However, the MPA assessment system is relatively single in its existing incentive and punishment mechanism (differentiated legal deposit reserve ratio). We should link the results of MPA assessment with the market access and qualifications so as to strengthen the regulation and restriction. Besides, we should also carry out microprudential regulation to break the trading structure of arbitrage between banks and nonbank institutions and make up for regulatory failure of macroprudential regulation.

Regulation has changed from increasing leverage to deleveraging, driving commercial banks to adjust their balance sheet. At present, the proportion of investment on the asset side of the balance sheet continues to increase. The proportion of standard bond investment decreases while the proportion of nonstandard and equity assets increases. The proportion of off balance sheet assets dominated by financial management increased from 6.5% at the end of 2014 to 16.5% at the end of 2016. At the same time, the growth rate of broad credit under the framework of MPA is much higher than that of loans, and the forms of asset expansion are more diversified. At present, the process of deleveraging can be regarded as an inverse process of increasing leverage in the past two or three years, which has a multifaceted impact on the whole market structure. For example, the proportion of deposits, loans and foreign exchange, which were originally regarded as traditional business, began to rise, while the growth rate of other businesses regarded as innovative slowed down. In terms of market concentration, in the process of increasing leverage, some small banks broke through the constraints of capital, branches and product lines, and thrived with expanded business scope, resulting in slightly lower market concentration. Therefore, in the process of deleveraging, we should see higher concentration of the market again, which will affect the existing pattern of the banking industry and put pressure on small banks.

The regulatory authorities attached greater importance to the allocation of assets on and off the balance sheet and strove to strengthen the principle of penetration. They tracked the flow of investment and financial business and included the rapidly expanded interbank certificates of deposit; interbank financial management and outsourcing investment in 2016 in the statistics, and regulatory loopholes were constantly filled. For nesting asset management products and income rights, the authorities strengthened the regulation principle of penetrating underlying assets, so as to track the capital flow.

The regulatory authorities attached greater importance to liquidity risk management, and interbank business becomes the top priority. Special inspection and regulation on interbank and financial services were carried out. The on balance sheet and off balance sheet expansion by means of active liabilities and off balance sheet financing was strictly controlled. Liquidity maturity gap monitoring and LCR index regulation will be strengthened.

The regulatory authorities encourage the development of innovative businesses. Top priority will be given to the promotion of innovative businesses such as asset securitization, credit asset transfer, market-oriented debt-to-equity swaps, government industrial funds, and investment and loan linkage.

3. Impacts of Such External Factors as Financial Technology on Commercial Banks

Financial technology has brought great challenges to the traditional business modes of the banking industry, and the banking industry is also actively exploring ways, trying to make use of these external challenges to enhance its competitiveness. Large banks actively develop financial technology on their own, while small and medium-sized banks take the initiative to cooperate with financial technology companies. However, at present, banks are still approaching financial technology with a traditional way of thinking, and they are still influenced by the traditional ideas concerning information technology. We are still focusing on the core trading system, credit management system, risk management system, and payment and settlement system. We mainly rely on the information technology platform and regard financial technology as a substitute for the existing branch business, that is, as a sales channel of existing products. We are not talking about financial technology from the perspective of channel or the flow of Internet financial technology, or from the perspective of improving customer experience, which is totally different from the perspective based on the integration of technology with finance.

Financial technology is the use of science and technology by the financial side or the use financial tools by the technology side. In fact, they go from different ends of a path toward each other. For example, the new business growth points of banks often center on new scenarios and the biggest challenge for banks lies in that many new scenarios have nothing to do with banks. Scenarios constructed by the real economy and Internet enterprises can realize self-information collection and self-risk assessment and thus provide financial services, but it has nothing to do with traditional banks. In the future, banks need to establish their own scenarios or make good use of existing scenarios to collect user information. With the accumulation of data, banks can develop their business through big data processing. Their business should not simply involve mobile payment and network sales.

Financial institutions should take the initiative to apply the financial technology when implementing the strategy of removing the operating pain points of the banking industry. The institutions need to undergo a process of trial and error in their application of any new technology and new model. Venture capital institutions are the best at dealing with such technological entrepreneurship projects. Only by cooperating with professional investment institutions can the banking industry effectively control the extra costs brought about by exploration and innovation, so as to better participate in the innovation ecology. In the construction of the ecology for the financial industry of science and technology, the cooperation and innovation of various institutions can be realized in a variety of ways.

Firstly, banking institutions borrow the innovative ideas of the financial technological industry and carry out independent research and development of innovative financial technology so as to construct industrial ecology;

Secondly, the banking institutions cooperate with financial technology companies to promote the research, development and application of banking financial technologies by using the innovative achievements of these financial technology companies;

Finally, the banking institutions take advantage of the favorable industrial policies such as "investment and loan linkage," promote cooperation through investment, and cooperate with professional investment institutions. Financial institutions invest or participate in financial technology start-ups so as to build the foundation for deep business cooperation between the two sides.

12.3 Evaluation of the Banking Industry's Transformation

As a typical industry of procyclicality, commercial banks often face the pressure of asset quality and profitability decline in the period of economic downturn. On the one hand, it is a test of the asset liability portfolio formed in the period of economic expansion; on the other hand, it forces commercial banks to innovate their business modes and promote business transformation. In 2008, a stimulus package estimated at RMB 4 trillion to deal with the financial crisis resulted in the phased recovery of China's economy. China's economy boomed at the beginning of 2010, and began to experience years of decline under the pressure of cyclical economic downturn and economic transformation. In the past few years, China's banking industry has withstood the severe test of cyclical economic downturn. The banking industry has experienced the increasingly high pressure from non-performing assets in the initial stage of the economic downturn, but now the pressure from asset quality has been significantly alleviated, and the profitability has witnessed steady improvement. At the same time, commercial banks actively adapt themselves to the new economic environment and promote economic transformation. The efforts to promote their own business transformation have also made remarkable progress, and the overall competitiveness has been steadily improved. Commercial banks have also significantly improved their ability to provide financial support for the sustained and steady growth of China's economy in the new growth platform for a period of time in the future.

1. China's Economic Growth and Improved Economic Structure

In 2017, thanks to the cyclical recovery of major global economies and the continuous progress in China's economic transformation, China's economic growth shows strong resilience against its steady decline. At the same time, the replacement of old growth drivers of China's economy with new ones has been steadily advancing. Gradual change has taken place in the traditional extensive growth model mainly driven by investment in the real estate and infrastructure. With the deepening of supply side structural reform, industries have begun to cut overcapacity, industry concentration has begun to increase and consumption upgrading has gradually become the main contributor to the rise of total demand. These favorable economic changes are reflected in the operating indicators of China's banking industry, and the profitability of China's banking industry became stable and showed signs of improvement in 2017 after falling from a high level at the initial stage of economic downturn.

2. Decreased Pressure from Bank Asset Quality

In the early stage of this round of slower economic growth and rapid structural adjustment, the asset quality has brought about great pressure on China's banking industry. However, after China's banking industry's active industrial restructuring, strengthened risk management and successful handling of diversified assets in recent years, the formation of non-performing assets of the overall banking industry began to slow down. The banking industry has successfully withstood the test of asset quality risks in the market-oriented environment, and the ability of cross-cycle operation has also been tested and improved. According to the data disclosed by CBRC at the end of the first half of 2017, the overall non-performing asset ratio of the industry has stabilized at 1.74%, and the ratio of non-performing assets in some banks and regions has witnessed year-on-year and month-on-month drop. Sufficient provisions have provided a solid foundation for digesting possible non-performing assets and supporting future profit growth. After the test of this cycle, China's banking industry attached greater importance to improving the ability to make strategic layout of asset quality, explored new methods such as non-performing assets transfer or securitization, debt-to-equity swaps, etc. The ability of risk resolution and disposal has been strengthened. As for the regional difference of non-performing assets, the non-performing assets ratio increased significantly in this round of economic downturn, which started from such cities as Wenzhou of Zhejiang Province in the Yangtze River Delta. The newly added non-performing assets in the region accounted for a large proportion of the newly added non-performing assets in the banking industry of the whole country. After several years of digesting non-performing assets and transforming banking business modes, the operation of banks in the Yangtze River Delta region has begun to improve significantly, and the ratio of non-performing assets has shown a trend of steady decline.

3. Effective Regulation and China's Banking Industry

With the restructuring and reform of China's banking industry, on the basis of summing up China's experience, the regulatory system of China's banking industry has been approaching the international standards in a confident manner. With the continuous improvement of regulatory transparency and system, a clear regulatory framework has been formed for the banking industry to adapt to the new market environment. In April 2011, the CBRC issued the guidelines on the implementation of the new regulatory standards for China's banking industry, and China was one of the first major global economies to localize the results of consensus on international financial regulatory reform such as Basel II and Basel III. On the basis of traditional prudential regulatory tools such as liquidity, provision coverage, risk concentration and non-performing asset ratio, the CBRC has introduced and updated the banking regulation tools such as capital, provision, liquidity and leverage ratio. The tools for banking regulation have been constantly enriched and improved. At the beginning of

2016, the macroprudential assessment system was introduced, combining macroprudential assessment and microprudential assessment, and the regulatory framework was constantly improved. In 2017, China attached greater importance to resolving financial risks and serving the real economy in its regulation of the banking industry. After the fifth national financial work conference, the ability of regulatory coordination and cross-market regulation was improved, which played an important role in promoting the steady development of the banking industry.

4. Active Transformation of China's Banking Industry during Economic Downturn

Under the new normal of China's economic growth, China's banking industry has constantly expanded new business growth points, reached new customers and markets, and explored new business growth modes so as to improve its risk response ability and market competitiveness. For example, the importance of traditional credit assets in bank balance sheets began to decline and the banking industry began to refrain itself from the blind pursuit of the growth supported by the expansion of credit scale. Some banks choose to shrink their balance sheets and adjust their income structure so as to become light banks with low capital consumption. Since 2015, the scale growth of China's banking system began to decouple from profit growth. Some banks began to step up their effort to become light banks, and the proportion of retail business with low capital consumption and that of non-interest income increased continuously. In the first half of 2017, the weighted average proportion of non-interest income of 16 listed banks reached 33.33%, which is close to the average level of international advanced banks. Investment banking and asset management business have become the active areas to drive the transformation of banks. Banks can better meet customers' needs of asset allocation by improving their product design capabilities and enhancing their service integration capabilities for upstream and downstream financial institutions. At the same time, China's banking industry also actively embraces the latest developments in the field of financial technology. Through the establishment of its own application scenarios and the continuous accumulation of business data, it improves the customer experience. The industry also strives to turn the challenges brought by external financial technology into the factors to improve their competitiveness.

Chapter 13
Retail Banking and Transformation and Development of Commercial Banks

In 2017, the banking industry is still facing a severe and complex economic environment at home and abroad in its reform and development. According to the requirements of the 2017 work meeting held by the CBRC, the banking industry should keep deepening the supply side structural reform, attach greater importance to the prevention and control of financial risks and strive to improve the quality and efficiency of serving the real economy so as to provide new financial momentum for stable and healthy economic and social development.

Retail banks have unique advantages in obtaining stable and low-cost funds and controlling the risks of corporate and interbank service. With the rapid economic transformation, customer demand differentiation and interest rate liberalization, the retail banking business is becoming the area of greatest profit growth in the process of transformation and development of domestic commercial banks.

13.1 Retail Banking: Status Quo, Opportunities and Challenges

At present, joint-stock banks are huge in scale, and small banks are developing rapidly. The individual loans of joint-stock banks account for more than 90% of the total loans of small and medium-sized banks. In the past three years, individual loans have also maintained a relatively high-speed growth of about 20%. Compared with the joint-stock banks with larger scale and complete business, agricultural commercial banks and urban commercial banks have developed retail business thanks to geographical advantages and achieved certain results. Their growth rate is faster than that of other types of banks, their proportion is also increasing year by year and they have greater potential for development. Small and medium-sized banks have different structures of individual loans, and they have caught up with the five major banks in terms of financial management business. However, compared with that in the mature markets, the profit contribution of retail banking in China is relatively

S. Ba, *The New Cycle and New Finance in China*,
https://doi.org/10.1007/978-981-16-8209-4_13

low. Besides, the asset quality of individual loans is better than that of corporate loans, and there are risks in housing loans.

China's economic and financial structure is in the process of transformation, and retail banking industry is facing both opportunities and challenges. Commercial banks are facing the problems of how to achieve breakthrough and innovation, and realize leapfrog development. In the era of Internet finance, retail banks are facing the threat of e-commerce and third-party payment platforms, but they are also constantly innovating ways to accelerate the research and development as well as the promotion of Internet financial products. The competition among banks also becomes the competition for channels and better user experience. Internet banking in North America and Europe has begun to develop from direct banking in the era of Internet banking 1.0 to mobile banking in the era of Internet banking 2.0. In the future, the Asia Pacific region will become the most important region in the world for the development of retail banking represented by mobile banking.

13.2 Retail Banking: Key Development Direction of Commercial Banks

The banking sector has reached the consensus that commercial banks should actively expand the retail banking business in response to the economic and financial transformation. At present, there is a popular remark in China's banking sector: "if we had not done well in corporate business, commercial banks would not have been able to get this far if they had failed to carry out successful corporate business; if commercial banks fail to do well in retail business, they will not have a bright future." This remark reveals two basic facts: first, the income from retail business targeting individual customers and small and medium-sized enterprises still accounts for a small proportion of the total income of China's commercial banks, usually less than 50%, but there is still a relatively broad space for development; second, in recent years, retail banking business represented by individual loans, housing mortgage loans and credit card business has grown rapidly. The retail banking business has many advantages, such as less capital occupation, small cycle disturbance, high economic value added (EVA) and low business risk, which makes it the key development direction of most banks. In addition, there are better reasons for Chinese commercial banks to regard retail business as their future development direction.

1. Significance of Retail Banking to Commercial Banks

Traditionally, the high-risk operation of small and microenterprises is inconsistent with the bank's traditional idea of prudent credit, so small and microenterprises can only obtain small amount of loans from financial institutions. However, in reality, most small and microenterprises are concentrated in light-asset industries such as circulation trade and service industry. Although the collateral is insufficient, their profitability is sustainable and guaranteed, so they are high-quality finance customers. The commercial banks do not have sufficient ability to identify these customers; as a result, the shadow banking system represented by a variety of private financing platforms is actually occupying the service market of small and microenterprises and making huge profits. The practice shows that it is the commercial banks' abilities of comprehensive service and risk prevention and control that decide whether commercial banks can occupy the market.

2. Retail Banking: An Indicator of Commercial Banks' Asset Management and Allocation Capabilities

At present, China is in the process of transforming bank savings into diversified financial assets. The financial assets of residents are no longer limited to savings and treasury bonds. The proportion of assets like bank financial products, funds and trusts in total financial assets has increased year by year, and the savings service for individual customers can no longer meet the diversified financial needs of customers. The competition among banks also involves the capability of asset management and allocation. Retail banking business reflects the customer's needs for asset allocation, and it also connects and maintains the wealth management products in the asset pool of commercial banks and various asset management platforms. Therefore, the retail banking is most sensitive to the asset management ability of commercial banks, and it also reflects the ability of a bank to meet the customers' needs for diversified financial assets. With deepened interest rate reform and intensified competition among banks, the level of retail banking business and related asset management and allocation will exert an increasingly great impact on the profitability and asset size of commercial banks.

3. Retail Banking: A Powerful Tool for Commercial Banks to Integrate External Resources and Build a Comprehensive Service Platform

From the practical experience, the service ability of commercial banks is reflected not only in financing, but also in the integration of external resources to meet diversified needs of customers. A survey shows that the customers' loyalty to a bank depends on the number of services provided by the bank. The more types of services customers get, the more loyal they will be. These services include both direct and indirect services provided by the bank. For example, the competition of credit cards involves not only the competition in the appearance, service and credit limit, but also the integration of third-party resources such as value-added services, manufacturer's discounts and credit card discounts. The integration of third-party resources is more important to private banks. An extreme example is the family office. In order to establish family offices for customers, European and American private banks have to integrate 30 or more third-party institutions so as to meet the customers' various financial and non-financial needs. A private bank in Canada even integrated 65 third-party institutions for its customers to meet their family's needs of car repair, aircraft leasing, clothes making, legal and taxation consulting, etc. Founded in Canyonville, Oregon, Umpqua, was just a small community bank, but just in 20 years, it stood out from many community banks in the United States to have an asset size of 22.5 billion US dollars and become a large commercial bank with nearly 400 branches. Umpqua's success is attributed to its competitive strategy of differentiated operation and community-intensive cultivation, and its success is also owing to its business philosophy of putting customers first. Generally speaking, the retail banking business represented by credit cards and private banking business can integrate external resources more easily than corporate business, and it is also easier for them to form an integrated service platform, which will play an important role in the competition among banks in the future.

Of course, China's retail banking business is still facing many realistic constraints and challenges. However, with accelerated financial transformation, diversified customer demands and interest rate liberalization, retail banking business is becoming the area of fastest profit growth during the transformation and development of China's commercial banks.

References

1. Ba Shusong. Ways to Expand Retail Banking Business [J]. China Urban Rural Financial News. 2012 (6)
2. Boston Consulting Company. Perfect Retail Bank 2020: Humanity, Technology, Transformation and Profitability [R]. 2015.
3. Intelligent Research Consulting. Report on China's Retail Banking Market Operation Situation and Development Prospect from 2017 to 2022 [R]. 2016.

Chapter 14
Future of Direct Banks

On September 16, 2013, China Minsheng Bank (CMB) and Alibaba Group jointly announced that they were preparing to establish a direct bank. On September 18 of the same year, Bank of Beijing (BOB) announced the establishment of China's first direct bank in cooperation with ING group of the Netherlands, and China started the development of direct banks. On July 18, 2015, ten departments, including the People's Bank of China and the Ministry of Industry and Information Technology, jointly issued *Guiding Opinions of the People's Bank of China, the Ministry of Industry and Information Technology, the Ministry of Public Security, et al, on Promoting the Sound Development of Internet Finance*, which encouraged and further promoted the development of direct banks. On January 5, 2017, Aibank, the first independent legal person direct bank in China, was officially approved to be established, which marks that the development of direct banks has entered a new stage. According to the latest report released by Analysys think tank in May 2017, there are currently 93 commercial banks with independent direct banking APPs.

The study of direct banks must be based on the current ecological environment of Internet finance and focus on the functions and positioning of direct banks in the new environment. Different from traditional finance, Internet finance is a symbiotic and competitive ecology. China's direct banks will experience the evolution from internal competition and cooperation to external competition and cooperation. Grasping the opportunities in this process is the key to the success of direct banks.

14.1 Key to the Development of Direct Banks

1. Differentiated Strategic Positioning

In the face of different competitors, differentiated strategic positioning is most important for direct banks to establish a reasonable competitive relationship (Fig. 14.1).

S. Ba, *The New Cycle and New Finance in China*,
https://doi.org/10.1007/978-981-16-8209-4_14

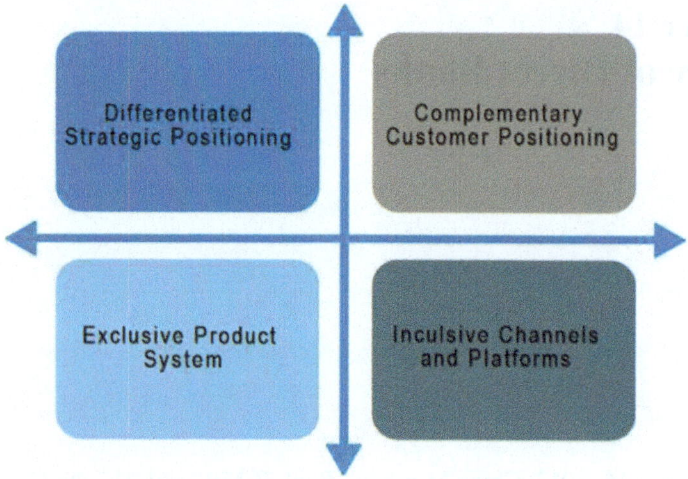

Fig. 14.1 Key to the development of direct banks

Examples:

ING Direct—It positions itself as "the first direct bank in the markets of target countries" and "the second option of customers" and meets the main financial needs of customers with the simplest and most basic banking products and services.

Openbank—It develops business for digital elites and has become the experiment field of innovations for the customers' host and parent banks.

Fineco—It relies on the strong investment banking platform and asset management capability of Unicredit, its parent bank, and strives to become an innovative, high-value and differentiated high-end direct bank.

HSBC Direct—Its main strategic positioning is to attract deposit customers through Internet.

2. Complementary Customer Positioning

The key to carry out competitive cooperation between direct banks and traditional outlets is to take attracting new customers as the main purpose, focus on the exclusive customer group and serve as a supplement to the traditional outlets, rather than encroaching on the customer resources of the traditional outlets.

Target customers: They are mainly digital elites who have a high degree of acceptance of electronic channels and low dependence on outlets. They readily accept direct sales channels such as Internet and telephone and value convenience very much. According to relevant reports, most of these customers are young people with high requirements for convenience. This is why Ping An Bank positions itself as a "bank for the young people."

Exclusive customers: as sub-brands, direct banks need to establish their own exclusive customer groups. For example, the three banks of Deutsche Bank Group aim at different customer groups, and there is little intersection between them. Most of Deutsche Bank and Postbank customers need to transact business in outlets, while Norisbank focuses on the customer group of digital elites. The major goal of HSBC Direct is to absorb deposits, rather than to provide comprehensive banking services through electronic channels. HSBC Direct focuses on its customers' adjunct accounts rather than their primary accounts. It has developed innovative and low-cost business model to serve and attract customers without significantly encroaching on the customer resources of its traditional outlets.

3. Exclusive Product System

Whether as an independent subsidiary or as a business department, a direct bank should establish an exclusive product system, subdivide customer groups and conduct independent channel sales, so as to establish and improve its own business mode.

In order to establish their own business modes, the direct banks have generally established their exclusive product systems with simple product design and reasonable pricing as compared with traditional channel products. The product categories of direct banks are few but complete, covering the fields of payment, investment and financing, and the number of products of each type is limited. For example, ING Direct started from a simple savings account and eventually expanded to five categories: savings account, mortgage loans, stock account, pension account and enterprise savings account, but the total number of products provided by ING Direct is decreasing. Product design is often aimed at the limited scope of direct channels to minimize the need for customer interaction so as to reduce costs. At the same time, simple and easy exclusive direct sales channels, which are different from traditional electronic channels in design and function, are established, focusing on integrating sales elements. Relying on the advantage of scale cost of the Internet, ING Direct yields profit from the interest rate spread, rather than from the international mainstream non-interest rate spread. However, it adopts the way of absorbing deposits with high interest rate and issuing loans at low interest rate.

4. Inclusive Channels and Platforms

The operation of international direct banks shows that, due to such factors as regulatory policies, legal environment and customer experience, pure network banking is not enough to form closed-loop financial services for customers and the business mode is relatively fragile. Direct banks must establish inclusive channels and platforms in order to establish a sound business mode in the environment of competitive cooperation of Internet finance.

International direct banks have accumulated some experience in this respect. Firstly, the outlets of direct banks are not entirely non-physical ones. Direct banks such as Openbank rely on the physical outlets of their parent banks; as a bank serving high-end direct customers, Fineco establishes its own exclusive network and financial consultant team; ING Direct not only carries out business through Internet but also supports online business through offline ING Coffee houses and trains coffee bar clerks into financial consultants who can communicate with customers and provide product suggestions without jargon-free language. Secondly, in terms of the operation platforms, ING Direct has established a completely independent organizational structure, and most of the direct banks as sub-brands have independent front systems, sharing the middle and back systems with their parent banks. Thirdly, in terms of marketing platforms, many direct banks value the purely online classic marketing mode without relying on the existing customers of their parent banks, but the subsidiaries like Openbank do not exclude outlet recommendation and even third-party cooperation. Finally, there are a large number of direct banks in Germany, a European country. with high market maturity and low concentration. ING Direct has established its own ATM system, and other direct banks either join ATM consortia, such as cash group or cash pool, or provide VISA or Mastercard for customers to withdraw money free of charge.

14.2 Policy Suggestions for China's Direct Banks

At present, the corporate license of direct banks has not been fully opened up. Therefore, the development of direct banks at this stage depends on whether an independent entity of competitive cooperation can be established within the banks. The key points are as follows (see Fig. 14.2).

Firstly, the direct banks should focus on the customers of the digital generation and establish an independent product system. The product should be simple, exclusive, advantageous, innovative and standard with a simple design and a clean user interface.

Secondly, we should properly handle competitive cooperation between direct banks and bank outlets and establish a business division system. Direct banks

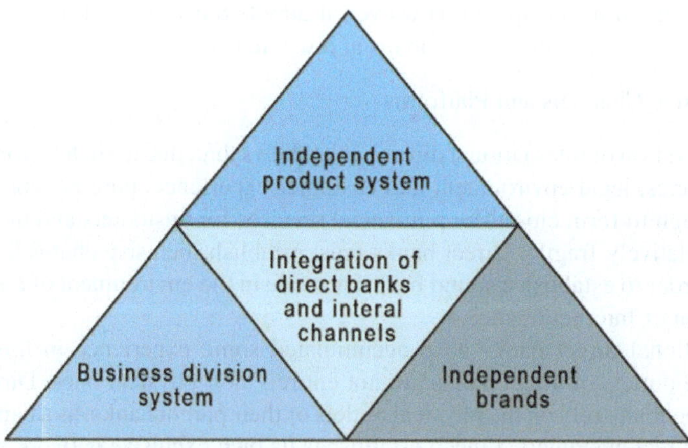

Fig. 14.2 Policy suggestions for China's direct banks

should establish an independent accounting system and product pricing system, and avoid developing existing customers for the second time or developing customers of traditional outlets.

Thirdly, we should promote proper integration of direct banks and internal channels. As mentioned above, direct banks in other countries have independent front systems and share the middle and back systems with their parent banks. At present, the electronic channels such as online and mobile banking of China's banks have witnessed a relatively high degree of development. Although direct banks are independent sales channels, under the current regulatory environment, they have to share with other channels such technologies as mobile operation, video face-to-face signature and image recognition.

Finally, direct banks need to sort out customers and products and establish their own independent brands as soon as possible. China's direct banks should consider the characteristics of the digital generation and learn from international direct banks, establish their own unique brands and strengthen the marketing of online consumer loans.

China's Internet finance will be the result of symbiosis and competitive cooperation between Internet and financial enterprises. From the international experience, we can say that in the field of direct banks, the bank side is in a strong position. In the United States, although physical outlets handle some cash and business online, the functional requirements of customer development and marketing have been strengthened. The total number of banking institutions has been decreasing year by year since 1980s, but the number of bank branches has been growing steadily.

Therefore, in order to get rid of the strong position of traditional channels, a direct bank, as a banking department, must make use of the current competitive cooperation of Internet finance, strengthen internal integration, obtain the favorable position of external competitive cooperation and make use of external platforms so as to rapidly expand its scale (Fig. 14.3).

Firstly, direct banks should promote internal integration, forming a unified interface of external competition and cooperation. They should also integrate their internal systems and connect with the account of Internet companies with a unified virtual account.

Secondly, direct banks should seize opportunities to actively carry out cooperation with large-scale e-commerce platforms. The Internet enterprises are the

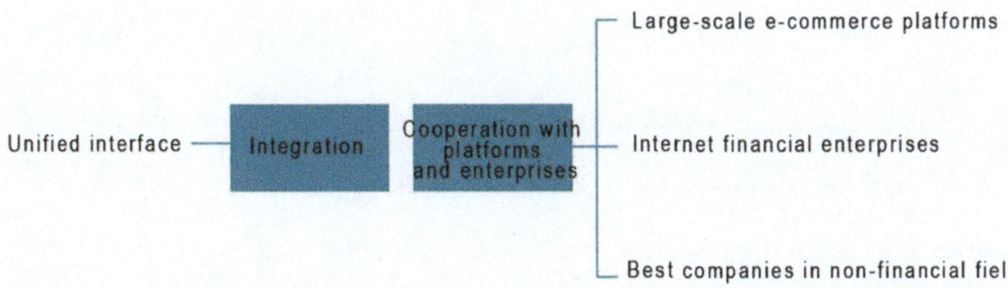

Fig. 14.3 The strategies for a direct bank to get rig of the strong position of traditional channels

main entrance and portals for the digital generation. Direct banks should seize the opportunities, actively cooperate with large-scale e-commerce platforms and attract customers in large numbers.

Thirdly, direct banks should actively carry out cooperation with new Internet financial enterprises such as third-party payment. The development of China's Internet finance shows that it is difficult for Internet enterprises such as third-party payment to develop into direct banks as it is difficult for them to bypass the regulatory policies, and they also lack internal motivation. As an independent sales channel, direct banks should strengthen cooperation with third-party payment companies in payment and customer settlement.

Finally, direct banks should promote cooperation with best companies in non-financial fields because the long-term goal of direct banks is to develop from business departments into independent subsidiaries.

ING Direct, as a global entity, is successful because it shares the best practices globally. Therefore, the direct banks should speed up the cooperation with the companies with best practices in service and brand, so as to establish their own brands and service as soon as possible form a unique customer group and have a unique positioning.

References

1. Ba Shusong, Ji Meng. Analysis of Business Model of Direct Bank [J]. *China Rural Finance*, 2015(17).
2. You Chun. International Experience and Enlightenment of Direct Banks: Taking Germany and Japan as Examples [J]. *Computer World*, 2016(5).
3. Analysys, Oneconnect, China Direct Banking Market Special Analysis 2017 [R]. 2017.

Chapter 15
Risks of Bank Financing

Recently, an article published by overseas financial media pointed out that CMB is the bank with the greatest risks in China because it relies heavily on financial products, the balance of which is about RMB2.1 trillion, and that it has made many so-called asset management plans, which may be the hiding place for many non-performing loans.

Some international rating agencies have also lowered the basic credit rating of a certain Chinese commercial bank, downgrading it from investment grade to junk grade. The reason for the downgrading is that the bank has a poor performance in financing, and its profitability is also poor due to the pressure from rising costs of market financing.

These two events have triggered off heated debates, but in fact, the two events are closely related to the financial management of commercial banks. In a certain sense, some overseas media made the assessment of CMB according to its development of financial products. The financing of commercial banks is directly affected by the development of financial market.

First of all, it should be pointed out that both the overseas financial media and the international rating agencies may have ignored that China's regulatory authorities have taken a series of regulatory measures on the financial management business of commercial banks. The financial management business of China's commercial banks is going toward the normal track. Although there are local risks, the overall risks are controllable. Statistical data show that, under the guidance of regulatory policies, the proportion of high-yield asset allocation of bank financial products is gradually declining. The income level of bank financial products is gradually falling, which is conducive to relieving commercial banks' pressure of rising financing costs in the previous stage. Along with this, in the first half of 2017, under the guidance of regulatory policies, the scale of interbank assets and liabilities of China's banking industry both fell for the first time since 2010. Statistics show that at the end of the second quarter, the balance of assets and liabilities of commercial banks in China decreased by RMB1.8 trillion compared with that at the beginning of the year. This shows that the regulatory policies were playing an active role, enabling commercial

S. Ba, *The New Cycle and New Finance in China*,
https://doi.org/10.1007/978-981-16-8209-4_15

banks to gradually release the risks in financial management business accumulated in the period of rapid development and enter the stage of rational development.

15.1 Status Quo of Commercial Banks' Financial Management

1. After rapid expansion, the financial management of commercial banks is entering the period of stable adjustment under the guidance of regulatory policies. The financial management business of China's banking industry started in 2004. After 12 years of development, it reached RMB29.05 trillion in 2016 (see Fig. 15.1). The bank financing management business has undoubtedly played a positive role in promoting the adjustment of financial structure and enabling China's banking industry to adapt to the environment of market-oriented interest rates. However, there were also certain risks in the process of rapid development. Since 2017, the regulatory authorities have continued to carry out a series of activities governing market chaos in bank financial management, and strengthened the regulation on financial management business. Statistics show that, after reaching a peak of RMB30.31 trillion at the end of January 2017, the scale of financial management business continued to decrease. After falling to RMB29.15 trillion at the end of the first quarter, it further dropped to RMB28.4 trillion at the end of the second quarter, a decrease of 2.23% compared with that at the end of 2016. Among them, the interbank financial management business witnessed the most obvious decrease, and outsourcing

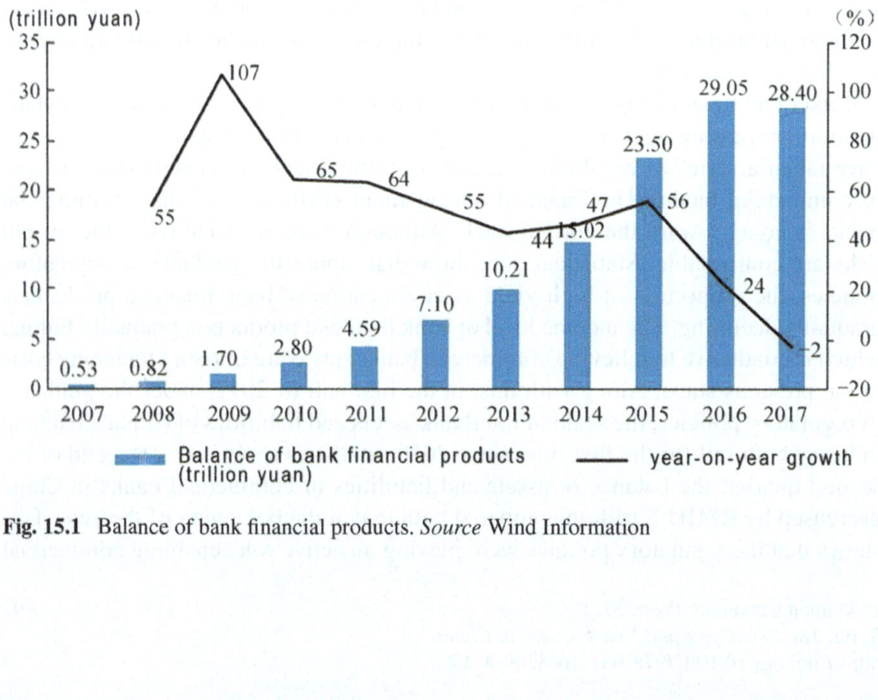

Fig. 15.1 Balance of bank financial products. *Source* Wind Information

Table 15.1 Fund raising of financial products with different risk levels

Risk level		Level I	Level II	Level III	Level IV	Level V	Total
2016	Fund raised (Trillion yuan)	41.81	95.82	29.81	0.34	0.15	167.94
	Percentage	24.90%	57.06%	17.75%	0.20%	0.09%	100%
2015	Fund raised (Trillion yuan)	42.37	94.42	20.75	0.75	0.12	158.41
	Percentage	26.75%	59.60	13.10%	0.47%	0.08%	100%

investment witnessed a decrease of more than RMB530 billion compared with that before the governance.

According to the *Annual Report of Financial Management Market of China's Banking Industry (2016)* (hereafter referred to as *the Annual Report*) released by the Banking Financial Management Registration and Custody Center, the total amount of funds raised through financial products with risk level of "grade II (medium low)" and below was RMB137.63 trillion in 2016, accounting for 81.96% of the total amount of funds raised in the whole market, a decrease of 4.39% compared with that in 2015. Under the background of financial deleveraging, the banking financial market is gradually releasing risks under the guidance of regulatory policies and returning to the track of stable development (Table 15.1).

2. Off balance sheet financing accounts for most of the remaining balance of financial products, and guiding the healthy development of off balance sheet financing has become one of the focuses of regulation. According to the *Annual Report*, the balance of the financial products with non-guaranteed principal, that is, off balance sheet financing, was RMB23.11 trillion, accounting for 79.56% of the total remaining balance of all financial products, an increase of 5.39% over the beginning of the year. The remaining balance of financial products with guaranteed principal was RMB5.94% trillion, accounting for 20.44% of the remaining balance of all financial products (see Fig. 15.2). Off balance sheet financing accounts for most of the remaining balance of financial products.

3. Bonds, deposits and money market tools are the top three major types of assets allocated through financial products, and the overall asset quality is good. By the end of 2016, the balance accounted for 73.52%, of which 43.76% were bonds, accounting for the highest proportion among the assets invested by wealth management funds (see Fig. 15.3). Treasury bonds, local treasury bonds, central bank bills, bonds of government-support agencies and policy financial bonds accounted for 8.69% of the balance of wealth management and investment assets, while commercial financial bonds, corporate bonds, corporate debt financing instruments, asset-backed securities, foreign bonds and other bonds accounted for 35.07%. In 2016, a total of RMB19.65 trillion of wealth management funds were invested in the real economy through the allocation of bonds, nonstandard creditor assets and equity assets, accounting for 67.41% of the balance of various assets invested through wealth management funds. There

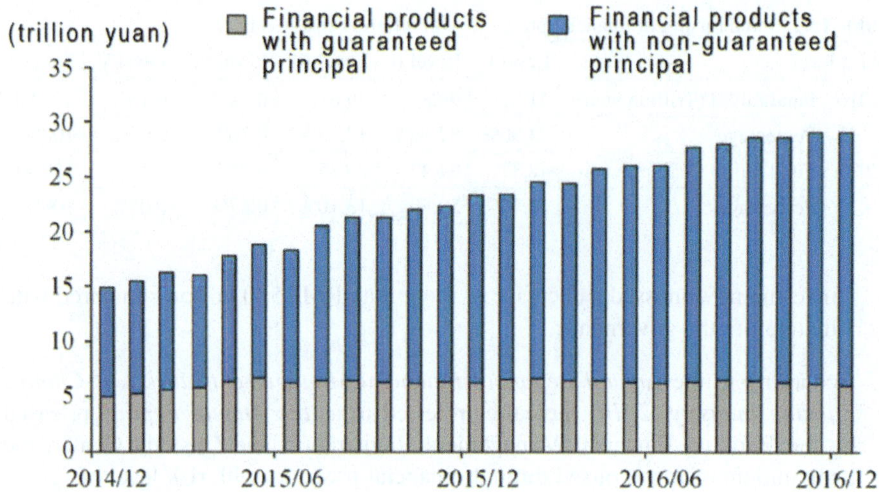

Fig. 15.2 Balance of financial products with different income types

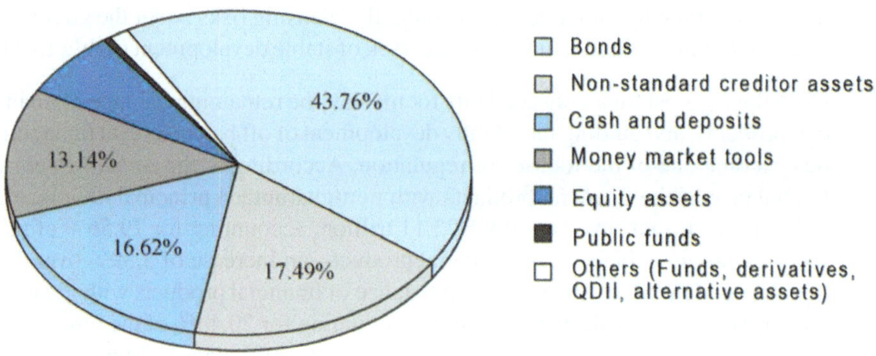

Fig. 15.3 Assets allocation of financial products at the end of 2016

was an increase of RMB3.77 trillion at the end of 2016 as compared with that at the beginning of the year, an increase of 23.75%.

4. Under the guidance of regulatory policies, the yield of financial products in the market witnessed steady decline. In 2016, a total of 192,200 products were cashed in the banking financial market (of which 184,400 products were due), and the total income of cashing customers was RMB977.27 billion, an increase of 12.97% as compared with that in 2015. In 2016, the return rate of cashing customers of closed-end financial products showed a downward trend. The annualized return rate of cashing customers decreased from about 4.2% at the beginning of the year to about 3.5% at the end of the year (see Fig. 15.4). In 2016, 88 matured financial products suffered losses, accounting for 0.05% of all the products that came due.

Fig. 15.4 Trend of annualized return rate closed-end financial products

15.2 Possible Local Risks in Financial Management Business of Commercial Banks and Their Causes

The financial management business of commercial banks plays an important role in serving the real economy and broadening the investment and financing channels. However, the rapid expansion of financial management business in its early stage may also result in local risks and problems.

1. Risk transfer as a result of multilayer nesting. A small number of financial products of commercial banks have the problems of multilayer nesting and complex transaction structure, which makes it difficult to truly achieve penetration management and understand the real risks of underlying assets, resulting in hidden business risks; multilayer nesting also leads to high leverage. All participants in the transaction chain may not be able to grasp all the business information all the time, and the entrusted asset managers often lack the initiative to carry out risk management, resulting in the absence of risk management in the whole transaction chain. Besides, this business mode may also increase the possibility and speed of cross-industry and cross-market transmission of financial risks. Once problems occur in one link, they may spread to other areas.
2. Outsourcing risk. Commercial banks are growing rapidly in the scale of financial management business, but the banks' ability of investment management can't match the growth of scale for a while, so they turn to other investment institutions for investment management. However, a few banks lack the systematic screening mechanism of investment institutions, so they regard the level of expected return on investment of investment institutions as the criterion for selection. The post-event management of outsourcing institutions is also relatively extensive.

3. Liquidity risk. There is often a maturity mismatch between the raising and use of financial management funds. By rolling release, collective operation, separate pricing and other ways, low-cost and short-term funds are put into long-term claims or equity projects. When financial products are due, mutual transactions between financial products and financial business with self-operated funds are sometimes needed to provide liquidity support.
4. Hidden risk of rigid payment. Although no institution has publicly guaranteed rigid payment of any of its financial products at present, it is difficult to achieve one-to-one match between assets and liabilities due to the fact financial business is often carried out through fund pool. In addition, financial business customers, especially ordinary individual customers, cannot fully accept the assumption of risks. To prevent and control reputation risk, banks will often use on balance sheet assets or other assets in the asset pool to remove the risk of payment, which cannot achieve real risk isolation and deviates from the essence of asset management business.
5. Compliance risk. Previously, banks generally adopted the model of asset pool in their financial management business, and the financial management funds of some banks illegally flowed to the industries and field such as the real estate, financing platforms and the industries with high energy consumption, high pollution and overcapacity, which was contrary to the regulatory policy requirements. At this time, bank financing business has become a channel to evade the regulation's credit constraints on specific industries.

15.3 Development Trend of Bank Financial Management

At present, a series of regulatory policies are being implemented with a clear purpose, which requires banks to gradually eliminate the rigid payment, release local risks in a controllable way, and return to the essence of asset management. *The Financial Stability Report 2017* issued by the central bank on July 4 specifically pointed out the problems of capital pool, multilayer nesting, shadow banking and rigid payment in China's asset management industry. Previously, CBRC have clearly expressed the same regulatory intention in its various regulatory documents. The policies issued from March to April had consistent policy orientation, emphasizing the regulation and implementation of measures regarding these problems.

The regulation on bank financial management business in the future should aim to achieve controllable release of risks, gradually unify regulation standards, implement penetrating regulation and strengthen inspection and rectification. *The Financial Stability Report 2017* pointed out that we need to put forward targeted solution, unify the regulation standards of similar products and establish an effective regulatory system for asset management business so as to address the outstanding risks and problems exposed during the rapid expansion of asset management business.

Under the guidance of these policies, the commercial banks are also starting to reposition their asset management business and carry out the asset management business to finance for others. Specifically, some commercial banks begin to strengthen team building by setting up asset management centers or business divisions; some strengthen the cultivation of asset management customers, carry out studies on the risk preference of potential customers and attach greater importance to improving their ability of asset allocation; after the current round of market reshuffle, commercial banks will be more prudent in carrying out outsourcing business, and the investment and research ability of the outsourcing institutions as well as the stability of the these institutions have become important criteria for selection.

The regulation has been constantly strengthened; the regulatory policies have been unified and improved; bank compliance and risk management has been strengthened; and asset management ability has improved. As a result, commercial banks will carry out sound financial management business, home local risks will be gradually eliminated, and commercial banks in China will undergo more stable and healthy development in its financial management business.

References

1. Ba Shusong, Wang Yuexiang. Bank financing will return to the essence of asset management [N]. *International Financial Journal*, 2017–01–02 (005).
2. Financial management registration and custody center of banking industry. Annual Report on Financial Management Market of China's Banking Industry (2016) [R]. 2017–05–19.
3. *Financial Stability Analysis Group of the People's Bank of China. China Financial Stability Report 2017* [M]. Beijing: China financial press, 2017.

Chapter 16
On Cash Loan Business

In recent years, the cash loan business in China has witnessed rapid development, and it has become a representative product of the integration of Internet finance and consumer finance. Cash loan mainly model itself on Payday Loan, a business in foreign countries mainly for customers with low income and inability to obtain loans from banks. The average term ranges from 7 to 30 days, and the amount of loans ranges from \$100 to \$1000. It can be availed without mortgage guarantee, scenario, or designated purpose. It is called Payday Loan because customers get small amount of funds in case of emergency or urgent need and repay them with salary on payday.

Payday Loan originated in the United States in the late 1980s. In 1983, Cash America Pawn took the lead in developing Payday Loan business. First Cash and EZcorp followed and provided various products such as cash advances, prepaid debit cards, pawns, auto-loans and consumer loans. Around 2006, Payday Loan business began to develop in the UK, and Wonga, a representative financing platform, was built and began to operate in early 2007. By the end of 2014, the loans granted through Payday Loan in the United States reached about 46 billion US dollars. There were more than 1000 Payday Loan service providers and 12 million active loan users in the market, accounting for more than 3% of the total population. In the UK, Payday Loan reached its heyday in 2013, with more than 400 enterprises serving 1.6 million customers, and the market value reached 2.5 billion pounds.

More and more disputes and doubts about Payday Loan came with the rapid expansion of the business. The regulatory authorities in the United States and the UK have taken special measures to comprehensively regulate the business. Since then, Payday Loan in the UK and the US markets has gradually entered a period of adjustment, and development speed gave way to service quality.

Wang Zhifeng and Shu Tianzhi participated in the drafting and discussion of this paper, which was published in China Banking on April 15, 2017.

S. Ba, *The New Cycle and New Finance in China*,
https://doi.org/10.1007/978-981-16-8209-4_16

16.1 Controversy Over Payday Loan

The most typical mode of Payday Loan is "bank check holding," that is, after credit review, the borrower instructs the bank to write a check from his or her own account according to the requirements of Payday Loan enterprise. The Payday Loan enterprise holds the check for a period of time and issues a small credit loan to the borrower after a certain proportion of discount of the check amount. On the borrower's payday, Payday Loan enterprise will ask the bank to cash the check to complete the repayment. It has the following features: firstly, the service is highly efficient. In particular, relying on the Internet and big data technology, PaydayLoan is able to accept online business 24 h a day and grant loans within 15 min, which perfectly satisfies the users' urgent needs of funds and brings unprecedented good experience to users. Secondly, it is accompanied by high risks. According to statistics, the non-performing loan ratio of Payday Loan in the United States is between 10 and 20%. According to the research of the Consumer Financial Protection Bureau (CFPB), 23% of online loan borrowers face the problem of account closure after the end of the 18 month sample period, which is far higher than the 6% account closure rate announced by banks. Finally, the cost of short-term loan is lower than that of other petty cash products, but the interest rates of long-term loans are very high. The original term of each loan is very short, and the interest rate is usually set daily at an average of 5–1%. It is estimated that if the repayment can be made on schedule, the cost will be lower than the penalty interest of bad checks and bank credit cards. However, the annualized interest rate is as high as 180–400%. It is high enough to be regarded as usury.

From the main features of Payday Loan, we can see that it grants small loans to low-income people at high interest rate. As a result, Payday Loan raised moral concerns despite its great social value. In fact, this kind of product is nothing new. There is a description of similar business in Shakespeare's *Merchant of Venice*, which also caused great controversy at that time.

On the one hand, low-income people need to borrow money to get through the difficulties. According to *The Economist*, in the United States, 8% of households with an annual income of less than 15,000 US dollars (about RMB100, 000) have not opened bank accounts. According to the Federal Reserve Board, 50% of Americans cannot afford to spend $400 in case of an emergency. Similarly, people in the UK are not in the habit of saving money, so they have the rigid demand for loans in case of emergencies. According to the statistics of the British regulatory authorities, affected by the financial crisis, 1.2 million users turned to the platform for small loans due to temporary financial difficulties around 2008.

On the other hand, Payday Loan, like the merchant of Venice, faces moral condemnation. Firstly, most Payday Loan users cannot make a lump sum repayment, but they have to postpone it. As a result, users will have to bear huge interest, making their life all the more difficult. According to statistics, more than 80% of Payday Loan users in the United States will renew their loans within one month. Secondly, if the balance of the check account is insufficient, Payday Loan company will try to cash the check frequently, and the failure of the check deduction will lead to repeated fines. Finally, users who fail to make the repayment will face high-handed collection.

16.2 US and UK's Regulation on Payday Loan and Its Influence

At the beginning, the UK and the United States did not have special regulatory rules concerning the service platform of Payday Loan but carried out unified regulation on the platform, regarding it as an institution with loan qualifications. For example, Payday Loan in the United States, like other lending institutions, is regulated by the *Federal Loan Act, the Fair Credit Reporting Act*, the *Equal Credit Opportunity Act*, and *Truth in Lending Act*. With the gradual exposure of Payday Loan's hazards, the Financial Conduct Authority (FCA) of the UK promulgated *Rules for Management of Consumer Loans* in April 2014, imposing regulation on high-cost short-term loans such as Payday Loan. On June 2, 2016, the Consumer Financial Protection Bureau (CFPB) released a draft regulation on Payday Loan, which will be applicable throughout the country and affect the vast majority of financial products in the market.

The Payday Loan regulatory bills in the United States and Britain mainly include the following six aspects:

1. Regulatory objectives. The regulation aims to make the lending institutions only grant loans to the right group of people and make the consumers fully understand the obligations and risks of borrowing.
2. Scope of regulation. The United States regulates Payday Loan products and car loans. The UK includes P2P loans and products with APR (annualized interest rate) higher than 100% in the category of high-cost short-term loans.
3. Access mechanism. Payday Loan institutions in the United States and the UK need to apply to the competent authorities for certification.
4. Loan element restrictions. Specifically, restrictions on such elements as borrowing cost, loan limit, loan extension limit and penalty management are imposed, so as to avoid the debt trap of users who bear much more than their total amount of loadable debt through continuous renewal of loans and borrowing from multiple sources.
5. Guidance on the optimization of products and services. For example, the US regulatory authorities advice Payday Loan to provide low-risk long-term loan products, that is, the lenders are allowed to provide two options of long-term loans: one is the loan with an annual interest rate of no more than 28% and the application fee of no more than $20; the other is the loan with a term of no more than two years and an annual interest rate of no more than 36%, but the default rate needs to be controlled within 5%.

6. Establishment of a regulatory reporting mechanism. Both the USA and the UK require lenders to report all credit data, including full repayment test or principal repayment options, through the credit reporting system.

The regulatory rules of the UK and the USA have exerted a profound impact on the Payday Loan industry. In the United States, the listed Payday Loan service providers such as First Cash, EZCorp, Cash America all said that the scale of Payday Loan service will be adjusted according to regulatory rules. In the UK, six months after the implementation of the regulatory rules, the number of customers applying for loans, the credit passing rate and the loan amount of Payday Loan decreased by 20%, 50% and 35%, respectively. FCA assessed the possible impact of the regulatory system on the market and concluded that only one quarter of Payday Loan institutions could survive in the market. However, it still remains a question whether strict regulation will help to better protect consumer rights and interests, and research institutions, media and users also hold different opinions in this regard. Researchers believe that the mandatory measures help to protect consumers from falling into debt, but some studies show that this reduces the scale of Payday Loan and damages the market mechanism. However, the survey of telephone and Internet complaint channels shows that the original problems have not been completely solved.

16.3 Status Quo of Cash Loan in China

With the rapid development of Internet finance, cash loan appeared in China in 2015. According to the incomplete statistics of the third-party media, there are more than 1000 Internet platforms providing cash loan service in the market, with about 30 million active users.

Similar to that in foreign countries, China's cash loan has the characteristics of convenience, small amount, short term, high interest rate and no scenario, which is mainly used for small sum consumption or emergent needs. Its customers are mainly young people under 30 years old, with low income, light economic burden, strong willingness of debt-financed consumption and preference to improve their quality of life through borrowing. From the perspective of service mode, the rise of China's cash loan is closely related to Internet and it mainly operates and provides services through the Internet; therefore, it is as convenient as its British and American counterparts. From the perspective of risk control technology, China's cash loan, relying on big data technology, improves the level and efficiency of risk control through such tools and means as data modeling, credit scoring, intelligent anti-fraud, which has provided strong support for the rapid development of cash loan business in China.

Similar to Payday Loan in its early stage of development, cash loan is widely accepted by the market, but it also has many problems. For example, it has also caused moral concern. The cash loan with high interest and general loan renewal (compound interest) puts a heavy burden on users. In particular, some platforms set too high interest rates, provide no clear information concerning charges and fees, induce users to renew their loans (long-term turnover), and deliberately give no clear or prompt warnings to the consumers to cause users' overdue interest penalty. All these behaviors have seriously hurt the rights and interests of consumers and brought ill reputation to the cash loan business. It has also caused concerns about risk control. At present, the cash loan industry is still in its infancy and has not yet experienced a complete risk cycle. The influx of customers and capital has brought huge short-term profits. As a result, some platforms have relaxed risk control standards, and a large number of users without repayment ability have been granted loans. Some platforms have weak risk control ability, but in order to enhance their competitiveness, they blindly compete for loan efficiency and credit limit, thereby giving rise to potential risks. In addition, China's credit system is far less developed than that of foreign countries, which makes it more difficult to guard against loans from multiple sources and malicious fraud.

16.4 Implications and Suggestions

Generally speaking, cash loan should be given space for survival and development as it has great social value of promoting financial marketization, improving financial supply system, enriching financial market and providing more options for consumers. However, cash loan also involves high interest lending, which runs counter to the moral principles and harms public order and good customs of modern civilized society. It is likely to be abused by market subjects lacking self-discipline and needs to be restricted and regulated by a perfect regulatory system.

According to the British and American experience, legislation and regulation concerning cash loan should be strengthened. It mainly includes three aspects: the first is to clarify the regulatory authorities. We can learn from the P2P regulation mode to carry out both institutional and behavioral regulation by the local financial office and CBRC. The second is to establish an access system, such as clarifying the subject qualification and business scope requirements of cash loan in the process of industrial and commercial registration and establishing the legal status of industry practitioners. The third is to establish appropriate industry norms to limit the prominent problems such as high loan interest rate, loans from multiple sources and continuous renewal of loans. In particular, the explicit legal provisions of interest rate in China can be found in *the General Principles of the Civil Law of the People's Republic of China*, which stipulates that the interest rate within four times of the bank's loan interest rate in the same period is legal while loans with interest rate over four times of the bank's loan interest rate in the same period belong to usury, and thus is not protected by law. From the British and American experience, this interest rate cap is too low, which should not be applicable to loans with ultra-short term, and, therefore, is not conducive to the sustainable development of cash loan business. The last is to establish a clear and powerful mechanism for law enforcement. At present, cash loan business is mainly conducted through the Internet; therefore, we should also base our law enforcement measures on the Internet and big data so as to achieve efficient regulation.

In addition to strengthened legislation and regulation, a good industry environment is needed for the healthy development of cash loan business. The following measures can be taken to improve the environment: firstly, we need to strengthen the construction of basic credit information system and the sharing of credit information, so as to help Payday Loan platform effectively guard against fraud, and identify loans from multiple sources and users of bad credit, so as to improve the overall risk control level of the industry. Secondly, we need to build industry self-discipline and information disclosure mechanisms to enhance information transparency so as to effectively reduce deception and improper inducement to consumers. We can give full play to the role of National Internet Finance Association of China to introduce industry standards and guide the industry discipline itself. Finally, we need to strengthen education to provide consumers with financial knowledge and enhance their awareness of credit, so that the borrowers can understand the responsibilities and risks of borrowing.

Chapter 17
On Development of Bank Financing

The central working conference held at the end of 2016 put higher requirements on the prevention and resolution of financial risks, stating clearly that "we should attach greater importance to the prevention and control of financial risks, resolve to remove a number of risk points, focus on the prevention and control of asset bubbles and improve regulatory capabilities so as to guard against systemic financial risks."

This is the extension of the idea of risk prevention and leverage reduction in China's financial regulation since 2016. The explosive scale expansion of China's bank financing business resulted in hidden industry risks and possible macroliquidity risks, which cannot be underestimated. We need to focus on these risks in this round of financial risk management and control and bring it into the scope of macroprudential regulation. This is of far-reaching significance for the healthy development of the banking industry.

17.1 Origin of Bank Financing Business

The financial management business of China's banking industry started in 2004. After 12 years of rapid development, its volume has reached RMB26.28 trillion by the end of the first half of 2016, and it has become the largest sub-industry in the asset management industry. The development of the business is the product of interest rate liberalization in China and benefits from the dual drivers of assets and liabilities. On the asset side, the financing business makes use of some of the traditional credit assets on the original balance sheet, expanding the financing channels of the real economy; on the liability side, the financing business caters to the residents' needs of maintaining and increasing the value of their rapidly growing assets. With the promotion of the net value of financing products, the financing business is also

---

Wang Yuexiang participated in the drafting and discussion of this article, which was published in the international financial Journal on December 31, 2016.

S. Ba, *The New Cycle and New Finance in China*,
https://doi.org/10.1007/978-981-16-8209-4_17

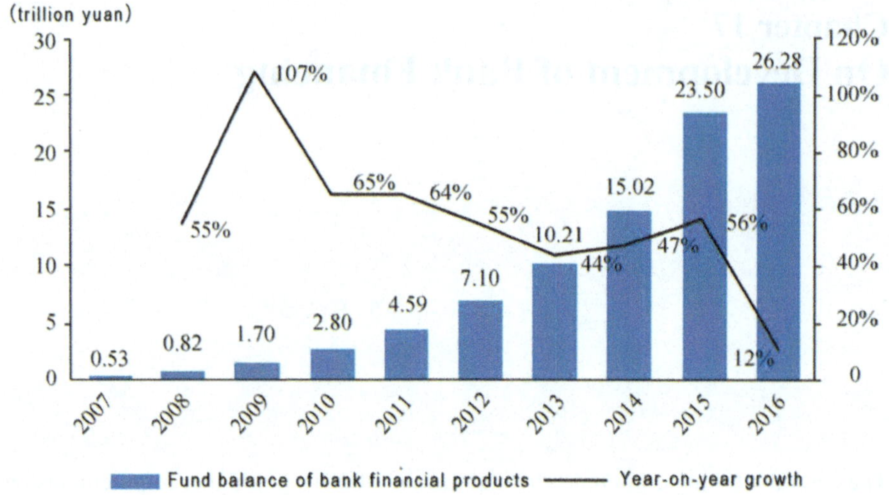

Fig. 17.1 Growth trend of fund balance of bank financial products. *Source* Wind information

playing the role of providing education for investors to inform them of relevant risks (Fig. 17.1).

Financial management products can be divided into the products with guaranteed income, the products with guaranteed floating income and the products with non-guaranteed floating income. The first two categories should be included in the bank's balance sheet for statistics. At the liability side, they should be included in the categories of general deposits, structural deposits or financial liabilities which are measured at fair value and whose changes are included in asset impairment losses. At the asset side, the capital pool operation is carried out according to the overall asset structure of the banks. These two categories of financial management can be clearly reflected in the banks' balance sheet. The bank, as a credit and liquidity intermediary, plays the function of indirect financing, so there is no essential difference between the first two categories of financial management and the traditional deposit and loan business of the banks.

For the non-guaranteed floating income, because the assets and liabilities are reflected on the off balance sheet, its operation is more flexible, and the requirements on information disclosure are relatively low. Only the total amount of information is disclosed in the equity of structured entities not included in the scope of consolidated financial statements, and there are no disclosure requirements for the disclosure of income of asset management and asset allocation.

According to *the Financial Management Market Report of China's Banking Industry* issued by the Financial Management Registration and Custody Center of China's Banking Industry, products with non-guaranteed floating income, namely off balance sheet financial products, basically contributed to the total new scale in the first half of 2016, accounting for 76.8%, and showing an upward trend (see Fig. 17.2).

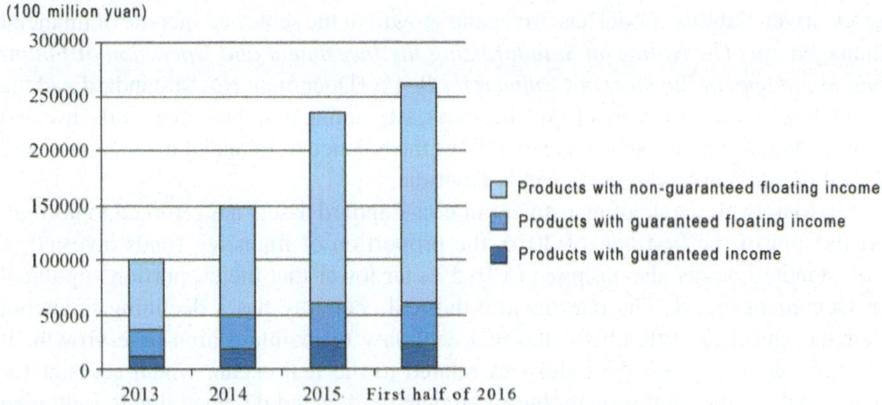

Fig. 17.2 Scale of financial management business in recent years

Therefore, the logic behind the explosive development of off balance sheet financing has become an important focus of regulation.

17.2 Logic Behind the Development of Off Balance Sheet Financing

After the scale of bank financial management exceeded RMB10 trillion in 2013, the logic behind its development began to be clear. Relaxed regulation created the external environment for financial innovation, and the profit seeking of large asset allocation has become the internal factor contributing to scale expansion.

17.2.1 Regulatory Arbitrage: On Balance Sheet Assets Moves into off Balance Sheet

In 2013, channel-type business represented by bank-trust business has become the main direction of financial investment. According to statistics, at the end of 2010, the asset balance of bank-trust cooperation accounted for more than half of the total trust scale, which then gradually decreased to about 30% at the end of 2012. The bank cooperated with various financial institutions to transfer their on balance sheet assets to off balance sheet assets through various non-standardized creditor's rights channels, including trust products, entrusted bonds and various kinds of income (beneficial) rights, so as to avoid regulatory restrictions on credit scale and the industry. At the same time, the off balance sheet operation is not subject to the regulation on capital occupation, which, in theory, can expand credit supply indefinitely. The asset-driven liability model has driven the growth of the scale and income of financial management. *The Notice on Standardizing the Investment and Operation of Financial Management Business of Commercial Banks* (Document No. 8) standardized the rapid development of channel-type business, stipulating that financing funds invested in non-standard assets shall exceed 35% of the balance of financial management and 4% of the total assets of the banks at any time.

Up to now, the scale of investment in non-standard assets has returned to normal. At the end of the first half of 2016, the proportion of financing funds invested in non-standard assets also dropped to 16.5%, far lower that the proportion stipulated in Document No. 8. The reasons are: the real economy has a declining financing demand, and it is difficult for the real economy to maintain high-base growth. It is especially true with the industries related to the real estate, which account for nearly half of the total growth, but the financing demand declined due to tightened external regulatory policies; besides, with lower investment yields, there were fewer projects that could meet the standards while on balance sheet credit and proprietary investment also competed for high-yield assets, and non-standard assets tend to be transformed into on balance sheet assets.

17.2.2 Income Driven: Emergence of Large Asset Allocation

The asset allocation of financial management is mainly determined by the risk preference and tolerance of the liability side, and the products with different risk levels need to match the corresponding risk assets. As the risk preference of bank customers is, on the whole, lower than that of the customers of other asset management sub-industries, the risk preference of the general individuals (accounting for 49%) is also low. According to the statistical data at the end of the first half of 2016, in asset allocation, cash and bank deposits, money market tools and bonds accounted for 74% of the total, becoming the main body of asset allocation (see Fig. 17.3).

The asset allocation of private banks and institutions with high-risk tolerance reflects the profit seeking nature of capital. Since 2010, the yield of bank financial management has been influenced by nonstandard assets, the bond market and the stock market, resulting in rotation of major types of assets.

Take CMB as an example. By the end of the first half of 2016, its balance of financial management was RMB2.04 trillion, ranking second in the whole industry and only next to ICBC. The balance of off balance sheet financing accounted for 38.9% of interest-bearing assets, ranking first in the industry. In terms of product structure, net worth products accounted for 68.44%. CMB benefited a lot from its large number of retail customers, its investors' relatively high-risk preference of financial products and more radical asset allocation. In the allocation of major types of assets, the allocation and financing of the equity market accounted for as much as 6%. In bond investment, credit bonds accounted for 63%, and entrusted bond investment accounted for 24%.

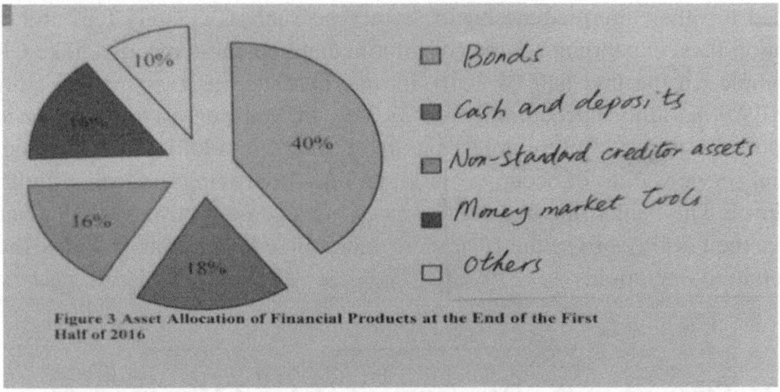

Figure 3 Asset Allocation of Financial Products at the End of the First Half of 2016

Fig. 17.3 Asset allocation of financial products at the end of the first half of 2016. *Note* Other products in the pie chart include equity investment, public funds, private funds, financial derivatives, industrial investment funds, new investable assets, direct financing tools, overseas financial investment under QDII program and alternative assets

17.3 Behind the Explosive Expansion: Prominent Macroliquidity Risks

With the continuous scale expansion of financial management, off balance sheet financial management has become the largest sub-industry in the asset management industry, forming a market pattern with large state-owned banks and national joint-stock banks as the main body. Within this pattern, urban commercial banks and rural financial institutions have been developing rapidly. By the end of the first half of 2016, the financial balance of national joint-stock banks was more than RMB10 trillion, accounting for 41.4% of the total, and that of the large state-owned banks was RMB9 trillion, accounting for 34.2% of the total. The development of financial management has made an important contribution not only to the commercial banks themselves but also to the whole asset management industry, and it has also provided financial support for the real economy. At the same time, we should also see that the rapid scale expansion has also caused more significant disturbance to the credit supply and liquidity at the macroeconomic level.

17.3.1 Improve the Income Structure of Banks and Enhance Their Light Operation Level

The most direct benefit of financial management is the improvement in the income structure of banks. China's banks have been relying on interest rate spread for their development for a long time. Under this backdrop, the rapid development of financial management gave rise to relevant handling and management fees, which then extended to other intermediate business income such as custody fees and project promotion fees, expanding sources of intermediate business income. Take CMB as an example. In the first half of 2016, its intermediate business income amounted to RMB9.908 billion, accounting for 23.35% of non-interest income, becoming an important source of non-interest income growth; in addition, off balance sheet financial services did not occupy capital, thereby improving the banks' light operation level. The banks' involvement in asset management business helps banks to improve their ability of serving customers under mixed operation, and raise the level of diversified operation.

17.3.2 Strengthen the Development of Asset Management Industry

Commercial banks enjoy the largest number of customers and have natural advantages in capital acquisition. In the period of relaxed regulation and interbank cooperation, such a large volume directly promotes the growth of asset management industries such as trust, securities asset management and fund subsidiaries. For nearly 20 years of development, the scale of assets under the management of the traditional public fund industry has not exceeded RMB8 trillion by the end of the first half of 2016. However, in the past two years, the scale of assets of fund subsidiaries has increased from RMB 3.74 trillion to RMB 10 trillion, and reached RMB 11.06 trillion by the end of the first half of 2016. The targeted asset management products of securities companies reached RMB12.56 trillion at the end of the first half of this year, accounting for more than 80% of all securities companies' asset management products (see Figs. 17.4 and 17.5). The rapid expansion of both depends on the funds of banks. The capital is invested in the real economy in the form of asset management products of plan, and the asset management industry plays an irreplaceable role in providing finance for the real economy.

But it should be noted that the nesting of multilayer channels and the expansion of the interbank industry chain increased both the financing costs and the intermediate risks. Intensified competition resulted in lower channel rates, and the new financial regulations and regulatory system limited the channels through new requirements on registered capital. As a result, the pure channel-type business will eventually disappear, forcing different types of asset management sub-industries to reposition themselves and give full play to their different advantages. In the future, asset management industry will be differentiated and undergo further development.

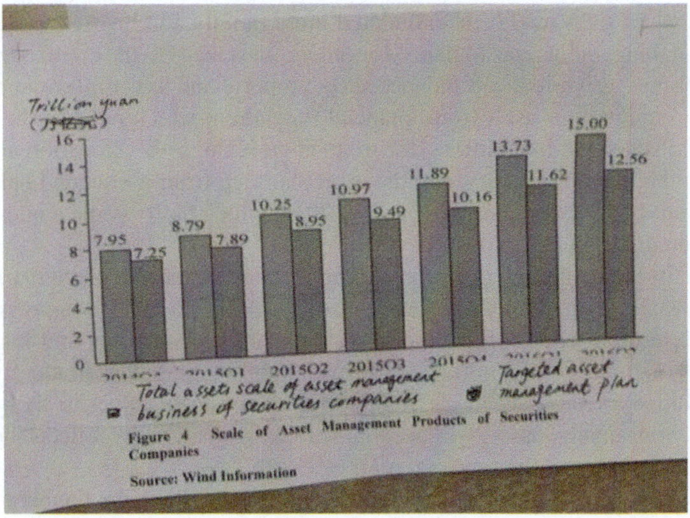

Fig. 17.4 Scale of asset management products of securities companies

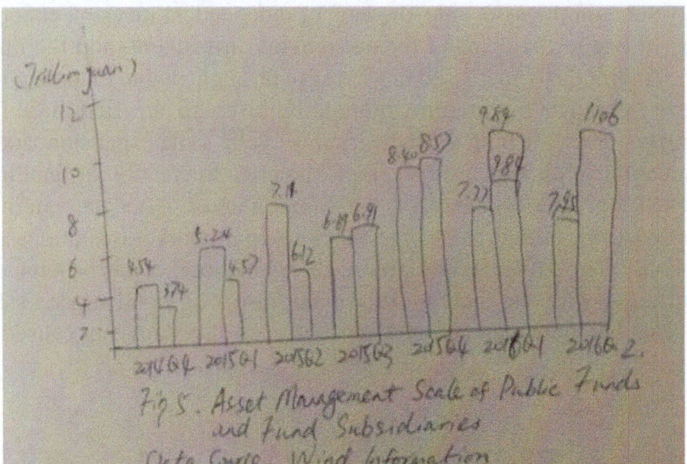

Fig. 17.5 Asset management scale of public funds and fund subsidiaries. *Source* Wind information

17.3.3 From Asset Shortage to Capital Shortage and Its Influence on Liquidity

At the present stage, the rigid payment has not been broken, and financial management has not entered the mature period of the industry. Risks continue to accumulate amid rapid development, especially in the period of superimposed economic downturn when risks may be accumulated more rapidly and involve a wider range. Financial management aims to fiancé for others. This leads to the credit expansion in the whole society, while its off balance sheet property and lower information disclosure requirements free itself from financial regulation, which reduces the accuracy of financial statistics; in addition, due to its large scale, asset allocation also has an impact on the overall liquidity, and the asset shortage from the second half of 2015 changed into capital shortage at the end of 2016, which has become a manifestation of risk accumulation and exposure.

Competition intensifies in the expanding financial management market, asset value depression is gradually filled and income space is gradually compressed. Asset shortage appeared when the inertia of scale expansion continues and high-quality assets are sought after. The initial asset-driven liability model has gradually evolved into a liability-driven asset mode. When there is a ratchet effect in the growth of liabilities, high-quality assets will become scarcer, which vividly reflects the primary excessive expansion of the financial market.

Small and medium-sized banks scrambled to participate in the financial management business, thus extending the risk chain. On the liability side, because it was difficult for retail funds to accumulate rapidly in a short period of time, interbank financial management, as a wholesale fund, became a means to quickly supplement the liability side; on the asset side, the lack of independent investment and research capacity gave rise to the demand for outsourcing investment, and the outsourcing institutions continuously increased the leverage through pledge financing in order to improve the yield. The high returns brought by leverage attracted more funds into outsourcing business, pushing the industry into cyclic scale expansion, and the risks are accumulating. With increased leverage, the price fluctuation of final investment assets exerted a greater influence on the whole market. After the external money supply shifted from foreign exchange funds to open market operations and funds injected via MLF in 2013, the liquidity of the whole market has become extremely fragile and tense with the increase of capital cost. The bond market's long-term departure from the fundamentals and the occurrence of defaults has caused the chain fracture.

17.4 Development Direction of Bank Financial Management

The regulation shows that we need to restrain the development of some areas while promoting the development in other areas regarding financial management business.

On the one hand, we should bring some business back to its balance sheet in line with the principle of constraining asset expansion through capital control. This part of business is essentially the same as the on balance sheet business, but the bank bears the credit and liquidity risks; on the other hand, we should encourage the industry to serve the original purpose of asset management

The assets of off balance sheet financing and on balance sheet assets of banks have certain homogeneity and substitutability, and the fluctuation of homogeneous assets will have a consistent impact on the on balance sheet and off balance sheet assets. Therefore, the regulation aims to carry out comprehensive risk management under the full scope. *The Measures for the Supervision and Administration of Financial Management Business of Commercial Banks* (Draft for comments) and *the Guidelines for Risk Management of Off Balance Sheet Business of Commercial Banks* (Revised Draft for comments) require the provision of risk reserves and the occupation of capital according to the risk situation. At the same time, we should break the long chain between financial institutions, strengthen the regulatory coordination of market and industry expansion, limit channels and reduce costs, so as to form a differentiated asset management pattern.

Emphasis should be placed on macroprudential regulation. From the first quarter of 2017, we will guide reasonable scale growth by bringing off balance sheet financing into the scope of broad credit of macroprudential assessment (MPA) system. Broad credit means that the proportion of credit assets in credit expansion is gradually decreasing after fully considering the innovation and transformation of banking business. It is difficult to calculate credit expansion by traditional satisfactory credit regulatory indicators, including the bond investment, equity investment, interbank buy back sale and the part of off balance sheet financing deducting cash and deposits. By restricting the growth of generalized credit and linking the macroprudential capital adequacy ratio to banks, it will help to strengthen information transparency, eliminate the worries of shadow banks, avoid capital idle, and thus inhibit asset bubbles, and transfer the funds from the virtual economy to the real economy. Under the constraint of broad credit, it is expected that the growth of wealth management business will slow down in 2017 and enter a period of stable growth, so that the expansion of social credit scale will be under regulation and calculation and guide the industry to serve the original purpose of asset management.

Commercial banks have begun to reposition their asset management business, trying to carry out the asset management business for the original purpose of financing for others. Specifically, some commercial banks begin to strengthen team building by setting up asset management centers or business divisions; some strengthen the cultivation of asset management customers, carry out studies on the risk preference of potential customers and attach greater importance to improving their ability of asset allocation; after the current round of market reshuffle, commercial banks will be more prudent in outsourcing business, and the investment and research ability of the outsourcing institutions as well as the stability of the these institutions have become important criteria for selection.

Chapter 18
New Third Board: Development Trend and Risk Management

The government work report published at the fifth session of the 12th National People's Congress held on March 5, 2017, stressed that: "We will deepen the reform of the multi-tiered capital market, improve the basic systems of the main board, actively develop the ChiNext stock market and the new third board, and see that regional equity markets develop in a well-regulated way." The report juxtaposes the new third board and the ChiNext stock market and calls for its active development, which is directly related to the greater role of the new third board in the multi-tiered capital market. The national small and medium-sized enterprise share transfer system, also known as the new third board, originated in Zhongguancun Software Park of Beijing City in 2006, a park home to high-tech enterprises.

18.1 Rapid Development of New Third Board

Before 2012, the new third board only covered the pilot market in Zhongguancun. On August 3, 2012, CSRC announced that the new third board will be expanded to the other three national high-tech parks, namely Shanghai Zhangjiang High-tech Development Zone, Wuhan East Lake high-tech Development Zone and Tianjin High-tech Area. In January 2013, the National Equities Exchange and Quotations (NEEQ) were officially launched. On December 13, 2013, the State Council promulgated *the Decision of the State Council on Issues concerning the National Equities Exchange and Quotations* (hereinafter referred to as *the Decision*), urging to give full play to the role of the National Equities Exchange and Quotations (NEEQ) and ease the financing difficulties of micro, small and medium-sized enterprises. At the end of 2013, CSRC announced that the new third board had broken the geographical restrictions, and expanded from the four high-tech parks to the whole country, resulting in the rapid development of the new third board. At the same time, a series of important institutional innovations appeared. On August 25, 2014, the market maker rule was introduced. On March 18, 2015, the index of the new third board was officially

S. Ba, *The New Cycle and New Finance in China*,
https://doi.org/10.1007/978-981-16-8209-4_18

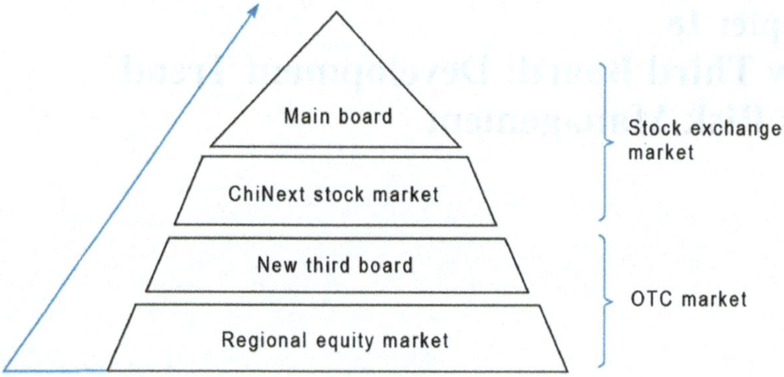

Fig. 18.1 Multilayer capital market

released; on June 27, 2016, the internal stratification system of the new third board was set up.

Driven by a series of factors, the number of enterprises listed on the new third board increased from 1572 at the end of 2014 to 10,163 at the end of 2016, and by August 2017, the number has already exceeded the total number of listed companies in Shanghai and Shenzhen stock exchange markets, reaching 11,551. It has become an important part of and plays a connecting role in China's multi-tiered capital market (see Fig. 18.1).

On December 13, 2013, the State Council issued the decision, positioning the new third board as a national securities trading venue that mainly provides services for the development of innovative, entrepreneurial, or growth-oriented micro, small and medium-sized enterprises, thereby adding new financing channels for small and medium-sized enterprises. It plays an important connecting role in the multi-tiered capital market system because the enterprises listed on the new third board can be transferred to the ChiNext stock market and the main board, and it can receive the listing of enterprises in the regional equity trading market.

The main institutional framework of the new third board as an over-the-counter market was established between 2014 and 2016. On August 25, 2014, the market maker rule was introduced. On June 27, 2016, the multilayered listing system was implemented. On October 25, 2016, the new third board issued the Rules for the Delisting of Shares of Listed Companies in the NEEQ system (draft for comments), which is also the draft for the delisting system (see Fig. 18.2). In August 2014, after the introduction of the market maker rule in the new third board, the trading of the company's shares can be carried out through market making transfer and agreement transfer. As of December 31, 2016, among the 10,163 enterprises in the new third board, 1654 have adopted market making transfer and 8509 have adopted agreement transfer.

The market maker rule of the new third board drawed on the experience of mature markets, but it has made adjustments according to the specific situation of the Chinese market in terms of market maker conditions, market making transaction methods,

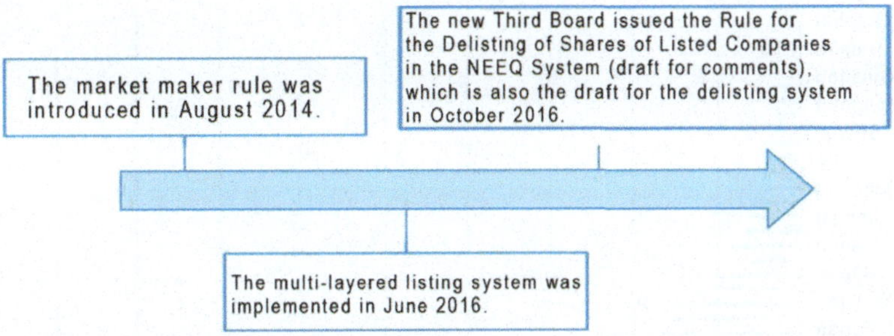

Fig. 18.2 Establishment of the institutional framework of the new third board

minimum market making period and two-way immunity. For example, due to the inventory risk of market makers, they are given certain two-way immunity (specific exemption standards are different); the market makers are given a certain bid-offer spread (5% of the new third board spread), considering that there is the problem of transaction cost.

In 2016, the multilayered mechanism of the new third board was established. The large number of listed companies and the uneven quality of enterprises will increase the costs of investors in their investment decision making, which is not conducive to the investment and financing functions of the market. The multilayered mechanism screens investment targets for investors with different risk preferences, thereby reducing the costs of information collection for investors. If the new third board enterprises want to be innovative ones, they will put forward many requirements on the company's finance, scale and transaction mode, which is also the difference between the innovative enterprises and the enterprises at the base layer. At the end of 2016, there were 952 enterprises in the innovation layer and 9511 enterprises in the base layer. In October 2016, the NEEQ system released the draft of delisting system. The establishment of this system ended the situation that the enterprises listed on the new third board will never be delisted.

As for the regions home to enterprises listed on the new third board, the top five are Guangdong Province, Beijing City, Jiangsu Province, Zhejiang Province and Shanghai City. Among the 10,163 listed enterprises, 6100 enterprises are located in these five provinces and cities, accounting for 60% of all enterprises (see Fig. 18.3). These five regions are located in the Bohai Rim, the Yangtze River Delta and the Pearl River Delta, which enjoy certain geographical and resource advantages and are also home to a galaxy of innovative enterprises.

As for industry distribution, the main industries of the new third board are manufacturing industry and information technology service industry, in which the number of manufacturing enterprises has reached 5153, accounting for 50.70% of the total number of listed enterprises (see Fig. 18.4). The number of enterprises in the information technology service industry has also reached 2003, accounting for about 19.71%. Besides, the financial industry, transportation and postal industry and public facilities

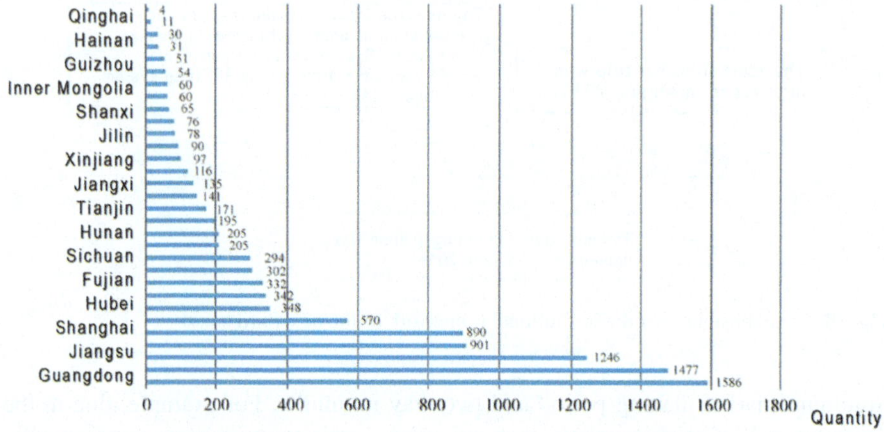

Fig. 18.3 Regional distribution of enterprises listed on the new third board

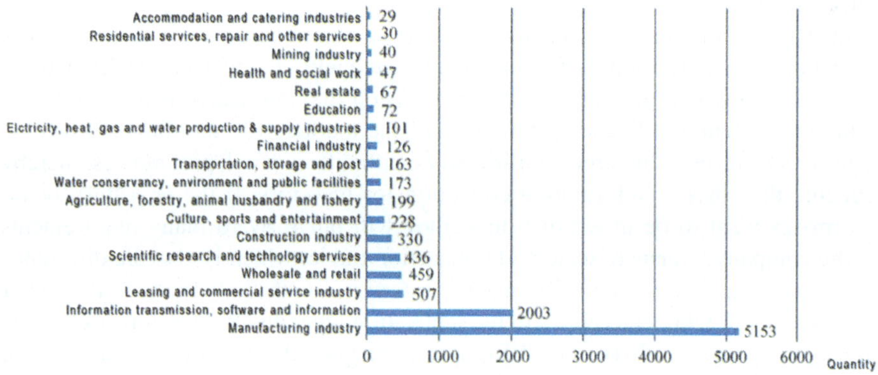

Fig. 18.4 Industry distribution of enterprises listed on the new third board

management industry accounted for about 1%, respectively. There are only 29 listed enterprises in the accommodation and catering industry.

18.2 Management of the Investment Risks of the New Third Board

Comparatively speaking, the investment in listed companies on the new third board is equity investment of higher risks. The listed companies on the new third board belong to non-listed public companies. The new third board was established to promote the development of micro, small medium-sized enterprises, so the requirement for the company's duration as one of the listing conditions is relatively low, and there are no rigid requirements for financial indicators such as financial status and profitability. The requirements for sustainable operation ability, corporate governance and legal compliance are also unspecific. Therefore, the risk of investment in the companies listed on the new third board is higher than that of other types of listed companies. There are many excellent listed companies in the new third board, and many of them have very good growth prospects. However, it is very necessary for us to warn against the risks of investing in the companies listed in the new third board in advance and take corresponding risk management measures. We also see that the regulatory authorities have been actively improving the regulatory system and taking many effective regulatory measures to cope with the risks of investing in the companies listed on the new third board.

We should realize that it is very likely for us to face risks when investing in companies listed on the new third board. Investors need to conduct professional analysis of the unique risks of investment in the stock market from the perspective of the industry. We divide the risks into the main risks faced by the micro, small and medium-sized enterprises and those faced by the non-listed public companies.

1. Main Risks Faced by Micro, Small and Medium-sized Enterprises
(a) Imperfect Corporate Governance and Violation of Commitment due to Lack of Integrity

Many examples show that imperfect corporate governance and lack of integrity are likely to result in the violation of the commitment when the company got listed on the stock market. The direct risks include the occupation of the listed company's funds by its actual controllers, controlling shareholders and related controlling parties, illegal guarantee of the listed company, horizontal competition, etc. The macro, small and medium-sized enterprises mainly rely on controlling shareholders and actual controllers in their management at the early stage of their development, and only these people have the say on the matters concerning the management of the enterprises. After the enterprises get listed on the new third board, the internal governance of these enterprises has been improved at the institutional level, but, in practice, it is very difficult for the controlling shareholders and actual controllers to change the traditional management mode. Besides, the listed companies do not have an accurate understanding of the companies' related parties; therefore, it is very likely for them to intentionally or unconsciously neglect related parties or transactions. The possible results are as follows:

The controlling shareholders, actual controllers and related controlling parties occupy funds of listed companies, including the companies' own funds and funds raised through private placement, some of which are funds borrowed by related party before implementing the review procedures, or funds occupied through other unnecessary, unfair or fictitious related party transactions. The illegal change of the use of funds will bring adverse effects on the companies' normal operation; according to incomplete statistics, From January 1, 2016 to August 31, 2017, about 184 tickets were issued by the stock share transfer system and local securities regulatory authorities to punish controlling shareholders, actual controllers and related controlling parties for such violations.

The listed companies give illegal guarantee, that is, the guarantee made by the controlling shareholders, actual controllers or non-related parties before implementing the review procedures. When the debtors fail to perform their obligations, the listed companies need to bear the corresponding responsibilities, which increase the risk to the normal operation of the listed companies. According to incomplete statistics, from January 1, 2016 to August 31, 2017, about 53 tickets were issued by the stock share transfer system and local securities regulatory authorities to punish controlling shareholders, actual controllers and non-related parties for such violations.

Horizontal competition exists. In order to ensure independent development of a listed company, there is usually no horizontal competition when the company gets listed. In addition, after the company gets listed, the company itself, its controlling shareholders, actual controllers, directors, supervisors and senior managers will also make corresponding commitments to avoid horizontal competition. However, after the company gets listed, compliance operation results in higher costs. In order to improve the efficiency, the listed company will often violate its commitment to avoid horizontal competition and entrust related parties to do part of its business.

In response to this risk, when making investment decisions, the investors should pay close attention to the listed company's governance regulations and their actual implementation as well as the integrity of the directors, executives, controlling shareholders and the actual controllers, and conduct full and comprehensive verification on the related parties of the listed company.

(b) Financial Fraud

On the one hand, although there are no rigid requirements for financial indicators as the listing conditions of the new third board, some listed companies still have the motivation to exaggerate their performance and make financial fraud so as to attract investors, seek the ideal stock price, win the gambling or realize performance commitment. On the other hand, a great majority of the small and medium-sized enterprises have such nonstandard practices as multiple sets of accounts and cash receipts and payments before they get listed on the stock markets. When a company gets listed, the financial standardization has been improved to a certain extent thanks to the work of intermediary agencies, but this is closely related to the professional ethics of the corresponding accounting firms and the specific employees of the securities companies. After a company gets listed, it is a mandatory requirement for the annual report of the company to be audited by an accounting firm qualified to audit securities and futures business activities. However, in practice, the annual reports of all listed companies need to be audited and disclosed before April 30; therefore, the accounting firms may have very tight work schedules. In addition, the fees for auditing the annual reports of the new third board are relatively low. As a result, the authenticity, integrity and accuracy of the financial statements in the annual reports of listed companies might be problematic.

In response to this risk, when investors participate in the investment of companies listed on the new third board, they should make a reasonable investment decision by taking the actual business situation of the listed companies into consideration, and if necessary, seeking help from customers or suppliers to verify the authenticity, integrity and accuracy of the statements, whether it is the audited financial statements in the public transfer prospectus or the audited financial statements in the annual reports. When an accounting firm cannot express opinions, express negative opinions or reserve its opinions about an annual report, we should analyze the reasons behind and try to locate possible risks.

(c) Violation of Laws and Regulations in Business Operation

Many companies on the new third board are micro, small and medium-sized enterprises. Due to the needs of their development, these enterprises fail to pay due attention to compliance operation. After a company gets listed, the sponsor securities company will carry out continuous supervision, but the supervision still focuses on information disclosure and major issues discussed by the board of shareholders, the board of directors and the board of auditors. Compliance operation can only be achieved through the listed company's own efforts. At the same time, the regulatory authorities usually carry out dynamic management, which exists in the whole development process of listed companies. Listed companies value direct economic interests, so they may not pay enough attention to compliance operation, resulting in administrative penalties by relevant departments. According to incomplete statistics, from January 1, 2016 to August 31, 2017, 72 listed companies were subject to administrative punishment by the environmental department, and 40 listed companies were subject to administrative punishment by the work safety supervision department. More than 200 penalty notices were issued by the departments of taxation, customs, public security, market supervision and administration, food and drug supervision and administration, city administration, cultural administration and other relevant departments. These business risks have a negative impact on the normal operation of listed companies.

In response to this risk, when making investment decisions, investors should not only pay close attention to the compliance operation in the history of the company but also examine the attitude of the management, controlling shareholders and actual controllers toward legal and standardized operation.

(d) Consequences of Rapid Development, High Leverage and Difficult Capital Turnover

After getting listed on the new third board, enterprises are usually able to gain more customers, orders, suppliers, partners and other resources due to their improved reputation, thereby entering the stage of rapid development. At this stage, listed companies usually expand their production capacity, relax the sales credit term, and increase foreign investment so as to promote production and sales. Most of the listed companies are small and medium-sized private enterprises, so if accidental events or policy changes occur, banks will immediately tighten credit for risk considerations, resulting in the difficulty of capital turnover of listed companies. In order to alleviate the problem of capital turnover, listed companies may resort to private borrowing, which brings corresponding risks. Improper solution of this problem will seriously affect the normal production and operation of these companies. In addition, at this stage, if the actual customer market of listed companies is quite different from what has been expected before expansion or investment, the companies will also face the decline of corporate profits caused by excessive amortization of fixed assets and failure of foreign investment, making it more difficult for them to obtain new funds. Many listed companies have but a small size and limited financing channels, resulting in fewer shareholders and limited resources. These companies will never be able to recover in the face of capital turnover difficulties and ensuing problems, and it will take them a longer time and greater efforts to resume normal production and operation.

In response to this risk, when making investment decisions, investors should fully understand the litigation and debt disputes of the company through ways like network inquiry and interview, and fully understand the company's debts and solvency; as for the development strategies of listed companies, the investors should fully understand the corresponding capital planning and risk response measures by consulting the company's management, controlling shareholders and actual controllers.

2. Main Risks Faced by Non-listed Public Companies

The listed companies on the new third board take information disclosure, corporate autonomy and market constraints as the basis of their development and establish a market constraint mechanism integrating self-regulation, intermediary regulation and social regulation. Therefore, when investing in the new third board, the investors also need to consider the risks brought about by the listed companies' failure to fully fulfill the obligation of information disclosure, including false records, misleading statements or major omissions in the disclosure. It might be failed or incomplete disclosure of important matters that might influence the decision making of the investor, or failure to perform corresponding review procedures before the event occurs. The important matters include: documents related to listing, equity change, gambling agreement, pending litigation, major contract disputes, related parties and related transactions, foreign investment, external guarantee, major asset restructuring, and major asset disposal. It is very likely that investors will be misled by this kind of information asymmetry to make unreasonable investment decisions. In addition, after investors invest in the new third board, as shareholders of listed companies, they have the corresponding right to learn the truth and vote. They must fully exercise their own rights to protect their own interests.

In response to this risk, investors should collect and sort out the announcements of listed companies on the designated information disclosure platform of the stock exchange system and pay close attention to the reasons for the reissue and correction of the announcements made by listed companies, so as to analyze the reliability of the information disclosed by these companies. Besides, when making investment decisions, investors need to be prudent and make every effort to fully understand the situation of the listed companies through different ways, such as paying on-the-spot visit to the company, observing the actual production and delivery, visiting customers and suppliers, and searching the Internet for information. After becoming shareholders of listed companies, the investors must also pay close attention to the information disclosure of the listed companies and the discussions of the board of shareholders, the board of directors and the board of supervisors and fully exercise the rights of shareholders to protect their own interests.

To sum up, there are a large number of companies listed on the new third board, covering a wide range of industries. When investors decide to invest in the new third board, their goal is to invest in companies with core competitiveness. Some of these companies have the potential to become the leader of the sub-sectors in the future; some have huge development space in the future, and the listed companies can enjoy the dividends of the rapid growth of the industry. Investors mainly choose investment targets on the basis of the information disclosed by listed companies. They need to prudent and verify the authenticity, integrity and accuracy of the information through a variety of means and angles. Besides, investors must also understand that the companies listed on the new third board are mainly macro, small, medium-sized ones in the growth period. The characteristics of these enterprises determine that they may not attach great importance to the legal compliance of production and operation in the process of their development. They may choose radical enterprise development strategies and financing plans and have certain motives to exaggerate their performance and make fraudulent financial statements. Besides, the corporate governance is far from perfect. All of this brings risks and may have adverse effects on the future development of these listed companies. After careful consideration and analysis, investors can make corresponding countermeasures for the possible risks before investing in the new third board. After this, the listed companies, with the help of the capital market, will be able to develop rapidly, carry out standardized operation and eventually become the leader of the sub-sector. They will witness continuous improvement of market share and capital appreciation, which brings income to the investors.

References

1. Ba Shusong. Investment Risk Analysis of New Third Board [EB OL]. Wukong Q&A. September 4, 2017.
2. New Third Board Research Institute. *Annual Report of China's New Third Board (2016)* [M]. Beijing: China Machine Press, 2017.

Chapter 19
Rigid Payment and Reshuffle of the Asset Management Industry

19.1 How Rigid Payment Came into Being

In recent years, the broad asset management of China's financial institutions has expanded rapidly in scale, from about RMB18 trillion in 2012 to about RMB100 trillion in 2017. The rapid expansion has promoted the transformation of China's financial structure, but it has also caused wide concerns about some institutional risks, one of which is rigid payment.

The so-called rigid payment occurs when a financial institution of an asset management product pays the investors the principal of the product and a certain amount of earnings promised or implicitly promised by the institution regardless of its actual investment performance and the actual performance of the underlying assets.

Rigid payment is not confirmed and supported by any legal provisions of the existing laws and regulations concerning China's asset management industry. On the contrary, Article 34 of Measures for the Administration of Trust Companies clearly stipulates that "when engaging in trust business, a trust and investment corporation must not promise that no loss will be incurred in respect of the trust property or guarantee minimum earnings". Then, how did the hidden rules of local rigid payment come into being?

1. In some early cases, there were implicit requirements for rigid payment, which gradually formed the path dependence. For example, after the failure of a certain trust plan in 2004, in order to maintain market stability, the regulatory authorities proposed that the trust company should guarantee to pay the investors the principal when the trust product expired. After that, other similar cases were dealt with in the same spirit. For example, in the notice on strengthening the supervision of real estate and securities business of trust companies issued by a regulatory department in 2008, the timely payment of trust projects was regarded as a very important indicator of regulatory evaluation. Gradually, some asset

Source Selected from the "2017 China asset management industry development report", published on the public platform "financial reading club" on October 1, 2017.

S. Ba, *The New Cycle and New Finance in China*,
https://doi.org/10.1007/978-981-16-8209-4_19

management institutions regarded rigid payment as a de facto hidden rule of the industry, and it may also result in the investors' wrong potential perception that rigid payment must be provided for some asset management products.

2. It is also attributed to the financial institutions' need to maintain the license value and their own reputation. Some financial institutions may weigh the pros and cons and carry out rigid payment, choosing to pay in advance with their own funds or in other ways even though the yield of individual financial products fails to meet the expectations or investment losses occur.
3. The legal support needs to be improved. Under the existing legal framework, the responsibilities of all parties need to be further clarified when the asset management products cannot be cashed at maturity. For example, if financial products or asset management products in China fail to be cashed at maturity, the responsibilities of the financial institutions need to be further clarified.
4. The risk disclosure for investors needs to be strengthened. In a market with vague risk disclosure for investors, it is not easy to cultivate the investment idea that the investors shall assume investment risks by themselves.

19.2 Rigid Payment Distorts the Ecological Environment of China's Asset Management Industry

For the asset management industry as a whole, rigid payment distorts the risk distribution of China's asset management industry and actually increases the financial risk actually borne by the asset management industry as a whole. For financial institutions, rigid payment gives debt attributes to investment products. In other words, rigid payment actually leads to the transfer of investment risks from investors to financial institutions. The asset management industry mainly involves different links from the source of funds to the use of funds. When there is rigid payment, the relevant products often extend from banks to trust and asset management. On the asset side, there is often a lack of reasonable risk pricing for the underlying assets, which naturally makes it difficult to implement the constraint mechanism of risk assumption by investors themselves.

For asset management institutions, the existence of rigid payment will distort the relationship between the return of the real economy and the return of financial investment. Rigid payment might give rise to a higher risk-free rate of return in the market. If the return rate of the real economy is lower than that of the financial investment raised by rigid payment, the social funds will naturally be divorced from the real economy and mainly circulate in the financial sector. According to the statistical data of China's listed companies for many years, the return on equity of listed companies in China's non-financial industry fluctuated at about 6%. In recent years, the return on equity of financial industry is gradually approaching this level. However, the returns of asset management products sold by many financial institutions are significantly higher than 6%. For a period of time, rigid payment resulted in the distorted pattern that the return of financial investment is higher than that of the investment in the real economy in China's market.

Once rigid payment becomes the hidden rules of the industry, it may reduce investors' ability to identify risks and objectively encourage investors to invest in high-risk products, which is not conducive to the establishment of the constraint mechanism of risk assumption by investors themselves.

19.3 Rigid Payment is Being Broken

The risks brought by rigid payment have received wide attention. Since 2016, the regulatory authorities have issued many policies to control and guide the asset management industry to gradually break the rigid payment.

At the Fifth National Financial Work Conference in 2017, a series of important arrangements were made to strengthen regulation and promote regulatory coordination. The policies on asset management regulation are basically consistent with the expectation of asset management regulatory framework adjustment. In April 2017, the CBRC issued a number of documents on strengthening regulation; fund pool was prohibited in securities companies' asset management, and new policies on insurance asset management were frequently introduced. Strict regulation will undoubtedly become the new policy keynote in 2017 impacting bank financing, trust, securities companies' asset management and fund subsidiaries. The regulatory authorities put forward requirements for the asset management industry to gradually break rigid payment and guide the industry to serve the original purpose of asset management. Regulatory standards for asset management products will be unified. All this will cause certain pressure on different types of asset management institutions and force them to think more about ways to improve their asset management ability and carry out transformation.

In recent years, there is the problem of rigid payment in the financial field such as bonds. But with the standardization of regulation, the cyclical decline of economy, structural transformation and financial deleveraging, local risks are gradually exposed, the default rate of bonds is gradually increasing, and the rigid payment of the bond market is gradually broken. In March 2014, the default of Shenzhen-listed Shanghai Chaori Solar Energy Science and Technology Co became the first interest default in China's corporate bond market. Since then, the subjects and industries involved in credit default have been expanding. The second half of 2015 and the first half of 2016 witnessed the eruption of defaults. As of December 15, 2016, a total of 88 bonds were in default, involving 52 issuers, with a default scale of RMB 49.694 billion. Among default issuers, there were 33 private enterprises with a default scale of RMB 15.794 billion, three public enterprises with a default scale of RMB 2.07 billion, four foreign-funded enterprises with a default scale of RMB 8.890 billion, four central enterprises with a default scale of RMB 8.100 billion and six local state-owned enterprises with a default scale of RMB14.84 billion.

From the above data, it can be seen that bond risks are gradually released, and rigid payment is gradually broken. In particular, rigid payment has also been broken in central enterprises and local state-owned enterprises that may be considered by investors to have obvious characteristics of rigid payment. This shows that the breaking of rigid payment represented by bond default has been gradually normalized.

19.4 Changes in Asset Management Industry After Breaking Rigid Payment

Rigid payment is a risk factor caused by the extensive development of asset management industry. Since 2016, People's Bank of China, China Banking Regulatory Commission, China Securities Regulatory Commission and China Insurance Regulatory Commission have continuously strengthened regulation to make asset management products serve their original purpose. As previously mentioned, rigid payment is being gradually broken, and it is an inevitable trend. What new changes will the asset management industry face after the breaking of rigid payment?

Breaking rigid payment will gradually promote the return of risk-free rate of return. In the long run, the rate of return of financial investment is expected to gradually become lower than that of the real economy, which will also drive the asset management industry to attach greater importance to serving the real economy.

Breaking rigid payment will help promote the rational allocation of risk returns and responsibilities in all links of asset management. It will help to clarify the basic functions of different areas and links of asset management and their relationships. After the default of asset management products, the risks and responsibilities of managers, sellers, intermediaries and investors will be clarified.

Breaking rigid payment will help to promote the establishment of the investment culture that risks should be assumed by the investors themselves. It will help investors to strengthen the rational evaluation of product risk returns and their own risk preferences. The risk preferences of different investors give rise to diversified demand for asset management products.

Breaking rigid payment will help to promote the concentration of funds in institutions with excellent management ability and promote the optimization of the industry structure. After rigid payment has been broken, the operation mechanism and institutional relationship of the asset management industry are facing reconstruction, the original systems dominated by the commercial banking system are expected to be changed, and the asset management ability will become the focus of the investment of funds. High-quality asset management companies will eliminate poor-quality asset management companies, and the funds will be concentrated in institutions and enterprises with excellent management ability; therefore, the industry concentration is enhanced.

Breaking rigid payment will make asset management products more diversified. For the existing asset management products, after the pressure of rigid payment on the supply side is eliminated, the institutions have more space to design products with different risk levels. The different risk preferences of investors on the demand side will be taken into consideration through reasonable product design, and the market demand will be diversified. After rigid payment has been broken, the supply and demand sides will make asset management products more diversified, and the transparency and risk return of products will become crucial.

Chapter 20
Core Competitiveness of Asset Management Industry

Now, there is a popular concept—broad asset management. The banking, trust and insurance industries have been developing very fast, and the assets of China's financial market have reached RMB80 trillion. The capital market has gradually changed. In the past, some market players such as public funds played a leading role; but in the face of fierce competition under the background of broad asset management, they now have to find a strategic positioning and unique business model that can highlight their own advantages.

Among the RMB 80 trillion assets of China's asset management industry, the asset of the banks ranks first, totaling more than RMB 20 trillion and accounting for nearly 30%. The asset of the trust industry ranks second, amounting to RMB15 trillion to 16 trillion, most of which is channel-type business. The asset of funds ranks third, with an overall value of about RMB16 trillion. We can further divide the asset of funds into the asset of fast-growing major subsidiaries, totaling more than RMB 8 trillion yuan, the asset of special accounts and that of private funds with the nature of alternative investment, totaling more than RMB 4 trillion, respectively. It can be seen that it is not the traditional secondary market-oriented public funds, but new business areas such as special accounts and subsidiaries that grew rapidly in recent years. In the current market environment, as long as most of the public funds can continue to beat the market indices, it means that the competition in the asset management market is not intense enough, and there is still a lot of space for development.

Both public and private funds are facing the problem of imperfect governance structure.

Recently, many examples have proved that the professional excellence of managers is the key to the success of the asset management industry. You can never expect to hire the best fund managers and supervisors to serve you at a low cost. If a company can establish effective incentive mechanism, it will lose these excellent fund managers who will turn to private equity funds to serve a few high-end customers.

The development of fund industry needs to be tested by the market cycle. At present, in China's public fund industry, fund managers with less than two years'

S. Ba, *The New Cycle and New Finance in China*,
https://doi.org/10.1007/978-981-16-8209-4_20

experience account for about 52% of all the fund managers. Compared with those in the mature markets, China's fund managers are generally younger and more energetic, but fund managers also need to be tested by the market cycle. Just like the development of the banking industry needs to go through a complete cycle test, a manager cannot be said to be mature if he or she has not gone through the test of a complete cycle of the market.

In the early days, there was a dispute in the fund industry, whether it is more important for a large-scale fund to start with an IPO of big size or for a fund manager to sell continuously after making outstanding performance in the later period. This is worth thinking, because it decides which links of the company are in need of reasonable allocation of resources. However, from the early development of the public fund industry, we can see that the development of many of the public funds can be attributed to the big size of the IPO. After many funds had been issued, there were not enough professional and excellent fund managers to continuously monitor and manage them.

The proportion of truly excellent fund managers among those who survived two cycles of bull and bear markets is undoubtedly much higher. Incentive mechanism plays an important role in retaining these excellent managers.

In order to stand the test of the market cycle, fund managers need constant accumulation of experience, independent thinking, and, in particular, the ability to reflect on the market, so as to better understand the market.

China's stock market witnessed large fluctuations in 2015, and it is also the case with the US stock market disaster in the 1980s. After paying a heavy price in the stock market crash, the United States reflected on the disaster and produced more than 400 professional research reports, which directly contributed to the improvement of the US capital market system. Should we also reflect on the current fluctuations in China's capital market?

The author found that in the implementation of China's stock disaster relief in 2015, all financial institutions such as securities companies, fund companies, banks and insurance companies were mobilized and tied together. It was originally only a local problem of the stock market, but now the risk of the stock market was likely to quickly transmit to other parts of the financial system. If the volatility of the stock market continues, the local microrisk might become a systematic risk and have to be relieved.

With the development of the financial market, the asset management industry has also undergone profound changes. Some time ago, I often heard about the concept of broad asset management. In the first stage of broad asset management, different industries are interested in each other's business field, regarding it as something new, so they actively enter each other's field. Now, this stage has basically come to an end. The price difference and arbitrage space brought by the division of business segments have disappeared. During the second stage, each type of asset management institutions should understand its own comparative advantages and find their own core competence, especially the ability of active management.

If asset management industries in Hong Kong and Taiwan want to enter the market of the Chinese mainland, channel-type business and preferential policies at the early stage are not enough for sustainable development. The sustainable development of an asset management institution can only be achieved when the institution has the ability to carry out active management according to market demand. In the market adjustment, the institutions with and without the ability of active management will show obvious differences immediately.

Chapter 21
On the Trend of Financial Structure Reform

I am much honored to have the opportunity to address you at the grand meeting hosted by Shenzhen Ma Hong Foundation for the Economic Improvement Research. Mr. Ma Hong is one of the pioneers of China's economic policy consultation. I have worked in the Development Research Center of the State Council initiated and led by him for more than ten years. Mr. Ma Hong has been providing training for young researchers, urging them to be pragmatic, open and stay close to the economic reality. This style of training has become a research tradition highly valued by the researchers of the development research center.

21.1 Expanding Coverage of Asset Management

Today, I would like to discuss the development of the asset management industry. Ten years ago, I expected that the asset management industry would gradually cause profound changes to China's financial structure, so I have been following the changes of this industry and presiding over the publishing of an annual development report on the development and changes of China's asset management industry every year. Up to now, ten annual reports have been published.

The meaning of asset management has been constantly changing and broadening over the past decade. The asset management we talked about ten years ago mainly referred to the public funds. Later, the term gradually expanded to cover banks, trusts and insurance, and then, the term of broad asset management appeared. Then, asset management expanded to cover the areas such as Internet finance and international asset allocation. Strictly speaking, the asset management that we are discussing now is no longer just a sub-sector of the financial industry, but a basic financial function with wide influence.

Now, many financial institutions get more and more deeply involved in the asset management business, making them a bit like asset management institutions. In this process, both high-quality and poor-quality institutions appeared in the market. Some

S. Ba, *The New Cycle and New Finance in China*,
https://doi.org/10.1007/978-981-16-8209-4_21

of them claimed to be asset management companies, but there were many problems with them, which have been exposed one after another. If we have a closer look at the industrial chain of these companies with problems, we will find where the problems lie.

21.2 Value Chain of Asset Management Industry

Asset management, an industry with expanding coverage, can be divided into several different parts from the perspective of value chain and industrial chain: The first is basic assets; the second is asset management institutions, which transform and design basic assets into investable financial products and then sell them to investors through specific sales channels. We usually say that the internal process of an asset management institution involves financing, investment, management and exit.

Besides some obvious violations such as self-financing there are some other problems with some asset management institutions, which results from the problems with basic assets. No matter how great Internet finance appears to be, many of the investment have been made in the basic assets of traditional industries and industries with overcapacity. Despite the wonderful designs of the Internet's sales channels, if the underlying assets are still traditional assets with relatively high risks, the risks will be relatively high. With economic adjustment, of course, problems will arise. Another important problem often occurs in the process of transforming basic assets into financial products. There may be distortions and problems in this process, such as incorrect assessment of risks, disclosure of risks and pricing risks. Besides, there may be some misleading information in the sales process, and a few investors have very strong motives for speculation.

If we make a more detailed analysis, the so-called basic assets satisfy the financing needs of the real economy, which may be direct financing needs, standardized financing needs or derivatives based on standardized financing needs. What do financial institutions do in the field of asset management? What is the value of financial institutions? In the asset management industry, it can be said that the main function of financial institutions is to standardize the non-standard financing needs in the form of products that can be accepted and invested by the public. Therefore, asset management institutions make use of the basic assets and then design, manage and sell financial products. They transform financial products into an important link between investors and basic assets. Investors invest in financial products, and investment is made in basic assets in the form of financial products. The core asset management ability of various types of asset management institutions is mainly shown in this process. Different types of asset management institutions get involved in the value chain and industrial chain from different links and in different ways.

If we do not consider the factors of economic growth, China's asset management has developed with China's financial market, accompanied by the gradual upgrading of China's financial institutions and the gradual deepening of the financial market. In fact, it can be said to be the process in which the capital is transferred from institutions with relatively low efficiency and return to more efficient departments through the competition of market-oriented products. The capital used to be put in the traditional commercial banks at the interest rates set by the government, so commercial banks were very profitable. With the development of the asset management industry, various types of asset management institutions have become competitors and distributors of savings by issuing their own financial products. Therefore, the capital flowed to more efficient financial institutions with the continuous development of the asset management industry. This process is in fact a process of gradually improving the efficiency of the asset management industry, and it is also a process of reducing the mismatch of China's financial system and improving the matching between the financing demand and the fund suppliers.

We can also see that the field and scope of basic assets are constantly expanding and that the unsatisfied financing needs are constantly being satisfied by new designed products. If we think of the customer's financing needs or the basic assets as a spectrum, the services provided by traditional commercial banks are most needed in the middle part, which is the mature and profitable period in an enterprise's life cycle. A new enterprise appeared, and then, it had a positive cash flow after going through difficulties in its development. And finally, it had a factory building—the fixed assets that can be used as collateral. At this stage, China's commercial banks provided very good services. But at the stages before and after the above-mentioned stage, under the traditional business system framework, it is very difficult for commercial banks to meet the financing needs as basic assets. We say that the asset management industry promotes the development of the financial system because it not only leads to the expansion in the basic assets, but also leads to the expansion of management institutions and financial assets. Thanks to the asset management industry, the sales channels are also increasing. With the change of connotation and extension of asset management industry, asset management has gradually changed from a relatively narrow financial sub-industry into a basic financial function which has a profound impact on the financial industry.

From the development of global financial markets, we can see that, in a country's investment and financing system, the higher the proportion of direct financing is, the higher the degree of marketization will be. This investment and financing system will show the characteristics of a broad domestic asset management system. Commercial banks, securities companies, fund companies or insurance companies all participate in asset management in different degrees, identify a kind of financing demand in the actual economic operation and then transform this financing demand into financial products that can be invested. The process of selling products is also the process of raising funds from investors.

This simple industrial chain and value chain of the asset management industry can be used to explain the phenomena in many asset management fields, and they can also be used to evaluate the competitiveness and operation efficiency of different financial institutions in this transformation. For example, the neologism of asset shortage has become popular in recent years. Theoretically speaking, there should not be an asset shortage because you should be able to buy the corresponding assets if you have the funds in hand. The word asset shortage actually reflects the challenge of the market to the asset management ability of financial institutions: In the financial market, due to the transformation of the economic structure and the competition in the financial market, the income of the asset side is obviously declining, but the cost of the liability side remains high because of the competition among financial institutions, and the decline is very slow. As a result, the cost of the liability side does not match the income of the asset side, giving rise to the so-called asset shortage. This shows that the asset management industry is now faced with higher requirements on their capabilities of matching and management regarding the term and costs of assets and liabilities.

From the perspective of function, the functions of asset management industry can be classified from three aspects: financiers, investors and countries. All kinds of financiers in the financial market are also the funds demanders in asset management industry; investors are the buyers of asset management products or the suppliers of funds in the financial market. For investors, asset management is a very important way of asset investment. It can redistribute the difference between the bank's deposit interests and the return of financial products in the market and transfer the net profit margin from the original commercial banks to the providers and investors of funds through the competition of various financial products provided by various types of asset management institutions.

From a macro point of view, this reflects the continuous improvement of efficiency in allocating financial resources and resource elements with the help of market forces. After the investment and financing system is more like asset management, the allocation of financial resources is correspondingly more market-oriented. From the perspective of risk identification, pricing and risk control, the risk system of asset management with high proportion of direct financing poses many new challenges to the financial institutions that are used to the environment of indirect financing. Therefore, we need to enhance new professional abilities.

The rapid development of asset management industry has also caused many problems worthy of study, such as the lack of functional definition of securities in basic law. What is an appropriate investor group? For the regulation of asset management and asset management innovation, which are for private high net worth group, and which can become public offering? Who will carry out the regulation? The current definition of these boundaries is not clear. Besides, at present, there is no uniform laws for asset management business. There are many channels for people to buy wealth management products. Securities companies provide asset management products, fund companies provide products of public offering, subsidiaries of fund companies provide private placement products and entrusted loan business, banks provide bank wealth management, and trust companies provide trust products, and insurance companies also provide asset management products. When investors invest in these products, they are often subject to different laws and regulations. At the same time, the scale of asset management industry is large enough, and the relationship between different markets is increasingly close. Taking institutional regulation as the starting point might lead to the unclear boundary and positioning of regulation on direct financing represented by asset management industry.

Premier Li Keqiang stressed a short time ago that after the violent fluctuations in the stock market have gradually subsided, we should now reflect on the stock market disaster and sum up the experience and lessons. There are many perspectives for reflection. One of the most important points is that different types of asset management industries have different ways of getting involved in the market, and their behaviors are regulated by different regulatory agencies. The persons in charge of the securities regulatory department cannot fully understand the whole picture of leverage distribution in the market. He might be able to see the changes of the securities margin trading in the market and of the companies. However, the securities regulatory authorities do not know the leverage of bank financial products and the intervention of trust products. They know even less about the allocation of funds to the Internet financial industry and high leverage allocation. This problem, as a result of the rapid development of our asset management industry, is worthy of study.

There are other problems in the actual operation. For example, after the asset management industry becomes larger in scale and deeper in development in the future, we will face the problems such as how to carry out risk consolidation and how to manage all kinds of off balance sheet and off balance sheet businesses under a unified risk management framework. Now, a commercial bank will be regarded as a very traditional one if it does not set up or cooperate with several asset management institutions. This actually shows a significant change in the current financial structure, that is, with the development of the asset management industry, the business model of financial institutions is undergoing profound changes. Now, when there is the demand for financing, financial institutions will consider the channels, the capital requirements and costs of different channels. Of course, this brings new challenges to financial regulation.

21.3 Development Trend of Global Asset Management Industry

From a global perspective, among the different sectors of the financial market, the asset management industry is also one of the fastest growing areas. At the end of 2014, the scale of global asset management was 74 trillion US dollars. As for the market share of the asset management industry, the asset management industry in North America ranks first in the world, accounting for about 50% of the global market share, while Europe accounts for 30%.The asset management industry in Asia is developing very fast, and China and India, two dynamic countries with large population, are the fastest growing countries in terms of the asset management industry, but the market share combined is just over 10%. So far, in terms of the regional distribution, we can say that the asset management industry is actually a typical industry dominated by European and American markets. China is an emerging market with large growth space, but so far, the asset management industry in China has relatively limited international influence.

The influence of asset management industry is shown in many aspects. For example, Chinese policymakers are increasingly concerned about communicating policy developments with international financial markets. Why is there the need for communication? This is because the European and American markets are managing about 80% of the assets in the financial market, the opinions of the management institutions managing the 80% of the assets and their fund managers and researchers are not only a matter of market share, but also related to development trends of specific industries, international capital flows, asset pricing in different markets, as well as the different impacts on different markets during the same period when the financial crisis led to significant fluctuations in the financial market. One of the important factors is "the preference for local market". As for the market share of asset management, North America occupies 50%, and Europe occupies 30% of the global market share. If there are problems in these markets, it is very likely for them to sell the assets of other markets. Therefore, even if the crisis and volatility are caused by their own problems, the result is that the emerging markets suffer from more violent fluctuations.

In this sense, China's asset management industry is still in its infancy, with a lot of room for development and a long way to go. At present, according to the statistics of the Asset Management Association of China (AMAC), there are currently 26,000 enterprises in China's private placement industry, which is quite a breakthrough compared with the initial stage when there was only the increase of several public fund companies in a year. The scale expansion of public funds is not small now, but it is much better compared with the initial stage. At that time, many fund companies were established and began to provide products, but their lofty ideal at that time was to manage assets of RMB 10 billion worth. Later, they set the goal at RMB100 billion. Once, a leader of the regulatory department said at a meeting that our fund companies would manage assets of RMB100 billion worth in the future. Some of the participants of the fund companies laughed, thinking that it was impossible for the companies to manage assets of such worth. They thought that it would be great for companies to manage assets of RMB 1 billion yuan and 2 billion. Now, the situation has changed a lot, but there is still a big gap between Chinese market and mature markets in the world.

For the past two years, as a senior visiting scholar at Columbia University, I have had the opportunity to visit professionals in various fields of the financial industry, including fund managers on the Wall Street. Once I met a fund manager of an established asset management institution. He was very pessimistic about China's economy at that time, so a warm-hearted friend of mine arranged an exchange meeting for us. How big is the stock fund managed by the institution where he worked as a fund manager? My friend told me that it was worth $90 billion at that time. At that time, I thought that, if monetary fund was excluded, few of the public fund companies in China could manage stock fund worth more than 90 billion US dollars. A well-known e-commerce enterprise was listed in New York at that time. On the second day of its successful listing, I met with a friend of an investment bank who participated in the listing project, and I asked their team about their opinions about the New York market. He said that many people in his team felt that the big market in New York is indeed full of liquidity. With such a large amount of financing, if their company wanted to get listed in the domestic market, the coordination and cooperation of several departments would be indispensable. When they got listed in the New York market, it seemed that it had little influence on the market, and the supporting products in all aspects were also very rich.

In the global market, the investment of hedge funds, sovereign funds and alternative financial assets in the sub-sectors of asset management industry is rising very fast. Investors have the demand for alternative investment, solution-oriented, multi-asset-oriented and passive investment products, and these products are beginning to erode the market share of the active products. The proportion of traditional active management products decreased from 59% in 2003 to 39% in 2014, and it is still on the decline. But the proportion of the passive products is on the rise, and so is the proportion of the solution-oriented products. This also shows that in the increasingly volatile market environment, it is difficult for fund managers to have a good performance all the time. Therefore, in actual product allocation, investors tend to go in opposite directions, either simply making passive index investment, or actively pursuing the return of active investment. They hope that asset management institutions can make a package of personalized solutions according to their own situations.

The change of products in the international market is also directly related to the development of the market. After the crisis, bond funds have replaced money market funds and become a very fast-growing product. Exchange traded funds (ETF) is an important product and carrier of index investment and passive investment. Passive investment in this area is widely welcomed. From the statistical data, we can see that the investment of ETF in the United States is dominant in these areas. A comparison between the private equity funds in China and the United States shows that private equity asset management industry in the United States has a larger scale and more diversified products, while China's private equity fund still has a long way to go and calls for continuous efforts. A simple analysis of the relevant business data is made to understand the distribution and differences of the asset size of private funds between China and the United States. In addition, the private equity funds and hedge funds with different strategies in the US market also have very different performance in this round of crisis.

The asset management industry in the world is becoming larger and larger in scale, exerting increasingly great impacts on the financial industry. Correspondingly, the regulation has become more and more strict. For example, many regulatory authorities have begun to carry out fund stress test and specific information disclosure and adjust the characteristics, service modes and sales channels of products. At the same time, such elements as Internet, computer technology and big data are also permeating the asset management industry. Developed in the Silicon Valley, robot investment advisors or financial management robots are developing fast, profoundly changing the business model of the asset management industry. Digitization has become a very important development trend of the industry. Many large asset management companies may be laying off employees in fields like market development, but they have been employing talents in IT and big data applications. This is an obvious trend, and the traditional asset management institutions are also undergoing significant changes. The traditional asset management institutions need to find ways to improve the product classification and product line. The professional asset management institutions need to launch financial products that meet the consumers' personalized needs. Correspondingly, diversified and large-scale asset management institutions coexist with personalized and professional ones.

21.4 Development of Asset Management Industry in China

The first is the bank financial management. In recent years, the financial management market of banks has been developing very fast. One of the main driving forces is the purpose of reducing the capital constraint through the expansion of off balance sheet assets. For example, a capital of RMB100, 000 is required if the balance sheet financing is RMB 1 million and the capital adequacy ratio is maintained at 10%. Rapid expansions of assets scale will create very big pressure on banks in capital supplement.

The second is the problem of rigid payment of financial products. In fact, there is no legal document requiring the financial management institutions to carry out rigid payment. In the first half of 2015, when the stock market underwent violent fluctuations, one of the reasons for supporting the rescue was the worry that the continuous decline of the stock market would lead to the disorderly breaking of the rigid payment of bank financial products. As for the development trend, the development speed of bank financial management will slow down in the future. In particular, the regulatory authorities have imposed 4 and 30% restrictions. In addition, the downward range of return on net assets under asset shortage is significantly greater than that of debt cost. Therefore, the return on financial management is declining, and bank financial management is becoming less attractive. Nevertheless, bank asset management is still an important development direction, and its development trend is mainly manifested in the net value and current financing as well as fixed term products. This is where the core competitiveness of commercial banks lies.

Third, the asset scale of the trust industry is growing, while the growth rate is declining, and the channel-type business is shrinking. At present, the main challenge of the trust industry is that the channel-type business is obviously shrinking, and the trust is beginning to face transformation. It is turning to asset securitization trust and land circulation socialized trust. The main purpose is to give full play to the functional advantages of trust and achieve personalized and diversified asset management.

Fourth, the insurance industry is growing very fast and has become the main body of market investment that cannot be ignored. The allocation is becoming more and more diversified. Of course, there are also areas that cause controversy and concern. For example, the rapid development of universal insurance and high debt cost lead to the increase of pressure in asset allocation.

Fifthly, public funds continue to develop steadily, and the number of sunshine private equity companies is growing very fast. Fund subsidiaries mainly got involved in channel-type business, and they now begin to carry out active management. At present, the futures asset management industry is relatively small in scale, but it is still growing quickly. Recently, private equity investment funds have developed rapidly, and the growth momentum has increased significantly. In recent years, the government guidance fund, a relatively new fund set up by governments at all levels, appeared with the purpose of encouraging entrepreneurship. The rapid development of the new third board is also an important factor to promote the development of private equity.

Sixth, the insurance funds begin to get involved in alternative investment more actively and do some equity investment related to their own upstream and downstream business. The private banking business and high-end financial management business are the two noteworthy areas in the asset management industry. Discretionary management and FOF are two areas that are recognized and have great potential for development.

Seventh, since 2015, the economic growth has been on the decline, the internal and external monetary policies are loose, and the supply of relatively safe and high-yielding assets has been decreasing, which has resulted in the asset shortage. Under this backdrop, there are several major policies affecting the asset management industry. One is the replacement of local debt. The central government bears part of the local debt, short-term debt is converted into long-term debt, and high-interest debt is converted into low-interest debt. In fact, this objectively aggravates asset shortage.

Eighth, asset securitization has been developing very fast in recent years. The combination of asset securitization and investment banking functions has become a new trend of concern. Commercial banks, securities companies and insurance companies have begun to attach importance to investment banking business., More products can be provided by combining asset securitization with asset management and investment banking business. Basic assets are constantly expanding thanks to the deepening of asset securitization. The recent economic adjustment has led to the rise of non-performing assets of banks, and the securitization of non-performing assets is receiving more and more attention. Under the background of asset shortage, the business model of "asset management plus investment banking" has attracted more and more attention. The fundamental economic growth rate is still falling, the cost of debt is still relatively high, and the income of the asset side is decreasing. All of this has pushed asset management institutions and investment banks to actively expand categories of new assets and turn them into investable products. Now, there is a saying that financial institutions used to do business with liabilities. Banks used to do business with deposits. Only by absorbing deposits can loans be made according to the deposit loan ratio. There is an interest margin between deposits and loans. Now, the market environment has changed dramatically. Especially, with the great development of the asset management industry, financial institutions have become asset-driven to varying degrees. The key to succeed in market competition is to get high-quality assets before looking for channels to match the funds. In fact, there are many sources of funds in the market, which can be allocated into deposits or different financial products.

Finally, let us talk about the asset management of the Internet. Although many Internet financial enterprises have different problems, the advantages of Internet and big data in the development of channels, products and platforms have not been fully made use of. How can we carry out targeted selling of products through the platform of Internet? How can we design new products based on big data and data analysis and mining? How can robot be used in financial management? The development of Internet finance gave rise to Internet asset management platforms covering many fields. In contrast, several so-called few of the Internet financial platforms that had problems in the early stage really make use of big data and the advantages of the Internet. They did not really use big data to identify risks, price risks and manage risks. However, Internet and big data technology will become a very important driving force to change the future asset management industry.

Chapter 22
Overseas Allocation of China's Insurance Asset Management

After years of development, the scale of China's insurance asset management has expanded to more than RMB10 trillion. Like other asset management businesses in the financial industry, overseas asset allocation has gradually become a trend.

22.1 Status Quo of Insurance Asset Management Industry

For nearly a decade, the total assets and the balance of insurance funds of the insurance industry have witnessed an annual increase of more than 20%. The scale of insurance assets is second only to that of banks and trusts. By the end of 2015, the scale of bank financial management exceeded RMB 23 trillion, the scale of trust assets exceeded RMB 16 trillion, and the balance of insurance funds exceeded RMB 11 trillion.

China ranks third in the world in terms of premium scale, second only to the United States and Japan. The original insurance premium income was RMB 2886.487 billion, a year-on-year increase of 28.88%. Among them, the original insurance premium income of property insurance business was RMB 777.305 billion, an increase of 8.73% year on year; the original insurance premium income of life insurance business was RMB1655.668 billion, an increase of 33.12% year on year; the original insurance premium income of health insurance business was RMB 384.180 billion, an increase of 73.08% year on year; the original insurance premium income of accident insurance business was RMB 69.334 billion, an increase of 17.37% year on year. In addition, the investment funds of the insured not included in the insurance contract accounting of life insurance companies and independent accounts increased by RMB 1211.453 billion this year, an increase of 65.17% year on year.

The main characteristics of insurance fund are as follows: (1) certainty of cost. Insurance fund is debt capital, and the cost of debt is certain, so it is necessary to match assets and liabilities; otherwise, it may bring systemic risks. (2) Low risk preference. Insurance fund requires long-term and stable yield. (3) Long term. The insurance policies have a longer duration. (4) Large size and stable growth. The scale

S. Ba, *The New Cycle and New Finance in China*,
https://doi.org/10.1007/978-981-16-8209-4_22

of insurance assets is second only to that of banks and trusts in the asset management market. (5) Funds as capital. Insurance funds can be used as the capital of enterprises for long-term equity investment, which can alleviate the problems of high debt ratio and high investment cost of the real economy to a certain extent.

By the end of November 2016, the total assets of China's insurance industry were RMB 1496.086 billion, an increase of 21.04% over the beginning of the year (see Fig. 22.1). Among them, the total assets of property insurance companies were RMB2346,359 million, an increase of 26.96% over the beginning of the year; the total assets of life insurance companies were RMB 12319.762 billion, an increase of 24.04% over the beginning of the year; the total assets of reinsurance companies were RMB 273.534 billion, a decrease of 47.27% over the beginning of the year; the total assets of asset management companies were RMB 40.762 billion, an increase of 15.67% over the beginning of the year. The balance of fund utilization was RMB13118.916 billion, an increase of 17.35% over the beginning of the year, accounting for 87.69% of the total assets of the insurance industry.

There are three fund utilization modes of insurance companies in the world: the establishment of internal investment department of insurance companies, the entrustment of independent third-party investment management companies and the establishment of investment management companies.

With the establishment of internal investment departments, insurance companies directly manage and operate insurance funds. The asset side and liability side of insurance funds are united within an insurance company, which is more conducive to asset liability matching and mutual driving and helps insurance companies to protect

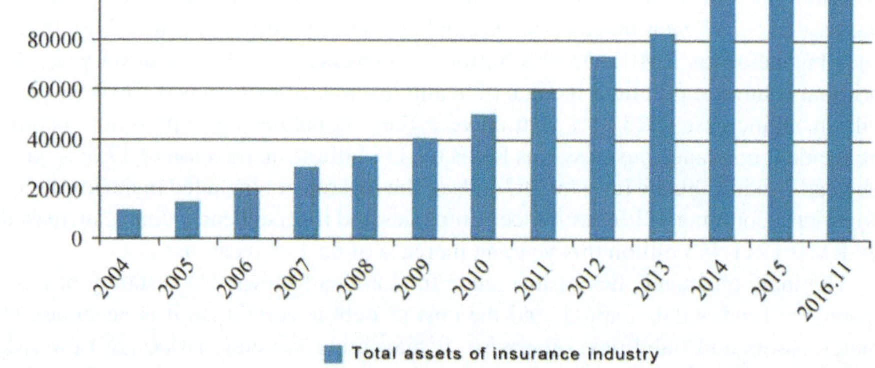

Fig. 22.1 Assets scale of insurance industry over the years. *Source* Web site of CIRC

their capital security and control liquidity risk. However, with the rapid expansion of the insurance assets, this mode of operation also leads to some problems, such as the internalization of transactions, the lack of effective market competition and the harm to the rate of return of insurance funds.

The entrustment of third-party investment management company is often adopted by most foreign property insurance companies, reinsurance companies and a small number of small life insurance companies. Companies with a relatively large proportion of third-party business have a high degree of marketization, and the comprehensive investment ability is approaching or has reached the standard of the fully competitive big asset management market. Of course, this mode may produce more "principal-agent" problems, which not only has investment risk, but also faces investment behavior deviation and investment operation risk of external investment companies.

The operation mode of establishing insurance asset management companies focuses more on the management of the parent company's funds. This mode can better attract talents in the use of funds and improve the efficiency of the use of funds; besides, it can help find new business growth points for the parent company by using the funds through professional asset management and thus promote the overall business development of the parent company. The professional operation can help the parent company expand the scope of asset management and improve the income of insurance funds; at the same time, it partly makes up for the shortcomings of internal investment departments and entrusted external investment institutions. At present, this mode has become the main operation mode of China's insurance industry. From the current business positioning of insurance asset management companies, most of them belong to various insurance companies, but the business scope is not limited to the internal business entrusted by related parties, but is expanded to the highly market-oriented asset management business, and the business structure is gradually diversified.

The main business development trends can be summarized as follows: First, the investment mode is expanded from public offering business to private offering business, from investment business to investment banking business and from domestic business to overseas business. Second, various operation mechanisms have been introduced, including asset full custody mechanism, risk responsible person mechanism, investment licensing mechanism, business division system and team system of alternative investment, and they have been playing an important role in strengthening the diversified resource allocation. Finally, the management mode has gradually changed from the account management mode to the product mode, and active expansion of the third-party asset management business has become an important trend. Insurance asset management institutions promote the standardization and marketization of insurance asset management through the development of debt investment plan, equity investment plan, portfolio investment plan, asset securitization and fund-like products.

As of the end of November 2016, fixed income assets accounted for 51.35% of the insurance assets, including RMB 4304.528 billion of bonds, accounting for 32.81%; bank deposits reached RMB 2352.239 billion, accounting for 17.93%. It can be seen that fixed income assets are still the main insurance assets, but the proportion has declined (At the end of November 2015) A, bond assets accounted for 34.82%, and bank deposits accounted for 23.3%). Equity assets amounted to RMB 1885.232 billion, accounting for 14.37%, with a year-on-year increase of 0.3%. Other investments reached RMB4576.917 billion, accounting for 34.89%, which was significantly higher than 27.81% at the end of November 2015 (see Fig. 22.2).

According to the report of CIRC, from 2011 to 2015, the investment income rates of China's insurance funds were 3.49, 3.39, 5.04, 6.3 and 7.56%, respectively (see Fig. 22.3). In 2015, the income from the use of insurance funds totaled RMB 780.363 billion, with an average return rate of 7.56%, reaching a new high in recent four years. From 2004 to 2014, the total investment income of insurance funds was RMB 2142.5

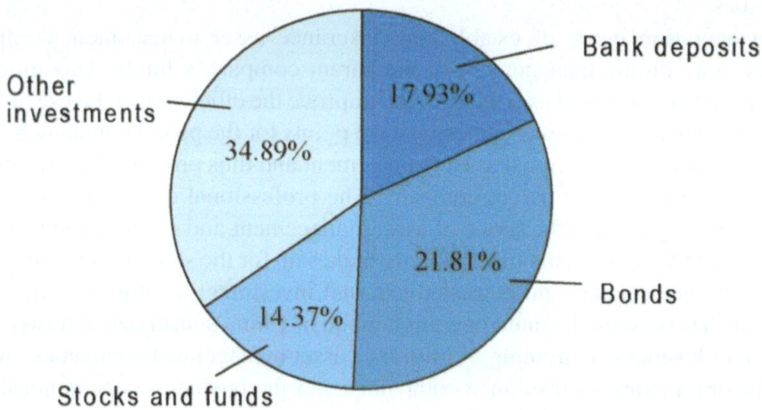

Fig. 22.2 Asset allocation structure of insurance funds (as of the end of November 2016). *Source* CIRC Web site

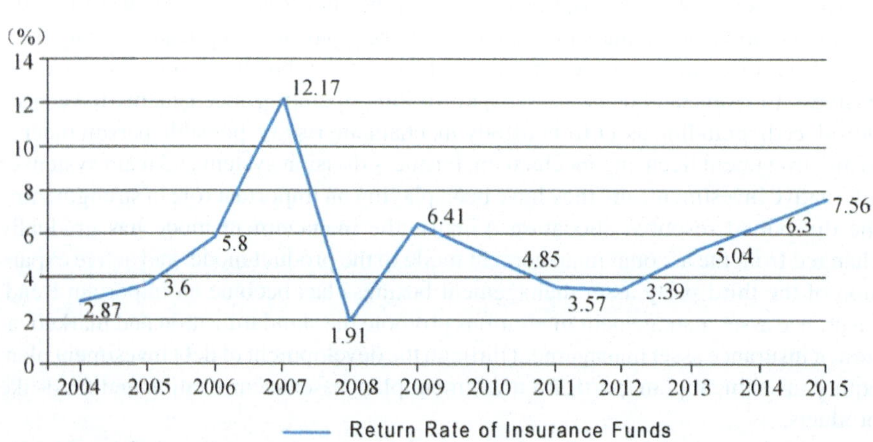

Fig. 22.3 Return rate of insurance funds

billion, with an average return rate of 5.32%, and an average annual contribution of nearly RMB 200 billion.

In terms of capital cost, Report on Insurance Asset Management Market Operation Report in 2015 shows that with the deepened reform of the insurance premium rate marketization, some insurance companies mainly promote products with high present value and financial nature, such as dividend insurance, and universal insurance. Insurance companies are faced with the difficulties of rising cost of liabilities and declining rate of return on the asset side, which makes the allocation of insurance funds and assets more difficult. The cost of liabilities of most insurance companies is still between 6 and 8%, and the cost of some companies even exceeds 10%.

22.2 Regulatory Provisions on Overseas Asset Allocation

In 2004, the CIRC and the People's Bank of China jointly promulgated the Interim Measures for the Administration of Overseas Use of Foreign Exchange Insurance Funds, allowing overseas use of foreign exchange insurance funds.

In July 2007, the CIRC, the People's Bank of China and the State Administration of Foreign Exchange (SAFE) jointly promulgated the Interim Measures for the Administration of Overseas Investment of Insurance Funds, which allows insurance institutions to entrust insurance asset management companies or other professional investment management institutions to be responsible for the overseas investment of insurance funds. The scope of overseas investment of insurance funds was expanded from fixed income products to equity products such as stocks and equity; the investment markets were expanded to globally developed capital markets; the total overseas investment of insurance funds increased to no more than 15% of the total assets at the end of last year.

In October 2012, the CIRC issued the Detailed Rules for the Implementation of the Interim Measures for the Administration of Overseas Investment of Insurance Funds, which clearly pointed out the internationalization of the insurance asset management industry, standardized the operation of overseas investment of insurance funds, prevented investment management risks and realized the value preservation and appreciation of insurance assets. The scope of investment was expanded to 45 countries or regions, including 25 developed markets and 20 emerging markets. The investment should be related to money market, fixed income, equity, real estate and overseas funds. The balance of overseas investment should not exceed 15% of the total assets at the end of last year, and the balance of investment in emerging markets should not exceed 10% of the total assets at the end of last year.

In August 2014, China Insurance Regulatory Commission (CIRC) issued Several Opinions on Accelerating the Development of Modern Insurance Service Industry (the "Ten New Provisions"), which proposed to improve the efficiency of insurance fund allocation, strengthen the insurance industry's support for enterprises to "go global", enhance the level of opening up to the outside world, introduce advanced management concepts and technologies and release and stimulate the vitality of sustainable development and innovation of the industry.

In March 2015, the CIRC issued the Notice of the CIRC on Adjusting the Policies Related to Overseas Investment of Insurance Funds, expanding the entrusted investment scope of insurance institutions from the Hong Kong market to the financial markets of 45 countries or regions and expanding the investment scope of overseas bonds, from bonds above BBB level to bonds above BBB level. It also allowed insurance funds to invest in Hong Kong GEM stocks.

In March 2016, the 13th Five-year Plan clearly pointed out that we should support the insurance industry to go global and expand the scope of overseas investment of insurance funds. We should promote the internationalization of financial institutions, strengthen the layout of overseas outlets, improve the global service network, and improve the opening level of the Chinese mainland's financial market to overseas institutions.

In September 2016, CIRC issued the Regulatory Guidelines on Investment of Insurance Funds in the Pilot Stocks of Shanghai–Hong Kong Stock Connect, allowing insurance funds to participate in the Shanghai–Hong Kong stock connect. The main contents include as follows: Insurance institutions should have the ability of stock investment when carrying out investment in Shanghai–Hong Kong stock connect, and those who do not have the ability should entrust qualified investment managers to carry out the investment; the portfolio insurance asset management initiated by insurance asset management can invest in the pilot stocks of Shanghai–Hong Kong stock connect; insurance institutions should include the book balance in the calculation of equity assets; the guidelines also clarify the detailed requirements for insurance asset management products to invest in Shanghai–Hong Kong stock connect.

In addition, since the first quarter of 2016, the Solvency II has been formally implemented. This system presents four major capital requirements for overseas assets: For fixed income varieties in developed markets, it prefers those with longer investment period; at present, it encourages investment in developed stock markets, because compared with other assets, stock investment saves more capital, faces relatively controllable risks, and the investment value is also high; the capital requirement for overseas real estate is significantly lower than that of Solvency I; it adopts a prudent investment strategy for emerging market investment.

22.3 Trend of Overseas Asset Allocation

In the environment of low interest rates, insurance institutions generally face the difficulties of decreasing investment income and increasing capital cost.

Since 2014, China's treasury bond interest rate has witnessed rapid decrease, and the treasury bond yield has continued to decline, which increases the pressure on the allocation of insurance capital. In the environment of low interest rates, there is a lack of high-yield fixed income assets allocated by insurance companies before, so it is difficult for insurance asset management institutions to find relatively high-yield low-risk assets for allocation, which creates huge pressure on the asset allocation of insurance companies.

The rising cost of debt of insurance companies is attributed to the following two factors: One is the competitive pricing inside and outside the industry. In order to gain the strategic advantage of scale, some insurance companies tend to sacrifice short-term interests and increase the costs of debt. In addition to product pricing competition within the insurance industry, bank financial products and various trust financial products are also competing with insurance companies for sources of funds. The other is the long duration of insurance fund liabilities. Insurance funds are characterized by liabilities with long duration, and the pricing of insurance products is based on the consideration of longer-term investment. As a result, the insurance companies have to face the relatively high cost of liabilities.

Under different interest rate cycles, the asset side of insurance has different goals. When the interest rate rises, the asset side takes higher yield as its primary goal. When the interest rate falls, the matching management of assets and liabilities is particularly prominent. In the current low interest rate cycle, insurance funds are facing great challenges at both the asset side and the liability side.

At present, the people in the market and industry generally believe that in the environment of low interest rate, the response measures of investors can be divided into five categories: increasing overseas asset allocation and carrying out global asset allocation; improving risk preference and risk tolerance on the premise of sound risk management and control; increasing the investment of equity assets relatively indirectly affected by interest rates; lengthening the duration of assets and increasing the proportion of alternative assets.

However, at present, the market of China's mainland is full of liquidity, and asset prices are relatively high, but there is a lack of long-term assets with high quality and yields. Due to various factors, the domestic asset portfolio cannot fully meet the demand of diversified allocation of insurance assets. But the international market has a larger capacity, the asset categories are more diversified, and the asset prices are more rational compared with the market of China's mainland. International asset allocation provides more options for insurance institutions. For example, overseas markets can provide rare treasury bonds with ultra-long term in the capital market of mainland China, such as 20-year, 30-year and 50 year long-term treasury bonds and inflation protected bonds.

The allocation of overseas assets helps expand investment channels for insurance funds, effectively disperses the risks of asset allocation and improves the return on investment of insurance funds. In addition, insurance asset management institutions increase investment in overseas high-quality assets, which also plays an important role in avoiding the risk of exchange rate fluctuation and regional risks.

By the end of July 2016, 53 insurance institutions had been approved to invest in the overseas market, with a total investment of US $44.579 billion, accounting for 2.14% of the total. Compared with that by the end of 2015, the balance of overseas investment of insurance funds witnessed an increase of 23%; the balance of overseas investment of insurance funds witnessed an increase of 459.58% compared with the balance of US $9.7 billion by the end of 2012. Before 2016, China's insurance funds were invested in overseas market mainly through the channel of QDII. In addition, China's regulatory authorities were more prudent in approving the amount of overseas investment. Under the pressure of renminbi depreciation, the amount of overseas investment of insurance funds grew slowly. Therefore, the strategic role of optimizing the allocation of insurance assets and improving the rate of return on investment through overseas investment was restricted to some extent.

In October 2012, the CIRC issued the Detailed Rules for the Implementation of the Interim Measures for the Administration of Overseas Investment of Insurance Funds, stating clearly that the balance of overseas investment in the insurance asset management industry should not exceed 15%, and the balance of investment in emerging markets should not exceed 10% of the total assets at the end of last year. Up to now, the proportion of overseas investment of China's insurance funds is about 2%, which is far lower than the proportion of overseas allocation of insurance funds in Japan, the UK and other markets. It can be seen that there is still a large space for the development of overseas asset allocation of China's insurance funds.

The overseas asset allocation of China's insurance funds has the following characteristics: First, the investment fields are relatively concentrated, covering bank deposits, real estate, stocks, bonds, funds, equity, etc. Second, the investment mode is relatively single. The overseas investment mode of insurance funds mainly includes direct equity investment, indirect equity investment and real estate purchase. Third, regional distribution of investment is highly concentrated: At present, the overseas investment markets of insurance funds mainly include Hong Kong market (mainly equity investment) and markets of developed countries such as Europe, America and Australia (equity investment of real estate and insurance enterprises). With the policies to control capital outflow and restrict QDII business, it is difficult for insurance institutions to directly obtain the opportunities to invest in overseas equity markets. In addition, compared with other overseas equity markets, the institutional investors of the Chinese mainland are more familiar with the equity market system and enterprises in Hong Kong and the enterprises in Hong Kong. Therefore, investing in Hong Kong stocks is often the first choice for insurance institutions to invest in the markets outside the Chinese mainland.

As of the middle of 2015, Hong Kong dollar assets of investment of China's insurance funds exceeded HK $170 billion, accounting for about 67% of the balance of investment outside the Chinese mainland. Fourth, asset allocation is concentrated in equity assets, while the proportion of alternative assets is increasing: mainly stock investment, equity investment and real estate investment. The proportion of stock is the largest type of assets, but judging from the recent trend, equity and real estate investment have increased rapidly, and the combined proportion of the two has gradually exceeded that of stock, becoming the largest type of assets. Alternative assets have become one of the main directions of investment outside the Chinese mainland. Meanwhile, market players attach greater importance to the allocation of financial products such as private equity funds, real estate trust investment funds and asset securitization. Some insurance companies, including overseas insurance companies, have purchased a number of high-quality office buildings or hotels in the core areas of London, New York and other core gateway cities and made financial investment in overseas high-quality enterprises through equity investment.

Due to the characteristics of insurance funds, the matching of risk characteristics is considered as the basic principle of insurance fund asset allocation. Under this principle, it has become an international common practice to carry out diversified, decentralized and globalized allocation of insurance assets.

Insurance funds are large in scale and are required to get some return on investment. But the local financial market has a limited capacity, and it is difficult to meet the requirements of the cost of insurance liabilities with limited return on investment. Besides, the regulatory policies of overseas investment are relatively loose, so the insurance industry in Britain and Japan allocates a large proportion of assets overseas.

From the experience of overseas asset allocation of Japanese insurance funds, we can see that the allocation of large assets is relatively flexible, which is highly related to economic development. It aims to obtain high returns by increasing the proportion of investment in overseas assets during domestic economic downturn. In terms of investment preference, insurance companies are relatively traditional, preferring the principles of security and liquidity.

Japan has a limited rate of return on its domestic investment, so its insurance industry attaches great importance to overseas investment. Especially after the financial crisis in 2008, with the continuous decrease of the yield of Japanese government bonds, Japanese insurance companies gradually increased the proportion of foreign assets. With the improvement of overseas investment income, the proportion of investment also increased year by year, reaching 19% in 2014.

The regulation on the UK insurance industry is relatively loose, and the UK insurance industry attaches greater importance to profitability rather than liquidity and security. Compared with fixed income investments such as bonds, the UK insurance industry prefers stock investment and has been actively investing overseas.

As for the overseas asset allocation of China's insurance asset management industry, it is the natural demand of insurance asset allocation to improve the equity allocation when the interest rate decreases. After the financial crisis in 2008, both Britain and Japan experienced a continuous decrease in bond interest rates. Insurance companies in both countries increased the proportion of equity asset to alleviate the impact of low interest rates on investment returns.

Compared with the capital market in the Chinese Mainland, Hong Kong, as an international financial center, has advantages in many aspects: more mature market; more diversified investor structure, which is suitable for long-term allocation; larger market capacity, more diversified asset categories, more rational asset prices, providing more choices for institutions; higher proportion of direct financing, stronger influence of institutional investors on the market and freer cross-border flow of capital, which contribute to the stability of the investment yield of insurance funds. In terms of valuation, market volatility, AH discount rate, dividend yield and global allocation, the Hong Kong stocks are more attractive to investors of insurance funds.

Since the beginning of 2016, a large number of insurance funds have been invested in Hong Kong stocks through the Shanghai–Hong Kong stock connect. In September

2016, the CIRC officially issued the Regulatory Guidelines on Investment of Insurance Funds in the Pilot Stocks of Shanghai–Hong Kong Stock Connect, and the Hong Kong stocks are becoming increasingly attractive to insurance fund investors.

In addition to the above advantages, a very important reason for the popularity of Hong Kong stocks is that the investment target of Shanghai–Hong Kong stock connect is more consistent with the investment preference of insurance fund investors. According to the regulations of the Shanghai–Hong Kong Stock Connect, at the initial stage of the pilot period, the Hong Kong Securities Regulatory Commission requires that domestic investors participating in the stock connect should be limited to institutional investors and individual investors whose total assets of securities accounts and capital accounts are not less than RMB 500,000. The stocks of the stock connect include the component stocks the Hang Seng Composite large stock index and Hang Seng Composite Medium stock index and the atocks of A + H-share companies listed both on the Stock Exchange of Hong Kong and Shanghai Stock Exchange. It can be seen from the above provisions that the investors of the stock connect are institutional or professional individual investors, and the investment targets are also index component stocks with larger market value, which is consistent with the investment preference of insurance fund investors.

The launch of Shenzhen–Hong Kong stock connects, especially with the cancellation of the total quota, has connected the Hong Kong, Shanghai and Shenzhen markets into a "common market". Meanwhile, insurance funds are allowed to be invested, which further expands the development space of insurance fund investment in overseas markets.

In addition, insurance funds can be used to indirectly purchase overseas assets through this channel. Among the 417 targets of Shanghai–Hong Kong stock connect and Shenzhen–Hong Kong stock connect, 29 companies listed on Hong Kong stock exchange possess overseas assets, and 102 companies carry out overseas business. The proportion of overseas business of 36 companies exceeds 50%. Hong Kong is also one of the largest equity financing markets in the world, with flexible financing and refinancing mechanisms. In the future, the listing of more overseas assets on the Hong Kong stock exchange will help allocate insurance funds globally, hedge the risks brought by the fall of a single market and help to stabilize the insurance investment yield. In the future, insurance funds can transform fixed income investments such as bank deposits and bonds into high-yield assets such as equity of listed companies through long-term equity investment of insurance funds so as to effectively deal with low interest rates and prolong asset duration.

In the environment of low interest rates, the alternative assets have a higher value for allocation than other large assets, and they are expected to have a greater growth potential in the future.

When the market interest rates fall, funds will be allocated to relatively high-yield and safe assets. The high return of alternative investment does not necessarily come from high risks, and excess returns rely more on the ability to obtain scarce resources, the value-added ability of post-investment management and the ability of cross-market arbitrage. Alternative investment also has the characteristics of high entry threshold and low flexibility of exit period, which is naturally consistent with the insurance funds' long duration and their pursuit of long-term and safe return on investment.

In the overseas asset allocation of insurance funds, there is still a large room for the proportion of overseas real estate to rise. Real estate investment accounts for 1.7 and 3.4%, respectively, of the total investment assets of Japan's life insurance and property insurance. The proportion of real estate investment in UK's insurance industry has been higher than 5% for a long time. At present, the proportion of real estate investment in China's insurance industry is still lower than this level, accounting for only about 1%, which is still far from the 30% upper limit set by the regulatory authorizes.

Solvency II framework encourages diversified allocation of insurance assets and encourages insurance funds to be invested in alternative assets. Under the Solvency II framework, the risk factor of real estate investment is somewhat reduced, and the capital consumption is significantly lower than that of stocks and funds.

The insurance characteristics of insurance asset management institutions determine that they are different from general asset management institutions. Due to the liability characteristics of insurance funds, "asset liability matching" and "risk management" are two very important basic principles.

Over the past year, the "black swan" incidents occurred frequently in the international financial market, and the prices of many asset categories witnessed varying degrees of violent fluctuations. It is expected that 2017 will still be a year of violent fluctuations and uncertainties. Market entities should focus on effective control of risks when they allocate assets in complex and changeable overseas markets. With more insurance funds entering the international market for asset allocation, the market will need more risk hedging and risk management tools. How to actively manage risks and make the existing risks measurable, recognizable and controllable will become an important constraint on the overseas asset allocation of insurance funds. It is foreseeable that the demand of market entities for various risk hedging tools in overseas markets will also increase significantly.

Chapter 23
On Treatment Level of China's Basic Endowment Insurance System

23.1 Introduction

In recent years, due to the aging of the population and the reduction of demographic dividend, the unfairness of the endowment insurance system has become a more and more prominent problem and has become the focus of public concern. The government should make efforts to reform the system and eliminate unfair treatment. In early 2014, Premier Li Keqiang pointed out at the executive meeting of the State Council that "it is decided to merge the new rural social endowment insurance and urban social endowment insurance and establish a unified nationwide basic endowment insurance system for urban and rural residents". In 2014, the State Council issued the Opinions on Establishing a Unified Basic Endowment Insurance System for Urban and Rural Residents, stipulating that a unified endowment insurance system for urban and rural residents would be established nationwide.

In January 2015, the State Council issued the "Decision on the Reform of the Endowment Insurance System for the Staff of Government Organs and Institutions", stipulating that nearly 40 million staff of government organs and institutions would pay the same endowment insurance as enterprise employees. After the implementation of the new policy, China's basic endowment system is mainly composed of basic endowment insurance for urban and rural residents and basic endowment insurance for urban workers. The 18th National Congress of the Communist Party of China proposed to achieve "universal coverage of social security". At present, the endowment insurance system for urban enterprise employees has basically achieved full coverage, while the coverage rate of urban and rural residents' endowment insurance is low, and the big difference in treatment is an important reason for the difference in coverage rate. Therefore, it is of great significance to calculate the treatment levels of endowment insurance for urban employees and urban and rural residents, find the treatment gap, and analyze its influencing factors.

There are three methods to measure the treatment level. The first method is to analyze the pension needs of microsubjects from the perspective of survival, so as to get the appropriate pension treatment level [1, 2]. The second is to get the

S. Ba, *The New Cycle and New Finance in China*,
https://doi.org/10.1007/978-981-16-8209-4_23

optimal pension treatment level from the perspective of the whole social welfare by applying the general equilibrium theory. Yang Zaigui [3] and Zhang Yingbin [4] used the overlapping generation's model to simulate the optimal social pension treatment level after reasonable setting of parameters. The third method is institutional, which measures the pension treatment level by measuring the expected income of the insured.

This method needs reasonable setting of parameters, which can include the pension insurance systems with different design mechanisms in the same framework for comparison and analysis of treatment level. China's basic endowment insurance system is composed of basic endowment insurance system for urban enterprise employees and that for urban and rural residents. There are great differences in the design of the two systems. The institutional method is more reasonable if we want to compare the treatment levels and analyze the influencing factors. This method is often used to measure the level of pension treatment at home and abroad.

Feldstein [5] first proposed the concept of pension property and its estimation method to measure the pension treatment level. Later, scholars such as Aldrich [6] and Whiteford [7] used the pension replacement rate index to measure the treatment level of the pension system. Compared with pension property, replacement rate is a relative index, which can measure the treatment level more comprehensively. In China, many scholars used the substitution rate index to compare the treatment levels of different systems. Wang Xiaojun [8] used the substitution rate index to compare the pension treatment levels of government institutions and enterprise employees and found that the treatment level of government institutions is higher than that of enterprise employees. Lin Donghai et al. [9] used the index to calculate the pension treatment levels of the basic endowment insurance for unban employees in 1997 and 2005. Deng Dasong [10] also used this index to calculate the personal account treatment level of China's new rural social endowment insurance and put forward policy suggestions such as raising the payment rate and increasing government subsidies.

Wang Yake [11] put the treatment level of urban workers, government organs and institutions, the new rural social security system and enterprise annuity into a unified framework and concluded that the pension treatment level of urban workers is higher than that of the new rural social security system. After the integration of the new agricultural insurance and the old-age insurance for urban and rural residents in 2014, Xue Huiyuan [12] put the old-age insurance for urban and rural residents and urban workers into a unified framework. By calculating the input–output ratio of the insured, it is found that the return of the old-age insurance for urban workers is higher than that of the old-age insurance for urban and rural residents.

It can be seen that most of the existing literatures focus on the calculation of the treatment level of endowment insurance for urban workers and the new agricultural insurance, and the research on the treatment level of endowment insurance for urban and rural residents is insufficient. Most of the existing studies estimate the treatment level by pension replacement rate, so the indicators to measure the treatment level are relatively single, and there is a lack of sufficient and comprehensive analysis of the treatment level.

OECD [13] held that the gross replacement rate of pension ignores the role and influence of social treatment payment, individual income tax and social average wage and therefore, fails to accurately measure the relative return of pension. The introduction of indicators such as the relative level of pension can more comprehensively measure the treatment level of pension. On this basis, this paper uses the research method of OECD for reference, measures the treatment level of China's basic pension system by using such indicators as gross replacement rate, net replacement rate, gross relative level and net relative level and further discusses the influence and role of retirement age, return on investment and treatment growth mechanism.

This paper intends to measure the treatment level of China's basic endowment system and analyze the differences in treatment. The questions to be discussed in this paper include: what is the level of treatment that urban workers and urban and rural residents can enjoy? And is there any difference between the treatment levels of the two systems? How big is the difference? What are the differences in the treatment levels of groups with different income levels? What are the different treatment levels for different genders? What are the effects of the factors such as delaying retirement age, increasing the rate of return on investment and setting up the return growth mechanism on the level of pension benefits?

This paper makes the following arrangements for the following sections: The second section compares the pension system for urban enterprise employees and that for urban and rural residents from the aspect of premium payment; the third section sets up the model and discusses the rationality of parameter selection; the fourth section analyzes the calculation results and carries out the sensitivity analysis of parameters to explore how the parameters affect the treatment level. In the last section, conclusions are drawn, and policy suggestions are put forward on the basis of the calculation results.

23.2 A Comparison of Systems

Before measuring the treatment level of China's basic endowment insurance system, it is necessary to compare the design of the endowment insurance system for urban workers and that for urban residents. The two systems are different in models and designs, so there are also great differences in the system details, as shown in Table 23.1.

Opinions on Establishing a Unified Basic Endowment Insurance System for Urban and Rural Residents is applicable to the endowment insurance for urban and rural residents, which is a pension plan based on DC (defined contribution). The payment of endowment insurance for urban and rural residents is very simple: Individuals pay at 12 levels, and local governments give a certain degree of subsidies according to the individual payment. In terms of treatment, the central government pays 55 yuan per month for the social pooling account, and the individual account pays the pension according to the previously accumulated calculation and payment coefficient stipulated by the state. The endowment insurance for urban employees consists of

Table 23.1 Comparison of the endowment insurance system for urban employees and that for urban and rural residents

System		Urban employees	Urban and rural residents
Contribution	Social pooling account	20% of wages paid by enterprises (monthly)	None
	Individual account	8% of individuals' salary (monthly)	Individual payment can be divided into 12 levels, between RMB100 and RMB2000 per year. The minimum subsidy of local finance is RMB 30 per year. The minimum subsidy for individual payment above RMB 500 is RMB 60 yuan per year
Retirement age (M / F)		50/60	60
Issuance	Social pooling account	The base is the average value of the local average wage of the previous year and the indexed monthly wage of the insured employee when he retires. 1% of the base will be paid for each full year of the payment period	The central government pays 55 yuan per month
	Individual account	The individual account savings of retired workers divided by the calculation and distribution coefficient prescribed by the state	The amount of savings in an individual account divided by the calculation and distribution coefficient prescribed by the state

two parts: social pooling account and individual account. The social pooling account is defined benefit (DB), type, and the individual account is DC type.

In terms of payment, the proportion of unit payment is 20% of the total wage of the unit, and the proportion of individual payment is 8% of individual wage. From the perspective of treatment, the base of social pooling account is the average value of the local average wage of the previous year and the indexed monthly wage of the insured employee when he retires. 1% of the base will be paid for each full year of the payment period; the pension of individual account is the amount of savings in an individual account divided by the calculation and distribution coefficient prescribed by the state. The pension system estimation model in this study is established on the basis of these rules.

23.3 Model Setting

In this paper, the gross replacement rate, net replacement rate, gross relative level and net relative level are used to measure the treatment level of the endowment insurance for urban workers and urban and rural residents. Among them, gross replacement rate (GRR) refers to the ratio of an individual's pension income to his last year's total wage; net replacement rate (NRR) refers to the ratio of an individual's pension income to his net wage after deducting social security contributions and personal income tax; gross relative level (GRL) is the ratio of individual pension to the average gross social wage in the year of retirement; net relative level (NRL) refers to the ratio of personal pension to the average social net wage in the year of retirement. For a detailed description of these indicators, please refer to the studies of Wang Yake et al. [11].[1] Pension replacement rate shows the replacement of personal pension income for personal wages; the relative level of pension shows the level of personal pension income relative to the average social wage, which can effectively measure the adequacy of pension income. Generally speaking, the net replacement rate is greater than the total replacement rate, and the net relative level is higher than the gross relative level. It can be seen that compared with the gross replacement rate and the gross relative level, the net replacement rate and the relative level can better reflect the treatment level of the pension system.

This paper mainly uses the following actuarial model for data processing and evaluation.

Gross replacement rate (GRR): the ratio of expected annual personal pension to gross income in the year before retirement.

Net replacement rate (NRR): the ratio of individual pension to net income of the year before retirement after deducting social insurance premium. To some extent, it reflects a more real replacement rate.

Gross relative level (GRL): the ratio of individual pension to the average gross social income in the year of retirement.

Net relative level (NRL): the ratio of individual pension to the average net social income after deducting social insurance premium in the year of retirement. It can effectively measure the adequacy of pension income.

This paper constructs the model on the basis of the above four indicators. The model usually assumes that the basic endowment insurance system is sustainable and will remain unchanged in the future; that is, it estimates the treatment level of "new insured persons" under this system. At the same time, some basic parameters need to be set for model construction. We assume that the rate of wage growth is g, the rate of return on investment of individual account is i, the age of insured person is a, and retirement age is r, the individual wage and social average wage at the age of a are W_a and $\overline{W}_a$, respectively, the income tax paid by individuals is T, C_s, C_p and C_g refer to social security payment, individual payment and government subsidy

[1] Wang Yake, Wang Bin, Han Bingjie, Gao Yun. Research on the difference of pension security level in China—Based on the comparative analysis of substitution rate and relative level. *Management world*, 2013, (08): 109–117.

payment, respectively, and the calculation and distribution coefficient of individual account is M.

23.4 Pension Replacement Rate and Relative Level Model of Urban Employees

We take RMB 62,029, the annual average wage of urban employees in 2015, as $\overline{W_a}$. According to the endowment insurance system for urban employees, the lower limit and the upper limit of the payment base are 60% and 300%, respectively, of the social average wage. According to this index, we divide employees into low-income, middle-income and high-income groups; on the basis of this index, low-income group refers to people with income 0.6 to 0.8 times of average social wage; middle-income group refers to people with income 1–1.2 times of average social wage; the high-income group refers to people with income 1.5–3 times of average social wage.

The annual pension income of urban employees when they retire is as follows:

$$\mathrm{PB}_1 = \frac{1}{2}(\overline{W_{a-1}} + \overline{W_{a-1}} \times \frac{1}{N} \times \sum_{n=a}^{r-1} \frac{w_n}{\overline{W_{n-1}}}) \times N\% \times (1+g)^{r-a} + \frac{1}{M} \times \sum_{n=a}^{r-1} w_a \times (1+g)^{(n-a)} \times \mathrm{C}_1 \times (1+i)^{r-1-n}$$

Gross replacement rate

$$GRR_1 = \frac{\frac{1}{2}(\overline{W_{a-1}} + \overline{W_{a-1}} \times \frac{1}{N} \times \sum_{n=a}^{r-1} \frac{w_n}{\overline{W_{n-1}}}) \times N\% \times (1+g)^{r-a} + \frac{1}{M} \times \sum_{n=a}^{r-1} w_a \times (1+g)^{(n-a)} \times \mathrm{C}_1 \times (1+i)^{r-1-n}}{w_a \times (1+g)^{r-1-a}}$$

Net replacement rate

$$NRR_1 = \frac{\frac{1}{2}(\overline{W_{a-1}} + \overline{W_{a-1}} \times \frac{1}{N} \times \sum_{n=a}^{r-1} \frac{w_n}{\overline{W_{n-1}}}) \times N\% \times (1+g)^{r-a} + \frac{1}{M} \times \sum_{n=a}^{r-1} w_a \times (1+g)^{n-a} \times \mathrm{C}_1 \times (1+i)^{r-1-n}}{[w_a \times (1 - C_s) - T] \times (1+g)^{r-1-a}}$$

Gross relative level

$$GRL_1 = \frac{\frac{1}{2}(\overline{W_{a-1}} + \overline{W_{a-1}} \times \frac{1}{N} \times \sum_{n=a}^{r-1} \frac{w_n}{\overline{W_{n-1}}}) \times N\% \times (1+g)^{r-a} + \frac{1}{M} \times \sum_{n=a}^{r-1} w_a \times (1+g)^{n-a} \times \mathrm{C}_1 \times (1+i)^{r-1-n}}{\overline{W_a} \times (1+g)^{r-a}}$$

Net relative level

$$NRL_1 = \frac{\frac{1}{2}(\overline{W_{a-1}} + \overline{W_{a-1}} \times \frac{1}{N} \times \sum_{n=a}^{r-1} \frac{w_n}{W_{n-1}}) \times N\% \times (1+g)^{r-a} + \frac{1}{M} \times \sum_{n=a}^{r-1} w_a \times (1+g)^{n-a} \times C_1 \times (1+i)^{r-1-n}}{\left[\overline{W_a} \times (1 - C_s) - T\right] \times (1+g)^{r-a}}$$

23.5 Pension Replacement Rate and Relative Level Model of Urban and Rural Residents

When setting up the model, the author of this paper will adjust the individual payment and government subsidies of urban and rural residents according to such factors as inflation, economic growth and income level. This study assumes that the annual net income growth rate of urban and rural residents is the same as that of urban workers' wages, and we take the per capita net income of rural residents as a replacement for wage income. As the data of National Bureau of Statistics on the per capita net income of rural residents in China are only updated to RMB 7917 yuan in 2012, for the convenience of research, this paper takes the per capita net income of rural residents in 2012 as the base, estimates the per capita net income of rural residents in 2015 as RMB 9164 with 5% wage growth rate and calculates the pension replacement rate and relative level of rural residents in China. The rural residents who participate in the endowment insurance for urban and rural residents are flexible workforce, and most of their work units are private small enterprises. We take RMB 39,589, the average wage of employees in rural private small enterprises in 2015, as $\overline{W}_a$.

When calculating the pension treatment level of urban and rural residents, in order to compare with the income level of urban workers, the farmers with an income 0.6 time, 0.8 time, 1 time, 1.2 times, 1.5 times, 2 times and 3 times of the rural per capita net income pay at the seven levels of RMB 100, RMB 200, RMB 300, RMB 400, RMB 500, RMB 600 and RMB 700, respectively, so as to distinguish the difference of replacement rate caused by different payments by different income groups in rural areas; the corresponding local government subsidies are RMB30, RMB 40, RMB 50, RMB 60, RMB 70, RMB 80 and RMB 90, respectively; The urban residents with an income 0.6 time, 0.8 time, 1 time, 1.2 times, 1.5 times, 2 times and 3 times of the unban per capita net income pay at the seven levels of RMB 600, RMB 700, RMB 800, RMB 900, RMB 1000, RMB 1500 and RMB 2000, respectively. The corresponding local government subsidies are RMB 60, RMB 65, RMB 70, RMB 75, RMB 80, RMB 85 and RMB 90, respectively.

The annual pension income of urban employees when they retire is as follows:

$$PB_2 = (12 \times 55) \times (1+g)^{r-a} + \frac{1}{M} \sum_{n=a}^{r-1} (C_p + C_g) \times (1+g)^{n-a} \times (1+i)^{r-1-n}$$

Gross replacement rate

$$GRR_2 = \frac{(12 \times 55) \times (1+g)^{r-a} + \frac{1}{M}\sum_{y=a}^{n-1}(C_p + C_g) \times (1+g)^{n-a} \times (1+i)^{r-1-n}}{w_a \times (1+g)^{r-1-a}}$$

Net replacement rate

$$NRR_2 = \frac{(12 \times 55) \times (1+g)^{r-a} + \frac{1}{M}\sum_{n=a}^{r-1}(C_p + C_g) \times (1+g)^{n-a} \times (1+i)^{r-1-n}}{(w_a - C_p - T) \times (1+g)^{r-1-a}}$$

Gross relative level

$$GRL_2 = \frac{(12 \times 55) \times (1+g)^{r-a} + \frac{1}{M}\sum_{n=a}^{n-1}(C_p + C_g) \times (1+g)^{n-a} \times (1+i)^{r-1-n}}{\overline{W_a} \times (1+g)^{r-a}}$$

Net relative level

$$NRL_2 = \frac{(12 \times 55) \times (1+g)^{r-a} + \frac{1}{M}\sum_{n=a}^{n-1}(C_p + C_g) \times (1+g)^{n-a} \times (1+i)^{r-1-n}}{\left[\overline{W_a} \times (1 - C_p) - T\right] \times (1+g)^{r-a}}$$

23.6 Parameter Hypothesis

In order to get a reasonable pension replacement rate and relative level, we need to set some parameters. We assume that the insured enter the labor market at the age of 25, and their personal wages increase synchronously with the average social wages, which means that their position in the overall income distribution remains unchanged. At present, the legal retirement age in China is 60 years old for male employees and 50 or 55 years old for female employees. Therefore, assuming that the calculation and payment coefficient of individual account pension is M, different retirement ages correspond to different calculation and payment coefficient M. If the retirement age is 50 years old, M is 195/12; if the retirement age is 55 years old, M is 170/12; if the retirement age is 60 years old, M is 139/12; if the retirement age is 65 years old, M is 101/12. When calculating net income, we need to consider the impact of social security individual payment and individual income tax. Specifically speaking, the social security contributions of urban employees include 8% of endowment insurance, 2% of medical insurance and 0.5% of unemployment

Table 23.2 CPI Growth Rate, Wage Growth Rate and Return on Investment (Unit: %)

Year	2007	2008	2009	2010	2011	2012	2013	2014
GDP growth rate	14.2	9.7	9.4	10.6	9.5	7.9	7.8	7.3
Wage growth rate of urban employee	18.5	16.9	11.6	13.3	14.4	11.9	10.1	9.5
Weighted return rate of enterprise annuity	41	−1.8	7.8	3.4	−0.8	5.7	3.7	9.3
CPI growth rate	4.8	5.9	−0.7	3.3	5.4	2.6	2.6	2.0

insurance,[2] and they pay personal income tax after deducting these social security contributions.[3]

According to *China Statistical Yearbook 2015* and *National Enterprise Annuity Data*[4] issued by the Ministry of Human Resources and Social Security, we can get the data as shown in Table 23.2.

23.7 Results of the Calculation of the Treatment Level

In this chapter, the author mainly uses the actuarial model mentioned above to calculate the differences in the treatment levels of different basic endowment insurance systems, that is, the gross replacement rate (GRR), net replacement rate (NRR), gross relative level (GRL) and net relative level (NRL) of urban workers and urban and rural residents with different income levels under their respective pension treatment systems within the same framework. See Table 23.3 for the results of the calculation through the actuarial model.

As for the middle-income group in the pension system for urban employees, the treatment level of insured male employees is higher than that of insured female employees. In the pension system for urban and rural residents, the treatment level of insured rural residents is higher than that of insured urban residents, and the treatment level of pension system for urban employees is higher than that of the pension system for urban and rural residents. Take the middle-income group with an income one time of the average social wage as an example. The GRR and NRR of urban male employees are 60% and 72.2%, respectively, while the GRR and NRR of urban female employees are 37.9% and 45.9%, respectively, showing a gap of 22.1% and 26.3%, respectively. The GRR and NRR of urban residents are 8.4%

[2] Unemployment insurance rates vary from place to place, ranging from 0 to 1%. We assume that unemployment insurance rate remains unchanged at 0.5%.

[3] At present, China's individual income tax adopts seven levels of progressive tax rate, and the starting point is RMB 3,500. We assume that this method of taxation is sustainable, and annuity income will also be taxed in the future according to this method.

[4] Ministry of Human Resources and Social Security: *National Enterprise Annuity Data* 2015 http://www.mohrss.gov.cn/gkml/xxgk/201603/t20160331_ 236,972. html.

Table 23.3 Replacement rate and relative level of different pension systems (Unit: %)

Income level		Indicator	Urban employees		Urban and rural residents	
			Male	Female	Urban areas	Rural areas
Low income	0.6	GRR	71.7	46.3	11.3	19.7
		NRR	80.1	51.7	16.2	25.3
		GRL	41.0	26.4	6.5	11.3
		NRL	49.62	32.0	8.5	18.6
	0.8	GRR	64.4	41.1	9.5	19.3
		NRR	74.5	47.5	9.6	28.8
		GRL	49.1	31.3	7.2	14.7
		NRL	59.4	37.9	9.5	24.3
Middle income	1	GRR	60.0	37.9	8.4	19.1
		NRR	72.7	45.9	11.1	31.5
		GRL	57.2	36.1	8.0	18.2
		NRL	69.3	43.7	10.5	30.0
	1.2	GRR	57.1	35.8	7.7	18.9
		NRR	69.5	43.6	9.9	33.6
		GRL	65.3	41.0	8.8	21.6
		NRL	79.1	49.6	11.6	35.6
High income	1.5	GRR	54.2	33.8	6.7	17.6
		NRR	66.2	41.2	8.6	31.2
		GRL	77.4	48.2	9.5	25.1
		NRL	93.8	58.4	12.6	41.3
	2	GRR	51.3	31.7	6.9	15.0
		NRR	66.6	41.2	9.7	24.7
		GRL	97.7	60.3	13.2	28.6
		NRL	118.3	73.1	17.4	47.0
	3	GRR	48.4	29.6	5.9	11.2
		NRR	65.7	40.2	8.1	16.1
		GRL	138.2	84.6	16.9	32.0
		NRL	167.4	102.4	22.3	52.7

and 11.1%, respectively, while the GRR and NRR of rural residents are 19.1% and 31.5%, respectively, showing a gap of 10.7% and 20.4%, respectively. In the pension system for urban workers, the GRR and NRR of urban female employees with the lowest level of treatment are still 18.8% and 14.4% higher than the indicators for rural residents with the highest level of treatment. From the indicator of relative level, we can find the same rule.

As for the low-income group, the treatment level of male employees is still higher than that of female employees in the pension system for urban employees, the treatment level of rural residents is still higher than that of urban residents, and the treatment level of urban employees is still higher than that of urban and rural residents. It can be seen from the index of replacement rate that the treatment of low-income group is higher than that of middle-income group under both the pension system for unban employees and the pension system for urban and rural residents. It can be seen from the index of relative level that the treatment of low-income group is lower than that of middle-income group. For example, the GRR, NRR, GRL and NRL were 71.7%, 80.1%, 41% and 49.6%, respectively, for urban male employees, and 46.3%, 51.7%, 26.4% and 32%, respectively, for urban female employees. The GRR, NRR, GRL and NRL were 11.3%, 16.2%, 6.5% and 8.5%, respectively, for urban residents and 19.7%, 25.3%, 11.3% and 18.6%, respectively, for rural residents.

As for the high-income group, the treatment level of men is still higher than that of women, the treatment level of rural residents is still higher than that of the urban residents, and the treatment level of urban employees is higher than urban and rural residents, but the gap between the treatment of urban employees and that of urban and rural residents is narrowing. As for net replacement rate, because individuals with higher income need to pay more individual income tax, the net replacement rate of all systems has increased, and the higher the income is, the more significant the role of social security payment and individual income tax, and the greater the rise of net replacement rate will be. As for the relative level, with the increase of income level, the relative level provided by the two systems also increases. Although the replacement rate of the people with higher income has declined, their security level is higher than that of the group with average social wage.

Generally speaking, in the pension system for urban employees, the treatment level of the insured male employees is higher than that of the insured female employees. This is mainly due to the design of pension system for urban workers with the incentive concept of "those who contribute more will be paid more". The retirement age of male is later than that of female, resulting in longer contribution period and more contribution.

In the endowment insurance for urban and rural residents, although it is assumed that the payment of urban residents is higher than that of rural residents, the treatment level of urban residents is lower than that of rural residents. This is mainly because the income of urban residents is higher than that of rural residents, and the improvement of treatment level in the design of the endowment insurance for urban and rural residents is slower than that of income level. It can be seen from the two systems that, regardless of the income level, the treatment level of urban employees is higher than that of urban and rural residents. This is mainly because urban employees have higher income and pay more, while urban and rural residents have lower income and pay less.

From the perspective of replacement rate, both the treatment level of urban employees and that of urban and rural residents decrease with the increase of income level. For example, the gross replacement rate of urban male employees decreased from 71.7 to 48.4%, and that of urban female employees decreased from 46.3 to

19.1%; the gross replacement rate of urban residents decreased from 11.3 to 5.9%, and that of rural residents decreased from 19.7 to 11.2%. As for urban employees, the social pooling account plays a role of redistribution, thus improving the treatment of low-income group while reducing that of high-income group, which fully reflects the fairness of the system. As for urban and rural residents, the individuals pay more, and the local governments provide more subsidies accordingly, but because the payment has limited incentive effect, and the improvement of payment level is slower than that of income level, so the replacement rate still presents a downward trend. From the indicator of relative level, we can see that the treatment levels provided by the two systems increase with the increase of income level. At the same time, the treatment gap between urban employees and urban and rural residents also expands with the increase of income level, which shows that the incentive of "those who contribute more will be paid more" is better than that of urban and rural residents. For example, when the insured have an income 0.6 times of the average social wage, the treatment gap between the urban male employees and the rural residents is 29.7%, and the treatment gap between the urban female employees and the urban residents is 20%. As for the insured with an income three times of the average social wage, the treatment gap between the urban male employees and the rural residents is 106.2%, and the treatment gap between the urban female employees and the urban residents is 52.6%.

23.8 Sensitivity Analysis

From the actuarial model, we can see that the retirement age, the rate of return on investment and the setting of treatment growth mechanism have an important impact on the pension treatment level. Next, we select the gross replacement rate of middle-income group for sensitivity analysis. An analysis of other income levels and indicators show the same characteristics, so we will not analyze them one by one.

23.9 Retirement Age

On November 12, 2013, it is pointed out in Decision of the Central Committee of the Communist Party of China on Several Major Issues Concerning Comprehensively Deepening Reform that "we will study and work out a policy to progressively raise the retirement age". In recent years, the Ministry of Human Resources and Social Security has also proposed to implement this policy. It can be seen that raising the retirement age is the reform trend of China's pension insurance system in the future. Based on this, we estimate the impact of raising the retirement age on the pension replacement rate. The results are shown in Fig. 23.1.

From Fig. 23.1, we can see that if the retirement age of urban employees is raised from 55 to 65, the replacement rate will rise from 47.7% to 79%, up 31.3%.

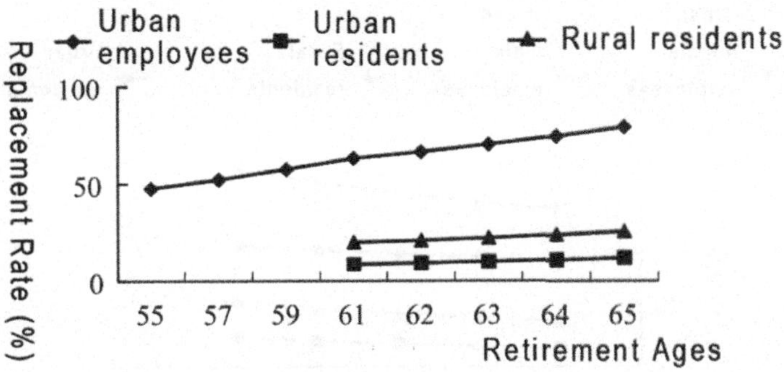

Fig. 23.1 Gross replacement rate at different retirement ages

When the retirement age of urban and rural residents is raised from 60 to 65, the replacement rate of urban residents will rise from 8.4% to 12.2%, and that of rural residents will rise from 19.1% to 25.7%, up 3.8% and 6.6%, respectively. The gross replacement rate is positively correlated with the extension of the retirement age. The later the retirement age is, the higher the replacement rate will be. This is because the extension of retirement age means the increase of contribution years and the accumulation of pension, so the replacement rate will increase accordingly. However, with the extension of retirement age, the treatment levels provided by the two systems continue to increase, and there is a greater increase in the treatment level of urban employees than that of urban and rural residents.

23.10 Return on Investment

According to the policies of basic endowment insurance, the interest of individual account is calculated according to the bookkeeping interest rate stipulated by the state every year. In August 2015, the State Council issued the Investment Measures for Basic Endowment Insurance Funds, stating clearly that we should carry out centralized and market-oriented operation of the basic endowment insurance funds for staff of government organs and institutions. The provincial governments collect the pension funds that can be invested into the provincial social security special account and entrust the funds to the pension fund management institutions authorized by the State Council for investment management. The measures stressed that in the investment and operation of pension funds, we must adhere to the principle of safety first and strictly control risks. The investment and operation of the funds should be diversified, and the funds should be allocated through multiple portfolio schemes to maintain a reasonable investment structure.

Assuming that an individual's wage growth rate is 5%, we calculate the change of replacement rate when the rate of return on investment changes from 2 to 6%. The results are shown in Fig. 23.2.

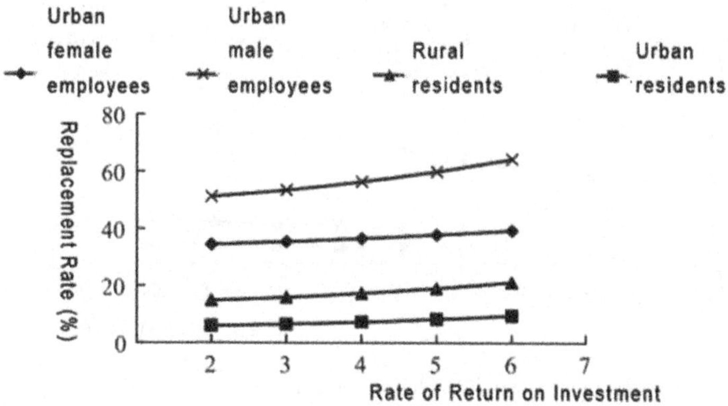

Fig. 23.2 Gross replacement rate under different of rate of return on investment

Since the growth rate of individual wage remains constant at 5%, when the rate of return on investment changes between 2 and 5%, the rate of personal wage growth will be higher than the rate of return on investment. When the rate of return on investment is 5%, the rate of personal wage growth will be the same as the rate of return on investment; when the rate of return on investment changes between 5 and 6%, the rate of personal wage growth will be lower than the rate of return on investment. From the results in Fig. 23.2, we can see that, whether it is urban employees or urban and rural residents, the gross replacement rate increases with the growth of return on investment. The replacement rate of urban male employees increased from 51.3% to 64.4% and that of urban female employees increased from 34.5% to 39.4%, up 13.1% and 4.9%, respectively. The replacement rate of rural residents increased from 14.9% to 21.2% and that of urban residents increased from 6% to 9.6%, up 6.3% and 3.6%, respectively. We can see that the treatment level of the pension system for urban and rural residents and urban employees improves with the increase of the rate of return on investment.

23.11 Treatment Growth Mechanism

In China's pension system, the individual account keeps value and increases in value through investment, while social pools are affected by the treatment growth mechanism, which, therefore, is also one of the important factors affecting the level of pension treatment. In the world, the mainstream way to adjust the pension treatment growth mechanism is to adjust the pension according to the consumer price index or the average wage growth rate of on-the-job employees. Therefore, we assume that the other parameters remain unchanged, and the treatment growth mechanism is adjusted according to the real wage growth rate. Influenced by historical payment wage level, the growth of retirees' pension will not be fully synchronized with the

Table 23.4 Gross replacement rate under different treatment growth mechanisms (Unit: %)

Age	Urban employees			Urban residents			Rural residents		
	50%	70%	80%	50%	70%	80%	50%	70%	80%
60	60.0	60.0	60.0	8.4	8.4	8.4	19.1	19.1	19.1
65	56.0	57.6	58.4	7.4	7.8	8.0	16.9	17.8	18.2
70	52.4	55.2	56.8	6.6	7.3	7.6	15.0	16.5	17.4
75	49.2	53.1	55.3	5.9	6.8	7.3	13.3	15.4	16.5
80	46.3	51.1	53.8	5.2	6.3	6.9	11.8	14.3	15.8
85	43.8	49.2	52.4	4.6	5.9	6.6	10.5	13.3	15.0
90	41.6	47.5	51.1	4.1	5.5	6.3	9.3	12.4	14.3

wage growth of employees. Assuming that the increase of treatment is 50%, 70% and 80% of the real wage growth rate, respectively, we will measure the impact of different treatment growth mechanisms on the gross replacement rate of urban employees and urban and rural residents. Assuming that the insured persons receive pension from 60 to 90 years old, we study the effect of treatment growth mechanism on the gross replacement rate under different conditions. The results are shown in Table 23.4.

It can be seen from Table 23.4 that, assuming that the monetary wages grow at 50%, 70% and 80%, and that the insured persons survive from 60 to 90 years old, for the pension system for urban employees, the gross replacement rate decreases from 60% to 41.6%, 47.5% and 51.1%; that of urban residents decreases from 8.4% to 4.1%, 5.5% and 6.3%; that of rural residents decreases from 19.1% to 9.3%, 12.4% and 14.3%. We can see clearly that, whether for the pension system for urban employees or that for urban and rural residents, the higher the monetary wage growth set by the treatment growth mechanism, the smaller the decline of the gross replacement rate and the higher the treatment level of the insured. Therefore, setting up a reasonable growth mechanism is the key factor to improve the level of pension treatment.

23.12 Conclusion and Policy Suggestions

Through the previous analysis, we find that, no matter from the replacement rate or the relative level, the treatment level provided by the endowment insurance system for urban employee is much higher than that of urban and rural residents. Gender and income level have an important impact on pension treatment level. In the endowment insurance system for urban employees, the treatment level of urban male employees is much higher than that of urban female employees, because men retire at an older age and pay more money into pensions.

In the endowment insurance system for urban and rural residents, the treatment level of rural residents is higher than that of urban residents probably because the income of rural residents is lower than that of urban residents, but there is little difference in the expected income of pension. Therefore, the ratio of expected income of pension to personal income of rural residents is higher than that of urban residents. At the same time, we also find that retirement age, return on investment and treatment growth mechanism have an important impact on the endowment insurance of urban employees and urban and rural residents. With the extension of the retirement age and the improvement of the rate of return on investment, the level of pension treatment of urban employees witnesses a higher increase than that of urban and rural residents. This is mainly due to the different incentive mechanisms of the two endowment insurance systems. The endowment insurance for urban and rural residents pays more attention to ensuring the basic security, while the endowment insurance for urban enterprise employees not only pays attention to ensuring the basic security, but also reflects the incentive concept of "those who pay more into pensions will be paid more".

From the perspective of system design, urban employees and urban and rural residents have different ways of paying into the pensions and getting paid, resulting in a big gap in pension treatment, which is very unfair and will lead to public criticism of the government. Therefore, it is suggested that the gap should be appropriately narrowed by increasing financial input at all levels, endowment insurance payment subsidies and basic pension of urban and rural residents. At the same time, we should implement the Interim Measures for the Link of Urban and Rural Endowment Insurance Systems, simplify the transfer procedures between the two systems and effectively protect the rights and interests of the insured persons in the transfer between the systems. The retirement age, the return on investment and the treatment growth mechanisms have a very important impact on the treatment level. At present, problems such as low return on investment, extended retirement age and poor treatment growth mechanism will have a negative impact on the treatment level of the insured. To solve these problems, system designers need to take a series of reform measures. First of all, we should promote the market-oriented operation of endowment insurance funds as soon as possible to improve the return on investment. Secondly, we should implement the policy of raising the retirement age as soon as possible. At present, due to different personal preferences and working environment, different insured persons hold different attitudes toward extended retirement age. Therefore, we can provide insured persons with more options concerning extended retirement age so as to reduce the pressure brought by the policy. Finally, the normal adjustment mechanism of basic pension should be established as soon as possible within the financial affordability of governments at all levels. At present, there is still no specific and detailed treatment growth mechanism for China's pension insurance, so it is necessary to formulate relevant rules as soon as possible to improve the level of pension treatment.

References

1. Bian Shu, Mu Huaizhong. Research on Micro Measurement and Dynamic Adjustment of the Appropriate Level of Rural Endowment Insurance [J]. *Social Security Research*, 2011, (06): 3-11.
2. Mu Huaizhong, Shen Yi. Research on the Path and Level of Endowment for Chinese Farmers with or without Land[J]. *China Soft Science*, 2012, (12): 78-89.
3. Yang Zaigui. Basic Endowment Insurance, Pension Replacement Rate and Population Growth Rate of Enterprise Employees[J]. *Statistical Research*, 2008, (05): 39-42
4. Zhang Yingbin, Liu Zhixin, Bo Manying, Luo Qiyao. Research on the Equilibrium System and Optimal Replacement Rate of China's Social Basic Endowment InsuranceAn Empirical Analysis Based on Intertemporal Iterative Model[J]. *Financial Research*, 2013, (01): 79-91.
5. Feldstein, MS. Social Security, Induced Retirement and Aggregate Capital Formation[J]. *Journal of Political Economy*, 1974(82): 905-926.
6. Aldrich, J. The Earnings Replacement Rate of Old-age Benefits in 12 Countries, 1969-80[J]. *Social Security Bulletin*, 1982, 45(11): 3-11.
7. Whiteford P. The Use of Replacement Rates in International Comparisons of Benefit Systems [J]. *International Social Security Review*, 1995, 48(2): 3-30.
8. Wang Xiaojun, Qiao Yang. Analysis on the gap of pension treatment between enterprises and institutions in China [J]. *Statistical Research*, 2007, (05): 36-40.
9. Lin Donghai, Ding Yu. New pension policy: Calculation of replacement rate of old and new pension policies [J]. *Population and Economy*, 2007, (01): 69-74.
10. Deng DASONG, Xue Huiyuan. Analysis of the difficulties in the implementation of the new rural social endowment insurance system—Also on the financing ability of individuals, collectives and governments [J]. *Economic System Reform*, 2010, (01): 86–92.
11. Wang Yake, Wang Bin, Han Bingjie, Gao Yun. Research on the difference of pension security level in China—Based on the comparative analysis of substitution rate and relative level [J]. *Management world*, 2013, (08): 109-117.
12. Xue Huiyuan, Wang Fan. Is it cost-effective to participate in the basic endowment insurance for urban workers? —on the input and output of the basic endowment insurance for urban workers [J]. *Economy and Management*, 2016, (06): 50-57.
13. OECD. Pensions at a Glance: Public Policies Across OECD Countries 2005 Edition Complete[J]. *Source OECD Social Issues/migration/health*, 2005(6): i-195(196).
14. OECD. Pensions at a Glance 2011: Retirement-Income System in OECD and G20 Countries[J]. *Source OECD Finance and Investment/Insurance and Pensions*, 2011(2): i-350(351).
15. National Bureau of statistics. *China Statistical Yearbook (2015)* [M]. Beijing: China Statistics Press, 2015.
16. Whitehouse, E. Pension systems in 15 countries compared: the value of entitlements[R]. *MPRA Papers*, 2001, (02/04).

Chapter 24
On Loan Guarantee Insurance of Micro and Small Enterprises in China

As an important part of the national economy, small and micro enterprises play an important role in China's economic development. Especially since the reform and opening up, with the gradual establishment of the market economy system, small and micro enterprises have been playing a great role in providing employment opportunities, increasing fiscal revenue, expanding export and promoting the growth of GDP. The effective supply and utilization of funds is an important driving force to promote the development of small and micro enterprises.

However, for a long time, due to poor financial system and lack of credit, small and micro enterprises have been facing financing difficulties. In addition, the economic crisis led to the overall economic downturn. Under this backdrop, the rise of factor prices and the imbalance between product supply and demand make the enterprise's profit margin continue to decrease. Small and micro enterprises are facing capital shortage, but they have insufficient repayment ability, making it more difficult to get loans from banks, which seriously restricts their development. At present, the government and financial institutions are faced with the problem of how to reduce the risk of loans and further increase the number of loans to small and micro enterprises.

In this context, the introduction of loan guarantee insurance has brought a solution to the financing problem of small and micro enterprises. It will not only improve the credit level and solve the financing difficulties of small and micro enterprises, but also strengthen the guarantee for loan providers, reduce the cost of internal risk control, relieve the worries after granting loans and help banks enter the financial market of small and micro enterprises. Better financing environment contributes to the rapid development of small and micro enterprises.

S. Ba, *The New Cycle and New Finance in China*,
https://doi.org/10.1007/978-981-16-8209-4_24

24.1 Overview of Loan Guarantee Insurance and Current Pilot Project

24.1.1 Overview of Loan Guarantee Insurance

Loan guarantee insurance is a type of insurance in which the right holder insures the credit risk of the debtor directly from the insurer. It is an insurance business used to manage enterprise risks, a guarantee insurance contract in which the debtor (the borrower) pays the premium to the insurer, and the insurer, in accordance with the agreement, makes compensation within the insured amount when the debtor fails to repay the loan granted by the insured (i.e. bank) as agreed in the loan contract.

Loan guarantee insurance system or similar system has been widely adopted in developed countries, especially in Japan. China began to carry out its guarantee insurance business relatively late, which mainly includes automobile consumer credit performance insurance and housing loan performance insurance. But the loan guarantee insurance for small and micro enterprises is still in the experimental stage. In terms of legislation, since the 1980s, the promulgation of Regulations of the People's Republic of China on Property Insurance, Interim Regulations on Insurance Enterprises and Insurance Law of the People's Republic of China marks the continuous improvement of China's insurance legislation. In the new insurance law of 2009, guarantee insurance is clearly listed under property insurance, which stipulates that "the business of insurance companies includes property loss insurance, liability insurance, credit insurance, guarantee insurance and other insurance business". It was the first time for guarantee insurance to appear in insurance law.

According to the experience of developed countries, loans through different forms of insurance, as a new way to solve the financing problem of China's small and micro enterprises, can reduce and pass on credit risk, indirectly improve the credit rating and financing ability, reduce the information asymmetry between the parties and break the financing bottleneck caused by small assets and weak solvency of small and micro enterprises.

24.1.2 Pilot Projects of Loan Guarantee Insurance

In September 2009, the government departments of Ningbo City began to promote the project of urban and rural small loan guarantee insurance. Whether enterprises can obtain insurance coverage is mainly determined by the risk control departments of banks and insurance companies. The default risk of enterprises is mainly shared by banks and insurance institutions. The Ningbo municipal government has established an excess compensation mechanism to provide reasonable compensation for the part of the total compensation under the insurance that exceeds 150% of that year's premium income. As of 2012, it has helped more than 1400 small and micro enterprises to get loans of more than RBM1.4 billion and has paid compensation of more than RMB1.2 million. Many enterprises have obtained bank loans for the first time.

In the Ningbo model, the procedure of applying for small loan guarantee insurance business is as follows: The enterprises submit application materials to banks or insurance companies, and the banks and insurance companies, respectively, review the submitted materials, investigate in enterprises, sign contracts and issue loans after they find out that the enterprises meet the conditions. The insurance institution undertakes the insurance liability for the principal and interest of the loan with the premium collected. Once the borrower of the small loan owes interest for more than three months continuously or fails to repay the principal within one month after the maturity of the loan, the bank fails to collect the principal, and the insurance institution shall compensate the bank according to the agreement. With the risk sharing mechanism, the banks are better protected from default risks of small loans, which enhance their willingness to grant loans to small and micro enterprises. Insurance strengthens the risk sharing mechanism, in which insurance institutions and loan issuers share the risks. Once the loss of loan principal occurs, the pilot bank and the operation center of small loan guarantee insurance will share the loss in the proportion of 3:7. The latter is an insurance corporate body composed of PICC Property Insurance Ningbo Branch and Pacific Property Insurance Ningbo Branch. They share premiums and risks according to a certain proportion. In addition, the RMB 10 million excess compensation fund set up by the government finance also provides more protection for the small loan guarantee insurance.

There are about 569,000 small and micro enterprises in Zhejiang Province, many of which do not meet the credit conditions of banks, so it is difficult for them to obtain loans. In 2011, the pilot project of small loan guarantee insurance was launched in Zhejiang Province. The cooperation between banks and insurance companies as well as that between small loan institutions and insurance companies makes it possible for these enterprises to obtain loans.

In September 2012, PICC Property Insurance Chongqing Branch signed a cooperation agreement with ICBC Chongqing Branch and began to carry out micro loan guarantee insurance as a pilot project. In the pilot project, the small and micro enterprises that have obtained the loan guarantee insurance loan should have the ability to fulfill the contract, good credit record, good market for products and the ability to repay the debt. Small and micro enterprises can obtain a loan of up to RMB3 million, and the loan cost is effectively reduced. The interest rate for the loan will not exceed 30% of the benchmark loan interest rate, and the insurance premium will not exceed 2.3% of the loan principal during the pilot period. Small and micro enterprises that meet the conditions of government support can also enjoy preferential treatment according to relevant policies.

In October 2011, the State Council issued nine financial, fiscal and taxation policies and measures to support the development of small and micro enterprises, including increasing credit support, widening financing channels and actively developing loan guarantee insurance and credit insurance for small and micro enterprises. In December 2011, the CIRC also required insurance companies to play a role in increasing insurance credit and improve credit risk management.

Ping An Insurance Co., Ltd. took the lead to respond to the national policy and launched the loan guarantee insurance business for small and micro enterprises on March 30, 2012. The company has launched the most thorough marketization of loan guarantee insurance, targeting small and micro enterprises in all industries in six pilot areas, including the six cities of Shanghai, Qingdao, Kunming, Fuzhou and Guangzhou. In the past year, it has carried out business for more than 100 small and micro enterprises, with insurance totaling more than RMB100 million. Only one city witnessed a high non-performing rate. Ping An adopted the credit records of the People's Bank of China on personal and corporate credit information. In addition, insurance underwriting specialists were employed in the pilot cities to get the specific information of small and micro enterprises through on-the-spot investigation, so as to effectively improve the quality of underwriting.

The loan guarantee insurance still occupies a very small market share in the overall insurance market, it is still seriously unbalanced in its development in various regions throughout the country, and the pilot development of loan guarantee insurance is utterly an inadequate measure. In addition, the insurance in the pilot project is short-term insurance, and the insurance period is only one year. Although short-term insurance can help insurance companies effectively control the cost, it is not conducive to the long-term risk data collection, risk control management and design of loan guarantee insurance products for small and micro enterprises.

24.2 Literature Review

In the financing of China's small and micro enterprises, the loans from commercial banks account for a large proportion. However, due to the low credit rating, it is difficult for small and micro enterprises to obtain loans. Financing difficulty is a major problem hindering the development of small and micro enterprises. Researchers have been carried out in this respect.

Wei (2010) pointed out that the alleviation of the financing difficulties of small and micro enterprises calls for the joint efforts of the banks, governments and society. The government should strengthen policy support and encourage banks to innovate and reform the financing channels in an optimized social environment, so as to provide more financial support for small and micro enterprises.

Xiong (2010) believes that the main reason for the difficulties in the development of small and micro enterprises is that there are few financing channels with insufficient funds for the operation of enterprises. The short life cycle, poor credit, insufficient collateral, asymmetric information with financial institutions, social environment and laws and policies have all caused the financing difficulties of small and micro enterprises. The article mentioned that only by combining the government, market system, self-development and legislation, can we effectively solve the financing problem of small and micro enterprises.

As for the guarantee insurance, the researchers believe that the introduction of loan guarantee insurance plays an important role in solving the financing problem of small- and medium-sized enterprises.

Zeng Ming pointed out that the financing difficulties of for small- and medium-sized enterprises can be effectively solved through loan guarantee insurance, which can be carried out through the combination of policy financial institutions and commercial insurance institutions. It can start as policy insurance, and then, commercial insurance can be introduced, so as to jointly solve the financing problem.

Zhuang (2003) discussed the feasibility and significance of the loan guarantee insurance system for small- and medium-sized enterprises. The article pointed out that the introduction of insurance mechanism can ravel out the concerns of banks after granting loans, improve the security of loans and provide guarantee for enterprise repayment. Insurance institutions should start loan guarantee insurance business for small- and medium-sized enterprises.

Bao et al. (2007) believed that the credit guarantee insurance system for small- and medium-sized enterprises should be established in China. They analyzed the feasibility and possible difficulties of establishing this system from many aspects and put forward the general idea for the establishment of this system.

The above researches briefed us on the financing difficulties that small and micro enterprises are facing and believed that we should introduce loan guarantee insurance as a way to ease the financing difficulties and help the healthy development of enterprises. This paper attempts to discuss the necessity, operation mode, existing risks and improvement suggestions of loan guarantee insurance.

24.3 Significance of Loan Guarantee Insurance

First, it helps to ease the information asymmetry between banks and enterprises. The unstable operation of small and micro enterprises and imperfect financial system make it difficult for banks to measure their risks, giving rise to serious information asymmetry. Besides, it is difficult for banks to evaluate the operation and financial conditions of enterprises before granting loans. Some enterprises deliberately conceal the true financial status from banks or forge financial statements, which might lead to the risk of adverse selection. In addition, banks lack the ability to control the actual use of funds after granting loans. In many cases, loans are used for high-risk investment and business activities. The moral hazard of enterprises increases the default risk of bank loans and makes it difficult for the banks to collect loans. After the introduction of loan guarantee insurance, insurance companies can get the credit status of insured companies through professional credit investigation, which helps to ease the information asymmetry of both sides of loan transaction and provide loan guarantee insurance to qualified loan applicants. The professional risk management ability of insurance companies will help banks control the default risk of enterprises applying for loans.

Secondly, it effectively reduces the financing cost of small and micro enterprises. The combination of insurance and loans effectively makes up for the deficiency of credit guarantee mechanism. Loan guarantee insurance results in reduced risk of lending and broadened scope of financial services. At the same time, the government subsidy for insurance expenditure reduces the financing cost.

Finally, it can effectively make up for the lack of credit guarantee and thus improve the financing ability of small and micro enterprises. Small and micro enterprises have difficulties in obtaining loans largely because they lack credit guarantee, and as a result, banks are unwilling to grant loans. Many problems existed during the development of credit guarantee institutions in China, such as disordered governance structure, lack of guarantee fund management, mismatch between risk and return and blind development in pursuit of profits. The credit guarantee institutions are faced with credit risks themselves because of these problems. Through the introduction of loan guarantee insurance, insurance companies bear part of the credit risk, and enterprises are able to obtain bank loans with less collateral. Besides, it reduces the risk of guarantee institutions, enabling these institutions to achieve sustainable development, improve their guarantee ability and help more enterprises to get loans.

24.4 Operation and Risk Control of Loan Guarantee Insurance

24.4.1 Operation of Loan Guarantee Insurance for Small and Micro Enterprises

Small and micro enterprises apply for loans from banks. The banks implement the unified audit standard and strictly examine the enterprises that meet the industrial policies and standards according to the examination procedure before granting loans. They should clarify the amount, purpose, term and repayment method of the loans and sign the loan contract after the audit.

Enterprises buy loan guarantee insurance policy. In order to prevent the enterprise from breaking the contract and bear the risk brought by the enterprise's failure to repay the loan due to unintentional reasons, the enterprise takes the loan principal and interest as the subject to take out the loan guarantee insurance from the insurance company; the insurance company signs the insurance contract with the enterprise after audit and bears the risk of breach of contract.

Bank grants loans. After signing the loan contract with the enterprise, the bank grants the loan to the enterprise. The bank should monitor the whole process of loan operation to verify the use of loan funds, so as to avoid higher risks caused by enterprises diverting funds for other purposes.

The insurance companies take out insurance from the reinsurance companies. The loan guarantee insurance transfers the credit risk to the insurance company. The insurance requires professional knowledge. However, at present, China's insurance companies lack relevant technology and experience, so the insurance companies are facing huge risks. The reinsurance is established to transfer the risks of insurance companies, which can help control the risks within a certain range, expand the underwriting capacity of insurance companies and promote the development of loan guarantee insurance.

The borrower uses the loan funds and repays the principal and interest of the loan funds according to the loan contract signed with the bank.

The insurance company pays insurance compensation to the bank. When a small and micro enterprise is unable to repay the loan, the bank determines that the borrower is in breach of contract and the bank can apply to the insurance company for claim settlement. After the insurance company confirms that it is within the scope of the insurance contract, it will pay the bank compensation according to the scope of retention, and the compensation amount shall not exceed the insurance amount.

The reinsurance company shall pay compensation to the insurance company according to the proportion of insurance ceded after the insurance company has determined the claim.

The insurance company pays the indemnity and then obtains the right to recover the loan from the borrower. After paying the indemnity to the bank, the insurance company obtains the right of subrogation to the defaulting enterprise and then pays the amount of indemnity to the reinsurance company according to the proportion of premium. The insurance company cannot only recover the amount of indemnity, but also have the right to deal with the enterprise property or collateral, so as to protect the rights and interests of the insurance company and the reinsurance company (Fig. 24.1).

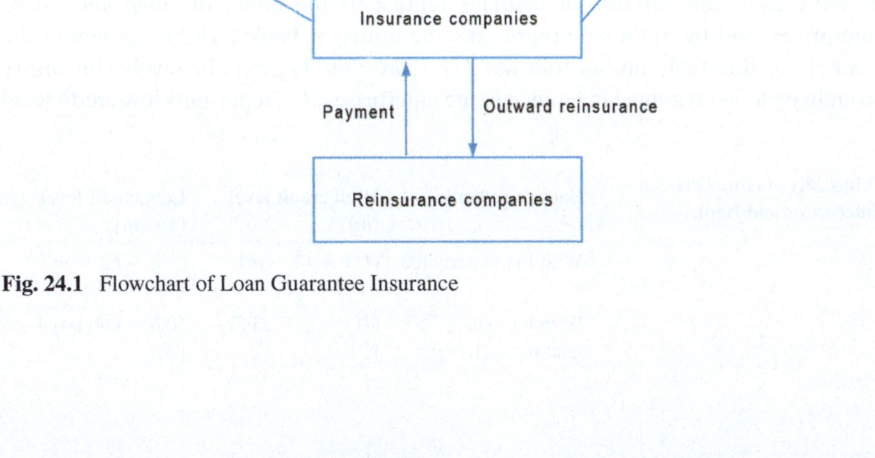

Fig. 24.1 Flowchart of Loan Guarantee Insurance

24.4.2 Risk Control of Loan Guarantee Insurance for Small and Micro Enterprises

Both banks and insurance companies investigate the credit status of applicants, and the two complement each other. The bank shall examine the applicant's financial status, the use of loan funds and the repayment ability. The review of insurance companies mainly focuses on credit records, in order to prevent the moral hazard of enterprises. Banks and insurance companies work together to complete the review of the applicant's application before granting loans, which can effectively control the risks in the business.

Reinsurance mechanism is introduced. Insurance companies carry out loan guarantee insurance, resulting in increasing risks, declining underwriting capacity and unstable enterprise operation. Therefore, it is necessary for insurance companies to disperse their own risks. At this time, the insurance company can take out reinsurance from the reinsurance company, so that the insurance company can better bear its own responsibility, enhance its underwriting ability and promote the sustainable development of loan guarantee insurance business.

The governments set up special fund for loan guarantee insurance compensation. China has established a socialist market economy, and the government should play a regulatory role. For the new business of loan guarantee insurance for small and micro enterprises, the government finance establishes a risk compensation fund in case the insurance institution is unable to bear the compensation liability. In this way, the government mobilizes the enthusiasm of all parties and promotes the further development of the insurance business.

24.5 A Theoretical Analysis of Relaxing Financing Constraints on Loan Guarantee Insurance of Small and Micro enterprises—A Game Model

In Table 24.1, the left side of brackets represents the utility of small and micro enterprises, and the right side represents the utility of banks. The meanings of the symbols in this table are as follows: $U1$ represents high credit level with utility brought by loan guarantee insurance to the enterprises, $U2$ represents low credit level

Table 24.1 Game between Enterprises and Banks

Enterprise/bank	High credit level (m)	Low credit level $(1-m)$
With loan guarantee p	$(U1-f1-m1, q1u1-v1)$	$(U2-f2-m2, q2u2-v2)$
Without loan guarantee $(1-p)$	$(U3-m3, q3u3-v3)$	$(U4-m4, q4u4-v4)$

with utility brought by loan guarantee insurance to the enterprises, $U3$ represents high credit level without utility brought by loan guarantee insurance to the enterprises, $U4$ represents the low credit level without utility brought by loan guarantee insurance to the enterprises; $f1$ and $f2$ represent the insurance premium paid to the insurance company; $m1$, $m2$, $m3$ and $m4$ represent the price paid by the enterprise to achieve a high credit level; $q1$,$q2$, $q3$ and $q4$ represent the rate of return of the bank; $v1$, $v2$, $v3$ and $v4$ represent the default losses brought by enterprises to banks; p, 1-p, m and 1-m represent their respective probabilities.

The expected income of the enterprise is

$$\begin{aligned} U = {} & pm(U1 - f1 - m1) + p(1 - m)(U2 - f2 - m2) \\ & + m(1 - p)(U3 - m3) + (1 - p)(1 - m)(U4 - m4) \end{aligned}$$

The partial derivatives of expected return u for p and m are obtained

$$\begin{aligned} \partial u/\partial p = {} & m(U1 - f1 - m1) + (1 - m)(U2 - f2 - m2) \\ & - m(U3 - m3) - (1 - m)(U4 - m4) = 0 \\ \partial u/\partial p = {} & p(U1 - f1 - m1) - p(U2 - f2 - m2) \\ & - p(U3 - m3) - (1 - p)(U4 - m4) = 0 \end{aligned}$$

From the above three formulas, we can get

$$\begin{aligned} p &= (U4 - m4)/(U1 - f1 - m1 - U2 + f2 + m2 - U3 + m3 + U4 - m4); \\ m &= (U4 - m4 + f2 + m2 - U2) \\ & \quad (U1 - f1 - m1 - U2 + f2 + m2 - U3 + m3 + U4 - m4 \end{aligned}$$

Therefore, the mixed strategy Nash equilibrium of the game model can be obtained; that is, if the enterprise chooses the loan guarantee with the probability of p, does not choose the loan guarantee with the probability of $1 - p$, the bank chooses the enterprise with high credit level with the probability of m and chooses the enterprise with low credit level with the probability of $1 - m$, and then, the mixed strategy combination constitutes a Nash equilibrium.

When the enterprise chooses the loan guarantee with the probability of p, the bank will choose the enterprise with low credit level with the probability of 1-m. At this time, the players of both sides of the game will not unilaterally deviate from their established strategies. In this case, enterprises with low credit can obtain bank loans through loan guarantee, and thus, financing constraints are reduced.

24.6 Problems in the Development of Loan Guarantee Insurance

24.6.1 Imperfect Credit Environment

A good social credit environment is an important factor for the sound development of the insurance industry. For the loan guarantee insurance of small and micro enterprises, the credit review of enterprises before insurance is particularly important. However, there is no perfect credit environment and guarantee system in China at present, so it is difficult for the insurance companies to obtain real-time, true and complete enterprise credit information. There is no incentive system for enterprises to abide by credit, and there is no effective system to punish enterprises for breach of contract. The information between insurance companies and policy holders is asymmetric.

The insurance industry has an imperfect credit information system on the credit records of small and micro enterprises, so the insurance companies do not have sufficient ability to audit the credit of the enterprises, which increases the underwriting risks. It is difficult for the insurance companies to restrain the policyholders when these enterprises perform poorly. At the same time, enterprises will seek profits at the cost of their credit, which leads to moral hazard and causes huge losses to the insurer. To a great extent, this dampens the enthusiasm of insurance companies to promote loan guarantee insurance.

24.6.2 Loopholes in Operation and Lack of Professional Talents

The guarantee insurance business is faced with higher operation cost, higher risk and relatively higher requirements for professional personnel of insurance companies. At present, insurance companies and banks generally lack all-round financial talents who are proficient in insurance market operation and familiar with the credit business procedure of bank financial institutions. In t credit investigation, professionals with risk judgment experience are needed, but at the present stage, there is a lack of such personnel in insurance companies, and there are technical difficulties in enterprise credit evaluation, which greatly affects the judgment of the risks. In the underwriting stage, most insurance companies in the insurance industry adopt the method of centralized underwriting by headquarters, and this method relies heavily on the transmission of information and data. Once the financial data and credit information transmitted by small and micro enterprises are tampered, it will bring risks to the insurance company; after t compensation, the insurance company begins to collect the loan. The insurance companies rely too much on call collection and the operation of debt collection companies, which will damage the overall image of insurance companies and have a negative impact on the development of the industry.

24.6.3 Small Pilot Scale

At the present stage, the loan guarantee insurance for small and micro enterprises is still in its infancy. There are only a small number of insurance companies carrying out guarantee insurance business in the market, and there are obvious geographical restrictions. The pilot business is only carried out in very few cities at the beginning, and the development in the limited pilot areas cannot fully reflect the real market environment of guarantee insurance. Moreover, many insurance companies carry out pilot projects for enterprises in specific industries. Many guaranteed insurance loans can only be used for productive purposes. Borrowers, such as large agricultural growers, small start-ups, and urban and rural entrepreneurs, cannot use the funds for consumption or other purposes. Many small and micro enterprises applying for loans are in the early stage of development, and they are faced with high capital pressure and high risk of bad debt loss. Some insurance companies will avoid providing service for such applicants.

24.6.4 Lack of Government Support

As a business facilitating financing, guarantee insurance can be regarded as quasi-public goods, which undertakes part of the social management functions for the government, and need the government's incentive and support policies to support its development. I China has introduced a series of policies, such as multiple tax incentives, exemption of business tax for qualified guarantee institutions and deduction of default risk reserve before tax, to promote the development of credit guarantee institutions. But when insurance companies carry out the guarantee insurance business, the premium income is included in the operating income, and worse still, the default risk reserve is not deducted in the calculation of income tax; therefore, insurance companies are faced with unfair tax burden. At present, in the whole system, the government mainly provides external support, but it fails to provide direct support, so the policy environment has not been formed to support the development of guarantee insurance business.

24.7 Suggestions on Perfecting Loan Guarantee Insurance

In May 2012, the State Council issued Opinions of the State Council on Further Supporting the Healthy Development of Small and Micro Enterprises (hereinafter referred to as the Opinions), requiring all localities and relevant departments to further increase financial and tax support for small and micro enterprises to alleviate their financing difficulties, promote the innovative development and structural adjustment these, and create a good environment for the healthy development of small and micro enterprises.

In order to give full play to the supporting role of the insurance industry, the opinions pointed out that it is necessary to broaden financing channels and support small and micro enterprises to adopt various financing methods, such as intellectual property pledge, warehouse receipt pledge, shop operation right pledge, commercial credit insurance policy pledge, commercial factoring and pawn. The opinions encourage the insurance industry to provide equipment financial leasing services and actively develop loan guarantee insurance and credit insurance for small and micro enterprises and call for the construction of financing service system for these enterprises.

24.7.1 Strengthen Internal Control System

Faced with more and more complex risks, insurance companies need to improve their risk control ability, optimize business processes and prevent and control internal risks. It is necessary to strengthen the identification and analysis of risks, make prompt response, carry out reasonable quantitative assessment and continuous tracking and effectively control risks.

At the same time, in the process of underwriting and settling claims, banks should investigate and evaluate the repayment period, the credit of borrowers and the profitability of enterprises. They should also cooperate with insurance companies to jointly control the risks of guarantee insurance business. In addition to risk control, insurance companies should communicate more with banks to share information, which will facilitate the settling of claims.

The credit rating system and legal system for small and micro enterprises need to be further improved and updated. In the rating index system, quantitative and qualitative rating indexes and adjustment rules in line with the business characteristics of small and micro enterprises should be set up, and a standardized and professional credit evaluation model should be established to focus on the authenticity of their financial information and the existing legal risks, and make a scientific prediction of their future cash flow. This can not only save the cost of the insurance companies, but also help the insurance companies to focus on the follow-up service and improve the level of risk management.

24.7.2 Strengthen Professional Personnel Training

The insurance industry cannot develop without the help of human resources. At present, the loan guarantee insurance of small and micro enterprises is in the initial stage, and there is a shortage of professional personnels. Therefore, we should establish a perfect system of professional talent selection and a scientific concept of talent. We should not only train professional personnel in actuarial, underwriting, claims settling and investment, but also cultivate talents with interdisciplinary knowledge. We should innovate our ideas and form the concept of great education and training, focusing on the cultivation of the learning ability, the practical ability and especially the innovation ability of professional personnel for the insurance industry.

We should strengthen the effective incentive and guarantee for insurance talents. We should actively explore ways for various elements to participate in the distribution and link the contribution, risks, responsibilities and distribution of business management talents and various professionals. We should establish a distribution system that can mobilize the enthusiasm of employees and reflect the company's performance, so as to fully stimulate the enthusiasm of insurance talents. We should expand our horizons, eliminate the industry barriers for the insurance industry to absorb all kinds of talents and actively attract talents from relevant departments, localities and even overseas to the insurance industry. We can employ talents who are familiar with legal and financial affairs and who have working experiences in banking, securities and other industries. We should give full play to the functions of all factors of production conducive to the rapid development of the insurance industry, such as capital, knowledge, technology and management. This will not only help to meet the demand for talents, but will also help to introduce advanced technology and management experience from other industries.

24.7.3 Strengthen Product Innovation and Optimize Resource Allocation

From the development experience of foreign guarantee insurance business, commercial insurance mechanism can be established to improve the guarantee insurance mode. The insurers are faced with huge risks due to the unstable operation of small and micro enterprises and the information asymmetry between the insurance companies and the applicants. And they have to bear the risks exceeding its solvency on their own. Reinsurance business can be introduced to pass on the risks, so as to ensure the safety of the insurance companies' business. This not only solves the financing difficulties of small and micro enterprises, but also expands the business scope and service field of insurance companies with more profitable projects.

Usually, the insurance company that carries out guarantee insurance obtains the creditor's rights of the enterprise after compensation, but the enterprise cannot repay the debt due to funds shortage. At this time, other means can be adopted; for example, insurance companies and banks can obtain the equity of the enterprise in accordance with the proportion of their own losses, and they can manage the small and micro enterprises as shareholders or sell their shares to obtain funds to compensate for the losses.

24.7.4 Increase Government Support

As for legislation, there are not many provisions on guarantee insurance in China's insurance law, guarantee law and other relevant laws at present, and the existing provisions are vague. When the borrower has such dishonest behavior as malicious fraud, evasion of debt, insurance fraud and loan fraud, the insurance company cannot restrain the borrower due to a lack of laws and regulations. Therefore, on the basis of foreign advanced legislative experience and the actual development of domestic small and micro enterprises, China should improve the existing laws and regulations, issue more relevant legal documents for new problems, improve the punishment measures for borrowers' dishonest behaviors and increase the punishment for malicious default and financial debt evasion, so as to provide legal support for the healthy development of financing guarantee system of small and micro enterprises and guarantee for legal and effective financing. At the same time, we should give tax preference to guarantee insurance or reduce the business tax and income tax of the insurance companies, which reduces not only the operating cost of the insurance companies, but also the financing cost of small and micro enterprises. We should give premium subsidies to enterprises applying for loans and implement different rates for enterprises with different risk categories. This will contribute to the stable operation of insurance companies and enterprises.

References

Bao Jinghai, Zhou Wenhai, Li Haoran. Construction of Credit Guarantee Insurance System for Small and Medium-sized Enterprises in China [J]. *Insurance Research*, 2007 (4): 33–35.

Cui Jingjing. Research on Financing Behavior of Small and Micro Enterprises—Based on the Survey of Small and Micro Enterprises in Gansu Province. Lanzhou University. 2011:1.

Tang Jincheng, Liu Xinxin, Gong Yongbing. Research on Credit Guarantee Insurance and Financing of Small and Medium-sized Enterprises [J]. Selected papers of annual conference of China Insurance Society, 2011: 474.

Wei Guoxiong. Increasing Financing Supply to Ease the Financing Difficulty of Small and Micro Enterprises [J]. *China Finance*, 2010 (3): 39–41.

Xiong Jin. Analysis and Suggestions on Financing Difficulties of Small and Micro Enterprises in China [J]. Learning Monthly, 2012 (2): 82–83.

Xiong Mengqian. Analysis of Guarantee Insurance's Support for SME Loans [J]. *Shanghai Insurance*, 2010 (5): 32.

Xu Wengang, Wei Jiufeng. Problems and Policy Suggestions of Loan Guarantee Insurance for Small and Micro Enterprises[n]. China Insurance Journal, 2012-05-17: 7th Edition.

Zeng Ming. Discussion on Establishing Loan Guarantee Insurance for Small and Medium-sized Enterprises [J]. Shanghai Finance, 2006 (5): 78–79.

Zhuang Qing. Thoughts on Establishing Loan Insurance System for Small and Medium-sized Enterprises [J]. *Shanghai Finance*, 2003 (11): 51–52.

Part III
Payment-Clearing Sector

Chapter 25
Online Payment in China at Present: Impetus, Risk Assessment and Supervision

25.1 Four Driving Forces for Development of Online Payment[1]

There are four major driving forces for the development of online payment in China in the future.

Firstly, the further development and transformation of economy is the material driving force for the development of online payment in China.

With regard to economic aggregate, China will witness a steady and relatively fast growth in the coming 10–20 years. There is still a considerable gap between the urbanization level of China and the world average, creating a relatively big space externally for further economic growth; the fourth revolution of science and technology is still forging ahead fast after the Industrial Revolution. The technological progress mainly in the fields of the Internet and modern logistics leads to the increase of production efficiency, creating a space internally for further economic growth in China; the second version of reform and opening-up, including reform in the political system and the second round of opening-up characterized with the going abroad of its capital, will also create institutional dividend and favorable international environment for the development of China's economy.

With regard to economic structure, China's economic structure has undergone gradual adjustment since the entry into the twenty-first century, with the importance of consumption, one of the three major driving forces for GDP growth, becoming more prominent. The general trend remains unchanged despite the surge of investment demand since 2008 as a result of the financial crisis.

[1] This section was published on October 20 of 2014 in International Finance News.

A group of experts joined the discussion when this report was being drafted. They are Yang Biao, Wu Bo, Zhu Haiming, Wu Xin, Qiu Sijun, Gao Yang and Yu Lu. Advice was also sought from directors of safety affairs in some online payment agencies. This report was published on September 10th of 2013 in China Economic Times.

S. Ba, *The New Cycle and New Finance in China*,
https://doi.org/10.1007/978-981-16-8209-4_25

With the relatively fast increase of economic aggregate and the gradual adjustment of economic structure, the total retail sales of consumer goods have maintained a relatively high speed of growth. This material basis ensures a great demand for development in the sector of online payment, which is mainly dependent on e-commerce.

Secondly, the evolution of consumption culture and payment habit is the mental driving force for the development of online payment. The consumption culture is changing unnoticeably with the fast development of the Internet and modern logistics. In the major cities, the Internet and modern logistics have gradually attracted shoppers away from high streets and malls. Even traditional leisurely window-shopping is being slowly replaced with surfing on the Internet and visiting online shopping malls. Although experiential shopping in offline shops is still popular, many of the shops are even put at the risk of being marginalized as "fitting rooms" as a result of the accessibility of different categories of goods in online malls.

As the Internet and modern logistics are changing the consumption culture bit by bit, the general pattern of behavior including payment habit is evolving unknowingly. Online payment, which is closely connected with E-commerce, gradually finds its way into the payment activities and becomes the payment habit of the general public. It develops into a habitual "common sense" in the mindset of people.

Physical behavior and mentality exert influence on each other mutually. Once online payment becomes "common sense" among the public, there will inevitably be a powerful drive for its further development.

Thirdly, technological progress, with network technology at the core, is the internal driving force for the development of online payment. No matter it is the material driving force derived from economic development or the mental driving force derived from change of payment habit, it can only become real with the support of technological progress, with network technology at its core. At Barcelona Mobile World Congress (MWC), the exhibition section of China Mobile remained a big eye catcher for most of the time with its terminal products and solutions of TD-LTE (4G). With the advent of the Internet era, "mobile electronic currency" will become increasingly popular. It not only helps to establish a paperless payment system but also replaces bank cards and thus ushers in a "card-free" age, bringing convenience to the users and cutting down the cost of the transaction system. It is predicted that, by the end of 2013, there will be 500 million people worldwide using mobile payment service, and by the end of 2014, there will be approximately three billion adults worldwide performing transactions of electronic currency through mobile communication and the Internet, indicating a giant business opportunity in the mobile payment system. Mobile communication technologies, led by 4G technology, will become another powerful engine for online payment in the age of new economy.

At last, the perfection of legal system, the improvement of supervision and the development of the sector's self-regulatory organizations are the external driving forces for the growth of online payment. The fast growth of online payment substantially facilitates the development of e-commerce and makes modern payment and credit systems more diversified; on the other hand, as a new type of payment, its emergence gives rise to new economic and social risks in the modern financial system. Online payment service cannot maintain a firm and long-lasting development without a sound legal system, a mature governmental supervision system and an optimized self-regulatory system of the sector.

25.2 Assessment of Status Quo of Online Payment Safety

The period between 1998 and 2012 saw the emergence and expansion of online payment in China. The fast growth of online payment has exerted a profound influence on and brought far-reaching changes to the payment system, payment habit and even the financial service. In general, the public attention to online payment safety shows obvious "excessiveness and inadequacy" in the awareness of the following aspects:

Firstly, focus is mainly on microscopic factors directly connected with online payment safety, including market access, product service, safety technology, operational risk control and supervision and administration. However, inadequate attention has been paid to the factors indirectly connected with online payment, such as user experience, the balance between safety and efficiency, the benign interaction between innovation and regulation and the external environment for the development of the sector, and systematic measures have not been adopted in this regard either.

Secondly, there is relatively adequate consciousness of and precaution against "single risks" of different types that have influence on online payment safety, but the consciousness of "complex risks" caused by overlaid risk factors of different types is relatively weak; great importance is attached to the risk control of single online payment institutions, but insufficient importance is given to the coordination in the industry chain in prevention and control of online payment risks.

With a look into the bigger picture, the whole payment sector should be taken into account when the safety problem is addressed currently. This helps to avert the situation of "achieving only half the result for double effort," which happens when the misjudgment of individual payment institutions is heavily relied on or stopgap and piecemeal solutions are adopted in problem solving. With a look into the actual situation, there are a large number of payment institutions, which are evidently different from each other in many aspects, including products and service, the capacity of internal operation and management and the orientation of strategic development. Besides, different payment institutions tend to choose different operation strategies on the basis of their own interest demands, market positions and unique features. Therefore, the study on the payment safety of the whole sector should not be confined to the differences of various payment institutions. In fact, it is hard to find a microscopic and workable measure up to the demands of all the individual institutions. It is more likely, however, to find common factors that can promote a sound development of the whole sector if the interests of the whole are taken into account.

25.3 Current Safety Status of the Whole Sector of Online Payment in China

With a look into the whole payment sector, there are a wide range of problems related to payment safety due to the development and change of online payment. Here are some problems that are used to be neglected yet need to be closely watched in the future:

25.3.1 Balance Between Safety and Efficiency of Online Payment

One of the crucial goals of online payment development is to strike a balance between safety and efficiency. Excessive safety control will greatly reduce the operation efficiency of the payment agencies and cause inconvenience to the users; negligence of safety, however, will also cause loss to the users and the payment agencies as well. It is important to notice that the goal of risk control should not be achieved at the cost of efficiency and user experience, because e-commerce has a long industry chain, and cooperation with an appropriate division of labor should be promoted among the different links in the chain so as to expand the market and reap more profit. If efficiency is sacrificed for safety, the revenue of the industry chain will fail to cover the cost and the industry will be knocked out quickly in the competition.

With regard to risk control in online payment, Asia is featured with a dense population, a less well-established credit system and more investment in safety when compared with other parts of the world, but it enjoys a relatively leading status in technological innovation of risk control. The existence of some risk in the payment system to a bearable extent will give impetus to relevant enterprises in their effort to explore and develop more effective safety technologies and thus promote the efficiency of online payment.

25.3.2 Relationship of Competition and Cooperation Among Major Online Payment Service Providers

The different participants involved in the effort to maintain online payment safety exert influence on each other and blend with each other. Together they decide the general level of the online payment safety. Although the transaction conducted via online payment agencies is less than 1% of that conducted via traditional payment agencies, it facilitates the development of online financial service of banks. Both cooperation and competition can be found between banks and online payment agencies. With direct service to small- and medium-sized businesses and individuals, online payment agencies, compared with commercial banks, have more advantages in financial service innovation and service experience provision for customers. Banks have significant potential advantages in promoting the development of online payment with their complete banking service license, brand and HR as well as risk control capacity. In 2012, a major commercial bank called for aborting the operation of Lakala, an emerging online payment enterprise in China, and cutting off its payment channels. This counter-example shows that a sensible and constructive competition-and-cooperation relationship is more needed in the future. From a microscopic perspective, it is probably beyond reproach for a business to take advantage of its powerful status to restrain the development of its potential competitors. From a broader viewpoint, however, it is not helpful for the improvement of efficiency of the whole sector. The relationship of irrational competition will increase the uncertainty of online payment market and affect the safety experience of online payment users.

25.3.3 Policy Framework Facilitating Benign Interaction of Innovation and Regulation

Innovation is the source power for the existence and development of the online payment sector. For more than ten years in the past, the online payment agencies have seen a fast growth by constantly lowering payment threshold and improving the safety and efficiency of payment. The fast growth has won the relevant regulatory authorities' recognition of their principal status in the market. This gives new impetus to the further improvement of the safety and efficiency of online payment. The interaction of innovation and regulation is one of the important fields of study about the dynamics of online payment safety and efficiency. The establishment of a policy framework that enables a sound interaction of innovation and regulation also has a bearing on the safety and efficiency of online payment.

The policy framework for online payment regulating can be roughly divided into three levels: Firstly, the safety and efficiency of online payment system should be ensured to avoid systematic risk. This is also a common goal set up for regulating retail payment systems by regulatory authorities in different countries. Secondly, emphasis should be placed on preventing online payment innovation from disrupting and impacting the implementation of monetary policies, the policies against money laundering and illegal cash advances or other polices aimed for maintaining economic and financial order. Lastly, the protection of online payment consumers should be enhanced because of the information asymmetry between the payment agencies and the users.

With the above policy framework, the establishment of a mechanism of recognition, assessment, consultation, monitoring and reporting of various innovations will become an important safeguard for the sound interaction between innovation and regulation or between online payment agencies and regulatory authorities. As for the various innovations of online payment agencies in safety and efficiency, the regulatory authorities should reduce regulation and interference in the future if the innovations are not against the general goals of regulating and the specific framework of policies. Over recent years, online payment innovations such as quick payment and card-free payment aroused disputes on safety and risk when they were launched in the market. The increasing popularity of the innovative payment methods, however, indicates that the concern about the risk has slowly faded and the service providers have developed the required capacity of risk control. Meanwhile, it should be noticed that online payment agencies have also developed an awareness of the necessity to adjust their range of business to relevant regulations. For instance, in 2012, the online payment agencies shut down the function of recharging virtual accounts with credit cards one after another, aiming to eliminate illegal advances on credit cards.

25.4 A Look into Online Payment Safety from Perspective of Online Payment Agencies

25.4.1 Safety Risk of Online Payment in China Kept Under Control, with the Safety State Being Stabilized and in Good Prospect

Firstly, with development for about ten years, the online payment agencies in China have collectively made sizable investment on safety measures and seen a constant improvement of their safety technology. With the extensive use of measures including Usbkey, dynamic password, digital certificates and real-time interception of phishing Web sites, the agencies have continuously improved their capacity of risk control and upgraded their measures for risk prevention and control.

Secondly, the safety risk of the market entities and the whole sector is kept under control. Since 2011, over 80 agencies have been granted license for online payment business. While the market entities have enjoyed profit from license ownership, they also have substantially improved their standards of operation; the online payment companies with leading market shares in different fields, such as Alipay, Tenpay, Unionpay, 99bill and Huifu, have constantly increased their consciousness of risk prevention and their capacity of risk management.

Thirdly, the government has strengthened its regulatory measures targeted at online payment, which helps promote the sector's development evidently in a healthy and standard way. With the adoption of the "Administrative Measures for the Payment Services Provided by Non-financial Agencies," the People's Bank of China (PBC) has stipulated the tatus and business attributes of the payment services provided by non-financial agencies. Apart from setting up the threshold for industry access, PBC has also established and continuously refined administrative principles about safety of provisions, real-name registration, anti-money laundering, anti-terrorist financing, payment risk management, the protection of the rights and interests of the users, etc.

Over the recent two years since its establishment, the Payment and Clearing Association of China (PCAC) has made great efforts on the supervision of self-regulation and policy compliance of the online payment agencies and has conducted a lot of research into the sector. Meanwhile, with importance attached to high-tech enterprises, the local government at different levels has also paid greater attention and offered greater support to online payment agencies.

Lastly, there is still a trend toward the enhancement of online payment safety. With the increasing popularity of the Internet and the wide spread of online banking service and e-commerce, greater emphasis is placed on the safety of online payment. Faced with the pressure of market competition and the widespread concern of the public, the different enterprises engaging in online payment service will keep on strengthening their safety measures.

25.4.2 Major Risks Facing Online Payment Agencies in China

Online payment safety is subject to various and intricately correlated factors with different connotations. Generally, the four most prominent risk factors affecting the safety and efficiency of online payment in China are as follows:

Unlawful Practice Involving Basic Legal Relationship

The unlawful practice involves the safety problem that comes into being when online payment service is taken advantage of by criminals or is found to have been used in criminal acts. It is mainly associated with the online payment service exploited in pornography, gambling, drug abuse and trafficking and illegal transaction of hazardous goods.

Inappropriate Internal Administration

It refers to the misconducts and negligence of online payment agencies in their internal administrative affairs, including procedures, technology and information safety, capital safety, rules and regulations and integrity of the staff. The inappropriateness can be found in cases involving defects in product service, embezzlement of customer deposit and leakage of customer information.

Successive Emergence of Fraud Conducted by Outsiders

In various ways, outsiders may trick the agencies out of the information and data relevant to online payment or just steal them. Then, they will manipulate or intervene in payment transactions, infringing on the lawful rights and interests of the payment transaction parties. Such fraud can be found in cases involving phishing Web sites, Trojan viruses and business fraud like Ponzi scheme and pyramid selling.

Absence of Supporting Environment and Its Influence on Safety Experience

There is potential risk in network environment, whereas the users have insufficient safety education and consciousness. And, a standard and efficient mechanism has not yet been established to investigate and deal with online payment risk.

Among the above risk factors, transactions violating laws and rules, inappropriate internal administration and external fraud on the Internet are more likely to cause direct capital losses to the users and the operators or result in the termination of business operation; Nonetheless, the lack of supporting environment will mainly have negative influence on the safety feeling of the users, with the potential influence being more extensive and immeasurable.

25.4.3 Supervision of Online Payment Safety in China

To promote the sound development of online payment agencies and the whole sector, supervision should be carried out with different intensities and frequencies on the basis of different risk factors in actual situations. In view of the above-mentioned status quo and major problems, the problems of online payment safety should be tackled mainly in three ways:

Firstly, measures should be enhanced to create a favorable external environment that is mainly supported by the supervision authority to prevent external fraud and the unfavorable influence of network environment on online payment safety.

The potential risk of external fraud and network environment remains the most important factor affecting online payment safety in the foreseeable future. According to the Proposals on Online Payment Safety, which was released by European Central Bank, supervisors, law makers, payment service providers and the general public share the perception that online payment is faced with greater chance of fraud than the traditional way of payment. The incidence of account number theft involving online payment averages 0.01% in China, with the average for the country's mainstream online payment agencies being much lower, as against the world average of 1–2% and the payment dishonoring rate of 0.27% for PayPal, the internationally leading online payment corporation. Nonetheless, with the "subjective feeling" of the users about online payment safety taken into account, it is still essential to purify network environment and improve the supporting mechanisms that deal with refunding, claim settlement, complaint filing, safety issue investigation, and other affairs intensely affecting the safety experience of the users to create a favorable eco-environment for the sound and standard development of online payment service.

Secondly, to address the influence of unlawful practice involving basic legal relationship and the lack of supporting environment on the safety of online payment, efforts should be strengthened to improve the sector's capacity of risk prevention and control through cooperation in the industry chain.

Risk management in this respect should focus on external fraud, market risk, transactions against laws and rules and consumer education to eliminate the various risk factors facing the whole industry chain. As major service providers in the sector, online payment agencies and commercial banks should strengthen cooperation to ensure online payment safety instead of benefiting oneself at the other's expense. To be specific, they should join hands in safety education among online businesses and consumers. They should also team up to research into a cooperation-based safety mechanism covering the complete process of online payment and to facilitate the implementation of specific measures like the development of safety technology, anti-fraud, anti-money laundering, anti-phishing and "black list" sharing. With a view to improving efficiency, online payment agencies and commercial banks should collaborate in e-commerce financing, dada mining, cross-marketing and mobile financing, etc., to facilitate the innovation of their own business models and the integration of each other's models. By reinforcing each other, they can work together to establish an efficient, balanced and sound eco-system of e-commerce and Internet-based finance. Besides, consensus and efforts of the whole industry chain of online payment and e-commerce are needed to create a favorable external environment, involving the sector-specific infrastructure, legal environment and the protection of the users' rights and interests.

Investigations reveal a gradual downward trend in the level of internal risk management and safety protection, along with the weakening awareness of banks, online payment agencies and the users about risk prevention and control in the industry chain. The level of safety protection is also found irregular in the industry chain. Accordingly, the supervision authorities should give guidance to small- and medium-sized online payment agencies for them to increase investment on safety measures; the relevant authorities should pay close attention to the agencies' investment on infrastructure and their capacity to maintain sustainable operations; the departments concerned should also work at preventing the small- and medium-sized agencies from exerting negative influence on the whole sector with their risk incidents.

Thirdly, to deal with the influence of online payment agencies' inappropriate internal administration on payment safety, greater efforts should be made to optimize the risk management mechanism centering around online payment agencies.

Risk management in this respect is aimed to enhance the capacity of risk prevention and control of online payment agencies, especially in the fields mainly dependent on their own capacity, including the management of operation risk, technology risk, information safety, etc. The primary purpose is to improve the industry chain's capacity to detect, control and mitigate various actual and potential risks facing critical links of the chain, with major enterprises playing a leading role in the process. For online payment agencies, it is critical to explore risk management procedures up to the characteristics and demand of online financial service in the future, covering internal and external environment, internal control mechanism and safety technology, by learning from the risk management procedures and experience of commercial banks and other institutions.

25.5 Trend of Online Payment Risk Management in China

25.5.1 Attention Should Be Paid to Dynamics of Online Payment Category

According to the Bank for International Settlements (BIS), online or mobile payment is termed mainly on the basis of the path or channel by which the command of payment is put into the payment system. Accordingly, the connotation of online payment will keep expanding with the progress of information technology. The expansion of the connotation can be found in the change of the relevant terms adopted by the People's Bank of China from "electronic payment" in the Guidelines of Electronic Payment (File No. 1) to "online payment" in the Administrative Measures for the Payment Services Provided by Non-financial Institutions. The expansion of the connotation is mainly attributable to technology innovations, which bring forth an increasing variety of payment commands and network channels. The appearance of the payment commands applying bio-identification technologies involving acoustic wave, finger print or iris (or retina), along with the appearance of the network channels such as digital TV network and 4G smart phone network, is expected to expand the category of online payment further.

25.5.2 Attention Should Be Paid to Great Influence of User Experience on Online Payment Safety

In reality, many users regard undesirable experiences in online shopping, such as dishonesty of shop runners, poor quality of goods and inefficiency of logistics, as the safety problems of online payment. It exerts obvious adverse effect on a sound judgment of online payment safety, leading to underestimation or even misjudgment of the safety of online payment environment. Fundamentally, the safety of online payment refers to the safety of monetary capital transfer on line. For an accurate measurement and effective improvement of online payment safety, focus should be placed on the safety of monetary capital transfer.

25.5.3 *Two Important Principles to Follow in Establishing Online Payment Risk Management System*

To prevent online payment risk in the future, focus should be put on the two effective basic principles: The first is the balance between safety and efficiency; the second is the balance between risk and profit—that is, an emphasis on safety should not bring forth an evident unfavorable influence on efficiency, and the profit from risk taking should cover the cost.

25.5.4 *Adherence to Notion of Innovation-Driven Development*

As for online payment safety, the concept of solving safety problems through technology innovations is to be upheld. With the trend of payment safety technology taken into account, we should pay special attention to the development in two fields. The first is the establishment of an intelligent real-time system of risk prevention and control. It is a monitoring system that enables a real-time screening of transactions by using corresponding rules. Along with human verification, the system can be used to discover risky transactions and control risky accounts. This improves the efficiency of risk prevention and control with the change from post-event response to concurrent response. The second is the application of big data in safety measures. With the support of Internet technologies, behavior patterns related to the use of mobile phones and fixed-line telephones can be recorded and then stored in cloud servers. With the help of the records, comprehensive analyses can be conducted in the future on the continuity of human behaviors instead of passwords and keys only. To develop inclusive finance, banks and online payment institutions should be encouraged to remove barriers through safety technology innovations to make convenient and safe payment service accessible to migrant workers and people in rural or remote areas.

Chapter 26
Prospective Changes in Third-Party Payment in China with Emergence of NetsUnion Clearing Corporation (NUCC)

26.1 Third-Party Payment Market: An Increasingly Competitive Market Featuring Co-Existence of Competitive Businesses

According to the Administrative Measures for the Payment Services Provided by Non-financial Institutions issued by the People's Bank of China (PBC), third-party payment refers to the online payment (including Internet-based payment, mobile payment, fixed-line telephone-based payment and digital TV-based payment), prepaid card service, bank card acquiring service and other payment service stipulated by PBC (as is indicated in Fig. 26.1), with non-financial agencies as the payment mediators for either payees or payers.This article will focus on an introduction to bank card acquiring service and online payment (including mobile payment and Internet-based payment), because fixed-line telephone-based and digital TV-based payment is less popularly received in the market. The same is true for prepaid card service, including card issuing and card-related business acceptance.

26.1.1 Market for Bank Card Acquiring Service: Bank Card-Based Transaction Remains Steady yet with a Slowing Growth

According to the General Operation of Payment System in China (2016), a global look into the bank card-based transaction (as is indicated in Fig. 26.2) shows that there were 3115.474 billion transactions via bank cards, involving a total of RMB 741.8 trillion, a growth of 35.49% and 10.75%, respectively, year-on-year. The higher growth rate of the number of transactions, compared with that of transaction amount,

Source: Headline Today on September14th, 2017.

S. Ba, *The New Cycle and New Finance in China*,
https://doi.org/10.1007/978-981-16-8209-4_26

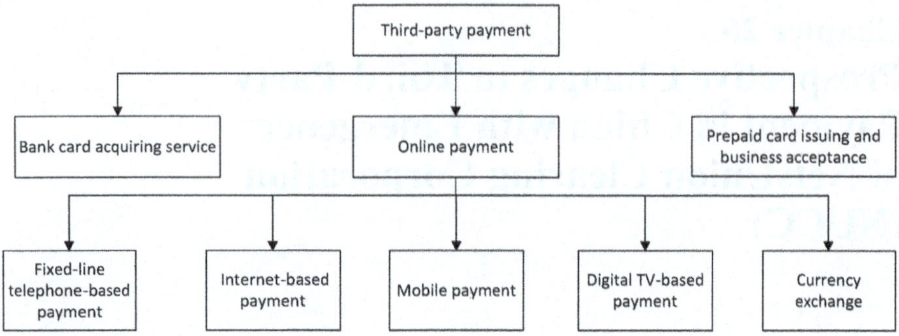

Fig. 26.1 Third-party payment categories (classified in terms of licenses). *Source* Administrative Measures for the Payment Services Provided by Non-financial Institutions issued in 2010 by PBC

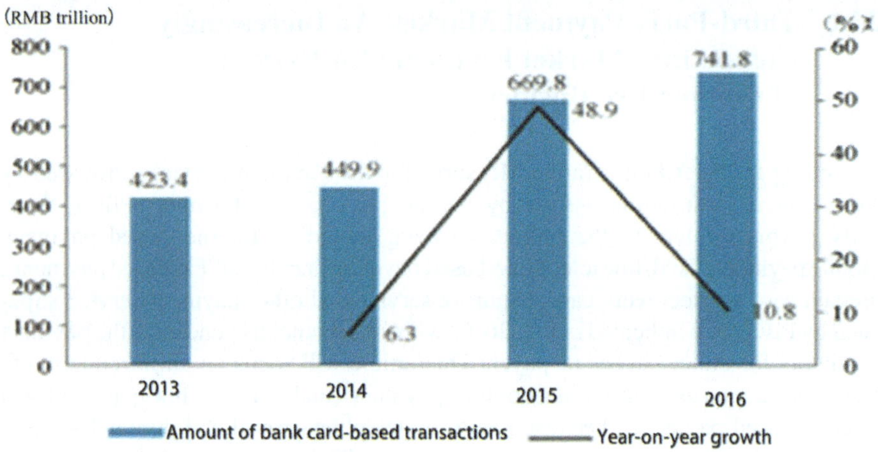

Fig. 26.2 Amount of bank card-based transactions in China between 2013 and 2016. *Source* General Operation of Payment System in China (2013–2016)

reveals that the increased binding of bank cards with third-party payment platforms in the mobile Internet era has extended the pattern of bank card-based consumption from transaction in big amount with lower frequency to transaction in small amount with higher frequency. However, an evident slowing growth can be found in the total amount of bank card-based transactions.

A microscopic investigation into bank card-related transactions, as is indicated in Fig. 26.3, reveals that, with per capita ownership of 4.47 bank cards, the rate of bank card penetration hit 48.47% in China by the end of 2016, a rise of 0.47% over the previous year. In view of the high rate of possession per capita and penetration, there is limited room for the growth of bank card issuance. As is shown in Fig. 26.4, the amount of bank card-based consumption averaged RMB 9,593, a decline of 5.08%

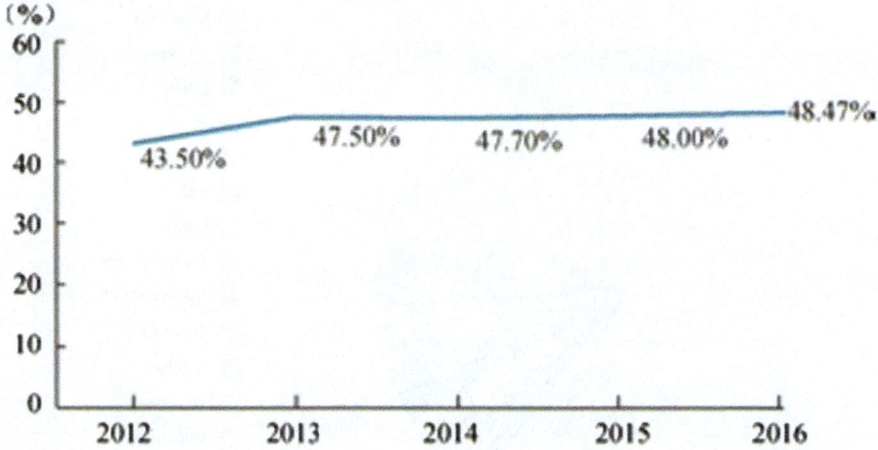

Fig. 26.3 Rate of bank card penetration in China (2012–2016). *Source* General Operation of Payment System in China (2012–2016)

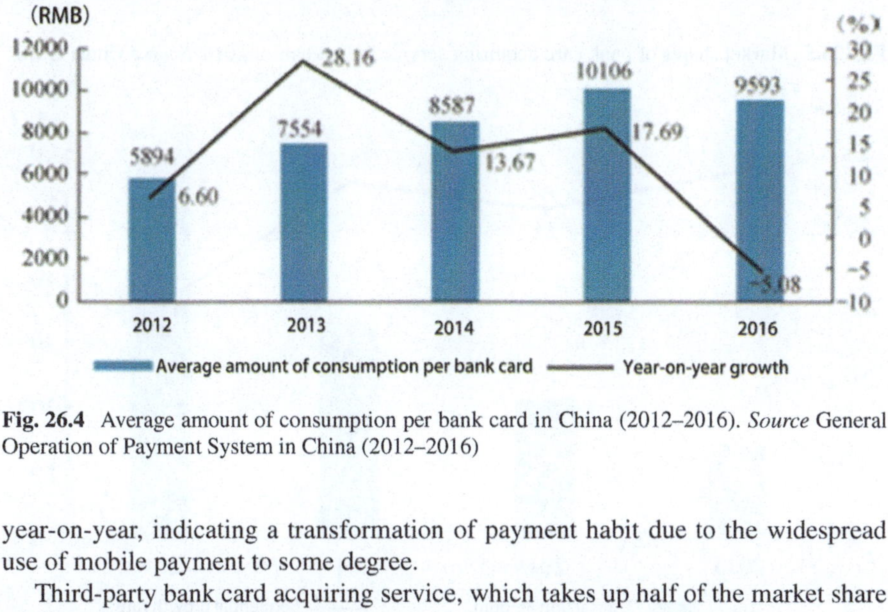

Fig. 26.4 Average amount of consumption per bank card in China (2012–2016). *Source* General Operation of Payment System in China (2012–2016)

year-on-year, indicating a transformation of payment habit due to the widespread use of mobile payment to some degree.

Third-party bank card acquiring service, which takes up half of the market share of the whole bank card acquiring service, saw a downturn of growth due to the influence of mobile payment. Statistics from China UnionPay Merchant Services Co., Ltd. (hereinafter referred to as China UMS) show that third-party bank card acquiring service took up 43% of the market in the first half of 2016, as is depicted in Fig. 26.5. The growth rate of third-party acquiring service saw a decline but ran higher than that of the whole bank acquiring service, as can be seen in Fig. 26.6. With its capacity of innovation and convenient service, third-party acquiring service

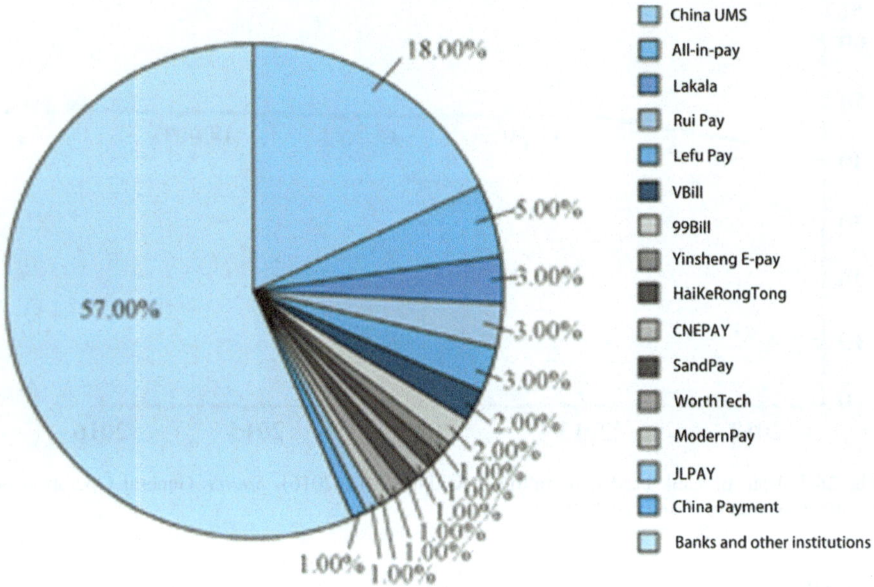

Fig. 26.5 Market shares of bank card acquiring service in first half of 2016. *Source* China UMS

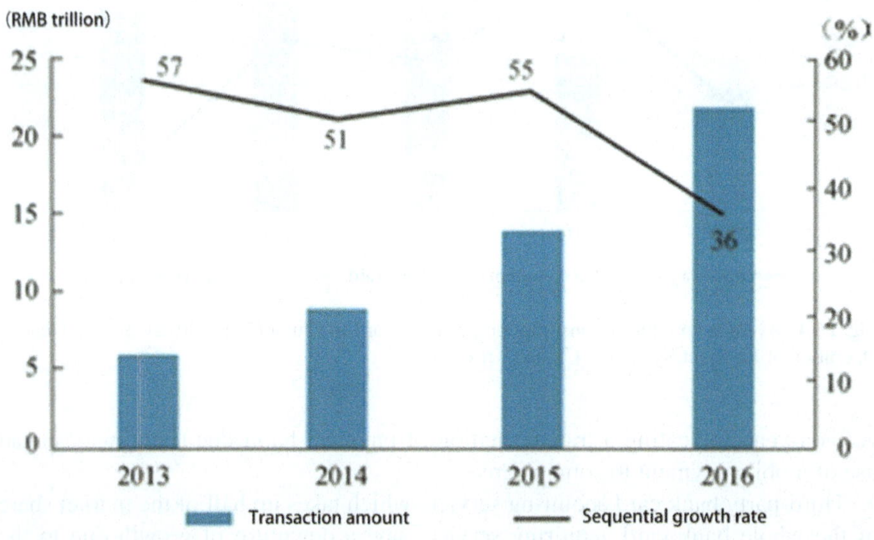

Fig. 26.6 Amount of transaction in third-party acquiring service. *Source* iResearch Consulting Group

is expected to play an increasingly important role in the whole bank card acquiring service.

26.1.2 Online Payment: Online Payment Sees Rapid Growth, with Mobile Payment Playing the Leading Role

Online payment has seen a fast growth in China. There were 470 million online payment users in 2016, a growth of 14.01% year-on-year. Among these people, 469 million were mobile payment users, an increase of 31.17% year-on-year. The rate of mobile payment has witnessed a gradual increase over the recent four years, hitting 64.90% in 2016 and matching the rate of online payment in the same year. It shows that mobile payment has become an increasingly popular way of online payment.

The online payment market shows an obvious feature of oligopoly. The statistics of the amount of third-party payment and Internet-based payment in Q4 of 2016 reveal a feature of dual oligopoly in the market, with Alipay and Tenpay as the dominant players. As can be seen in Figs. 26.7 and 26.8, the market shares of Alipay and Tenpay went up by 92% and 61.9%, respectively, in Q4 of 2016.

Mobile payment has taken the place of Internet-based payment as the new leader in the online payment market. A look into the transaction amount of the subdivided sectors of third-party online payment shows that the market shares of Internet-based payment, which took up 96.5% of the total in 2011, fell sharply to 25.4% in 2016. And, the trend of mobile payment taking shares away from Internet-based payment will remain unchanged in the foreseeable future (Figs. 26.9 and 26.10).

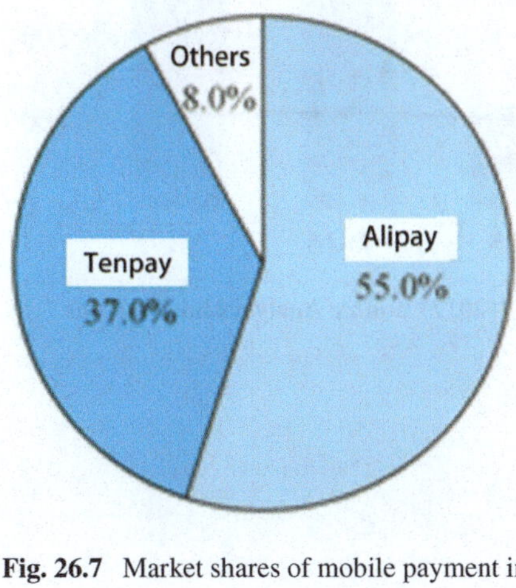

Payment service businesses	Amount of transaction (RMB 100 million)
1qianbao	4963.4
Union Mobile Pay	1694.0
LianLian Pay	1647.4
JDpay	1621.5
99Bill	1315.3
YeePay	1184.3
Suning Pay	710.3

Fig. 26.7 Market shares of mobile payment in Q4 of 2016. *Source* iResearch Consulting Group

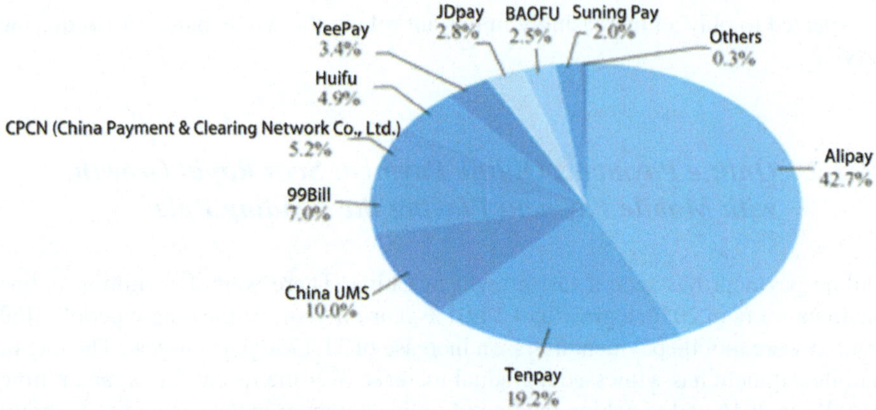

Fig. 26.8 Market shares of Internet-based payment in Q4 of 2016. *Source* iResearch Consulting Group

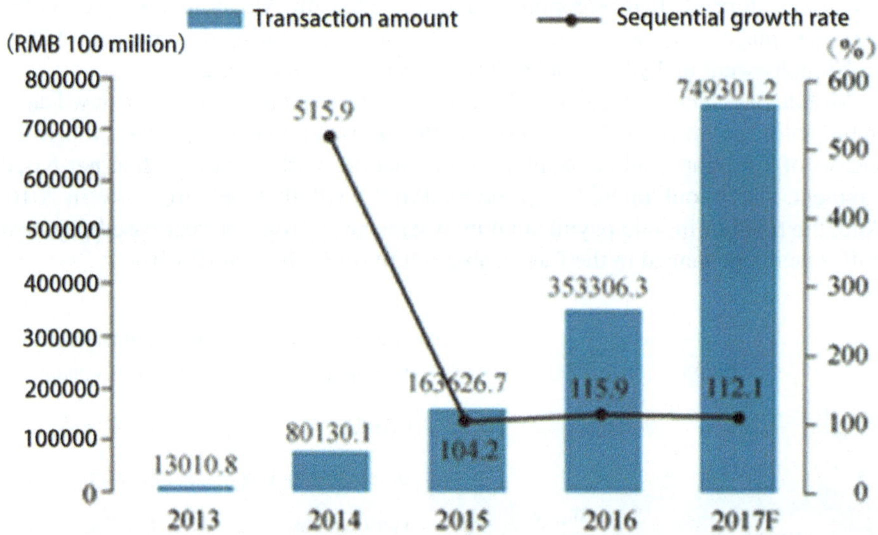

Fig. 26.9 Mobile payment transaction amount (2013–2017). *Source* Analysys International

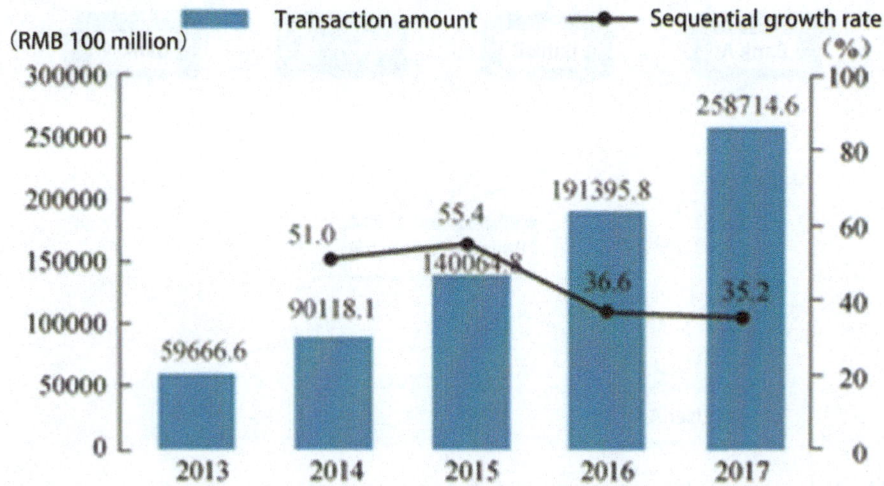

Fig. 26.10 Transaction amount of Internet-based payment (2013–2017). *Source* Analysys International

26.2 Expectation on NetsUnion Clearing Corporation (NUCC): What is the Supervision Authorities' Concern of About Payment Service?

26.2.1 Potential Supervision Loopholes in Third-Party Payment Based on Direct-Link Operation

Before NUCC was founded, the third-party payment agencies in China operated in a pattern featuring a direct link with banks. In this pattern of business, as is shown in Fig. 26.11, the third-party payment agencies directly connect with the banking system on the one hand and the users on the other, with the transaction data beyond the reach of supervision. As stated earlier, Alipay and Tenpay are the leading players in the online payment market. With stronger capacity of price negotiating and big efforts in expanding their direct connection with banks, they have more competitive rates than the other third-party payment agencies. The non-banking payment agencies undertake the function of clearing in practical operation. Together with merchants and custodian banks, they complete the payment procedures in a new three-party framework.

From the perspective of the regulatory authorities, there are potential supervision loopholes in the business pattern featuring a direct link between third-party payment agencies and banking institutions. In the direct-link pattern of operation, a payment agency can open accounts in many different banks simultaneously, and the flow of the capital in the accounts, which are held by the same agency, enables it to complete all the payment procedures by simply adjusting the amount of money in different

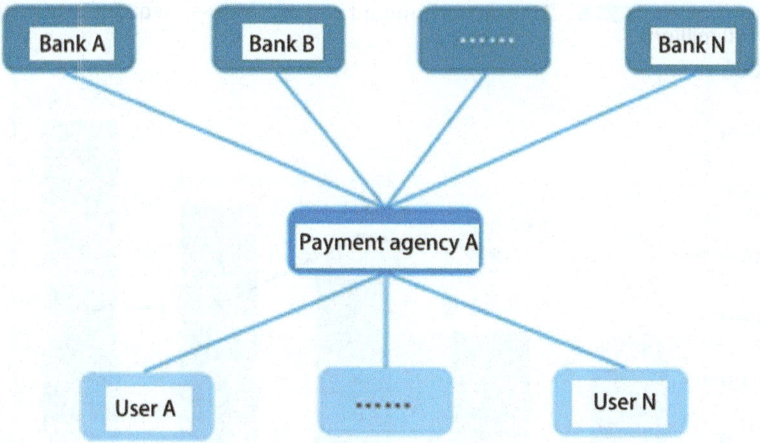

Fig. 26.11 Direct-link operation pattern of third-party payment agencies

accounts after balance offsetting. As the detailed information of the transaction is kept within the payment agencies, the regulatory authorities can only see the change of capital in the different bank accounts, but they cannot supervise potential law or rule-breaking behaviors in the process of payment, including money laundering, tax-related risks or illegal accounts held by the agencies. Apart from that, although the third-party agencies were granted payment licenses, they often expand their operations to cover banking, securities and insurance and even partly perform the function of the central bank. Furthermore, the total capital involved in third-party operation has hit a level of approximately RMB 1 trillion. These hidden risk factors have naturally raised concern of the supervision authorities.

26.2.2 NetsUnion Clearing Corporation (NUCC) is Established to Close Supervision Loopholes and Help Third-Party Payment Return to Essence of Online Payment Service

The establishment of NUCC (as is indicated in Fig. 26.12) was not unexpected. It is a natural outcome of PBC's efforts in adopting a series of relevant policies over recent couple of years. The measures introduced by PBC in the last year or two, including the classification of accounts and the centralized custody of payment agencies' customer provisions, along with its recent move to transfer transactions to the NUCC platform, show PBC's increasingly clear strategy of supervision. It is the primary concern of the central bank to guard against financial risks to ensure the safety of the money of the general public. The establishment of NUCC provides a technical means for the supervision of the payment agencies. It is also an indication

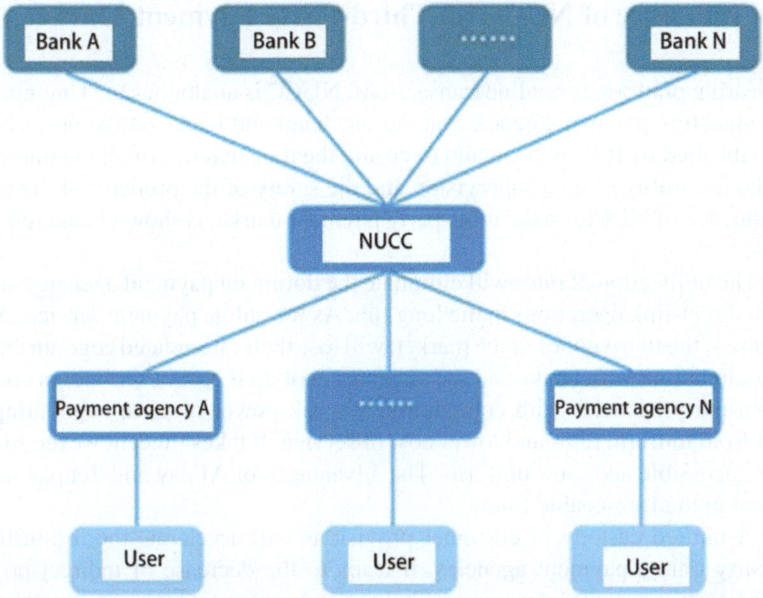

Fig. 26.12 Four-party operation pattern with involvement of NUCC

that PBC has begun to seek a breakthrough from third-party payment service in the institutional innovation of financial supervision, taking Internet-based financial service and financial supervision of online consumption as the important fields. The unified platform of payment agencies provides both accessing and clearing service and helps to improve payment efficiency, avoid overlapping projects and optimize the supervision of third-party payment. This helps reduce risks in an all-round way and protect the rights and interests of the general public. It is important to lead third-party payment service to return to the essence of online payment service, that is, "small-amount and convenient transaction to the benefit of the general public," and lead the service to a track of sound and orderly development.

The third-party payment agencies used to operate in a pattern of direct financial link with banks and users, with Unionpay kept away from the transaction. In this pattern of operation, neither the PBC nor the banks could keep track of all the transaction information and capital flows on a real-time basis from a global perspective. This caused comparatively great challenges for PBC in its various financial operations, including money laundering prevention, financial supervision, monetary policy regulation, and financial data analysis. After being put in operation, NUCC is expected to change the status quo featuring passive supervision or after-the-event investigation into a proactive mechanism characterized with in-process supervision or even before-the-event precautions. This will effectively promote the efficiency of financial supervision of online payment service.

26.3 Influence of NUCC on Third-Party Payment Market

As a clearing platform for online transactions, NUCC is analogous to "Unionpay" on line, connecting payment agencies on the one hand and banks on the other. NUCC was established by PBC with an aim to ensure the transparency of all the transaction data, the feasibility of data supervision and the safety of the property of the public. The influence of NUCC on the third-party payment market is shown in the following aspects:

3.1 The unification of rates will eliminate the dominant payment agencies' advantages in direct-link operations in the long run. As for online payment service, Alipay and Tenpay, the two tycoons of the market, will lose their rate-related edge attributable to their direct link with banks and see an increase of their cost of service. In contrast, the third-party agencies with comparatively weak power of price negotiating will benefit from uniform rates and lower cost of service. It takes time, however, to make NUCC accessible and rates uniform. The advantages of Alipay and Tenpay in rates still exist in the foreseeable future.

3.2 A unified custody of customer provisions will accelerate the reshuffling of third-party online payment agencies. It leads to the decrease of indirect profit of the third-party payment agencies and helps them return to payment service per se gradually as the unification of rates spares them efforts to develop links with banks. To tackle the pressure resulting from the drop of actual profit, the agencies should increase their market shares and promote the quality of their service. Hence, they are likely to face an accelerated reshuffle of the market.

3.3 For the agencies specialized in bank card acquiring service in a four-party pattern, the establishment of NUCC will not exert direct influence on them in view of the status quo.

3.4 In accordance with the stipulation of the regulatory authorities, NUCC will only engage in clearing instead of payment service. Hence, it is not a direct competitor for the third-party payment agencies.

References

1. Ba Shusong. Categorized supervision of payment accounts: experience for reference and policy framework [N]. *Financial News*, 24–09–2014 (002).
2. Ba Shusong & Yang Biao. Study of international practice and experience of third-party payment supervision [J]. *Public Finance Research*, 2012 (04): 72-75.

Chapter 27
Development of Payment-Clearing Sector in Financial Reform of China

With economic restructuring and financial reform in progress across different sectors, the payment-clearing sector in China is also forging ahead continuously. In 2016, it witnessed two major changes: The first is the adoption of the reform-and-opening-up policy for the payment-clearing sector; the second is the kicking off the project of online payment-clearing platform dedicated to the payment agencies. These two measures will exert a major influence on the country's payment-clearing market, pushing ahead the reshaping of the market with regard to its form and structure. Of the two measures taken, the opening up of the bank card-related payment-clearing market is expected to facilitate the development of a market of fair play and accelerate the further reform and innovative restructuring of payment service in China. It is also expected to promote a sound development of the economic and financial market, push forward economic restructuring and upgrading and strengthen international economic cooperation. The establishment of the online payment platform will help, among others, save social resources, improve the efficiency of payment and clearing, optimize the structure for market competition and ensure the transparency of supervision.

With demand, supply and other factors taken into account, a more effective, market-oriented and flexible payment-clearing sector is needed in economic restructuring and financial reform to undertake the responsibility of building the infrastructure for its microscopic operations. The payment-clearing sector is also expected to develop in a direction inextricably linked to the general trend of financial reform in China.

1. **With demand taken into account, economic restructuring and financial reform calls for an effective, market-oriented and flexible service of payment and clearing.**

With a look into the general trend of financial reform, a more effective, market-driven and flexible financial system is needed to support economic restructuring.

Source Headline Today on June 24, 2017.

S. Ba, *The New Cycle and New Finance in China*,
https://doi.org/10.1007/978-981-16-8209-4_27

The new round of economic reform is aimed at increasing the total factor growth rate and facilitating the economic restructuring. In the foreseeable future, the economic growth of China will shift from a resource-driven pattern to an innovation-driven pattern focusing on the efficiency of resource allocation, with an aim to increase the total factor productivity. As an important part of the economic reform, the financial reform calls for the establishment of a more effective financial market and more market-oriented financial institutions to tackle various risks in the existing economic and financial systems. It also calls for the establishment of a more flexible financial system to obtain greater momentum. Besides, efforts should be made to coordinate financial reform with the reform in other fields of economy. With economic restructuring and financial reform under way, a more effective, market-oriented and flexible payment-clearing sector is therefore needed to assume the responsibility of infrastructure building in support of microscopic operations in the sector.

In view of the law of development for payment service, the payment system in most countries runs with a trend toward a more effective and market-oriented system. Firstly, the emergence of cash-free payment is attributable to people's pursuit of a more effective service of payment and clearing. The great improvement of payment efficiency, which is supported by electronic payment technology, gives impetus to the reform of payment system in various countries. A couple of developed nations, like Norway, Belgium and Finland, have already established a system of non-cash payment or a system supporting limited use of cash. Secondly, the increasingly diversified demand on payment service pushes ahead the division of the sector and the appearance of various service providers. This facilitates a market-oriented reform of payment service.

2. **With supply taken into account, the payment system in China is seeing improvement in efficiency and progress in market-oriented reform, but a more balanced and coordinated development is needed.**

Since 2002, with the fast growth of economy and finance in China, the payment system has undergone a "golden period" of development and shown three prominent features typical of the period:

Firstly, the perfection of payment infrastructure and the innovation of payment service, both of which are driven by modern science and technology, have significantly improved the safety and efficiency of payment and clearing countrywide. This is attributable to the widespread application of technologies in different links of payment transactions, including the technologies of Internet, communications, imaging, electronic autographing and receipt counterfeiting prevention. Meanwhile, in a trend toward the popular application of electronic and information technologies, innovations are emerging endlessly in the patterns of payment service covering transactions and operation processing, with a focus on the prominent feature of "convenience in payment" and the foremost goal of "safety and efficiency." This has greatly facilitated the diversification of payment approaches in the society and has satisfied to some extent the increasingly diversified demands on payment in a market-driven economy.

Secondly, the payment system has become increasingly connected with the market-oriented and internationalized pattern of operation, with the latter exerting an intensifying influence on the former. Generally, the rapid growth of the payment system in China in more than a decade is mainly attributable to structural reform and infrastructure improvement. For instance, with the unified efforts to establish a large-scale inter-bank system of payment and clearing, the system has been successfully upgraded, and the payment-related financial infrastructure has been improved to world standard; China has also stipulated the core principles of its payment system by referring to the regulatory standards in practice worldwide, following the trend toward an internationalized payment system.

Thirdly, increasing importance will be attached to a balanced and coordinated development of the different components of the payment system. To achieve this goal in its effort to develop and optimize the payment system, it is advisable for PBC to shift its focus from massive development of financial infrastructure to the perfection of laws and regulations on payment and clearing, the promotion of non-cash payment tools and the increase of the efficiency of payment-clearing administration. As the financial institutions in the banking industry undertake the function as the "arteries" of public capital flow, it is advisable for the third-party or non-financial payment service agencies, which are the mainstay of the sector, to place emphasis on enriching and perfecting the "veins" of the payment system continuously through intensive efforts in specializing and individualizing service applications and through the innovation and upgrading of product service as well as the building of well-matched infrastructure.

3. **Non-cash payment service—powerful impetus for development of the sector.**

The recent years has witnessed a fast growth of the overall scale of non-cash payment service and a widespread use of non-cash payment tools in China. A set of payment tools have been developed, with receipts and bank cards as the major tools and electronic payment as the supplementary tool, including Internet-based payment and mobile payment. This period has also seen continuous improvement in different fields, including the infrastructure of payment, clearing and settlement, the system of laws and regulations on payment and clearing and the multi-dimensional supervision of the sector. With the increasingly extensive coverage of the Internet, non-cash payment service has become a powerful impetus for the development of the payment-clearing sector in China.

4. **Major fields to propel payment-clearing sector forward on the basis of the trend.**

The first is diversification, which involves the entities of the sector and the means of payment. The diversification of the entities helps prevent low efficiency incurred by monopoly and reduce the negative influence of individual market entities on the whole society when they fail to maintain the continuity of their operations; the diversification of payment means can meet the multiple demands of the market. And, the different means of payment with the same function can be each other's backup. This makes the function of payment more flexible.

The second is the unity of principles and flexibility. For example, in the year-end settlement of banks, PBC will appropriately adjust the operation time for both large payment and small payment systems, showing a unity of principles and flexibility. In the retail payment system, great flexibility is also needed for an efficient and convenient mechanism of dispute settlement. The payment-clearing sector should balance principles with adaptability in its different services, as a way to enhance its flexibility; in some periods when inter-bank liquidity becomes tight, time limit can be extended accordingly for day-end processing of PBC's large payment system.

The third is variety and priority. In view of the variety and divergence of market demands, a sound and sustainable payment system should also be multi-layered and diversified. The co-existence of the systems of large payment, retail payment and designated payment matches the various demands of payment transactions; the multiple functions of debit, credit and different credit payment tools can satisfy the demands of economic activities subject to different rules of transactions; pre-paid card service, mobile payment and Internet payment also have their respective roles to play in the market.

There will be all kinds of evolution in the payment-clearing system and payment tools at different levels and in different categories and fields. But it remains a fundamental principle to refer to their different levels of importance in the whole system while deciding on the intensity of supervision needed to ensure the flexibility of the payment-clearing sector. In other words, the flexibility of supervision over the payment-clearing sector should be determined on the basis of a principle of priority.

5. **Major development fields to help promote flexibility of payment system**

With a look into the trend of the payment sector, the three major fields, namely retail payment, cross-border payment and inclusive finance, are where the demand for greater flexibility of the payment system can be satisfied. They are also the major fields that can well integrate into the development of payment system in the important phase of economic and financial restructuring.

Firstly, with convenience and safety of payment as the main goals, efforts should be made to facilitate innovation in retail payment system for convenience of consumption and boost of domestic demand. A major step in China's economic restructuring is to shift from investment-driven to consumption-driven economy. It is important that the reform involved should promote the development of systems and mechanisms supportive of a moderate-speed growth driven by domestic demand. The innovation and development of retail payment system evidently contributes to a boost in consumption.

Secondly, efforts should be made to develop cross-border payment to promote the internationalization of RMB. In light of international practices, cross-border payment is the starting point and foundation for the internationalization of RMB. With a look into the payment system, cross-border payment service helps to build a financial market that is in-depth and far-reaching and enables the domestic payment-clearing sector to be geared to international standards in a more flexible way.

Thirdly, efforts should be made to further promote non-cash payment tools to facilitate the development of inclusive finance and enhance the function of account-based financial service. The promotion of non-cash payment tools helps to increase and popularize the payment accounts, the number of which has already become huge in China. With regard to the flexibility of the payment system, however, the popularization of accounts is only part of the picture, and a system of multiple payment tools and a multi-layer system of payment and clearing are needed as a support for enhancing the function of account-based financial service.

In the last decade or so, China has made great progress in developing an efficient and market-oriented payment system. The finance sector in China is now ushering in an era of rapid transformation of both the market and the supervision. The drive behind the transformation is derived from reflections on the financial crisis, the new demand of the real economy and the infusion of new forces such as the Internet. With the economic and financial systems becoming increasingly complex, the payment-clearing sector will inevitably take on a new trend in China, which is well worth our follow-up study.

References

1. Ba Shusong. Study on development of China's payment-clearing sector in light of financial reform trend [N]. *Financial News*, 25-07-2013: 002.
2. Wang Ying. Major changes of payment-clearing market in China in 2016 [J]. *China Credit Card*, 2016 (12): 14-16.
3. Wang Ganyin. Status quo of payment system in China and solutions to related problems [J]. *China Credit Card*, 2016 (03): 50-53.

Part IV
Inclusive Finance

Chapter 28
Technological Innovation of Inclusive Finance and Its Path of Development in "New Normal" of China's Economy

Inclusive finance is a way of financial service characterized with broad coverage, easy accessibility and prominent long-tail effect. It is realized through mass, efficient and low-cost operations. With capacity of data mining, quantitative storage and fast processing, big data technology well matches the demand of inclusive finance.

28.1 Technological Innovation of Inclusive Finance

Firstly, a look into the effect of technological innovation on the infrastructure of inclusive finance shows that technological innovation offers potential solutions for further development of inclusive finance, including a broader coverage of service and sustainable operations. The development of infrastructure mainly involves fundamental fields. Computer technology and cloud computing technology should be relied on to make inclusive finance more easily accessible. Meanwhile, the infrastructure platform based on Docker, a container technology, is a distributed framework popularly applied in inclusive finance worldwide. Compared with traditional frameworks, Docker-based framework features lower cost in big data processing. Furthermore, the sharing of infrastructure can cut down the cost of IT significantly while increasing productivity and efficiency, which ensures a steady operation of inclusive finance.

Secondly, technological innovation helps to enhance the capacity of inclusive finance in customer service. Inclusive finance companies in the broad sense do not have distinct advantages over traditional financial institutions or even have disadvantages in risk control measures. Therefore, the key to a sustainable development of inclusive finance is to solve risk control problems. There has been a frequent argument about risk control between the young people working in online finance institutions and the people engaging in risk control at banks. The former often stress the capacity of their institutions in making breakthroughs and innovations, while the

This article was published in 21st Century Business Herald on June 8, 2016

S. Ba, *The New Cycle and New Finance in China*,
https://doi.org/10.1007/978-981-16-8209-4_28

latter emphasize the importance of risk control, holding that it is more important to recover loans than to grant loans. It appears that they have reached a consensus that the key to the development of inclusive finance is to tackle problems of risk control. Risk control based on technological means mainly involves creating personalized graphic background of the people requesting financial service through mass data collecting and computing to determine the degree of the risk.

Thirdly, in an effort to promote the innovation of inclusive finance through technological transformation, the following points should be taken into account: (1) Data processing technology can be explored to conduct credit rating of loan applicants and divide customers into finely categorized groups so as to launch credit products matching the demand of different groups and conforming to different risk features; (2) innovation should be made in the ways of process management and risk control and should be represented in the description of relevant products. Risk control on the basis of process or system management is more reliable than that conducted by human; (3) loans on credit should be promoted in light of the characteristics of customers. And, credit products should be designed with labor skill training, science and technology popularization and entrepreneurship training taken into account; (4) efforts should be made to render financial service more easily accessible to the public and expand the scope of its service to offer optimal solutions that meet the capital needs of manufacturers.

Fourthly, as for the creation of credit value, it is intimately linked with transactions in economic activities. It depends on not only the retaining of credit but also an effective management of credit, covering credit investigation management, credit conferring management, account control and management and the utilization of credit database in market tapping or the promotion of credit payment tools. With the support of big data technology, which is characterized with the capacity of data mining, quantifying, mass storage and rapid processing, the management of modern credit system is expected to be upgraded to some extent. To deal with the challenges facing China in the development of the credit system, big data technology, with its massive amount of comprehensive information and advanced data processing technology and with the novel ways of thinking that form on the basis of data analysis, is applied and has helped break through the limitation of traditional methods in credit investigation, pressing for and facilitating the establishment and optimization of the credit system in China. Without the breakthrough, financial institutions have to turn to traditional methods in credit rating. For instance, banks will continue to depend on collateral-backed guarantee, whereas the customers of inclusive finance may happen to have no assets that can be used as collateral. This forces banks to adopt a technological means to investigate the credit of the customers.

Fifthly, a look into the effect of technological innovation on the development of credit management shows that big data technology helps extend the scale of credit data to include untraditional credit data as an important source of information for credit rating and to cover the group of people unregistered in the traditional credit system. Meanwhile, big data technology can provide real-time information of customers apart from the historical information. In addition, big data technology makes credit management more objective, as it helps expand the scope of data samples or even expand the scope to cover the entire data. The application of big data ensures the objectivity of credit management, and data mining technology ensures the authenticity and effectiveness of the data. Furthermore, big data technology helps improve the economic efficiency of credit management by solving some common problems of credit and cutting down human cost. It can also increase the sources of credit information, which ensures not only the authenticity of the information but also the fast, efficient and real-time communication of the information.

Sixthly, information technology can be applied to optimize the process of risk management. As a result of the adverse-selection effect in inclusive finance, the clients who undertake the higher interest rate bring with them greater risk. Meanwhile, it is difficult to conduct ethical risk assessment and identify potential risks through in-advance credit examination. With big data technology, however, in-depth analyses can be made on a company's production and operation data of past years to reveal its path of development and status quo. Big data technology also helps track the company's operations on a quantified and around-the-clock basis to better identify risks. Big data technology also helps match risks with the characteristics of clients and transfer risks or disperse them more effectively. For example, it can match the clients who have the capacity to undertake higher-level risks with capital of higher risk. Furthermore, big data technology helps predict the occurrence of future events, transfer and disperse potential risks accordingly and match clients with appropriate credit products on the basis of the predicted risks and profits. It still has many other applications in terms of risk monitoring, precaution and prevention. It can be applied to help establish a risk precaution mechanism, conduct real-time risk monitoring and make visualized analysis to display the whole process of risk prevention and control. For banks, the restructuring of credit procedures poses a great challenge. For institutions engaging in inclusive finance, it can be pushed forward and implemented from a higher starting point.

Seventhly, the effect of technological innovation on risk management methods. Technological innovation helps enhance risk management in different aspects, the first of which is shown in its support for the acquisition of mass data. Risk management demands a good variety of data, such as the data of e-commerce Web sites, credit cards, social network sites, small loan sites and daily life service sites. The whole picture of a client's risk status cannot be seen clearly until the data from different sources are integrated. By following the big data-based procedures specific for risk control data processing, the management of risk-related decision making can be improved, and the information about loan applicants can be obtained on a more comprehensive, accurate and timely basis. In fact, when a client enters a bank, he or she is a black box to the bank. These data help us make clear judgment, find the internal link of different variables and make a more accurate decision. The use of big data increases both the efficiency and quality of risk-related decision making, facilitating a shift from idea and concept-based management to digitalized and more precise management.

Eighthly, the effect of technological innovation on the management of all-round customer experience. The clients' demand varies with the ways of economic growth and development. The application of the new technologies can meet their new demand, such as an emphasis on the importance of customer experience and involvement, the development of sensory experience and the development of a sense of identity in thoughts. Without the support of relevant technologies, the demand can hardly be satisfied.

Ninthly, the effect of technology on marketing patterns. Viewed with the traditional concept of marketing, a consumer's behavior of buying is a process of personal decision making. Viewed with the concept of big data-based marketing, however, the decision making of an individual consumer is greatly affected by the will of the consumer group and will exert influence on the group. Therefore, a video clip spread on the Internet can cause a stock to soar to a limit-up level or fall sharply to a limit-down level. People engaging in video and media-related work claim that the era of short videos has come and news dissemination has been transformed into the dissemination of short videos.

Tenthly, technological innovation helps optimize value-added service. Apart from the service of payment, clearing, investment, wealth management, loan financing, the financial institutions has launched multiple value-added service.

28.2 Seeking New Path of Development for Inclusive Finance in "New Normal" of China's Economy[1]

Many financial institutions in China, whether they are burgeoning institutions, who put a focus on inclusive finance, or commercial banks, who try to extend their business to reach ordinary customers under the pressure of market competition, carry out their financial service in a sustainable way and expand it to cover the people and businesses beyond the reach of traditional financial service. This strategy has developed into a common understanding among these institutions on their path to the "new normal" of the country's economy. In their process of exploring, the different institutions find in various ways that operation patterns, product forms and risk control systems different from those intended for the customers of traditional commercial banks should be used to reach the customers who are not covered by traditional financial systems. For example, through their practical experience, some commercial banks come to learn that new patterns of operation characterized with batch processing and fixed procedures should be adopted to take the place of traditional ones featuring examination and approval on a one-by-one basis to expand their financial service to cover small and microbusinesses that have been reached less frequently.

The financial institutions, represented by CreditEase, Alibaba and other emerging enterprises, have made significant exploration via different paths into the application of big data in the development of inclusive finance. It is certainly of great importance to sum up the experience of the exploration to promote further development of inclusive finance in the next phase. Some parts of the report *Practice of Inclusive*

[1] This part is a brief review made by researcher Ba Susong on the CreditEase's special report *Practice of Inclusive Finance in China: Big Data and Reform.*

Finance in China: Big Data and Reform are summaries of the experience. They can be used as valuable reference.

There are many metaphors about big data, and one of them is impressive. Financial businesses, no matter how big they are, have very limited capacity to integrate their operations if there is no support of big data technology. Business expansion without resource integration supported by big data will lead to very limited effectiveness and coping capacity. It is comparable to the effort of Cao Cao, a central figure in the Chinese classical novel the *Romance of the Three Kingdoms*, who tried to gain an edge by connecting war ships with chains in the battle of the Red Cliffs; A financial institution, with its operations integrated with the support of big data, resembles an aircraft carrier with a unified smart system. It is not only big in size but also powerful in its fighting force.

Big data technology helps extend financial service to reach the customers who were not covered in the traditional financial system because of the high cost of risk assessment conducted in the traditional way. Exploration of inclusive finance has begun to attract attention in both developed and emerging markets after the financial crisis. If there is a conflict in developed nations, with the United States as the representative, between Wall Street and Main Street after the crisis, the extension of financial service with the support of big data enables the former to provide more service to the latter. The significance of doing this is self-evident.

Internet finance has drawn much more attention in China than in the developed market represented by the United States. Despite the common operation principles, such as the emphasis on the application of big data, there is a remarkable difference between Chinese and American Internet finance businesses in terms of development paths, customer selection and profiting methods. It shows that more explorers are needed in China to accumulate experience of big data application in inclusive finance. It also calls for more adjustment in the economic and financial systems. For example, the regulatory authorities should set a clear-cut and flexible framework of supervision and strengthen supervision on fake online financial activities that violate laws and rules while giving support for the development of law-abiding businesses in the market to keep the sector's reputation and public confidence away from any harm caused by some businesses who take advantage of the situation when a clear supervision framework is not in place; The regulatory authorities should take measures to remove "information islands" so as to provide the businesses with better resources in information collecting and sharing and help them lower the cost. Meanwhile, a full consciousness of the inherent defects of big data is needed. For example, the risk assessment model based on big data is likely to be abused and misled; big data is likely to contain distorted or biased views and misunderstandings of the designer as it is a product designed by humans; and big data collection is likely to be incomprehensive, with some fields possibly not covered. As for these imperfections, explorers across the world should work together for better solutions. Proposed solutions to these problems can be found in the report *Practice of Inclusive Finance in China: Big Data and Reform*. They are well worth our attention and further exploration.

Chapter 29
Path of Development and Innovation of Small and Microbusiness-Targeted Finance During Economic Adjustment

With accelerating liberalization of interest rate, deepening disintermediation of finance and emerging of Internet finance in recent years, financial institutions of different types have included small and microbusiness-targeted finance as their important field of development, and a variety of business models of microfinance have developed, with the model of city commercial banks, the model of share-holding commercial banks and the model of Internet finance as the representatives. During the economic adjustment, the different business models are faced with adjustment pressure in different ways, prompting microfinance institutions to make innovation and breakthrough in the new economic and financial situation.

29.1 Business Models of Microfinance Facing Pressure Test During Economic Adjustment Cycle

29.1.1 Three Business Models of Microfinance

There are roughly three business models of microfinance in China, namely the model of city commercial banks, the model of share-holding commercial banks and the model of Internet finance. They are comparatively successful in practical operation and have attracted extensive attention in the market. But there is still room for improvement despite their respective advantages for different customers and fields.

The model of city commercial banks: This model stresses the importance of regional microfinance, with its operation being financing service-oriented. As the business of city commercial banks is comparatively confined to specific regions, they base decision making on the comprehensive information of the regional customers

---

This article was published in the 7th issue of *Finance and Economy* in 2016.

S. Ba, *The New Cycle and New Finance in China*,
https://doi.org/10.1007/978-981-16-8209-4_29

and promote business among customers with regional characteristics. The comprehensive information covers not only financial but also non-financial affairs. For the financial service providers for small and microbusinesses, the regulatory authorities mainly give guidance and adopt encouraging policies, with an emphasis placed on market repositioning and the change of business operation idea and with efforts made to encourage the establishment of professional mechanisms and systems to gradually improve their professional service. The typical banks of this model include Baoshang Bank Limited, Zhejiang Tailong Commercial Bank, etc.

The model of share-holding commercial banks: This model places an emphasis on fixed procedures and large scale and is comprehensive financial service-oriented. With more demands for loan satisfied, small and microbusinesses have seen rapid growth, and they need a more specific and comprehensive financial service. The national share-holding commercial banks, with their abundant financial products and competitive human resources, have developed a "credit factory" pattern of operation and a financial service pattern targeted at specific regions and industry chains. Both patterns can better satisfy the demand of small and microbusinesses. A typical bank of this model is China Minsheng Bank.

The model of Internet finance: This model stresses the importance of technological innovation in microfinance and is aimed at providing diversified and customized financial service. Thanks to the advancement of interest rate marketization and financial deregulation, more attention has been attracted to microfinance and many Internet companies have begun to engage in the business. These companies have come up with new paths of exploration into microfinance through the application of information technology, the Internet, cloud computing, big data technology, etc. With advantages in capital allocation efficiency, channels, data information, transaction cost and system technology, Internet finance is essentially a more democratic and inclusive way of finance targeted at the general public, and its features well match those of microfinance. Typical institutions of this model include Ant Financial Services Group (or Ant Financial in short) under Alibaba Group and CreditEase.

29.1.2 Business Models of Microfinance Under Test During Economic Adjustment Cycle

Different business models will undergo pressure test in every cycle of economic adjustment. If one type of credit service is excessively concentrated on some industries or regions, it will show a more evident periodicity and confront greater impact of the pressure from the economic adjustment. With China's economy shifting from a pattern of high growth to a pattern of medium–high growth, the percentage of non-performance loan is gradually going up (as is indicated in Fig. 29.1). As a new financing pattern emerging after 2008, microfinance has not undergone the test of a complete economic cycle, especially the test of the cycle of credit risk unleashing. The sustainability of different business models of microfinance remains to be seen.

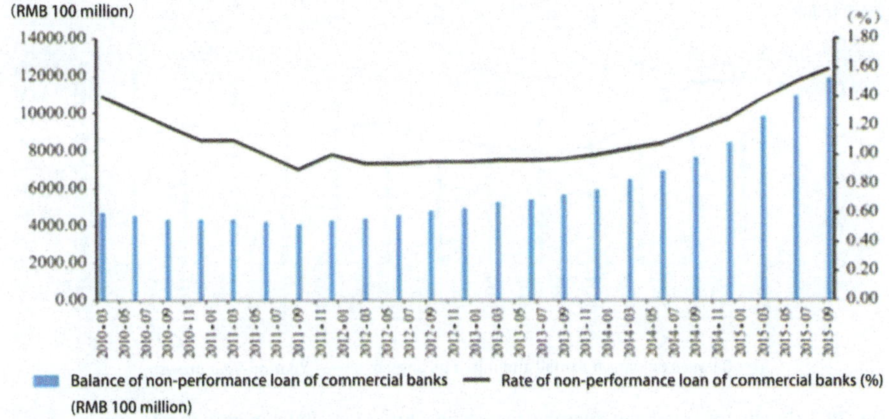

Fig. 29.1 China's commercial banks see rapid increase in NPL rate

As their operations are highly concentrated in certain regions or industries, the business models of city commercial banks and share-holding commercial banks face comparatively evident impact in the cycle of economic downturn. An example of this is the pattern of microfinance focusing on "specific regions and industry chains," a pattern characteristic of the share-holding commercial banks. The small and microbusinesses in the target regions will be divided into groups of different levels and categories specifically in terms of the duration of operation, revenue, etc. Then, specific credit plans will be worked out for the businesses accordingly. The industry chain consists of a central enterprise and a group of small businesses and proprietors serving the central enterprise. The banks provide comprehensive financial service to the small and microbusinesses in the upstream and downstream chain on the basis of the transaction data of the central enterprise. The share-holding commercial banks have adopted an operation pattern of mass marketing and mass credit conferring for the small and microbusinesses in the specific regions and chains. They have also adopted a policy supporting mutual guarantee in joint loan application to reduce credit risks of individual businesses. These measures help the banks carry out credit operations on a mass basis and maintain low cost of operations. This model of business was a significant attempt, but it has led to many cases of non-performance loan in the cycle of economic adjustment. The problem of joint loan application on the basis of mutual guarantee is especially severe in Jiangsu, Zhejiang and Shanxi provinces, creating a big impact on microfinance operations. Despite the fact that the model of Internet finance helps lower cost with technological means and manage risks with big data and cloud computing, a business model or a credit risk control model in the financial industry will only become mature after being tested in one or two economic cycles. The model of Internet finance, in which the Internet is a technological driving force, still cannot be regarded as a mature business model, because there have been no samples and data that show its operations in complete economic cycles.

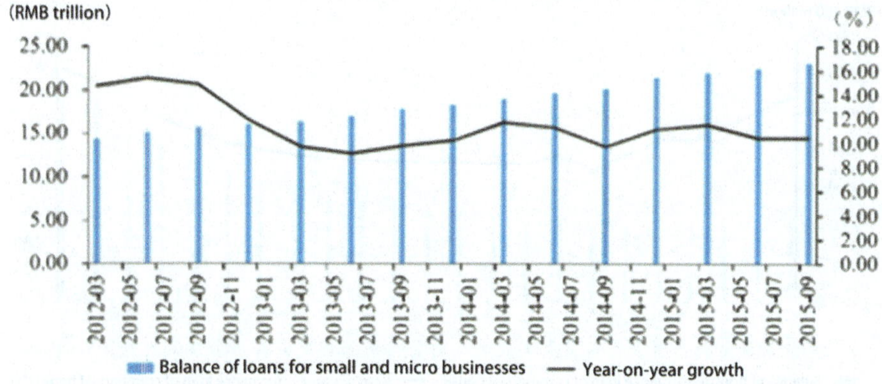

Fig. 29.2 Loans for small and microbusinesses in China slow down in growth rate

To sum up, no matter what type of business model is currently adopted for microfinance in China, the risk model is established on the basis of the customer behavior and economic data in the cycle of economic upturn, and the credit risk data have not undergone the test of a complete economic cycle. Consequently, different risks may emerge as a result of the underestimation of the extent of credit quality decline. Confronted with the pressure test in the cycle of economic downturn, some financial institutions have been hit hard in microfinance operations, with the balance of microloan taking a downturn in its growth rate (as is indicated in Fig. 29.2).

29.2 Exploration on Innovation of Microfinance in New Economic Situation

Confronted with the new situation of economic adjustment, microfinance institutions of different kinds have made great effort to explore new business patterns and improve their existing ones.

Traditional financial institutions have also adopted a series of measures to adjust their business models for microfinance. Firstly, the traditional business pattern focusing on specific regions and industry chains is improved so as to establish a more refined and professional financial model for industry clusters and supply chains. Secondly, by taking advantage of the diversification of their financial service, the business scale of microfinance is expanded to provide the proprietors of small and microbusinesses with service apart from financing, with the service covering account settlement, wealth management and consultancy to enhance customer stickiness. The deciding factor for a greater market share is the effective identification of customer demands and the adjustment of products, service and business models on the basis of the change of customer demands. Thirdly, the operation procedures are optimized in order to promote operation efficiency and lower operation cost. Currently, many city commercial banks and share-holding commercial banks are exploring and implementing new measures to improve the operation procedures for microfinance and cut down the cost, with an aim to develop an efficient "credit factory." Fourthly, for risk management, innovative risk management tools and credit rating technology are utilized, and risk control measures more adapted to the current situation are adopted.

Many burgeoning institutions have explored into technology-backed credit investigation and risk monitoring to different extent.

Firstly, new technologies are applied to upgrade and transform the traditional pattern of credit investigation. Banks used to assess the customers' credit status on the basis of their financial condition, behavior features, credit records, profession environment, default probability and credit rating. With Internet data sources put to use, big data-backed credit investigation is conducted on the basis of the data of the customers' activities, including online searching, social activities, travel and consumption. This makes customer analysis more valid and accurate and helps cut down the cost of credit investigation effectively in microfinance service. Secondly, technological revolution helps upgrade risk monitoring, pre-warning, prevention and control and other relevant measures. The development of cloud computing and search engine technologies makes possible an efficient analysis of big data and a low-cost assessment of the price of loan applicants' risk assets and their default probability, which reduces the operation cost of the whole financial activities. For example, with the support of online platforms and systems, a visualized system of prevention and control can be developed to integrate the information of the customers' historical transactions conducted via different channels, which helps remove the information islands of separate systems. Another example: big data can be used to visualize correlations, which helps enhance the effectiveness of the internal supervision of regulation compliance, anti-fraud service and credit risk prevention and control.

In reality, there is enormous value in data application. In the different phases of bull and bear markets, the major investor groups contributing to the growth of fund share sales are evolving in a stair-step pattern. At the beginning of a bull market, which has not been widely recognized by ordinary investors, the high-end investors in the first-tier cities are the major buyers of the shares of a certain fund; when the bull market matures, the middle-class investors in the second-tier cities become the major buyers; and when investors in the third-tier cities become the major buyers, other investors should be alert to the change of the market trend. These data already exist, but they seem irrelevant to each other. Internet finance institutions should explore ways to dig into the correlations among the information islands and provide visualized demonstration, support and decision making. Online loan service is another typical example indicative of the effective application of big data in credit investigation. A database can be built firstly to collect information about the customers. With some technical methods, investigations can be made into the internal link between the data of the customers' behaviors and their credit status to find out the probability of customer default and the prospective loss caused by default. After big data mining, Internet loan institutions can summarize the features of the customers and record their credit rating. When a customer files a loan application, Internet loan companies can assess the default risk of the customer in time on the basis of the data system in the computer and adjust the credit limit, lending rate and length of maturity flexibly. This well shows the advantage of technology application in efficiency improvement.

29.3 Development Trend of Microfinance in China

29.3.1 Microfinance Remains Important Field for Further Development of Banking Industry

Although it is still undergoing the test of economic downturn, the banking industry has not stopped listing microfinance as a major field of business. According to *Chinese Bankers Survey*, continuous follow-up interviews show that over the last three years Chinese bankers regard small and microbusinesses as the most important customers in their strategic development. In 2015, 86.9% of the bankers showed a positive attitude to the important status of these businesses (as is indicated in Fig. 29.3). Apart from the influence of external factors such as policies and fierce competition for customers among big companies, the high rate of profit contribution of small and microbusinesses is an important reason for the banks to continuously try to make the businesses their customers.

A look into the development of Wells Fargo reveals that a good performance in microfinance has helped it get through the test of complete economic cycles and the related business model is sustainable (as is indicated in Fig. 29.4). With the help of the credit rating system tailored to small and microbusinesses, Wells Fargo is able to deal with two million loans every year for the businesses with yearly sales of less than US$ two million each. And, two-thirds of the loan approving decisions is made by the system itself. After the release of a loan, the system will do a follow-up credit assessment of the customer on a monthly basis. The computer will automatically assess the customer's behavior connected with the loan and make adjustment about relevant loan policies if applicable.

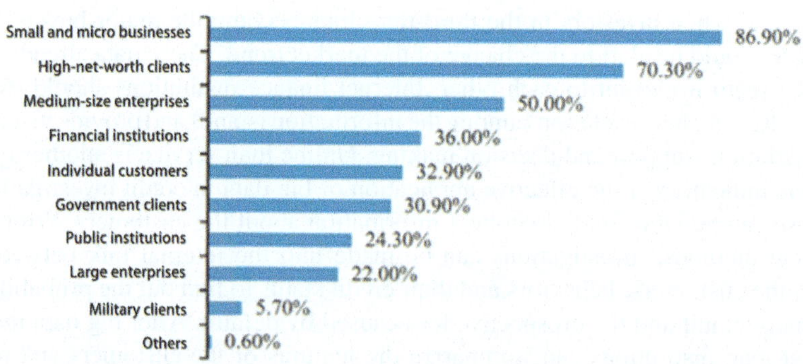

Fig. 29.3 Prospective major customers for Chinese banking industry in 2015

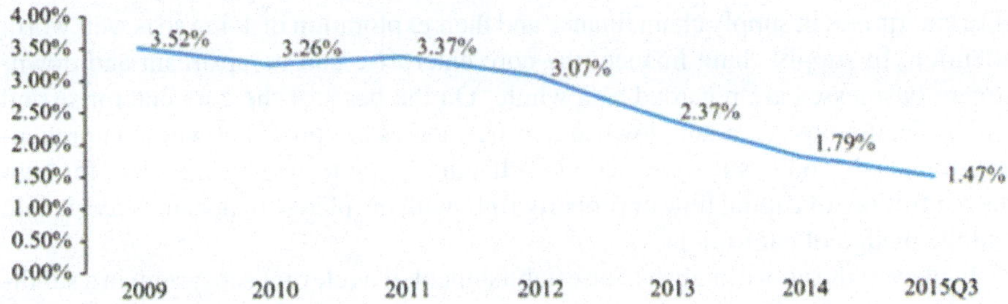

Fig. 29.4 Wells Fargo sees continuous decline in NPL rate

29.3.2 Reliability of Big Data-Based Credit Investigation and Online Loan Service in Internet Finance to Be Tested

Big data-based credit investigation and online loan service are still in the initial phase of development. They are much less mature than the credit investigation conducted and the loan service provided by traditional financial institutions such as banks in terms of the pattern and scale of business as well as the capacity of surviving complete economic cycles. Consequently, the sustainability of microloan service in Internet finance remains to be proved. Firstly, the big data mining platforms in China are still in their early stages, and there is a lack of core technology for the building of the platforms; Secondly, there is a lot of publicity about big data and Internet finance, but more efforts are needed to build fundamental databases of information resources; thirdly, data variables need to be pinpointed, and there is still enormous room for improvement in the selection and optimization of variables in data mining; fourthly, Internet finance still has potential risks related to information safety, including network malfunction, hacker attacks and internal privacy disclosure. They are yet to be solved properly.

29.3.3 Vertical Management to Become Solution to Microfinance Problems

Vertical management is going to be a solution to the problems of microfinance in the future. It is especially critical to build a financial ecosystem for the subdivided branches of the industry. For microfinance in the future, there is minimal likelihood to find a uniform solution or principle, which will vary still further depending on specific sectors, industries or even regions. Microfinance service will be improved to overcome the barriers between the upstream and the downstream of a sector to build microfinance ecosystems specific to industry chains and application scenarios. In the ecosystem of microfinance, the involvement of traditional financial institutions and core enterprises in supply chain finance and their exploration in doing so is well worth attention. In supply chain finance, the core enterprise and its upstream and downstream businesses are regarded as a whole. On the basis of the core enterprise and real trade, the upstream and downstream businesses are provided with comprehensive financial products and service via self-liquidating trade financing and through the controlling of capital flow or property right with the pledge of accounts receivable and the pledge of cargo right.

In view of the above analysis, the establishment of a relevant ecosystem in a subdivided branch of industry, which is not merely the demand of the overall situation of the macroeconomy, is especially critical to the sustainable development of microfinance in the related field. Mysteel Group, a Shanghai-based enterprise of steel and iron trade, has made exploration in this field successfully. By integrating banks with steel and iron trade agencies at a dedicated business-to-business platform, Mysteel Group helps remove the barrier of mutual trust and has therefore witnessed a rapid growth.

29.3.4 Comprehensive Application of Financial Tools to Become Important Field for In-Depth Development of Microfinance

Information technology revolution will become an external force to be reckoned with for the accelerated development of microfinance, and financial technology and products are still the essential internal factors supporting its development. The applications of innovative financial technology and products in microfinance will become more comprehensive and diversified. The major fields of development for microfinance will include a further division of the customer groups, the matching of the subdivided customer groups to the corresponding services and products and the provision of comprehensive service by integrating various means of financial service such as credit, leasing, factoring and crowd-funding. For example, risk diversification methods such as the securitization of assets are being actively introduced into the microfinance market. In addition, with the innovation of financial technology, it has become a feasible business model for small and microcompanies to provide customized service and products related to operation procedures, the term of repayment, the methods of repayment and the interest rate for financing.

Chapter 30
Influence of Aging Population on China's Financial System

A Look into Pace of Population Aging in China Against Background of the World

The problem of aging society is arising in many countries. According to the 2016 World Economic Outlook published by IMF, the problem of aging population is indicated not only by the slowing down of overall population growth but also by the negative growth of labor force and the sharp increase of aging labor force. Especially in China, population aging will become faster with shorter intervals and its burden on the overall society will become heavier in the short run.

30.1 Faster Pace of Population Aging

According to world standards, when the rate of the population aged above 65 has risen from 7 to 14% in a country, it is an indicator of population "aging." By this criterion, the transition to aging society for major developed countries takes a span of 40–100 years, such as 45, 69 and 115 years for the UK, the United States and France, respectively; in comparison, the time for the completion of the transition in Asian countries is much shorter than that in European countries and the United States. For example, it took 25 years for Japan and a span of 15–20 years for Viet Nam, Malaysia, Thailand, Indonesia and South Korea. According to the 6th national population census in China, people aged 65 or above accounted for 8.87% of the total population, a rise of 1.91% over the rate in 2000. And, the pace of population aging in China will be faster in the coming 10 years. The UN predicted that the aged population in China will reach to or even exceed 14% of the total as early as in 2025. In other words, China will complete the transition to an aging society in a span of 25 years as did Japan (as is indicated in Fig. 30.1).

In addition, as is shown in Figure Two and Figure Three, population aging in China is prospected to show the following three characteristics in a short- and medium-term

Zhu Hong has participated in the drafting and discussing of this article. It was published in 21st Century Business Herald on December 9, 2016.

S. Ba, *The New Cycle and New Finance in China*,
https://doi.org/10.1007/978-981-16-8209-4_30

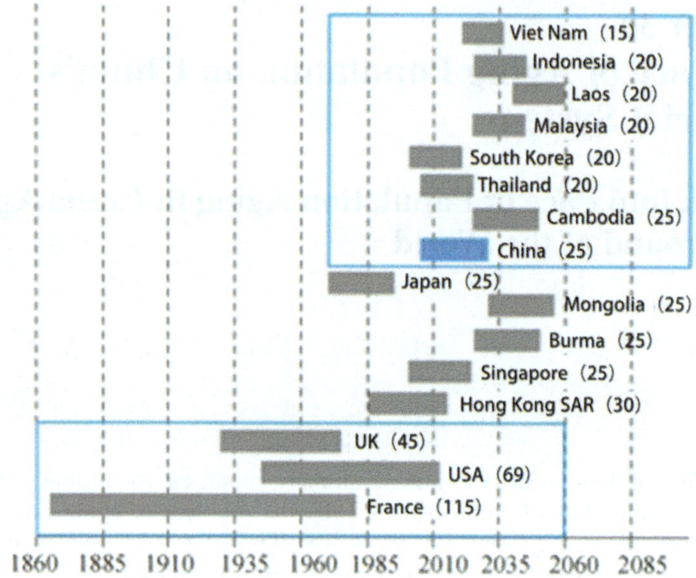

Fig. 30.1 Pace of population aging in different countries and regions

outlook covering a span from 2016 to 2021: Firstly, the growth rate of the overall population tends to become the same as that of developed economies but much lower than that of other emerging economies; secondly, the labor force is seeing a negative growth rate, which is expected to exceed that of traditional developed economies; thirdly, the proportion of aged labor force will grow continuously (Figs. 30.2 and 30.3).

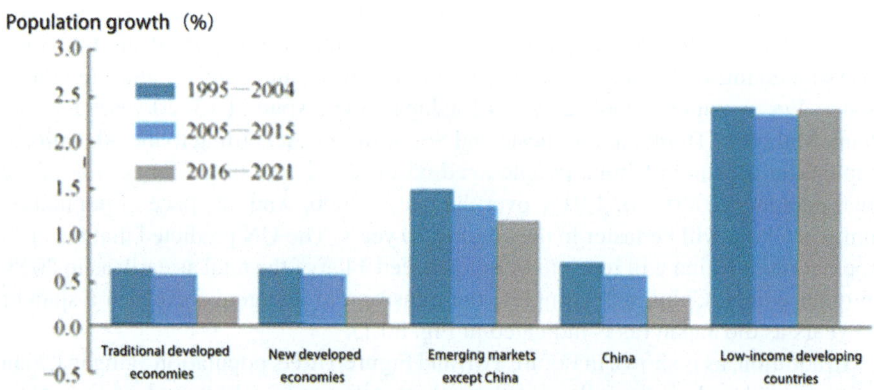

Fig. 30.2 Comparison of population growth trends in the world (1995–2021)

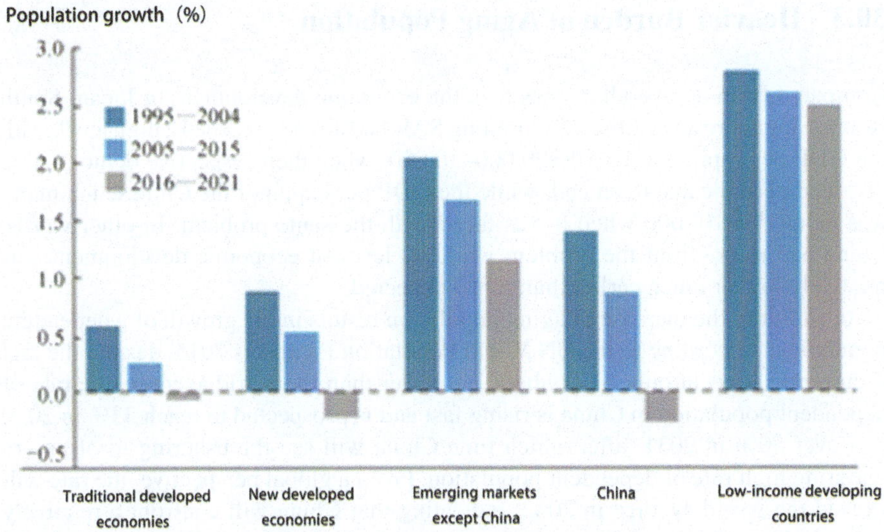

Fig. 30.3 Comparison of labor forcegrowth trends in the world (1995–2021)

30.2 Shorter Intervals Between Turning Points of Demographic Structure

If the following, indicators are taken as the four turning points of the demographic structure, that is, a fertility rate reaching 2.1% below average, the rate of people aged above 65 reaching over 14%, the zero growth of labor force aged 15–64 and the downturn of overall population; the three intervals among the four turning points are 30, 10 and 5 years, respectively, in Japan in comparison with 20, 0 and 5 years, respectively, in China. This is an indication that China will complete the transition through each turning point in a shorter span of time than did Japan. To some extent, it shows the negative effect of the strict family planning policy in China.

A further comparison shows that Japan crossed over the "Lewis Turning Point" in the late 1950s and the turning point of "demographic dividend period" in the middle 1990s, with an interval of nearly 40 years, during which time Japan successfully changed into a developed country. In comparison, China saw the coming of the "Lewis Turning Point" around 2003 and the end of "demographic dividend period" around 2015, with the interval lasting slightly longer than one decade. China is therefore confronting greater pressure than Japan from the change of the demographic structure. Given the prospect that India will continuously enjoy "demographic dividend" in the decades to come, China will face greater pressure from the competition with the neighboring markets.

30.3 Heavier Burden of Aging Population

Compared from an overall perspective, the economic development in Japan, South Korea, Singapore and China's Hong Kong SAR had already reached a high level, with the GDP per capita hitting US$20,000–30,000, when their respective demographic dividend period came to an end, while the GDP per capita of the Chinese mainland was below US$10,000 when it was faced with the same problem. In other words, China had to confront the problem while its level of economic development was relatively low or much earlier than it had expected.

In addition, the increase of aging population results in the growth of a dependent population. According to the UN World Population Prospects 2015, despite the fact it currently stays at only 31%, about 7% lower than the world average, the rate of dependent population in China is rising fast and is prospected to reach 33% in 2020 and over 50% in 2031, after which time China will see the ushering in of an era featuring high rate of dependent population. From a global perspective, the rate will exceed the world average in 2032, indicating that China will confront a relatively heavy burden of dependent population starting from the 2030s and the problem will become even worse.

30.4 Influence of Pension Finance on Development of Financial Industry

Population aging has a profound influence on economy and finance.

Firstly, population aging will lead to the decline of savings deposit. Age distribution is one of the major factors affecting the rate of savings deposit, because people aged 16–60 contribute to the main part of the deposit, and people aged above that range are likely to withdraw savings deposit for livelihood expenditure instead of continuing to deposit their savings. The increase of aging population will inevitably result in the decline of savings deposit rate.

Secondly, with a look into the whole life span, population aging will change the economic structure on the demand end. The consumption pattern of the aged shows that their expenditure is more on medical care, public goods and other consumables in comparison with that on real estate, transport and communications.

Thirdly, population aging will exert influence on the structure of the financial system, which is dominated by banks currently and will be dominated by both banks and institutional investors in the future. With the aging of the population, people tend to become conservative in risk control. Contract-based depository institutions can provide long-term and stable flow of income and meet the investment demand of the aged. Therefore, the status of the traditional service of banks will decline while that of institutional investors represented by depository institutions will be improved steadily. In terms of the composition of insurance investment in China, the rate of bank deposits fell from 30.32% to 18.00% between the end of 2006 and October of

2016, while that of bond investment rose from 18.46% to 33.66%; the rate of stock and fund investment increased from 9.26% to 14.42% in the same period; and the rate of other types of investment stays at 33.93% currently.

In the existing pension system, the unfunded pension burden will keep growing. According to World Bank statistics, China has seen a significant increase in the medical insurance coverage for the aged. With too much dependence on the first pillar pension, however, there is a big shortfall in its pension guarantee fund and the sustainability of the fund remains relatively weak. An estimation of the World Bank shows that the investment on social security in 2015 in China only took up 87% of the social security fund demanded. It is a great challenge for the government to fill the gap, which will become wider with the increase of the aged population. If the net present value of the balance of pension funding and spending between 2015 and 2050 is compared with the GDP of 2014, the accumulated deficit of the pension fund for urban government employees and that for urban and rural residents will be equivalent to 64% and 12% of the 2014 GDP, respectively. The combination of both takes up more than three quarters of the year's GDP. With a look into the distant future, the giant shortfall in the pension fund shows the necessity of reform on the pension system and means great potential opportunities for financial institutions as well.

The establishment of a pension system made up of three pillar schemes covering social security, employer-funded pension and personal savings pension is a common practice of developed countries and also a trend in China's pension system reform in the future.

In 2011, both the total pension assets and the total individual pension assets in America exceeded the general market value of the country's domestic stocks. The 2016 Investment Company Fact Book issued by the Investment Company Institute (or ICI) of America shows that the country's overall pension assets reached 24 trillion US dollars in 2015. The two biggest components of pension in America are Individual Retirement Account (or IRA) and Defined Contribution (or DC) scheme, with their assets amounting to 7.3 trillion and 6.7 trillion US dollars, respectively, and their combined assets taking up nearly 60% of the country's overall pension assets. Mutual funds make up about half of the overall pension assets, accounting for 48% of IRA and 54% of DC scheme, respectively. The development of pension finance has become an important channel linking real economy and the financial market in America.

The Pension Act 2008 promulgated by UK ushered in a new round of reform in its occupational pension system and accorded pension status as important as that of banks, securities and insurance. Since October 2012, the occupational pension has become a more compulsory occupational annuity. The in-service employees are automatically listed in the occupational pension scheme. A total of 8% of an individual pay check will be compulsorily credited to the personal pension account, with 4% covered by the employee, 3% covered by the employer and 1% covered by the government in the form of tax reduction.

The pension system reform in China should be focused on developing the second and the third pillar pension schemes and establishing a pension investment operation system. The burgeoning of the second and the third pillar pension schemes will create space for further development of the financial assets management sector in China. In regard to pension assets management, it will mainly involve the operation management of personal savings deposit at banks, pension payment entrusted to banks and enterprise annuity as well as commercial pension insurance.

The effective matching of pension with financial market will promote the development of both elderly service industry and financial industry. From the perspective of financial industry, elderly care service bears typical financial features and has a demand for asset allocation on an inter-temporal and inter-regional basis. Elderly care finance covers not only pension finance but also elderly service finance and elderly service industry finance, respectively, matching the demand for preserving and increasing the value of pension assets, the demand of the aged for financial consumption and the demand of the elderly service industry for investment and financing. Elderly care finance involves pension-related financial products, elderly care service and elderly care financial service. Of these different fields, pension finance is the most important, which mainly involves the system design and pension assets management.

The major component of retirement finance is the savings investment mechanism related to elderly care service, covering basic endowment insurance fund, enterprise annuity, commercial retirement insurance, retirement savings, reverse housing mortgage, pension trust and pension fund. The products of elderly care finance in China are mainly in the form of deposit products provided by banks. Although elderly care products have already been developed to some extent in the insurance sector, they are rarely developed in the sector of securities and are almost nil in the sectors of investment fund and trust fund. And pilot programs are still being actively planned to develop elderly care products related to real estate, such as reverse housing mortgage.

In 2015, the State Council of China issued and circulated the "Regulations on Investment of Basic Endowment Insurance Fund." According to the Regulations, the investment of the basic endowment fund on stocks, equity fund, hybrid fund and stock pension products should not exceed 30% of its total net value. The investment is mainly made in bank deposit and national debt. This way of investment can effectively mitigate risks, but it is hard for the interest rate to cover the inflation rate of the same period continuously. With limited capacity to have the value preserved and increased, pension assets are faced with the increasing pressure of value reduction.

The pension invested in capital market constitutes the central part of elderly care finance, and enterprise annuity and occupational annuity play an increasingly important role in it. At the end of 2015, the pension in market-based operation amounted to 24 trillion US dollars in the United States, an equivalent of 145% of the year's GDP. Pension management is entrusted to various financial institutes, including commercial banks, fund companies and insurance companies. Pension assets have their value preserved and increased via the capital market and are also a major source of institutional investment in the market, with as much as 60% of pension investment in stocks, venture capital (VC), private equity (PE) and other equity products. Pension investment facilitates not only the development of real economy but also the emergence of new industries as well as the innovation and upgrading of existing industries.

With a look into the overall elderly care industry, elderly care finance can be regarded as an independent link in the industry chain. It involves far more population and capital than the sectors of elderly care supplies, elderly service and retirement real estate. Elderly care finance can also be regarded as the financial part of the overall industry, as it covers a broad range of fields including banking, insurance, securities, fund, trust, retirement real estate and elderly service and is extensively linked to the financial industry chain. One can well perceive that elderly care finance is not only a major component of the whole financial system but also an essential part of the elderly care industry. It has a great influence on the development of the whole financial industry.

Chapter 31
Path to Sustainable Development for Small Loan Companies

Since 2008 when the local government in China launched a pilot project in support of the founding of small loan companies, small loan business has seen a rapid growth and played a significant role in the development of small-size enterprises and the mitigation of their financing pressure; over recent years, however, the development of these enterprises are obviously confronting challenges.

31.1 Small Loan Companies Face Development Bottleneck

In May 2008, China Banking Regulatory Commission (CBRC) and the People's Bank of China (PBC) jointly issued the Guidelines for Pilot Project of Small Loan Companies. With its flexibility and convenience, small loan business makes up for the deficiency of financial service in the small cities and the rural or remote areas and has seen a rapid growth. Over recent years, however, some small loan companies are faced with development bottleneck, which leads to shrinking business and unpromising state of operation.

31.1.1 Number of Small Loan Companies and Employees Shows Steady Downturn

Since 2015, the number of both small loan institutions and employees has shown a downward trend. By the end of June 2017, there were a total of 8,643 small loan companies with 108,100 employees in the country, 3.00% and 7.85% lower than in 2015, respectively (as is indicated in Figs. 31.1 and 31.2).

Source: Headline Today on October 18,2017

S. Ba, *The New Cycle and New Finance in China*,
https://doi.org/10.1007/978-981-16-8209-4_31

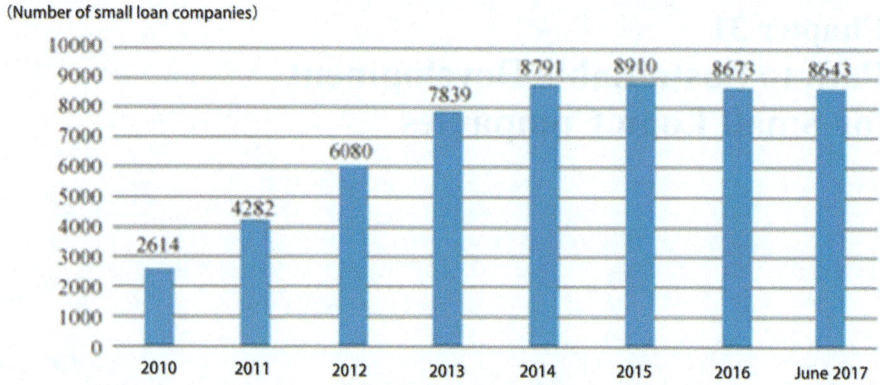

Fig. 31.1 Number of small loan companies in China. (Data Source: Wind Info)

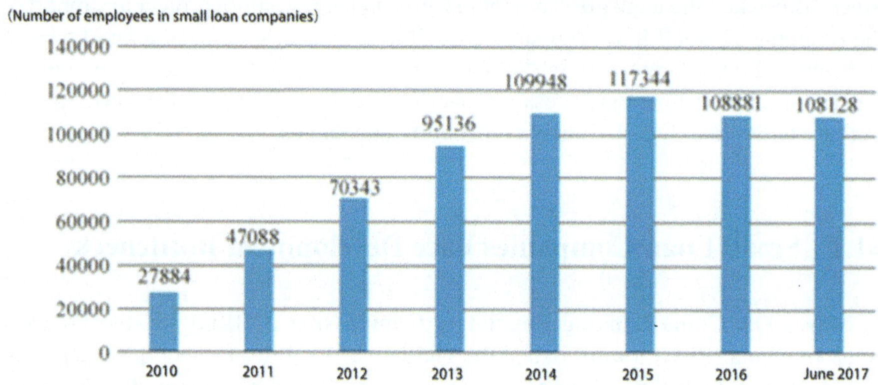

Fig. 31.2 Number of employees in small loan companies in China. (Data Source: Wind Info)

31.1.2 Proportion of Small Loan Companies' Loan Balance in Financial Institutions' Total Loan Balance Declines Continuously

Since 2014, the loan balance of the small loan companies has maintained stable on the whole, but its proportion in the total loan balance of the financial institutions has been going downward. By the end of June 2017, the loan balance of the small loan companies in China amounted to RMB 960.82 billion, making up 0.84% of the total loan balance of the financial institutions (as is indicated in Fig. 31.3).

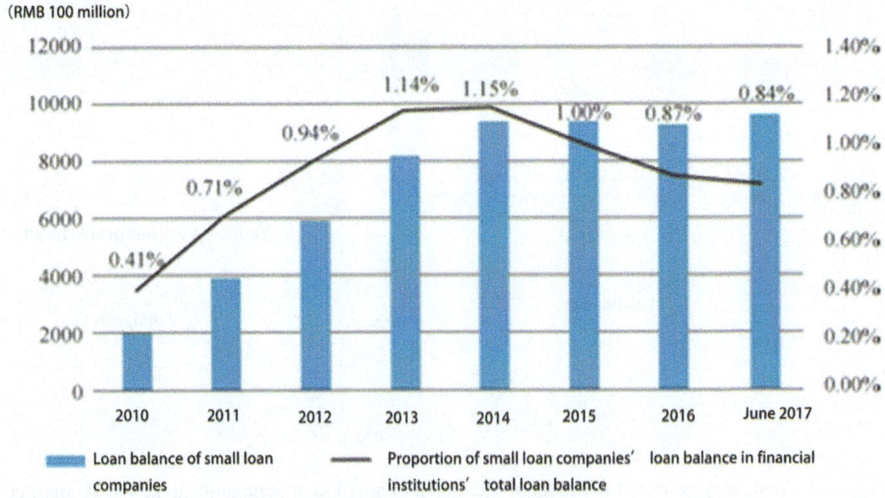

Fig. 31.3 Loan balance of small loan companies and its proportion in total loan balance of financial institutions. (Data Source: Wind Info)

31.1.3 Small Loan Companies See Big Drop in Revenue and Profit on Average

By the end of June 2017, there were 40 small loan companies in normal operation in the New Over-the-counter Market (or New OTC Market). According to their interim reports of 2017, the total revenue and the total net profit in the first half of the year dropped by 15.30% and 8.70% year-on-year, respectively. In addition, 20 of the 40 companies saw a year-on-year decline in both revenue and net profit, and only 10 of the companies saw a year-on-year increase in revenue (as is indicated in Fig. 31.4).

31.2 Development of Some Small Loan Companies Subject to Multiple Constraints

31.2.1 Constraints of Financing Channels

According to the Guidelines for Pilot Project of Small Loan Companies (hereinafter referred to as "Guidelines"), small loan companies are not allowed to pool public deposits as their capital, the sources of which should be confined to the capital injected by the shareholders, the capital injected by no more than two financial institutions of banking and capital endowment. The first two feasible channels of financing, however, are restricted by the Guidelines.

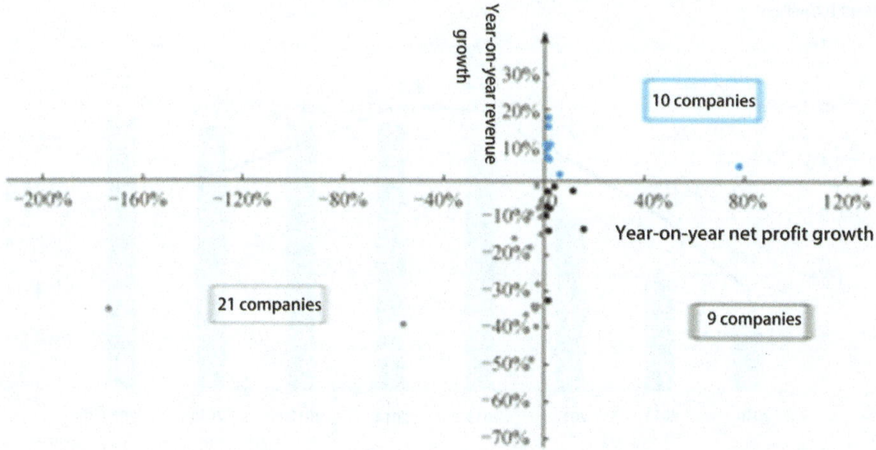

Fig. 31.4 Year-on-year growth of revenue and profit of small loan companies in new OTC market. (Data Source: Wind Info)

On the one hand, the Guidelines stipulates that "an individual natural person, corporate legal person or social organization of other types and its related parties should not hold more than 10% of the shares of a small loan company in terms of its registered capital." Although the restriction on shareholding is loosened at regional level, it fundamentally remains unchanged in most of the regions except South China's Guangdong Province, where the restriction is completely lifted. In Quanzhou City of Southeast China's Fujian Province, for example, the shareholding percentage can be only increased to 49% when certain conditions are met. The decentralization of equity makes it difficult for a small loan company to obtain adequate capital from a major shareholder.

On the other hand, the Guidelines stipulate that "the balance of the capital obtained by a small loan company from financial institutions of banking should not exceed 50% of its net capital." With the increase of non-performing loan (NPL) of commercial banks (as is indicated in Fig. 31.5), stricter examination and verification are conducted on the loans granted by small loan companies, as they are not officially listed as "financial institutions," making financing more difficult for the companies.

31.2.2 Ways for Small Loan Companies to Replace Private Usury

Viewed objectively from a certain standpoint, the development of small loan companies helps eliminate private financing, especially private usury. But the flow of private capital into small and microbusinesses through small loan companies involves a relatively high cost of license application, plus relevant taxes and fees payable such as

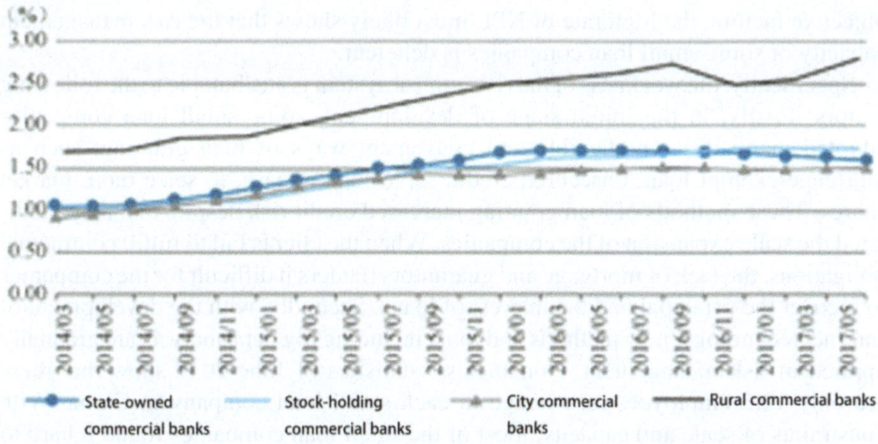

Fig. 31.5 Trend of NPL of commercial banks in China. (Data Source: Wind Info)

business tax and surcharges of daily operations at a rate of 5.5% and income tax at a rate of 25%. In contrast, private usury is actually not bound by regulations involving license application and tax payment. Nor is it subject to strict supervision of relevant government departments. The comparatively high cost of small loan makes it less competitive, making some private capital flow into private usury directly instead of entering the market via the small loan companies approved by the government.

The restriction on the shareholding ratio of an individual investor makes small loan company founders less motivated to make the enterprise bigger and stronger and less likely to plan their business on a long-term basis.

Cases show that the founders of small loan companies only enjoy a relatively small share of profit after the deduction of the cost of a license, risk control and operation management. This results in the flow of some capital into private usury. The capital will otherwise be invested on small loan companies.

31.2.3 Risk Control System of Some Small Loan Companies is Relatively Weak

In the first half of 2017, the NPL balance of the small loan companies in the New OTC Market totaled RMB 21.6618 million, with the NPL rate reaching 7.18% on average and 30% for some of the companies. The high rate of NPL is attributed to two factors: Firstly, the creditors of some small loan companies are mainly clients screened out by banks. As they have no bank loan records, the clients might bring credit risk; secondly, the regulations in force restrict trans-regional operation of small loan companies, making collective default on loans more likely to happen when natural disasters occur in certain places due to force majeure. Apart from the objective factors, the high rate of NPL most likely shows that the risk management capacity of some small loan companies is deficient.

Specifically, the weakness of the risk control system is attributable to the following factors: Firstly, in the initial stage of development, some small loan companies adopted many different flexible and convenient ways of loan granting, such as mortgage-exempt loan, unsecured credit, rapid loan release, to seize more market shares. These methods of loan granting increased credit risk despite that they facilitated the scale expansion of the companies. When the clients fail to fulfill contractual obligations, the lack of mortgage and guarantors renders it difficult for the companies to recover the principal and the interest of loans. Secondly, with the development of Internet technology, new methods and tools including big data analysis are gradually applied in risk management. Nonetheless, statistics of June 2017 show that there are only 12.5 employees on average in each small loan company in China. With constraints of scale and capacity, most of the small loan companies found it hard to set up independent internal risk control systems on their own.

31.2.4 Competition in the Sector Intensifies

As the demand for small-sum loan increases, small loan companies are facing growing pressure of competition with banks, peer-to-peer lending platforms and consumer finance companies. Banks have certain advantages in small loan service with their abundant capital sources, comparatively low cost of capital and widespread network. Peer-to-peer lending platforms and consumer finance companies have increased their sources of capital by making full use of the Internet to eliminate geographic restrictions. Their influence on the business of small loan companies is also growing.

31.3 Ways for Small Loan Companies to Lift Constraints on Sustainable Development

31.3.1 Concentration on Inclusive Finance as Prerequisite for Sustainable Development

The Plan for Development of Inclusive Finance (2016–2020), which was issued by the State Council, stresses that efforts should be made to promote small loan service among small and microbusinesses, college graduates, farmers, special disadvantaged groups and people covered by targeted poverty alleviation programs and make innovations in the relevant field. According to the Notification on Tax Policy for Small Loan Companies, which was jointly issued by the Ministry of Finance and the State Taxation Administration on 9th June, 2017, the interest income from small loans granted to farmers can be exempt from added-value tax under certain circumstances. It shows that small loan companies are encouraged and guided by the government to play an active role in the development of agriculture, rural areas, farmers and small and microbusinesses to better serve the real economy. With the support of favorable policies, the small loan companies should focus their business on inclusive finance and continue to take small and microbusinesses, the agricultural industry, rural areas and farmers as targets in their customer service. They should also seize the opportunity to relieve the bottleneck in their efforts to achieve the goal of sustainable development.

31.3.2 Multiple Channels of Financing as Critical Drive for Development

Small loan companies are confronted with many restrictions on financing, and the high cost of financing forces them to turn to high-risk customers who accept high interest rate. The "Administrative Procedures for Small Loan Companies (a draft for inviting recommendations)" jointly promulgated by the People's Bank of China (PBC) and China Banking Regulatory Commission (CBRC) in May 2014 allows the adoption of more approaches to financing and lifts restriction on the proportion of financing. But it has not been issued officially so far. The pressure from acquiring a relatively big amount of working capital renders it difficult for small loan companies to expand their business. It is advisable for relevant government departments to further lift restrictions on the financing of small loan companies, list the companies as "financial institutions" and allow the companies to provide value-added service for small and microbusinesses in such fields as investment, underwriting and consultation. It is also advisable for the departments concerned to encourage the companies with good business performance to go public to raise money in the capital market while conforming to laws and regulations. Small loan companies should adopt multiple approaches to financing, including the transfer of credit assets and the issuance of private placement bonds, to expand their business and promote sustainable development of their business.

31.3.3 Establishment of Business Model and Risk Control System with Special Features as Important Safeguard Measure

It is critical for small loan companies to develop a new business model with unique features. For example, pilot programs are launched in some regions to take small loan companies as platforms for supply chain finance to help the companies explore new business models and improve their risk management capacity by engaging in the service of supply chain finance. In view of practical cases, the companies should stick to a principle of "small loan" and "diversification" in lending to reduce the concentration of risks and avoid collective default on the loan. Besides, an all-round risk control system should be established via pre-loan due diligence and post-loan management. With regard to pre-loan due diligence, the companies should enhance the training of customer managers to improve their capacity of risk investigation and pledge assessment. The companies may also try to win new customers with the help of the "circle of acquaintances" or adopt the "model of joint guarantee on a group basis" initiated by Grameen Bank in Bangladesh to introduce the practice of mutual oversight among group members, with an aim to reduce the credit risk of customers. As for post-loan management, efforts should be strengthened to conduct customer supervision and give risk pre-warning. For example, small loan companies should conduct real-time follow-up on small and microbusinesses' operation and assess their capacity of loan repayment on the basis of the policy changes and development trend of the sector involved, with an aim to avoid default on the loan. Provided that their capacity is insufficient in this regard, the companies can turn to institutions specialized in big data-based financial information service to set up a strict risk control system.

References

1. Ba Shusong. Reform of Small Loan Companies [J]. *China Investment*, 2012 (8).
2. Ba Shusong. Challenges and Improvement of Small Loan Companies [J]. *Boao Review*, 2013 (2).
3. Ba Shusong. Beauty and Sadness of Small Loan Companies [J]. *Finance Economy*, 2015 (2).

Chapter 32
Green Finance: Challenges and Opportunities

32.1 Background, Opportunities and Challenges

"Low-carbon economy" and "low-carbon technology" are attracting increasing attention worldwide with the occurrence of global warming. As the world is recovering from the international financial crisis, the development pattern centering on low-carbon economy has become the main stream and has greatly facilitated the revival of the global economy.

Low-carbon economy, which involves efficient utilization of energy sources, exploitation of clean energy sources and a pursuit of green GDP, is another major progress of human society after the formation of agricultural civilization and industrial civilization.

As the largest developing country, China is faced with both opportunities and challenges in the development of low-carbon economy. In the long run, exploring a path to low-carbon development not only matches the global trend of low carbonization in the field of energy sources, but also is consistent with China's efforts in the transformation of growth pattern, the adjustment of industrial structure, the implementation of plans for energy conservation and emission reduction and the achievement of the goal of sustainable development. In the near and medium term, as China is still constrained by its phase of development, the target of low-carbon transformation is still faced with many unfavorable conditions, including the need for fast growing economy, the low-end positioning in international division of labor in trade, the enormous pressure of employment, a coal-dominant structure of energy sources, comparatively backward technology and institutional obstructions. Therefore, China is facing a hard choice between opportunities of economic growth and low-carbon transformation. China should not only observe the general rule of economic and social development and climate protection and follow the trend of low-carbon economy, but also try to find an appropriate path to low-carbon development on the basis of the basic national conditions and interests, a path that coordinates long-term and short-term benefits and balances different policy targets.

S. Ba, *The New Cycle and New Finance in China*,
https://doi.org/10.1007/978-981-16-8209-4_32

32.2 Necessity of Developing Green Finance

Green finance involves certain investment behaviors in the financial industry, including an emphasis on eco-environment protection and pollution abatement, and strengthened support for the development of environmental industries and technological innovation of the industries. It is intended to facilitate sustainable development of economy and harmonious development of eco-environment by promoting investment on natural ecological resources. According to the Chinese Bankers Survey (2016), 88.9% of the interviewed bankers agreed that green finance would have positive influence on the operation of banks, and 97% of the interviewees agreed that green finance would become an important part of banking in five years. Apart from the consensus of the bankers on supporting the development of green finance, the status quo of the low-carbon industries in China also calls for the development of green finance.

To begin with, green finance can provide support for low-carbon economy, which has a great capital demand, and the great economic benefits of low-carbon industries can create abundant capital backflow, a win–win situation for both the enterprises and the financial institutions; Secondly, as the global economy is turning low-carbon-oriented, green finance becomes an inevitable trend. Banks as special enterprises should consider both business risks and profits. Environmental risks are attracting increasing attention of financial institutions, because bad performance in environmental protection will weaken the profitability of financial investment clients and consequently threaten the safety of debts as the risk of the clients' non-performance in meeting their liabilities increases. Lastly, finance is the core of modern economy. The financing service for environmental industries will help promote capital investment in green industry. The investment is aimed at supporting the development of new technologies and inventions that will be applied in pollution abatement and eco-environment improvement to the benefit of sustainable development of economy.

32.3 Status Quo of Green Finance and the Existing Problems

The year 2016 marks the launching of green finance in China. Released on March 17th of 2016, the "13th Five-Year Plan for Economic and Social Development" proposes "establishing a green finance system, promoting green credit service and green bonds and setting up green development funds," an indication that the building of green finance system has become a national strategy. On August 31, 2016, the Guidelines for Establishing the Green Financial System was jointly issued by the People's Bank of China, the Ministry of Finance, the National Development and Reform Commission, the former Ministry of Environment Protection, the former China Banking Regulatory Commission, China Securities Regulatory Commission and the former China Insurance Regulatory Commission, as guidance on the top-level planning for "the development of green finance." At the G20 Summit held on September 4 in East China's Hangzhou City, China listed green finance on the agenda for the first time and proposed the founding of a green finance study group. At the summit, China also submitted the G20 Comprehensive Report of Green Finance, providing solid theoretical basis and data support for low-carbon-oriented transformation of the global economy.

Since the beginning of 2017, different sets of standards for green finance have gradually been established, covering green loan, green bonds and other fields, such as the Guidelines for Supporting Development of Green Bonds, which was issued by the China Securities Regulatory Commission's on March 2nd of 2017, and the Guidelines for Operation of Green Debt Financing Tools, which was issued by the National Association of Financial Market Institutional Investors on March 22nd. The "Standardization Project of Green Finance" was listed as a major project in the Plan for Establishment and Development of Financial Industry Standardization System (2016–2020), which was jointly released on June 8 by the People's Bank of China, the former China Banking Regulatory Commission, China Securities Regulatory Commission, the former China Insurance Regulatory Commission and the Standardization Administration.

So far green finance service in China mainly covers three fields, namely green securities, green loan and green insurance. In view of the status quo, green finance is faced with the following major problems:

Firstly, the capital market is still premature for implementing the policy of green securities, and the systems involving the inspection on environmental protection and the disclosure of environmental information are far from being perfect. To begin with, the capital market in China bears the dual features of an "emerging market in transition." This structural problem constrains the market from functioning effectively and results in the immaturity of the market access mechanism for environmental businesses. This has a major impact on the effectiveness of the policy of green securities. Besides, there is neither a system of inspection on a company's environmental activities before it goes public nor a system of supervision of the process control after it is listed. This contributes to the non-performance of some listed companies in implementing their promise of environment protection after they are successfully financed. Lastly, because of information asymmetry in the capital market, along with the resulting moral risk as well as adverse-selection effect, the quality and quantity of environmental information disclosure cannot be guaranteed.

Secondly, the standards of green loan service are incomplete and the related mechanisms and systems unsound. To begin with, the green finance administration system is not streamlined. Next, the internal incentive and discipline mechanism are ineffective. Besides, the mechanism of information communication remains to be improved. In addition, the existing standards of "green loan" are not fully specified, and there is a lack of specific guidance catalog and environmental risk rating standards. It is therefore difficult for commercial banks to adopt relevant supervision measures and internal enforcement regulations. This hampers the implementation of "green loan" policies. Lastly, there are no personnel, mechanisms or systems dedicated to green loan operation in banks.

Thirdly, the comparative shortage of laws and regulations relevant to green insurance make it difficult to prevent behaviors with moral risk. To begin with, the number of relevant laws and regulations adopted lags far behind the demand, making it difficult to introduce compulsory insurance of environment pollution liability. Next, moral risks are prone to occur after green insurance service is launched, but there is a lack of supervision mechanism required.

32.4 Suggestions on Policy Making

Firstly, optimize the laws and regulations of green finance to safeguard the development of low-carbon economy by financial means. Currently, the adoption and implementation of laws and regulations relevant to green finance lag behind market demand in China. The laws and regulations should be adjusted, optimized or amended in response to the changes of economic situations to provide a strong institutional and legal support for the implementation of green finance.

Secondly, optimize the mechanism of information communication and sharing between the government department of environment protection and financial institutions. For financial institutions, an access to timely and valid information about environmental behaviors of enterprises is a prerequisite for the provision of green finance service. The environmental protection administration and the financial institutions should strengthen cooperation and exchanges, with clear division of work between the two sides. They should enhance the training of related personnel about environmental knowledge while establishing standards for information sharing procedures and mechanisms of information sharing via information platforms and the corporate credit reporting system. The government should enhance its efforts to promote innovation in the financial administration system and set up a dual leadership model which centers on the vertical management of the central government. Under the leadership of the State Environmental Protection Administration (now the Ministry of Ecology and Environment), a high-level coordination mechanism can be set up to integrate the efforts of different participants to allow innovation to happen in the system of green finance administration.

Thirdly, include the factor of environment protection in the financing system to establish an effective system of standards for green finance. To begin with, financial companies should list environmental risk as a major target in their investment assessment and manage the environmental risks involved with the investment programs. They should research into the drawing up of green finance guidelines specific to China on the basis of the green credit criteria that are comparatively well-established worldwide. Next, the factor of environment protection should be included in the credit rating of financial institutions to establish a scientific system of rating standards for environmental credit. Besides, research should be conducted to develop a system of environmental performance appraisal on China's listed companies, and the indexes and the ranking of the companies' environmental performance should be released regularly. Lastly, systems related to green insurance should be established, covering insurance premiums, compensation procedures and other specific items.

Fourthly, design and establish an environmental accounting system of companies. The system can provide environmental accounting information of related companies for the environment supervision department and financial institutions. On the basis of the information, the financial institutions can make an assessment of the enterprises' future financial condition and their own green finance strategies.

Fifthly, strengthen international exchange and cooperation and draw on advanced international practices. To begin with, strengthen cooperation with international financial organizations including the World Bank, the International Finance Corporation and Asian Development Bank. Increase exchanges with these organizations in terms of carbon market, carbon funds and climate insurance while cooperating with them in energy efficiency projects. Next, strengthen cooperation with multi-national banks and draw on their advanced practices related to green finance products and service to develop green finance of Chinese characteristics. Lastly, strengthen international cooperation on greenhouse gas emission and trading, participate in the Clean Development Mechanism (CDM), draw on international experience in the trading of greenhouse gas emission and accelerate the development of a domestic market dedicated to the trading of greenhouse gas emission.

Sixthly, accelerate innovation in green finance service and products and accelerate the launching of the service and products newly developed. Innovate in the fields of green credit, green bonds and green fund. Support the development of green industry and facilitate the business restructuring of the financial industry.

References

1. Ba Shusong, Yan Min & Wu Dayi. Trend of China's Green Financial System in Post-financial-crisis Era. *Financial Management and Research: Journal of Hangzhou Financial Research and Training Institute*, 2010 (2).
2. China Banking Association, Price Waterhouse Coopers (PwC). *Chinese Bankers Survey (2016)*. Beijing: China Financial Publishing House, 2017
3. Lu Zhengwei & Tang Weiqi. Half-year Report of Green Finance (2016H1): China Starts to Lead Global Green Development. *Industrial Securities*, 2016.

[illegible] gradually. Lastly, sectors related to access to finance should be considered, covering [illegible] and other [illegible] standards [illegible] system of [illegible] This [illegible] a set of [illegible] companies [illegible] and [illegible] institutions. On the basis of the [illegible] assessment of the [illegible] financial [illegible] strategic.

This [illegible] and comparing, and draws [illegible] international practices. [illegible] with the international [illegible] including the World Bank [illegible] Development Bank [illegible] of [illegible] banks [illegible] efficiency [illegible] with multi-national banks and draws on their [illegible] practices [illegible] products and [illegible] characteristics [illegible]

[illegible]

[illegible]

Part V
Urbanization

Chapter 33 What is the Way Out for China's Reform in Rural Land System?

The reform of rural land system is the central part of China's efforts to launch economic restructuring, promote new-pattern urbanization and usher in a new round of institutional dividend. It is also a major challenge facing China in achieving these goals. A unified and open market system, where the order of competition is well observed, should be developed so that market can play a decisive role in resource allocation. A fundamental approach to this goal is to set up a unified market of construction land in both urban and rural areas, to ensure the same market status, including land use right and land price, for both collectively owned commercial land in rural areas and state-owned land.

33.1 Background: Why is Land Reform Imperative?

With three important features, that is, urban–rural dichotomy, government monopoly and non-market-oriented allocation, the existing land system in China is a unique and the most complicated system in the world.

Firstly, urban–rural dichotomy refers to the total separation between urban and rural areas in the system of land ownership. With the urban land under state ownership, the local government is entitled to transfer, dispose of and obtain benefit from the construction land. With the rural land under collective ownership, the peasants are entitled to use, transfer and obtain benefit from the land when it is used for farming purpose. But when the farm land is converted to land for non-farming purpose, the peasants will lose their entitlement to the land once they have received compensation, which is worth several times of the value of the land used for farming purpose.

Secondly, government monopoly refers to the fact that new urban land is only supplied by the local government to the market after it has expropriated some farm land. There are mainly three different ways of land transfer, and they are adopted

This article was published in the Journal of Chinese Rural Discovery (Issue 5, 2016).

S. Ba, *The New Cycle and New Finance in China*,
https://doi.org/10.1007/978-981-16-8209-4_33

according to different purposes of land use: The land for business use is put in the market via "bid invitation, auction and listing"; the land for public use is put in the market through "government allocation"; the land for industrial development used to be transferred on the basis of "agreements" before 2004, and in practice, it has been transferred basically at cost price since 2004 though the procedures would nominally be completed by way of "bid invitation, auction and listing."

Thirdly, non-market-oriented allocation refers to the practice that the possession of arable land should be examined and approved by the government. To ensure food security, China has enforced the strictest arable land protection system by adopting policies to protect the country's red line minimum acreage of arable land, which covers a total area of 1.8 billion Chinese mu or 120.06 million hectares. The supply of land for construction is under strict quota control. The plan of land supply and utilization is mapped out on the basis of the country's 15-year overall plan of land utilization, the 10-year overall urban plan and the one-year overall plan for the supply of new construction land in urban areas. Then land is expropriated and reserved by strictly following these plans and at last supplied and transferred in different ways.

The dichotomy of land ownership and property right in China leads to the separation of land markets, which is shown in the wide difference between the market of agricultural land and the market of urban construction land. The dichotomy of urban and rural land markets is the core issue of China's land system and the origin of a series of problems, which are becoming increasingly conspicuous restraints on China's economic restructuring and the urbanization of population. The problems mainly fall into three categories:

To begin with, the non-intensive land utilization against the law in urban villages. The land in the urban–rural fringes of China is the area where land use efficiency is the lowest and the land-related law breaching the most intense. As is stipulated in the relevant policies, the urban land is state owned and the rural land collectively owned, but the expansive land in the urban–rural fringes is collectively owned despite the fact that it is situated in urban areas. The land in these areas should be expropriated by the state according to the constitution, but the government cannot afford the huge expense involved in the requisition of the land.

Next, low efficiency in the utilization of the land for industrial use. Currently, the land for industrial use takes up a very high proportion in the cities. It is not intensively utilized, and it occupies a lot of livable space of the cities.

Lastly, the financial risk incurred by over dependence on fiscal revenue from land. The fund for urban development is raised by the local government by using land mortgage and governmental credit. 2013–2015 is the peak time for the repayment of land mortgage loan. The revenue from land transfer has even become the local government's source of income used for debt repayment. Yet the fall of land price and the decrease of land purchases caused by the fluctuation of the macro economy will lead to the rapid weakening of the government's capacity of debt repayment.

Given these outstanding problems, the existing land policies of China have seen a weakened sustainability. It is imperative to make a change and priority should be given to the reform of these policies.

33.2 Ways of Reform: Marketization as the Main Approach to Land Reform

A close look into the overall land reform plan released at the 3rd Plenary Session of the 18th CPC Central Committee reveals that the main approach to land reform is to allow market to play a decisive role in the allocation of land factors. With this approach taken into account, the land reform can be generalized with the following key words, that is, marketization, profit distribution and classified management.

33.2.1 Marketization

It is shown in the following aspects:

(1) The collectively owned rural land for business development should be allowed to be transferred, leased or taken as investment shares if these operations are conducted in accordance with relevant plans and purposes. It should have the same market status, the same right of use and the same price as the state-owned land.

(2) Efforts should be made to reduce land requisition and introduce standards to the proceedings of land requisition. The department concerned should establish and optimize a reasonable, standard and multifactor mechanism that ensures the benefits of the peasants who have their land expropriated. Meanwhile, it should extend the range of paid use of the state-owned land and reduce the allocation of land for profiting purpose.

(3) Efforts should be made to stabilize the policy of contracting rural land to farmers and keep it long-lasting. With the strictest arable land protection system maintained and optimized, the government should entitle the peasants to possess, utilize, transfer and reap benefits from the land that they have contracted to work on. The government should also entitle the peasants to use their right to contracted land management as mortgage and guarantee and allow them to engage in industrialized agricultural operations via taking the right as investment shares. The peasants should be encouraged to transfer the right to large families specialized in farming, family farms, peasants' cooperatives or agricultural enterprises, so as to develop scale management of rural land in different ways. It is the first time for the government to initiate a policy to support the use of the right to contracted land management as mortgage and guarantee, showing that the rural arable land's function as asset and financing tool is recognized by the top decision makers.

33.2.2 Profit Distribution

It is shown in the following aspects:

(1) Efforts should be made to set up a profit distribution mechanism in regard to the added value of land, with due attention paid to the state, collectives and individuals in profit distribution, while increasing the share of profit for individuals reasonably. If the original way of profit distribution, which is based on predetermined terms of land requisition compensation, can be adjusted to be market price-based, the peasants' earnings from land will increase by a big margin.

(2) Grant more property rights to the peasants. Protect the peasants' house site usufruct, and reform and optimize the policies related to rural house sites. Choose some places for pilot programs and discreetly promote the practice of taking peasants' housing property rights as mortgage and guarantee and making them transferable, to explore new ways for the peasants to increase their income from property. Set up a market for rural property right transaction and promote an open, fair and standard operation in the transaction.

(3) Allow the fund appropriated for financial projects to be channeled directly to eligible cooperatives. Allow the assets deriving from financial aid to be kept, managed and protected by cooperatives, and allow cooperatives to conduct credit cooperation. Encourage the investment of the capital used for industrial and commercial purposes on modern planting and breeding industries suitable for enterprise-oriented operation, and guide the investors to do so, to usher in essential modern production factors and modern business models in the agricultural industry.

33.2.3 Classified Management

Classified management refers to the fact that the land reform plan finalized at the 3rd Plenary Session of the 18th CPC Central Committee is in fact a classified program. It can be elaborated as follows:

(1) As for the arable land, the preservation of traditional collective ownership, which is the prerequisite of the reform, remains unchanged. And the fundamental principle of "farm land for agricultural use" is still followed. The focus of the reform is placed on the centralized management of cultivated land, with an aim to develop scale cultivation and modern agriculture.

(2) As for the transfer of rural collectively owned "land for business use," it should accord with the original plans and purposes. This precondition fundamentally decides the fact that there is still a long way to go for the marketization of the rural land for business development. The range of the land transfer is in fact restrained.

(3) As for the conversion of the use of rural land from farming to non-farming purpose, the existing mechanism of land requisition and "bid invitation, auction and listing" remains unchanged except that the range of land requisition has been narrowed and the compensation for the peasants increased. It indicates that the local government's intervention in the transaction process of the land market remains relatively strong.

33.3 Influence of the Reform: Exploration of New Land Dividend

Despite that there is still a long way to go before the complete marketization of China's land market, the 3rd Plenary Session of the 18th CPC Central Committee has embarked on a program toward the goal. This will have a whole range of influence, including the easing of the conflicts caused by the irrational part of the existing land policies and the creation of a new round of land reform dividend.

Firstly, the transfer of the rural collectively owned land for business use will alleviate the constraint of land use quota in urban areas and help increase the economic efficiency of land use. As for the increment in land supply, the land for construction use still takes up a small proportion in China, and the transfer of the collectively owned land for business use will create room for the increment of land supply in the future. As for the stock of land, the land that is reserved for construction use in the extended urban areas is still collectively owned and is generally utilized with low efficiency, despite the fact that it is currently used for industrial, commercial and housing (with limited property right) purposes. If the land of this type can be re-allocated in accordance with the policies adopted in the land reform, not only can the efficiency of land use improve, but also more land will become available for urban development. Besides, as the land is located in urban areas, it will generate greater economic value. Generally, the transfer of collectively owned land for construction use is faced with much less restriction, which helps alleviate the constraints of urban land quota.

Secondly, the transfer of collectively owned land for construction use will bring a change to the structure of stock land utilization in urban areas. The proportion of the land for industrial use will decline, while the proportion of the land for commercial use will go up. This leads to the transformation of a city and even the urbanization of an area. Generally, the structure of construction land allocation in urban areas will see regular changes with different phases of development, different predetermined functions of cities and different city development plans. More importantly, the structural change of urban construction land is actually a reflection of the transformation of a city. In the middle and later stages of industrialization and urbanization, major cities or central cities will generally become centers for the headquarters economy of the industrial sector and centers for production services, leading to the gradual relocation of factories occupying relatively large areas and the gradual decrease of industrial land in the center of these cities. So far the first-tier developed cities in China, including Beijing, Shanghai, Shenzhen and Tianjin, are gradually transitioning to this phase of development. As for the urban construction land in these cities, there will a decreasing proportion of industrial land as against an increasing proportion of the land for housing and commercial projects as well as infrastructure. With the combined influence of the transfer of rural collectively owned land for construction use and factory relocation, the new areas of industrial land will be concentrated in the collectively owned construction land on the fringes or suburbs of the major cities.

Thirdly, despite that the transfer of collectively owned construction land partly alleviates the constraints of urban land quota, land urbanization in China will shift from a focus on quantity to a focus on efficiency in the overall trend. As is widely believed, the urbanization process in China mainly goes with the expansion of urban area, but the land utilization efficiency is relatively low due to the comparatively slow growth of population. Under this circumstance, the core issue of land urbanization in China will be shifted from quantity increase to efficiency promotion in a fairly long period of time.

Fourthly, the reform in the distribution of the added value of land might generate certain property income for the migrant workers from rural areas, and it will potentially make a breakthrough in the efforts to urbanize the migrants. The biggest difference between migrant workers and citizens is wealth gap, which is difficult to be narrowed mainly due to the fact that the migrant workers' property cannot be converted to cash in the market, not because they have no property. The peasants' properties falls into three categories, that is, the right to farmland use, the right to house site use and house ownership. If these properties can be converted to cash through the market, the peasants' asset income per capita will increase dramatically and can cover a considerable part of migration cost. In addition, the pressure of cost involved in urbanizing migrant workers will be smaller than imagined, if the peasants can be granted a greater share of the added value generated from other uses of farmland and house site transfer, as was proposed at the 3rd Plenary Session of the 18th CPC Central Committee.

Fifthly, farmland transfer is the prerequisite of agricultural scale management and agricultural modernization. The transformation of the mode of agricultural production and operation will become a new highlight in the next phase. By the end of 2011, the farmland for contracted management on a household basis across the country covered 1.277 billion Chinese mu or about 85 million hectares, of which 228 million Chinese mu or about 15 million hectares had been transferred, with the year-on-year growth in the area of transferred farmland hitting 22.1%; Driven by the reform policy concerned, all the farmland across the country will have been transferred prior to 2020. This is projected on the basis of the statistics regarding the area of transferred farmland and the growth rate of farmland transfer in 2011. Farmland transfer and agricultural scale management is aimed at increasing agricultural labor productivity, reducing production cost and promoting crop quality. From an international perspective, the crop yield per unit area in China, being 1.6 times of world average, is only lower than that in such developed countries as the USA, the UK and Japan but much higher than that in India and Brazil. This may be due to the fact that scale planting alone cannot increase crop yield per unit area easily and will even lead to a decline of yield instead. Besides, the density of chemical fertilizer application in China, being 2.5 times of the world average, is much higher than that in the USA and the UK. Scale management will not increase the total amount of agricultural supplies used, but it will bring a change to the structure of the utilization of agricultural supplies. Therefore, the key to scale management is the promotion of labor productivity by mechanizing agricultural production and management. Currently, as the agricultural labor productivity in China is only 1% of that in Japan, 20% of that in the USA and

50% of the world average, there is a relatively big room for improvement in this respect, especially in the field of crop harvesting.

Chapter 34
"3+6" Pattern of Development in China's Urbanization Campaign

34.1 Shenzhen is Characterized by the Highest Circulation Rate of Second-Hand Housing in China

According to Ba Shusong, a "3+6" pattern of city grouping, which includes three city clusters and six central cities in China, will become the mainstay of the cities in the country and will remain as a major driving force for the development of city clusters for a certain period. In 2016, the population and the GDP of the city grouping accounted for 19.5% and 36.8% of the country's total, respectively, and the transaction amount of new housing and second-hand housing hit 46.2% and 73.5%, respectively. Major cities have become an increasingly strong magnet for new population and capital and are characterized by a high rate of real estate transaction. The real property developers in these cities have shifted their focus from real estate development and investment to multiple operations, with their business becoming increasingly concentrated.

The real estate industry's "era of growth-oriented development" is fading away, as a balance is forming between new housing supply and demand. According to a graph demonstrated by Ba Shusong about the growth of real estate investment in China, the United States and Japan, the growth-oriented pattern of real estate development is diminishing, and the contribution of housing development and investment to macroeconomy is decreasing. Since 2012, the growth rate of real estate investment in China, the United States and Japan has almost approached that of a mature market though at a slow pace and has returned to normal.

The rising circulation rate of second-hand housing marks the upcoming of an "era of existing real estate." Among different countries and typical cities, China's Shenzhen City ranks only next to Australia and is at the top in China in terms of the circulation rate of second-hand housing. According to Ba Shusong, the transaction amount of second-hand housing in China exceeded RMB 6 trillion in 2016 or 41%

This article was published in Shenzhen Economic Daily on September 11, 2017, and posted on the online public platform "Financial Reading Club" on September 12, 2017.

S. Ba, *The New Cycle and New Finance in China*,
https://doi.org/10.1007/978-981-16-8209-4_34

of the total amount of all housing transactions. The price trend will take on many new features in the market dominated by the existing housing, compared with that of the new housing-dominated market. In 2016, the transaction amount of second-hand housing in Beijing and Shanghai accounted for 74% and 72% respectively of the total amount of all housing transactions, meeting the level of a mature market in the world. The number of second-hand housing transactions in the two cities is already three times that of new housing. Various indicators show that the era of "existing real estate" has already arrived, and an increasing number of cities are seeing the advent of the era featuring a high rate of second-hand housing transactions.

According to Ba Shusong, the real estate market has already witnessed a structural change from being growth-oriented to being oriented toward the transaction of second-hand housing, which will also cause a shift of its focus from development to service. It indicates that, instead of real estate development and investment, the following divisions of the field will become new growth points in the future, including transaction service covering the circulation and leasing of second-hand housing, house tending service covering home decorating, cleaning and maintenance, house removal service, and financial service associated with rent and real estate monetization.

Meanwhile, there is an increasing demand for the purchase of housing in metropolitan areas, indicating the upcoming of an era of metropolitan areas bigger in size, and housing prices in different parts of the areas have become more closely correlated. With more public resources and development opportunities and with the clustering of industries, megalopolises are seeing the influx of people continuously. Beijing, for example, boasts nine key universities listed on the national 985 projects and 80 three-A hospitals, taking up 23% and 5% respectively of the country's total, and these resources have an obvious effect on the population flow from outside the city and therefore help boost housing demand in the city. Part of housing purchase demand in major cities has been transferring to the neighboring smaller cities under the influence of housing price and the relocation of industries.

34.2 The Leasing Market Will See the Fastest Growth in Ten Years to Come

Currently, the most outstanding feature of the real estate market is a continuous market splitting up, stated Ba Shusong. The number of housing transactions in the first-tier cities remains at a low level, with the housing price heading for stability, while the real estate market in the second-tier cities is split up seriously. The growth rate of real estate investment in China has witnessed a slight fall, as is shown in a graph indicating the country's year-on-year growth rate of accumulated real estate investment. Ba Shusong also predicted that the keynote of the relevant policy would remain unchanged and that the number of second-hand housing transactions and the prices in the second half year would keep stable at a comparatively low level. Due to the lack of favorable economic conditions, the third- and fourth-tier cities where the number of housing transactions and the prices have kept rising will face pullback of the market in the medium and long term.

As for the prospects of the market, Ba Shusong held that the keynote of relevant policies will remain unchanged and the government will encourage both housing leasing and purchase. As the current round of market adjustment and control has already lasted for long, the government is starting to shift its focus to the increase of housing supply and the development of housing leasing, the latter of which is of great importance in the residential patterns of developed nations. For example, over 35% of the families in the United States, Japan and the UK live in rental housing, compared with 21% or so in China.

The policy for "equality between the rights obtained from house leasing and the rights obtained from house purchase" and the policy for "shared property right" are both adopted in line with the idea that housing is for living in rather than for speculation. But the problem of housing speculation can only be cracked after the demand for living in has been satisfied. An important way out is the development of housing leasing market. Ba Shusong pointed out that the rise in the proportion of the people choosing to live in rental housing will facilitate the transformation of the real estate market. The industry chain of housing leasing is projected to stimulate GDP growth and increase job opportunities.

Housing leasing will have the biggest room for growth in China's real estate market in ten years to come, commented Ba Shusong. As housing leasing market provides products and service catering to demand of different levels, it helps the real estate market develop more steadily.

Chapter 35
Central Issues in Reform of Urbanization Financing

Urbanization financing in China is characterized with such problems as overdependence on land transfer receipts, inadequate supervision on local government debt and inadequate restriction on local government expenditure. A package of reform should be implemented in urbanization financing, to eliminate inequality of public service accessing between permanent urban residents and transient population. The reform should also be aimed at building infrastructure and providing public service for a new urban population of 300 million in 20 years to come. It involves establishing a system that makes local government's power match its spending responsibilities, rationalizing revenue division between central and local government, increasing local tax revenue, adjusting land finance policy, promoting the investment of the private sector and developing stable and sustainable debt financing.

35.1 Critical Issues of Reform and Methods of Coordination

It remains a great challenge for the fiscal system and the financial system of China to meet the new demand of financing for urban infrastructure and public service. To begin with, in the special setting of China, the fiscal system and the financial system are connected yet differentiated: On the one hand, the two systems interact in a pattern of mutual waning and waxing like the movement of a seesaw; on the other hand, the two systems are closely connected. For example, banking risks are likely to spread to the fiscal system eventually. So how should the roles of the fiscal system and the financial system be defined, divided and coordinated in urbanization financing in the future? Obviously, it is a problem to be tackled. Besides, with the

---

This article is an excerpt from *The New Urbanization Financing and Financial Reform* by Prof. Ba Shusong and Dr. Yang Xianling. The book was published and issued by China Workers Publishing House in December 2014.

S. Ba, *The New Cycle and New Finance in China*,
https://doi.org/10.1007/978-981-16-8209-4_35

"soft" constraint of budget, how should local government be encouraged to play an active role in infrastructure investment and financing while avoiding unlimited expansion of debt and excessive accumulation of risk? It may be imperative to draw up a transparent balance sheet of local government and set up a risk precaution and follow-up mechanism to address the aforementioned problems. In addition, is there a viable operation mechanism where land urbanization and population urbanization reinforce each other, with land financing still playing an active role? Can land quota be linked to population quota for this purpose? Furthermore, is the difficulty in financing for indemnificatory housing a problem of fund or mechanism? Generally, the allocation of land for indemnificatory housing involves a big opportunity cost for the local government, because the government can otherwise obtain a considerable amount of land transferring receipts when the land is transferred publicly in the market; meanwhile, indemnificatory housing is difficult to circulate on its own in the market and involves sizable amount of investment and maintenance cost. Is there a feasible business model that solves all these problems? The decision-makers of the government have realized these problems to some extent, regarding the problems as a bottleneck in the process of urbanization in the future. To overcome the bottleneck, a series of policies must be adopted to launch reform in fiscal and financial systems and priorities should be set when the reform starts in key areas.

Firstly, the key to the reform of the future fiscal system lies in how to deal with intergovernmental relations. Aimed at overcoming the asymmetry between fiscal power and routine power and the inadequate provision of public service, the reform can be carried out in three fields, covering fiscal power, routine power and financial transfer payment system. The purpose of fiscal power reform is to redefine the relationship among government of different levels in terms of taxation so as to enhance the taxation power of lower-level government. The key to routine power reform is to divide the responsibility for basic public service cost in a different way so as to transfer the responsibility from lower to upper-level government. The reform in financial transfer payment system calls for the transfer of certain revenue from upper to lower-level government to ensure adequate revenue for the government of each level to provide basic service with appropriate quality.

Secondly, the central government should undertake more responsibility in the public service sector in the future. According to the practice of mature economies, the central government undertakes responsibilities for national defense, foreign affairs, international trade, currency, national legislation and justice; the local government mainly undertakes the responsibility for the cost of transportation, public security, fire control and so on. In comparison, the central government of China undertakes smaller expenditure on education, medical service and other fields of public service. It undertakes less than 10% of the combined expenditure of primary and higher education, with the rate being much lower than that in countries like Australia, France and Belgium; The expenditure undertaken by the central government on public health accounts for 2% of the total, as against 97% undertaken by the federal or central government of Canada and Switzerland; and the expenditure undertaken by the central government on social security makes up a very small proportion of the total. This structure of expenditure is likely to cause inadequate supply of basic public products and imbalance among different regions of the country.

Thirdly, efforts should be made to reform land finance, which keeps playing a critical role in the financing plans of the local government. Via "bid invitation, auction and listing" in the secondary market, the land for business development can be used by the local government as the main source of land transfer receipts and extra-budgetary revenue and as the source of fund for the government's off-balance-sheet activities. As for the land for industrial development, the local government can use it to attract investment by offering low land prices or offering land for free use, with the expectation that the investment will create new fiscal revenue flow in the future. As for the land for infrastructure use, via "administrative allocation" and "agreement-based transfer," the local government can offer very low land prices or offer land for free use, to subsidize infrastructure investment and enhance the function of cities as public service providers. This helps increase the value and the remising price of the land earmarked for "bid invitation, auction and listing." The local government often uses the land of the government's land reserving centers, government policy-backed companies and the administrative committees of development zones as collateral for government debt. Likewise, land is more or less used as collateral for real estate development loans, residents' mortgage loans, the loans for the development of most industrial parks, and even the loans for the development of university towns and new campuses of universities in China. The use of land as a way of financing is in essence the capitalization and monetization of land. In this process, financial tools are applied so that future revenue flow can be created and used to cover the present expenditure on various investment projects of a local place.

The above analysis reveals that land finance is in fact an innovation of financing in China's certain phase of development and in the established structure of fiscal power and routine power. If innovation can be carried out to a reasonable extent on the existing mechanism of land finance, it can continue to play a certain role in urbanization financing in the foreseeable future. A look into the current trend reveals that the most workable reform in land finance involves the transfer of collectively owned construction land and the profit distribution of the added value of land. The reform in the former field helps ease the expenditure burden of the local government when the responsibility of urbanization is transferred to collective bodies; the reform in the latter field helps urbanize migrant workers from rural areas via distributing to them a bigger share of the increased value of their land after it is transferred in the market.

Fourthly, make house property tax a more important source of revenue for local government. As a kind of property tax, it is in essence one form of land finance and is only different from land finance in that it is levied on the existing land. In developed countries, house property tax, as a major category of tax, is the most important source of tax for local government. From an international perspective, house property tax takes up a comparatively high proportion of local tax revenues in developed countries as against a relatively low proportion in developing countries or countries undergoing economic transformation. It is safe to say that house property tax will become increasingly important to the tax revenues of local government with the rising of a country's economic level.

With the particular situation of China taken into account, house property tax can be used to change the time flow of land-related revenue and is a feasible solution to eliminate overdependence on "land finance" in urbanization financing. The existing pattern of land transfer actually involves a short-term move of obtaining the profit and the potential profit generated from the land all at one time. Whereas levying house property tax enables the government to receive revenue flow indefinitely after a house is built. And if house property tax revenue is put to use in urbanization projects, the time gap between investment making and profit gaining can be bridged effectively. Besides, the amount of house property tax revenue of a city is correlated to its level of urbanization in the future. An increase of investment on urbanization, along with the rise of municipal construction level, will lead to a continuous growth of the value of both the land and the housing in the city. This will eventually lead to the increase of the city's house property tax revenue and its greater capacity of repayment in the future for the debt involved in municipal construction.

The general pattern of development of mature markets reveals that levying house property tax is an inevitable choice in the future. In view of its pace of progress, the pilot program carried out in China's Chongqing and Shanghai municipalities can be expanded to cover more cities in the next phase, with an aim to gradually make house property tax a potential and sustainable source of revenue for local government.

Fifthly, with the fiscal and land reform in place, a reform in the financial sector of China is needed to enable sustainable financing for urbanization projects in the future. In view of the current circumstances, it can be predicted that the amount of M2 can hardly maintain an obvious growth in China. Given this constraint, it is advisable to increase the overall amount of nongovernmental financing so that the financial department can carry on with its support of infrastructure development. To make this workable, the proportion of direct financing should be increased, making it possible for corporate bond, municipal bond, Medium Term Note and other financing tools to play a more important role.

In the short run, it is of the greatest importance to objectively assess the role of financing platforms and shadow banking systems in the infrastructure financing of the present. They will still play a supporting role in urbanization financing in the future before long-term direct financing tools become workable effectively. Although the financial risk of local investment platforms is still likely to convert into fiscal risk, the overall risk is controllable to some extent after the platforms have been rectified and standardized. Besides, the relevant regulatory departments have conducted necessary assessment of the operation of the platforms. China Banking Regulatory Commission and the Ministry of Finance, for example, have conducted assessment of the platforms' loan business involving major banks and the financial guarantee involved in the operation of the platforms respectively. Apart from the assessment, it is also advisable to establish a set of relevant systems and standards. With potential risks brought under control, financing platforms should be allowed to continue to play their role in urbanization financing in the future while complying with standards. The same is basically true with shadow banking systems.

35.2 Framework, Priority Setting and Breakthrough Points of Reform

Reform is the key to and the footing of urbanization financing. A successful reform calls for a clearly defined framework, a workable priority setting and reasonable breakthrough points. To set priority and explore breakthrough points, the following major factors should be taken into account: Firstly, whether or not the reform facilitates people-centered and higher-quality urbanization so that the new measures can become efficient, inclusive and sustainable proceedings; Secondly, urgency and importance of relevant factors. Indemnificatory housing plays a critical role in the urbanization of population and therefore should be a top priority in the reform of financing mechanism in the future. Thirdly, level of consensus. Reform should be carried out on the basis of consensus. If consensus cannot be achieved within a limited period of time on the different roles of fiscal and financial systems in urbanization financing, efforts should be made to choose breakthrough points in other fields where there is consensus, and then the reform should be launched as soon as possible.

As a systematic and integral project, the reform in urbanization financing, calls for careful consideration about the interrelationship of and coordination among the different factors involved. Being a critical breakthrough point in the overall project, land reform is almost a prerequisite for all aspects of the reform in urbanization financing. The housing development fund, medical service and education programs involved in the urbanization of migrant population are to some extent all related to the status of the farming land and the house sites of the people. If they can be given a greater share of the market-based added value of their land in the reform, the cost involved in the urbanization of the population will be cut down significantly in the future. If the existing land system remains unchanged, however, it is hard for the local government to reduce its dependence on land finance, and it is also difficult for the government to weaken its impulse to increase investment on infrastructure while reducing investment on public service. Nonetheless, land reform is not a factor with independent linear relevance to the whole project. It plays an important role in the whole picture, along with fiscal and financial reform.

To bring fiscal, financial and private sectors into play in urbanization financing in the future, a package of reform should be conducted in the whole system instead of focusing on side issues. The reform in different fields of the existing system of urbanization financing, covering taxation, the division between financial power and routine power, land finance, urban infrastructure financing and the management of local governmental debt, is interrelated and interactive. Therefore, consideration should be given to the coordination of different parts of the reform package and their influence on the overall economy. Comparatively, the reform in some fields can be carried forward easily and consensus is likely to be achieved in these areas. For example, reform can be launched first in the effort to create new ways of direct financing for local government and promote asset securitization. Whereas the reform in some other fields is far-reaching and therefore can only be promoted in an all-round way after being fully tested, such as the adjustment of taxation relationship between the central and the local government and the adoption of house property tax.

It is therefore advisable that the reform be carried out phase by phase, each with different focuses, on the basis of the order of priority and timetable.

The first phase involves reform in a short term (2013–2015), with the reform mainly covering the following steps: (1) Rectifying and standardizing the existing financing models so that they can still play their proper role. An example is the standardization of financing platforms, shadow banking systems and the current practices of indemnificatory housing financing; (2) engaging private capital in the financing program, setting up the mechanism of admittance and retreat of project funds, and making institutional arrangement for the distribution of returns on ventures; (3) lifting restrictions on registered permanent residence along with the launching of land reform, linking the quota of registered residence to the quota of land, to carry forward the urbanization of population in an orderly manner.

The second phase involves reform in a medium term (2015–2020), with the reform mainly covering the following steps: (1) Studying the feasibility of levying house property tax in an all-round way on the basis of the pilot programs, to create potential new sources of tax for the local government; (2) launching reform in the tax sharing system, and redefining the routine power and the financial power of both the central and the local government; (3) studying the feasibility of reform intended for the establishment of a more fundamental and market-oriented land system.

It is predictable that, with the two-phase reform carried forward, the fiscal, financial and private sectors will play different roles and perform different functions in a sustainable financing system in the future. The fiscal reform should be aimed at improving the efficiency of labor and business flow so that they can flow to the places and the sectors with the highest productivity. The expenditure on public service should be aimed at urbanizing rural migrants and their families and helping them fully integrate into urban life. Financial reform should effectively satisfy the financing demand of local government for infrastructure development. As it is difficult for the total amount of loan to keep growing, local government should be allowed to raise funds via bond market on a larger scale and on a more market-oriented and transparent basis. However, it is imperative to impose necessary financial discipline on local government, to keep uncontrollable potential risk away from the financial sector. The private sector should play a more important role in the highly market-oriented fields that have a well-developed mechanism of admittance and retreat.

Chapter 36
Approaches to the Development of PPP with Chinese Characteristics

Over recent years, public–private partnership (or PPP) has attracted increasing attention in China. This is mainly due to the fact that increasingly rigorous restraints have been imposed on local government debt despite the arduous task of infrastructure development in the country. By pooling government and private funds and finalizing a series of agreements, PPP helps separate a project from government debt and attracts private investment at the same time. Therefore, it caters to the demand of both government and private investors.

Generally, PPP refers to a long-term partnership established in the fields of infrastructure and public service. In the normal pattern of PPP, private investors undertake most parts of the project, including the designing, construction, operation and maintenance of the infrastructure, and gain reasonable return on investment (ROI) via "user charges" and necessary "government payment"; the government departments concerned are responsible for supervising the price and quality of the infrastructure or public service to maximize public interests.

PPP is often defined in a broad or a narrow sense. In its broad sense, PPP refers to the various partnerships between government departments and private investors in providing public products and service. In its narrow sense, PPP is a general description of a series of project financing patterns, through which the government departments and private investors jointly invest on or put resources into certain projects and then the private investors hold responsibility for the construction and operation of the projects.

Viewed from its narrow sense, PPP is different from the traditional project financing models to some extent. There are both similarities and differences among PPP, privatization and the traditional pattern of contracting: PPP is similar to privatization in terms of the incentive mechanism; it is more like the traditional pattern of contracting, however, in regard to the budget accounting system. The businesses involved in PPP are responsible for the operational performance of a long-term

This article is the preface written by Prof. Ba Shusong for the New Model of PPP in Financial Reform—"City Development Pattern" for Restructuring Value of Infrastructure Assets.

S. Ba, *The New Cycle and New Finance in China*,
https://doi.org/10.1007/978-981-16-8209-4_36

project, while those involved in the traditional pattern of contracting do not hold responsibility for the operational performance of a project when it is out of warranty coverage. From an overall perspective, the major differences among PPP, privatization and the traditional pattern of contracting can be shown in three aspects, that is, the ownership and the right to the control of the assets of a certain project, whether businesses are set up to run the project, and the participants responsible for planning and management of the project. In the traditional pattern of contracting, the contractor is responsible for infrastructure construction only and is not responsible for project maintenance and operation; in PPP, the private businesses have interim ownership of the project assets, as against their indefinite ownership of their private assets, and the ownership of the latter is subject to common laws only. One of the shared advantages of PPP and the traditional pattern of contracting is that both reserve the right of the government to policy-making and efforts coordinating.

PPP is applicable in a broad range of fields, covering water, heat, gas and power supply, sewage and garbage treatment, government-subsidized housing projects, new-pattern urbanization, municipal engineering, water conservancy projects, resource environment and ecology protection, the construction of highways, railways, airports and multi-purpose tunnels for underground pipelines, rail transit projects, medical service, tourism, education and training, and elderly care service projects. As for PPP's scope of application, there are subtle differences in the interpretations given by the Ministry of Finance and the National Development and Reform Commission. The former includes infrastructure and public service in its range of application, while the latter puts public products and service on the list.

In terms of the charging mechanism, PPP projects can fall into three categories, that is, profit-oriented, quasi-profit-oriented and non-profit-oriented projects. Some projects cofunded by government and private investors have inadequate returns to cover the cost and the expected profit, yet they have comparatively good social benefits. It is advisable for the local financial department of different levels to subsidize these projects properly. And the relevant expenditures including the subsidies can be categorized and listed in the budget of the government of the same level and listed in the medium and long-term financial plans.

There are different interpretations of PPP between China and the West due to the different economic systems and circumstances. On the basis of China's national conditions and the practical applications of PPP in the country's public products and service, PPP can be defined from the following perspectives:

Firstly, the private sector is distinct from the public sector in PPP. In addition to privately-owned enterprises and foreign-invested enterprises, the private sector also includes the state-owned enterprises with independent legal person status, because the overall production value of China's state-owned enterprises takes up the vast majority of the country's gross domestic product (GDP) and the large enterprises that are able to provide public products and service are generally state-owned. Comparatively, the public sector usually refers to the government agencies and those state-owned enterprises that have no independent legal person status under certain government departments.

Secondly, the public sector and the private sector share both risks and benefits in the partnership. The risks are shared on the basis of the different capacities of the two sectors, because PPP is aimed at a win–win situation and the maximization of the overall benefits. And the benefits are distributed in line with both the cost and the risk undertaken by the two sectors. The private sector's demand for economic benefits can be satisfied when it does not infringe on the consumers' rights.

Lastly, the public sector and the private sector come into partnership on the basis of equality and mutual benefit. The government in China has been playing the roles of the "player" and the "referee" simultaneously for long when it provides public products and service. In the new pattern of partnership, the government should transform its functions and roles, and it should not enjoy any privilege in selecting private investors and sharing risks and profits. Once an agreement of cooperation has been signed with private investors, the government department represents one of the parties only and should not use its official power to interfere in the construction of the project and the action of the private investors. This is especially important in China due to its specific national conditions and is a deciding factor for the success of the PPP project.

With the partnership between public and private sectors being its essence, PPP stresses the importance of the harmonious integration of fairness and efficiency. In the partnership, the fairness in social development should be realized with the minimal cost of efficiency, and the comprehensive utilization efficiency of economic resources especially the resources of the public sector as well as and the benefits generated from the utilization of the resources should be increased with the minimal cost of fairness. Generally, the involvement of private investment in urbanization financing has four advantages as follows:

Firstly, it helps transform the function of the government and reduce the burden of public finance. As is one of its advantages, PPP helps reduce the expenditure of the public sector and the pressure of government budget, and it also helps transform the government's role from a provider to a supervisor of infrastructure and public service, with their quality further ensured. In launching infrastructure projects such as highways and railways, the government often allows the private sector to get involved due to the shortage of capital. The private sector can recoup its investment by charging for the use of the infrastructure or service. With PPP, the government is still likely to provide the society with certain infrastructure and service without making any investment and it can obtain the ownership of the infrastructure after a certain period of time.

Secondly, it gives full play to the private sector's efficiency in capital utilization and its advantage in operation management. In financing the projects launched by the public sector, PPP brings new technologies of production and management, which dramatically improves its efficiency and performance in providing public products and service. Meanwhile, on the basis of the "charging for use" mechanism and the involvement of private sector, PPP can meet the demand of the society to a greater extent without increasing tax burden on the general public. Besides, in the initial phase of a PPP project, the public sector and private enterprises jointly engage in the process, including project identification, feasibility study, facilities construction and financing. This ensures the feasibility of the technology and the capital needed, shortens the duration of the preliminary work and reduces the cost. In addition, the sustainability of PPP makes the intergenerational sharing of cost possible. As they normally last for 15–30 years, PPP projects can alleviate the existing generation's burden of the cost involved in building the infrastructure for future use.

Thirdly, it helps share risks rationally between the public and private sectors. By engaging in PPP, the two sectors share the risks involved in public products and service, which brings about a change in the traditional pattern where the risks are concentrated in the public sector only. Rational sharing of risks not only gives full play to the advantages of the private sector, but also enables the public sector to become better focused on its fundamental functions. Meanwhile, the government will not totally lose its right of control over the project when the risks are shared. Undoubtedly, risk-sharing can only become an advantage when necessary constraints are in place, because both parties in the partnership have the motive to minimize their own risks, as is known according to the principle of risk minimization in vested interests.

Fourthly, it makes profit reconciliation more flexible. In the financing model of PPP, the principle of "greater profit for greater risk" is followed as a way of profit distribution. The public sector and the private sector share profits on the basis of the risks taken respectively. In the administration model of PPP, however, the government shares no profit from the project but controls or regulates the share of profit allotted to the private sector.

From the perspective of the financial market, PPP projects can generate cash flow income, and this meets the basic requirement of asset securitization. Generally, the execution plan of a PPP project will stipulate that the future cash flow, including the outflow, inflow and net flow of cash, be calculated on the basis of the ROI mechanism of the project's deal structure. Meanwhile, the debt repayment capacity and the expenditure responsibility of the government should be assessed and included in its financial budget deliberation, to ensure that the government payment is confirmed and in place. These measures safeguard the predictability, sustainability and stability of the cash flow of a PPP project, and together they become the foundation for the securitization of the project assets.

In view of the aforementioned theories of PPP, along with the recent policy trends in China, including the neutralizing of government debt risk, the revealing of covert government debt, and the standardizing of government bond issuance and government expenditure, three central features of PPP can be extracted on the basis of the experience of PPP development in China:

To begin with, PPP attracts not only "investment" but also "talent." Apart from private capital, it is more important to involve the professional competence and managerial experience of the private investors in the partnership. In a market featuring full and effective competition, the capital from private investors with adequate experience and the capital characterized with high efficiency and low cost is most likely to be accepted. The private investors may have higher efficiency and better experience in project construction and operation management, compared with the traditional state-owned enterprises established by the government for a certain infrastructure project. Therefore, if the government allows certain projects to be undertaken by experienced and professional institutions rather than make investment on the projects and operate them by itself, the efficiency of the projects may be higher. Meanwhile, the private investors are willing to invest in the projects, because they are granted the right to project operation by the government and can enjoy the foreseeable income from the cash flow of the projects. And their one-time investment can be repaid with a long-term and steady economic return. The process involved is in fact the securitization of project assets in a special way. As can be seen, PPP integrates the professionalism of private investors and the public resources of the government, giving full play to their respective advantages, and maximizes their shared benefits.

Secondly, the pivot of PPP lies in the sharing of risks and profits. As it involves a market-oriented and contract-based business activity, PPP will inevitably change the traditional pattern of management in an infrastructure project initiated by the government. Acting as the provider of infrastructure projects in the traditional sense, the government is responsible for providing public infrastructure effectively, with less attention paid to the returns on its investment and with all the risks undertaken by itself. A system of this kind causes comparatively low efficiency of management. In PPP, however, through reasonable sharing of risks, the government allows the private investors to undertake some risks and obtain corresponding returns on their investment. This is not intended to transfer government risks but to bring the risks under control effectively. As public infrastructure projects are of limited profitability for private investors, who are always in pursuit of profits, they will naturally give full play to their own advantages and energy in controlling the risks of the projects all through the process with their greatest efforts possible to ensure their own reasonable interests. Meanwhile, the risks of the projects are controlled effectively when they are reasonably shared among the different parties of the partnership and when each side draws on its own strengths. Undoubtedly, the profits should be shared among the different partners. Only by doing so, can the motivation of the investors be stimulated.

Thirdly, PPP pushes ahead of the transformation of government administrative mechanism. We have been stressing the importance of separating the functions of the government from those of enterprises, with an emphasis placed at the same time on solving the problem of chaotic and misplaced roles of the government and enterprises. In effect, PPP pushes ahead the reform of government administrative mechanism in the field of infrastructure. In the traditional administrative pattern, where the government provides public products directly, the government acts as both the supervisor and the executor. This dual identity makes it difficult to develop effective compatibility of incentives and increase efficiency in providing public products. However, as infrastructure projects of PPP are put on the market, the government can only act as the rule maker and the industry supervisor. It helps rationalize the administrative mechanism and truly reflects the role of the market in optimizing resources allocation. It also enables the government to play its role of guidance and supervision in a more effective way.

Therefore, I am happy to see the publishing of the *New Model of PPP in Financial Reform—"City Development Pattern" for Restructuring Value of Infrastructure Assets,* which helps the people engaged in PPP projects and relevant learners in China develop a systematic command of the fundamentals of PPP, including the specific financing patterns of PPP projects, the advantages of PPP projects, and the financing of PPP projects on the basis of asset securitization. Especially the book shares many cases of urban development funds in restructuring the value of infrastructure assets through financial innovations over recent years. On the basis of the cases, it elaborates on the background and nature of the rise of PPP and the change it brings to the innovation of infrastructure investment and financing. The book covers not only the research on the macroscopic theories of PPP but also the analysis of typical PPP cases. As the book proceeds from the shallow to the deep and from the surface to the interior in its analysis, it enables the readers to explore the model of PPP from both macroscopic and microscopic perspectives.

Chapter 37
On How to Securitize Assets of PPP Projects

37.1 What is "PPP"?

PPP refers to a long-term partnership established in the fields of infrastructure and public service. In the normal pattern of PPP, private investors undertake most parts of the project, including the designing, construction, operation and maintenance of the infrastructure, and gain reasonable return on investment (ROI) via "user charges" and necessary "government payment"; the government departments concerned are responsible for supervising the price and quality of the infrastructure or public service to maximize public interests.

PPP is often defined in a broad or a narrow sense. In its broad sense, PPP refers to the various partnerships between government departments and private investors in providing public products and service. In its narrow sense, PPP is a general description of a series of project financing patterns, through which the government departments and private investors jointly invest on or put resources into certain projects and then the private investors hold responsibility for the construction and operation of the projects.

Viewed from its narrow sense, PPP is different from the traditional project financing models to some extent (as is indicated in Table 37.1 and Fig. 37.1). There are both similarities and differences among PPP, privatization and the traditional pattern of contracting: PPP is similar to privatization in terms of the incentive mechanism; it is more like the traditional pattern of contracting, however, in regard to the budget accounting system. The businesses involved in PPP are responsible for the operational performance of a long-term project, while those involved in the traditional pattern of contracting do not hold responsibility for the operational performance of a project when it is out of warranty coverage. From an overall perspective, the major differences among PPP, privatization and the traditional pattern of contracting can be shown in three aspects, that is, the ownership and the right to the control of the assets of a certain project, whether businesses are set up to run the project, and the participants

Source: Headline Today on July 10, 2017

S. Ba, *The New Cycle and New Finance in China*,
https://doi.org/10.1007/978-981-16-8209-4_37

Table 37.1 Differences between PPP and traditional pattern of government financing

Differences	Traditional pattern of government financing	PPP
Degree of recourse	Full recourse: The financial institution can demand debt repayment by the local financing platform with all its assets	Limited recourse or non-recourse: The debts should be paid off with the profit from the PPP project only. The financial institution cannot demand debt repayment on the basis of other assets, which are not PPP-related
Risk sharing	The risks of project financing are usually concentrated on the side of the government or the financing platform of the local government	The risks of project financing are undertaken by private investors
Financing cost	A normal rate of bank loan interest	The financing cost is associated with the financing capacity of the private investors, who can lower the financing cost-effectively by using their own resources

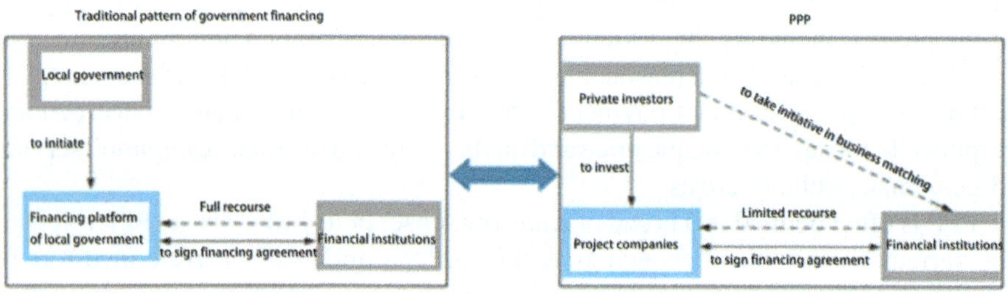

Fig. 37.1 Participants involved in PPP and traditional pattern of government financing

responsible for planning and management of the project. In the traditional pattern of contracting, the contractor is responsible for infrastructure construction only and is not responsible for project maintenance and operation; in PPP, the private businesses have interim ownership of the project assets, as against their indefinite ownership of their private assets, and the ownership of the latter is subject to common laws only. One of the shared advantages of PPP and the traditional pattern of contracting is that both reserve the right of the government to policymaking and efforts coordinating.

PPP is applicable in a broad range of fields, covering water, heat, gas and power supply, sewage and garbage treatment, government-subsidized housing projects, new-pattern urbanization, municipal engineering, water conservancy projects, resource environment and ecology protection, the construction of highways, railways, airports and multi-purpose tunnels for underground pipelines, rail transit projects, medical service, tourism, education and training, and elderly care service projects. As for PPP's scope of application, there are subtle differences in the interpretations given

Table 37.2 Different Interpretations of PPP's range of application

Government departments	Description of PPP's range of application	Document source
The Ministry of Finance	infrastructure and public service	Document ID: MOF Finance [2014] No. 76
The National Development and Reform Commission	public products and service	Document ID: NDRC Investment [2014] No. 2724

by the Ministry of Finance and the National Development and Reform Commission (as indicated in Table 37.2).

In terms of the charging mechanism, PPP projects can fall into three categories, that is, profit-oriented, quasi-profit-oriented and non-profit-oriented projects. Some projects cofunded by government and private investors have inadequate returns to cover the cost and the expected profit, yet they have comparatively good social benefits. It is advisable for the local financial department of different levels to subsidize these projects properly. And the relevant expenditures including the subsidies can be categorized and listed in the budget of the government of the same level and listed in the medium- and long-term financial plans.

37.2 Specific Forms of PPP Project Financing

The theoretical research and the practice of PPP in China lag behind that in developed nations to some extent. The government in China has a long-lasting monopoly on the provision of public products and service, featuring a comparatively high level of state intervention. As there is a big gap in respect to economic and political background, China and the West have different interpretations of PPP. On the basis of China's national conditions and the practical applications of PPP in the country's public products and service, PPP can be defined from the following perspectives:

Firstly, the private sector is distinct from the public sector in PPP. In addition to privately owned enterprises and foreign-invested enterprises, the private sector also includes the state-owned enterprises with independent legal person status, because the overall production value of China's state-owned enterprises takes up the vast majority of the country's gross domestic product (GDP) and the large enterprises that are able to provide public products and service are generally state-owned. Comparatively, the public sector usually refers to the government agencies and those state-owned enterprises that have no independent legal person status under certain government departments. Therefore, the notions of "public" or "private" should be redefined in China on the basis of the types of interests pursued, that is, the pursuit of public welfare or economic benefits, instead of the types of ownership.

Secondly, the public sector and the private sector share both risks and benefits in the partnership. The risks are shared on the basis of the different capacities of the two sectors, because PPP is aimed at a win–win situation and the maximization of the overall benefits. And the benefits are distributed in line with both the cost and the risk undertaken by the two sectors. The private sector's demand for economic benefits can be satisfied when it does not infringe on the consumers' rights.

Lastly, the public sector and the private sector come into partnership on the basis of equality and mutual benefit. The government in China has been playing the roles of the "player" and the "referee" simultaneously for long when it provides public products and service. In the new pattern of partnership, the government should transform its functions and roles, and it should not enjoy any privilege in selecting private investors and sharing risks and profits. Once an agreement of cooperation has been signed with private investors, the government department represents one of the parties only and should not use its official power to interfere in the construction of the project and the action of the private investors. This is especially important in China due to its specific national conditions and is a deciding factor for the success of the PPP project.

37.3 Advantages of PPP Projects

The partnership between public and private sectors, which is the essence of PPP, leads to the integration of planned economy and market-oriented economy in its operation mechanism. Compared with the separate economic patterns, the new management system and operation mechanism developed on the basis of the combination of both economic patterns have a better performance. PPP stresses the importance of the harmonious integration of fairness and efficiency. In the partnership, the fairness in social development should be realized with the minimal cost of efficiency, and the comprehensive utilization efficiency of economic resources especially the resources of the public sector as well as and the benefits generated from the utilization of the resources should be increased with the minimal cost of fairness. Generally, the involvement of private investment in urbanization financing has four advantages as follows (as indicated in Fig. 37.2):

Firstly, PPP helps transform the function of the government and reduce the burden of public finance.

As is one of its advantages, PPP helps reduce the expenditure of the public sector and the pressure of government budget, and it also helps transform the government's

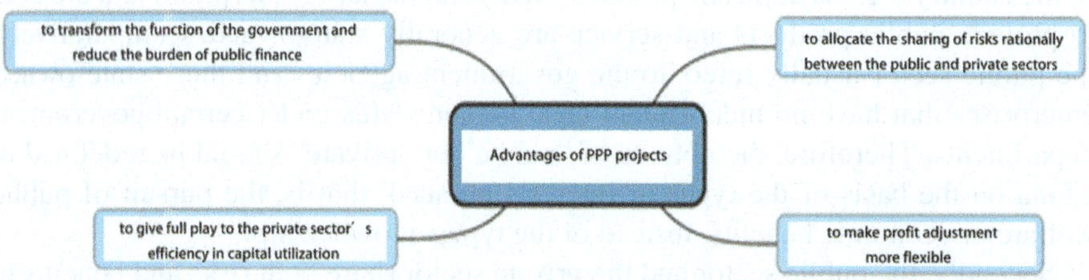

Fig. 37.2 Advantages of PPP projects

role from a provider to a supervisor of infrastructure and public service, with their quality further ensured. In launching infrastructure projects such as highways and railways, the government often allows the private sector to get involved due to the shortage of capital. The private sector can recoup its investment by charging for the use of the infrastructure or service. With PPP, the government is still likely to provide the society with certain infrastructure and service without making any investment and it can obtain the ownership of the infrastructure after a certain period of time.

Secondly, PPP gives full play to the private sector's efficiency in capital utilization and its advantage in operation management.

In financing the projects launched by the public sector, PPP brings new technologies of production and management, which dramatically improves its efficiency and performance in providing public products and service. Meanwhile, on the basis of the "charging for use" mechanism and the involvement of private sector, PPP can meet the demand of the society to a greater extent without increasing tax burden on the general public. Besides, in the initial phase of a PPP project, the public sector and private enterprises jointly engage in the process, including project identification, feasibility study, facilities construction and financing. This ensures the feasibility of the technology and the capital needed, shortens the duration of the preliminary work and reduces the cost. In addition, the sustainability of PPP makes the intergenerational sharing of cost possible. As they normally last for 15–30 years, PPP projects can alleviate the existing generation's burden of the cost involved in building the infrastructure for future use.

Thirdly, PPP helps share risks rationally between the public and private sectors.

By engaging in PPP, the two sectors share the risks involved in public products and service, which brings about a change in the traditional pattern where the risks are concentrated in the public sector only. Rational sharing of risks not only gives full play to the advantages of the private sector, but also enables the public sector to become better focused on its fundamental functions, such as the procurement of public service, the formulation of public service criteria, the supervision of criteria enforcement and the protection of public interests. Meanwhile, the government will not totally lose its right of control over the project when the risks are shared. However, risk-sharing can only become an advantage when necessary constraints are in place, because both parties in the partnership have the motive to minimize their own risks, as is known according to the principle of risk minimization in vested interests.

Fourthly, PPP makes profit reconciliation more flexible.

In the financing model of PPP, the principle of "greater profit for greater risk" is followed as a way of profit distribution. The public sector and the private sector share profits on the basis of the risks taken, respectively. In the administration model of PPP, however, the government shares no profit from the project but controls or regulates the share of profit allotted to the private sector. The government can give subsidies to the private investors according to the contract, if the profit they have reaped from a PPP project is relatively small and the partnership might fail as a consequence. The government can also adjust the share of profit allotted to the private investors according to the contract, if they are expected to obtain excess profit from the project.

37.4 Applicability of Asset Securitization to PPP Projects

With PPP, a pattern of partnership between the government and private investors, the government can select private investors through bid inviting in the field of public products and services that the government holds responsible for and then delegate power to the investors to invest in and develop specific infrastructure and utility projects. With the projects completed, the private investors can recoup their investment and obtain reasonable ROI through project operation and charging for the use over a certain period, after which the projects will be transferred to the government for free. Throughout the process of cooperation, the government is responsible for supervision and payment that is made on the basis of performance assessment. During the period of project operation, the project company maintains continuous and steady cash flow with government payment and viability gap funding (VGF) as well as the income from charging for use (as indicated in Fig. 37.3).

Asset securitization refers to the real sale of the illiquid basic assets that can generate predictable and sustainable future cash flow to the specially established special-purpose vehicle (SPV) through legal means, to isolate risk from the assets of the original owner. The cash flow of the basic assets is then split into securities with different credit ratings and terms via certain structural design and is then sold to eligible investors. The asset management agency pays for the basic assets with the money obtained from the sale of the securities and then pays the investors for the principal and interest of their investment with the cash flow generated from the basic assets. The crucial requirement of asset securitization is that there be a stable, predictable and sustainable cash flow generated from basic assets.

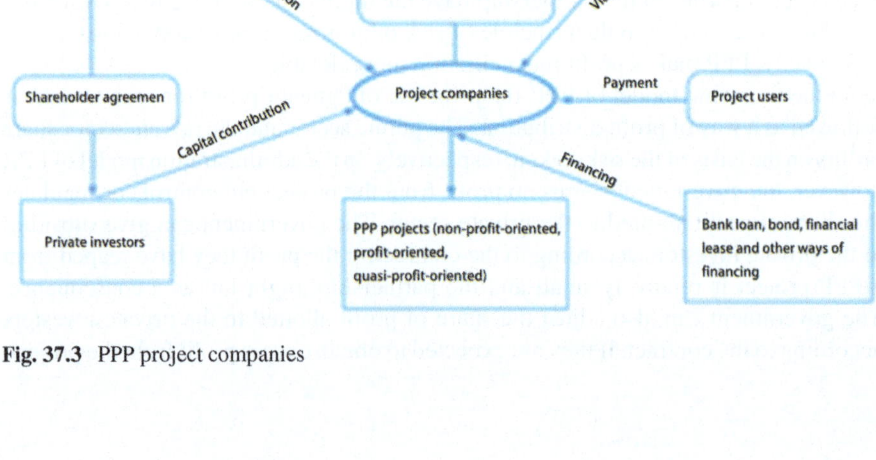

Fig. 37.3 PPP project companies

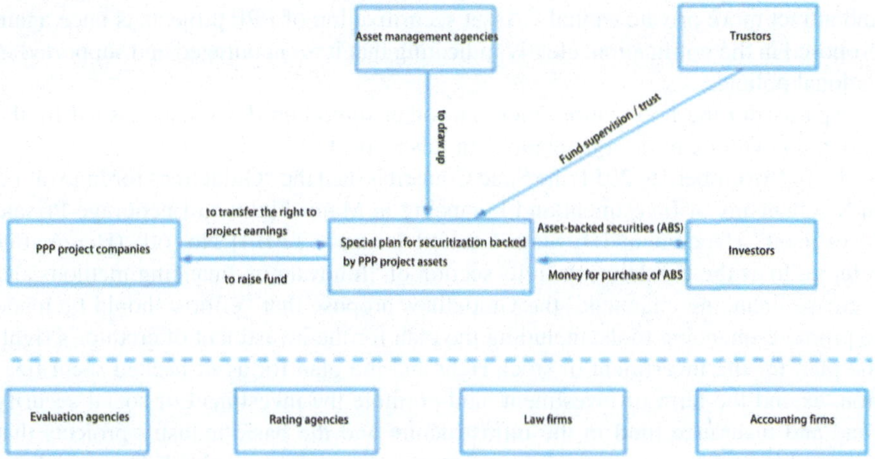

Fig. 37.4 Special plan for securitization backed by PPP project assets

On the basis of the concepts discussed above, it can be concluded that PPP projects can generate cash flow income, and this meets the basic requirement of asset securitization. Generally, the execution plan of a PPP project will stipulate that the future cash flow, including the outflow, inflow and net flow of cash, be calculated on the basis of the ROI mechanism of the project's deal structure (as indicated in Fig. 37.4). Meanwhile, the debt repayment capacity and the expenditure responsibility of the government should be assessed and included in its financial budget deliberation, to ensure that the government payment is confirmed and in place. These measures safeguard the predictability, sustainability and stability of the cash flow of a PPP project, and together they become the foundation for the securitization of the project assets.

37.5 Supporting Policies and Relevant Laws and Regulations

On August 10, 2016, the National Development and Reform Commission issued the "Notification about Promoting Partnership between Government and Private Investors in Construction of Traditional Infrastructure" (Document ID: NDRC Investment [2016] No. 1744) (Hereinafter referred to as the Notification). According to the Notification, "the integration of PPP projects with the further development of capital market should be promoted to increase the ways of withdrawal for the venture capital of PPP projects via stock right transfer, asset securitization and so on in various property right and stock right markets. The marketability of the right to charge for project use and the right to other prospective investment returns should be enhanced, and multiple, standard and market-oriented mechanisms for private capital withdrawal should be established, to promote the liquidity and the value of PPP projects and attract more private capital." Asset securitization of PPP projects is once again proposed in the notification, clearly indicating that it is encouraged and supported in national policies.

Apart from the notification, there are other important documents issued by the national government or organizations in this respect:

1. On November 16, 2014, the State Council issued the "Guidelines for Innovation in Mechanisms of Investment and Financing in Major Fields to Encourage Private Investment" (Document ID: State Council Issuance [2014] No. 60) (Hereinafter referred to as the Guidelines). In its section of "Innovate on financing methods and increase financing channels," the Guidelines propose that "efforts should be made to promote financing tools, including the plan for the investment of creditor's right, the plan for the investment of stock right and the plan for asset-backed securitization, extend the term of investment, and promote the investment of social security fund and insurance fund in the infrastructure and the basic-industry projects that have stable investment return and long-term investment recouping." The guidelines also propose "the securitization of the accounts receivable of the enterprises responsible for the construction of transportation projects including railways, highways and airports." The plan for asset-backed securitization and the securitization of enterprises' accounts receivable, as are proposed in the guidelines, is the top-level policy design for the securitization of PPP project assets.

2. On December 24, 2014, the Asset Management Association of China issued the "Guide to Negative List of Basic Assets for Securitization" (Hereinafter referred to as the Guide). According to the first clause of its attached file, the "Negative List of Basic Assets for Securitization," "the basic assets, with the local government being the direct or indirect debtor, should not be included as the basic assets to be used for securitization, except the financial subsidies payable by the local government according to the publicized provisions of profit-sharing in PPP." In other words, the government payment and subsidies for private investors in PPP projects can be included in the basic asset pool for securitization.

3. On April 25, 2015, six national government departments including the National Development and Reform Commission jointly issued the "Administrative Measures for Management of Infrastructure and Public Utility Franchise" (Document ID: NDRC Decree No. 25) (Hereinafter referred to as the Administrative Measures). The 24th clause of the Administrative Measures states that "franchised project companies in China are encouraged to engage in structured finance and issue project revenue notes (PRN) and asset-backed notes (ABN)." As a category of asset securitization products, ABN is a debt financing tool issued in the interbank bond market and backed with the prospective cash flow generated from the basic assets of non-financial businesses, with the capital and interest repaid within a certain period agreed.

The basic assets for securitization must be defined in accordance with specific laws and regulations. As is stated in the above documents, the right to the profit generated from charging for the use of PPP projects can be included as basic assets. This lays a foundation for asset securitization in the field of PPP.

References

1. Ba Shusong & Yang Xianling. *The New Urbanization Financing and Financial Reform* [M]. Beijing: China Workers Publishing House. 2014.
2. Jia Kang. "PPP–Innovation of Institutional Supply and Its Positive Effect" [N]. Guangming Daily, 2015–05–27.
3. "Notification from Ministry of Finance on Promotion of PPP" (Document ID: MOF Finance [2014] No. 76).
4. "Notification from Ministry of Finance on Issuance of Guide to PPP Operations (Trial Version)" (Document ID: MOF Finance [2014] No. 113).
5. "Notification from Ministry of Finance on Issuance of 'Guide to Assessment of Financial Capacity of PPP Projects'" (Document ID: MOF Finance [2015] No. 21).

Chapter 38
Four New Trends of Innovation in Financing Models

From my perspective, there are three crucial factors in the innovation of financing models.

The first crucial factor is "innovation."

Breakthroughs should be made in the existing financing model, and innovative ideas should be introduced into the new models. With the financial market undergoing drastic transformation at home and abroad, the leaders of many financial institutions have asked me to recommend candidates for the positions of senior executives and experts in the institutions. They all come up with an interesting criterion for the candidates. Against a background of drastic changes in economic and financial structure, they think it desirable that the candidates should not work in the field of securities or should not be so familiar with the business pattern of securities companies, so that they are not susceptible to the original way of thinking. As can be seen, of the strategic investment institutes that the Postal Savings Bank of China (PSBC) came into partnership with at this time, quite a few are from outside the banking industry. The interaction between these institutes and PSBC is expected to facilitate innovations in its business models and products.

The second crucial factor is "model."

I think that we should discover general rules and principles from sporadic and random financial innovations, have them institutionalized and transform them into products or develop them into a model that can be promoted and copied. In fact, it is a crucial capacity of the financial industry to transform the large number of assets into investible products in the market via special financial design. In the process, financial institutes can also give full play to their professional capacity. This facilitates the development of new models.

The third crucial factor is "financing."

In my personal opinion, the operation of commercial banks should be analyzed with a focus on financing or asset management, which is also a major problem facing

This article is written on the basis of the speeches by Prof. Ba Shusong at the PSBC Summit Forum held on December 11, 2015.

S. Ba, *The New Cycle and New Finance in China*,
https://doi.org/10.1007/978-981-16-8209-4_38

the whole banking industry in the transformation of operation management models. I was once the director of a state-owned bank at grassroots level. The commercial banks were "liabilities-oriented" or "deposits-centered" at that time. Because of inadequate funding, the banks could only provide loan service on a certain scale in line with the loan-to-deposit ratio required when the deposits were adequate and when the banks became creditors, and then they could release loans to gain a profit from interest margin. With the transformation of the market structure, the competition in terms of assets will become more decisive. The PSBC Summit Forum focuses its attention on financing and asset management. This happens to accord with my understanding of the trend of market transformation, that is, the transformation of the overall pattern of bank operation and management from "liabilities-oriented" to "assets-oriented." With abundant liquidity, capital source is no longer a major constraint, and the key to market success will lie in attracting high-quality assets through innovation in financing and asset management, because high-quality assets can naturally attract abundant capital when transformed into financial products up to standards. In fact, this is an important part of the background for the current discussion of the so-called asset shortage.

According to the financial statistics of November released by PBC on December 11, there was a moderate growth of M2 by 13.7% at the end of November, with the bank loan totaling RMB 708.9 billion only in the same period. The bank loan is RMB 234.7 billion less than expected on the basis of its growth rate compared with that of M2 in previous years. The monetary conditions for M2 have stayed relatively loose, yet the growth of bank loan has kept shrinking. This matches the trend of growing diversification in the innovation of financial products and the overall trend of financial restructuring as well.

As for the innovation of financing methods, the following four factors should be taken into account.

To begin with, the focus of financing model innovation during economic restructuring should be on the development of the capacity to shift from asset-heavy to asset-light business. Why? Because the commercial banks in China are good at mortgage guarantee service currently. Then what kinds of industries are more likely to use their assets as mortgage guarantee? Naturally, they are asset-heavy industries. In the period of economic restructuring, however, asset-heavy industries are exactly the upstream industries with excess production capacity. If the commercial banks continue to follow conventional models of financing, with a focus on asset-heavy industries, they will automatically give valuable financial resources to some asset-heavy industries with overcapacity, the industries that should have been shut down. Therefore, the banks should learn to shift from asset-heavy business, which they have already become used to and good at, to asset-light business, following the trend of economic restructuring in China. For example, many dynamic enterprises developing in the direction of the country's future economic transformation are often asset-light enterprises that are innovation or service-oriented, or knowledge-intensive. Such enterprises often have no assets to be used as mortgage guarantee, because their assets may just be an innovative idea or the patent for a product. If the banks stick to the traditional mindset, which focuses on asset-heavy business, how could they provide service for these emerging industries? As economic restructuring is going on, the financial industry should keep up with the trend, with emphasis laid on the improvement of the banks' capacity in the operation of the business associated with light assets.

Secondly, with a view to financing structure adjustment, deleveraging or asset securitization, an important trend of financing innovation should lie in a gradual shift from the dominance of indirect financing such as bank loan to the mutual development of direct and indirect financing, with an emphasis placed on increasing the proportion of direct financing. Why should direct financing especially equity financing be promoted? Because the development of bond market helps reduce maturity mismatch brought about by bank loan, and it helps establish a market-oriented interest rate mechanism and reveal a complete yield curve. It also facilitates the transformation of monetary policies. As for equity financing, it will lead to the formation of new capital, and the increase of capital reduces leverage. Accordingly, the financial sector can either cut down on debt or boost the growth of new capital as a way to decrease the numerator or increase the denominator in the leverage ratio. Therefore, the commercial banks are actively pushing ahead with the adjustment of financing structure to support the development of direct financing especially equity financing, which in fact helps reduce the leverage of the whole economic system. Meanwhile, the development of direct financing also helps establish a mechanism for risk diversification. If there is a big non-performing loan (NPL), it will exert a considerable influence on the quality of the bank assets when placed in a bank's account. If it is a bad loan based on direct financing in the capital market, the risk will be dispersed among thousands of investors. It can be safely concluded that the development of direct financing especially equity financing is a workable solution not only for deleveraging but also for reducing maturity mismatch and creating the mechanism of risk diversification.

Thirdly, the innovation in financing models should also be expanded to cover the financial service for an enterprise in its whole life cycle.

Objectively speaking, the commercial banks in China have become accustomed to serving enterprises when their business keeps a steady development with positive cash flow. The banks often compete fiercely for opportunities to conduct business with these enterprises in this phase of their life cycle. Therefore, it is hard to find any enterprise still short of financing service from banks in this phase. A look into the overall economic transformation, however, reveals that the so-called economic transformation and industrial restructuring actually foster the emergence of many new enterprises. A considerable number of them are still in their humble beginning or initial phase of development, and some are in need of a merger or reorganization because they are trapped in temporary difficulties in business operation. In these phases, however, they can hardly obtain service from commercial banks, as the banks often follow the conventional model of operation. It is in these phases that the enterprises need financial service the most badly. Therefore, commercial banks should shift from serving enterprises mainly in the period when they have positive cash flow and favorable balance with steady development to serving them in their whole life cycle. We have read some reports on PSBC's great efforts to explore ways to support start-ups. I think we still need to push ahead in this field.

Fourthly, the commercial banks should transform their operation from being "liabilities-oriented" to "assets-oriented" against the current background of innovation in financing models. Faced with the influence of a long-lasting emphasis on a business model that is "deposits-centered" and "liabilities-oriented," the banks should enhance their capacity to control high-quality assets. With relatively abundant liquidity, it is important to obtain high-quality assets and transform them into financial products available for investment through product design and risk management and then sell them out while complying with relevant regulations. A stress on the capacity of asset control is more important in the market where low-interest rate and "asset shortage" are expected to persist.

Chapter 39
Trends of Innovation in Financing for Small- and Medium-Sized Enterprises

In the ecosystem of B2B, finance is a link that plays a predominant role. I'd like to share my views of finance from this perspective. I will follow the example of Director Tong to confine my speech to three points as follows.

Firstly, in the period of economic downturn, the different business models of microfinance are under pressure tests. Some problems that are hard to find during economic upturn will probably be exposed.

Secondly, new explorations are being made worldwide about microfinance in the new situations.

Thirdly, I'd like to share my observations on the trend of microfinance.

As can be seen, some business models of microfinance are frequently discussed in the market. The first is the business model of city commercial banks, which reach their potential clients on the basis of the financial or non-financial data of the clients in specific regions. Some city commercial banks are widely acclaimed in the market, such as Baoshang Bank Limited and Zhejiang Tailong Commercial Bank.

The second is the business model of shareholding commercial banks, which provide nationwide microfinance service with a stress on standard procedures, such as China Minsheng Bank (CMBC). I was once the board director of CMBC and chairman of its risk management committee. I think the explorations of CMBC about microfinance bear different features in different economic cycles.

The third is Internet-based finance. Just now Director Zhang and Director Tong both discussed the innovation of Internet finance. How can emerging technologies push ahead financial reform and help create new paths for the development of microfinance? The aforementioned three business models of microfinance have their respective advantages in different fields and for different clients. Despite that, there are also problems exposed in these models.

This article is written on the basis of the speech entitled "Trends of Innovation in Financing for Small- and Medium-sized Enterprises" by Dr. Ba Shusong, chief China economist of Hong Kong Exchanges and Clearing Limited (HKEx), at the World Summit of B2B Ecosystem on January 12, 2016.

S. Ba, *The New Cycle and New Finance in China*,
https://doi.org/10.1007/978-981-16-8209-4_39

The regional microfinance model, with city commercial banks as its representatives, focuses on the clients that are not expected to develop into large-size enterprises according to the relevant policies adopted by the supervision department. It centers round the operation patterns that are local place-based and are distinct from those of major banks, with a focus on microfinance clients. It is aimed at establishing a specialized mechanism, institute and business model. The major restrictions on the regional microfinance model are information asymmetry, comparatively high unit cost and the comparative concentration of its business in a certain field. The excessive concentration of business in an industry or a field will incur major impact whenever a round of economic adjustment happens, raising doubts on the sustainability of the model. The service most typical of this model is the analysis of the cash flow and personal qualities of a borrower, with field study conducted to crosscheck the borrower's qualities, capacity, and financial and non-financial information.

As for the commercial banks with nationwide operation, they place more emphasis on providing special and different services, among others, in microfinance, to meet the requirement of supervision departments. Some of the banks, however, refer to microfinance as service for retail businesses and take it to be retail service, leading to a scattered operation in microfinance. This business model will suffer considerable impact in the period of economic downturn. The most typical example is the pattern involving "specific regions and industry chains." In the pattern involving "specific regions," small and micro-businesses in target business areas are managed on a multilayered and categorized basis. The businesses are divided in accordance with the timespan of their operation and their business income, and then different credit is conferred accordingly. As for the small- and medium-sized businesses involved in the pattern of "one specific region, two industry chains," the method of mass marketing and concentrated credit conferring is adopted in micro finance, and mutual guarantee for joint loan application is introduced to mitigate credit risk of individual businesses, This method, which helps bring down the cost-effectively, is a meaningful exploration in microfinance. In the period of economic downturn, however, many problems arise in the pattern of mutual guarantee for joint loan application. Over the recent couple of years, some nationwide commercial banks suffered from the failure of this pattern as 60% or even 70% of the new non-performing loans reported each year were formed in the Yangtze River delta area (mainly Jiangsu and Zhejiang provinces), which had long been regarded as a place with sound development and good financial conditions.

The rapid rise of Internet-based finance happens with a major change in the policy environment, that is, the marketization of interest rate and the gradual relaxation of financial restriction. Due to the change of relevant policies, greater attention has been drawn to Internet-based microfinance. Its trend of development lies in the application of technological means to lower cost and the use of data power to control risk. For example, the application of information technology, the Internet, cloud computing, big data and other technologies provides multiple directions for the innovation of microfinance. As can be seen, Alibaba Group has made some explorations in these fields.

The aforementioned different business models are faced with pressure tests in the periods of economic adjustment and downturn. As is known, a risk control model or a business model in the financial sector can only become credible after the test of one or two rounds of complete economic cycles, which should cover both economic expansion and economic adjustment. Those financial business models that have developed in the period of economic expansion or adjustment only are immature, whether it is based on the Internet or not.

Therefore, we saw the growth of microloan balance slow down countrywide in the period of economic downturn, especially in the third quarter of 2012 and the second quarter of 2013 as the growth slowed remarkably. The risk models currently used in microfinance, whatever categories they fall in, are set up on the basis of limited historical data, covering especially the client behavior and economic data in the period of economic upturn. This brings with them risks of different degree due to the underestimation of credit crisis and the decline of credit quality. To put it another way using technical terms of risk management, the database of non-performance loans has not been fully tested in economic cycles.

Under the new circumstances, financial institutes and Internet institutes of different kinds have made explorations to lower the cost of microfinance service proactively. For example, microfinance service in a rational range involves both credit cost and physical cost, and new technologies, including supply chain finance and big data-based credit information service, help cut down on the cost of investigations conducted into the operation of small and microbusinesses. Meanwhile, the specialized operation of industry chain and the tracking of big data also help reduce credit cost to some extent. As can be seen, the financial service models of traditional institutions and industry supply chains have been adjusted to the changes of industry clusters and supply chains. For example, industry clusters are promoted in specialized markets, specific regions or the supply chain of a specific industry, to develop into business area clusters and industry supply chains of unique characteristics.

Microfinance service has expanded its connotation. The demand of small and microbusiness owners has expanded from pure financing service to integrated financial service that covers financing, clearing, money management and consultation. Therefore the ability to identify the change of clients' demand is the deciding factor in the further development of a business model, no matter whether it is the business model of city commercial banks, shareholding commercial banks or Internet-based finance. Three or five years ago, we conducted a survey in some business areas about what kind of service is needed by our clients. Can you imagine the kind of response from the clients surveyed? They hoped that they could get an instant message once their payment for goods has been received by the consignor. That is actually a message of clearing. Therefore, with the changing of clients' demand, the concept and the business model of microfinance should be adjusted accordingly.

The traditional financial institutions have made some explorations in their business models, including, for example, the exploration of how to improve their operation procedures. This has become a focus of commercial banks in their drive to introduce patterns in their operation and optimize their business models. Especially it has basically become a focus of the domestic commercial banks in their effort to explore how to collectively optimize their operation procedures and lower the cost so as to create an efficient "credit factory." As can be seen, China Construction Bank (CCB) and China Minsheng Bank (CMBC) are pushing ahead with explorations in their operation models.

The innovation of technologies and the development of credit investigation system make it possible to assess different aspects of the clients, including financial status, behavior features, credit records, occupational environment, non-performance probability and credit rating. Based on big data, these methods of credit investigation make customer classification more rational and accurate with the support of new data sources, especially the fundamental core data collected by Internet companies, such as the data of online searching, social activities, travel and consumption. These are the data we tried to access when we were engaged in banking industry, but they were only accessible at high cost. Over 20 years ago when I was head of Hangzhou Branch of Bank of China (BOC), a shopping center applied for a loan from the bank. I could only learn about the condition of its assets by referring to its financial statement. Through investigations and analyses, we came to learn that a major factor deciding the repayment capacity of the shopping center is the structure of its customer group. It would involve a high cost at that time to collect such data as the customers' average expenditure per time and the proportion of regular customers. At present, however, the Internet provides favorable conditions for data collection at lower cost. Apart from the Internet, professional analysis and theoretical framework are undoubtedly indispensable.

The development of cloud computing and search engine technologies makes possible an efficient analysis of big data. These technologies can provide such data as risk-based pricing and non-performance probability of a loan applicant at a very low cost and then cut down on the overall cost of the financial operation. A visualized system of risk prevention and control, for example, helps ensure the safety of capital. Another example is the mechanism for risk precaution. We have developed a real-time risk-monitoring system on the basis of online platforms and other online systems, to gather the data of a customer's historical transactions completed in different ways and to link information islands among different systems.

In fact we held a symposium online yesterday. I spoke to a leader of a commercial bank at the meeting, saying that there are actually a mass of data in the possession of commercial banks but they are not put to use comprehensively according to the finding of a data analysis I had made earlier. As can be discovered, for example, in the different phases of bull and bear markets, the major investor groups contributing to the growth of fund share sales are evolving in a stair-step pattern. At the beginning of a bull market, which has not been widely recognized by ordinary investors, the high-end investors in the first-tier cities are the major buyers of the shares of a certain fund; when the bull market matures, the middle-class investors in the second-tier cities become the major buyers; and when investors in the third-tier cities become the major buyers, other investors should stay alert to the change of the market trend. These data already exist but they are separated. It is important to link the information islands by exploring their correlations and providing visualized demonstration, support and decision making.

As is known, Internet loan service is an effective application of credit investigation based on big data. Both Internet loan service and traditional loan service have the same essential elements, covering credit risk management, risk control and risk-based pricing. As for risk-based pricing, the two most important data are the customers' overdue repayment probability and default probability. They are worked out on the basis of the intrinsic connection between customer behavior and customer credit, with the correlation discovered through certain methods and via a database of the customer group's information collected earlier. By referring to the customers' features summarized and the customers' credit rating recorded by financial institutions, Internet loan service agencies can assess the customers' default risk via the computer-based data system and adjust the line of credit, the interest rate of a loan and the length of maturity flexibly for certain customers.

As a hobby, I regularly read the annual reports of different banks. If consumer finance is not mentioned in a bank's annual report, it seems that the bank has lagged behind others. This is mainly due to the new trend in the sector: As the interest rate has already become market-oriented, banks do not have much room for negotiation with big clients, who have many ways of financing. The liberalization of the interest rate and the development of direct financing pushes the banking industry to shift its focus further and further to the service of small and microbusinesses after the test of economic cycles and devote its efforts to exploring new growth points in the field.

I have noticed that my banks show their ambition to become the Wells Fargo of China in their annual reports. As can be seen, the case of Wells Fargo has proved that a bank can survive economic cycles and its business can become sustainable if it has a good performance in microfinance. With the support of a credit rating system tailored to small and microbusinesses, Wells Fargo will accept and deal with two million loan applications annually from small and microbusinesses whose yearly sales volume is below USD two million each. Two-thirds of the loan approval decisions are made by the system itself. And after the release of the loan, the customers' credit status will be assessed monthly and adjustment will be made accordingly.

Big data-based credit investigation and Internet loan service are still in the initial phase of development. Their business models and their capacity to survive economic cycles are yet to be tested. As we know, there are no core technologies in either Internet loan service or platforms, and the capacity of big data mining platforms is inadequate. Despite the fact that Internet finance and big data are frequently discussed by many people, they can be applied in the real process of credit decision making only in very few business models. And the basic database is yet to be set up. So far, traditional banks have been stressing the importance of big data and Internet finance as concepts, but they have not devoted as much effort to building the database of basic information resources and the accuracy of the data remains to be improved.

The basic problems of data mining are found in the quantity, quality and dimensionality of the data. In addition, the variables selected in the process of data mining should be optimized, and the safety of the information be improved. To ensure the safety of Internet finance, special attention should be paid to such operation risks as network malfunction, hacker attack and internal privacy disclosure. With a look into microfinance solutions, we can find that the market has evolved further into a vertically structured financial ecosystem with subdivision of sectors. It is very unlikely that there will be a single solution to the problems with microfinance models. Nor is it likely that there will be a single rule of microfinance models in the future. Instead, microfinance models will become more connected with specific sectors, industries or even regions. Links will be built between the upstream and downstream of a sector's industry chain, and then microfinance service will be provided in specific industry chains and specific application scenarios. Microfinance involves not only Internet platforms but also banks and even the capital market at home and abroad, such as the Main-board Market, the Growth Enterprise Market (GEM) and the New OTC (over-the-counter) Market in China. The involvement of the core enterprises of the traditional financial institutions in supply chain finance and their exploration in this field is well worth our attention. In supply chain finance, the core enterprises and the related upstream and downstream firms in the supply chain are viewed as a whole, with the core enterprises as the central pillar and real trade as the foundation, and the whole capital flow or the real right is managed in a closed-off pattern on the basis of self-liquidating trade financing, the pledge of accounts receivable and the pledge of property in goods, to provide comprehensive products and services to the upstream and downstream businesses.

In view of the above analysis, the building of a sound ecosystem is more important than the sustainability of microfinance in the subdivided fields of a sector, and it does not merely depend on the performance of the macroeconomy. In the system of the steel trade sector, for instance, we can find vertically structured B2B platforms, steel dealers and banks. There will be a more comprehensive and diversified application of financial technologies and products in microfinance in the future, with the customer group subdivided further and with the service better tailored to different customers. And there will be a trend toward an integrated application of various means of financial service. Moreover, it will become possible to provide customized products in terms of operational procedures, repayment time limit, repayment methods, the interest rate of financing, etc. Risk diversification measures such as asset securitization will also be used proactively.

Part VI
Financial Supervision

Chapter 40
China's Implementation of Basel III: Progress and Solutions

From the perspective of implementation progress, it can be concluded that China has higher regulatory capital requirements than Basel III. China's banking sector basically meets the new regulatory requirements, but small- and medium-sized commercial banks are under great funding pressure. And myriad problems existent in the regulatory tools and banks are likely to compromise the process and efficiency of implementing Basel III.

40.1 The Status Quo of China's Banking Sector

As of the end of 2012, the assets of China's 511 commercial banks amounted to RMB129 trillion, around 240% of its GDP. The total assets of the five large commercial banks (Industrial and Commercial Bank of China, Agricultural Bank of China, Bank of China, China Construction Bank, and Bank of Communications) accounted for about 60% of the total assets of the banking sector, among which, Bank of China is currently the only global systemically important bank (G-SIB). At the end of 2011, the China Banking Regulatory Commission (CBRC) issued a consultative document on the classification criteria of domestic systemically important banks and the specific regulatory framework is still being drawn up.

Table 40.1 provides a summary of the size of China's banking sector at the end of 2012.

Table 40.2 summarizes the capital adequacy of China's banking sector by the end of the second quarter of 2013. Calculated under the *Capital Rules for Commercial Banks (Provisional)*(hereinafter referred to as "the Rules"), in the second quarter of 2013, the average capital adequacy ratio of the banking sector has reached 12.24%, the Common Equity capital adequacy ratio 9.85%, the non-performing loan ratio 0.96% and the provisioning coverage ratio 292.50%. Under the rules, the capital adequacy

This paper appeared in the *South China Morning Post* (SCMP), dated October 3, 2013.

S. Ba, *The New Cycle and New Finance in China*,
https://doi.org/10.1007/978-981-16-8209-4_40

Table 40.1 Size of China's banking sector

Categories	Size
Total assets of the banking sector	RMB129.102585 trillion
Total assets of internationally active banks	RMB76.916507 trillion
Total assets of the banks subject to Basel III	RMB76.916507 trillion
Number of globally active banks	Six
Number of global systemically important banks (G-SIBs)	One

Source the CBRC website

Table 40.2 Capital adequacy of the banking sector

Categories	Size
Total capital	RMB 8745 billion
Tier 1 capital	RMB7036.6 billion
Common Equity Tier 1 capital	RMB7036.6 billion
Total risk-weighted capital	RMB71452.1 billion
Off-balance sheet assets of banks	RMB11127 billion
Credit risk-weighted assets/total risk-weighted assets	92.1%
Market risk-weighted assets/total risk-weighted assets	0.9%
Operational risk-weighted assets/total risk-weighted assets	6.9%
Capital adequacy ratio	12.24%
Tier 1 capital adequacy ratio	9.85%
Common Equity Tier 1 capital adequacy ratio	9.85%

ratios of the banks subject to the new Basel capital accord have met the eligibility criteria, while small- and medium-sized commercial banks are still greatly affected. Meanwhile, Common Equity Tier 1 capital and Tier 1 capital of Chinese banks are convergent and lack capital innovative instruments. In short, China's banking sector as a whole is well-capitalized, but great efforts still need to be devoted to developing diversified channels to replenish capital.

In terms of the indicators of leverage ratio and liquidity, according to the June 2010 version of the leverage ratio calculation method, the average leverage ratio of the five large Chinese banks is 4.7%, all exceeding 4%; the average leverage ratio of five midsize banks is 3.9%, around 4%, which would not affect their operations even in accordance with the eligibility criteria by the end of 2016. The test results released by the CBRC at the end of 2010 show that the average liquidity coverage ratio (LCR) of the five large banks in China is 118.5%, and their net stable funding ratio (NSFR) is 114.1%, which have basically met the eligibility criteria; the average LCR of five midsize banks is 92.9%, and their NSFR is 118.6%, indicating that the liquidity indicator of most large and midsize banks in China can also normally meet the eligibility criteria.

In addition, although China's banking assets continue to expand, the core business of banks still focuses on providing traditional credit products and services. According to the data at the end of June 2013, the ratio of bank loans to total assets is about 51.4%. The persistence in traditional business models leading to credit risk has been the most pressing risk facing China's banking sector, with the ratio of the credit risk-weighted assets to the total risk-weighted assets reaching 92.1%. Yet regulatory authorities have been cautious about banks' involvement in complex financial activities and paid close attention to the development of asset securitized products and complex over-the-counter (OTC) derivatives, giving rise to generally small scale of the trading book of commercial banks, with the ratio of the market risk-weighted assets to the total risk-weighted assets being less than 1%, and by the end of 2012, the total amount of their outstanding asset-backed securities was less than RMB20 billion.

Meanwhile, constrained by a cap on the deposit interest rate, the market for wealth management products, as an alternative to bank deposits, is growing rapidly. Banks have been expanding their off-balance sheet assets by issuing wealth management products directly or indirectly through trust companies. On March 27, 2013, the CBRC issued the *Notice on the Relevant Issues concerning Regulating the Investment Operations of the Wealth Management Business of Commercial Banks* focusing on risks associated with wealth management business. As for the economic nature of wealth management products, because the products have no credit risk tranching, they neither fit in with the definition of securitized products nor provide liquidity facilities. Therefore, the current regulatory standards applicable to wealth management products are the rules for credit risk rather than for securitized products.

It can be seen from the rules that compared with the international standards, the regulatory standards of the Chinese version are higher than those old international standards or those of Basel III, whether in provisions against expected losses, or in capital against non-expected losses, or in the regulatory standards for the leverage ratio. The Common Equity Tier 1 capital adequacy ratio is raised to 5% from 4.5% under Basel III, while Tier 1 capital adequacy ratio and capital adequacy ratio stay the same, at 6% and 8%, respectively, and conservation buffer (retained capital), countercyclical buffer and capital surcharge for systemically important institutions are tentatively consistent with Basel III. The leverage ratio is also increased from 3% under Basel III to 4%. Although it is a small percentile increase from the perspective of individual indicator, banks will face greater regulatory pressure in the short term as a result of higher capital adequacy ratio and leverage ratio, higher regulatory requirements and more detailed indicator definitions, as well as increase in both loss provisions and capital.

40.2 Implementation Problems in China's Banking Sector

On the whole, the rules are consistent with the international standard agreements, effectively implementing the formulation principles of the Basel Accord. At the same time, given the fact that Chinese large banks have strong risk tolerance and sufficient capital; commercial banks are classified into four categories in light of the status of their capital adequacy to implement differentiated supervision. Even under the premise that the requirements of some capital indicators are higher than the international requirements, China's banking sector as a whole can basically meet the new requirements, which, on the one hand, relieves the pressure of China's banking sector to implement Basel III, but on the other hand draws attention to the fact that how to find ways to enhance the quality of capital and optimize the capital structure is the pressing issue facing the banking sector and regulators. The major problems the banking sector is faced with are as follows:

Firstly, Common Equity Tier 1 capital and Tier 1 capital converge.

The financial crisis exposed the invalidation of Tier 2 and Tier 3 capital and the artificially highness of Tier 1 capital in the American and European banks according to the definition of capital under Basel II. There are many hybrid capital instruments in these banks' assets and liabilities structures. Before the crisis, hybrid Tier 1 capital instruments accounted for about 18% of the net Tier 1 capital in European banks and the proportion of the instruments was even higher in the US banking. To this, Basel III puts forward the concept of Common Equity Tier 1 capital to offset the fact that the ratio of Additional Tier 1 capital instruments to Tier 1 capital is too high. And some hybrid Tier 1 capital instruments, especially cumulative preferred stocks, can still receive recognition in Additional Tier 1 capital and become an important supplement apart from Common Equity Tier 1 capital. However, there are no instruments that meet the criteria for inclusion in Additional Tier 1 capital in China's financial market, and Tier 1 capital and Common Equity Tier 1 capital converge seriously, leading to the convergence of the indicators of Common Equity Tier 1 capital adequacy ratio and Tier 1 capital adequacy ratio. In addition, under Basel III qualified Tier 2 capital shall include the provisions of compulsory conversion or write-off under certain circumstances. If such provisions are directly adopted, the convertible bonds and subordinated debts issued by China's commercial banks will no longer meet the requirements, which may lead to a significant reduction in Tier 2 capital of domestic banks. For small banks, whose deposit-taking capacity and funding capacity through issuing common shares are lower than those of large banks, they will be more significantly affected by the new regulatory capital requirements.

Secondly, the effects of regulatory indicators accumulate.

Such regulatory tools as the indicators of capital adequacy ratio, leverage ratio, liquidity and loan provision can objectively enhance banks' risk tolerance, but banks are also required to maintain a higher level of profitability and net interest margin, which, to a certain extent, may force banks to reduce lending, and increase investment in bonds or other off-balance sheet items to reduce capital and provision requirements. In addition, the effect of regulating both the leverage ratio (the static capital adequacy ratio) and capital adequacy ratio will lead to the invalidation of Tier 1 capital adequacy ratio, while from the perspective of risk appetite, risk-based capital adequacy ratio and risk-neutral leverage ratio have mutually exclusive regulatory effects. Given the correlation between indicators and their cumulative effects, it is likely that banks will be required to maintain or further increase their current spread levels to cover higher regulatory implementation costs. And this will undoubtedly accelerate the transformation of bank operations, but it will also exert pressure on the whole process of interest rate liberalization.

Lastly, the supervision of Pillar 2 and Pillar 3 needs to be improved.

Currently, China's banking sector is relatively standard and comprehensive in the implementation of Pillar 1, but weak in the implementation of Pillar 2 and Pillar 3, with some requirements being lower than the international ones. In terms of Pillar 2, regulators differ in their assessments of the definition of default. Under Basel III, regulators shall assess banks' definitions of default and their effect on capital requirements, but neither the rules nor the internal capital adequacy assessment process (ICAAP) has mentioned any specific assessment requirements on regulators. As for the information disclosure requirements of Pillar 3, there is a lack of information disclosure of credit quality data. The rules require banks to provide relevant information exposure about securitization, but without asking for such information as the nature of other risks within securitized assets, the risk management process, the use of credit risk mitigation, and the types of institutions for special purposes. Besides, the accounting information about securitized ledger, and implicit and explicit adjustments of employee deferred compensation and retained compensation, grouped by category of risk exposure within reporting period, is not mentioned, either. At present, China's asset securitization market is still in its infancy. From the perspective of the current business carried out by banks, relevant disclosure information has met the international requirements. However, with the further development of the market, the missing information may have an impact.

40.3 Suggestions on the Implementation of Basel III in China's Banking Sector

The banking risk management has a significant impact on the stability of the financial system and economic growth with indirect funding being still dominant. In recent years, the introduction of the regulatory framework of the Basel Accord has greatly improved the professional level of China's banking supervision, and the effective implementation of the Basel Capital Accord will be of great benefit to the improvement of the banking risk management level and regulatory capital system.

40.3.1 Utilizing Innovative Capital Instruments to Achieve the Differentiation Between Common Equity Tier 1 Capital, Tier 1 Capital and Total Capital

Under the redefined capital of Basel III, in Chinese commercial banks there exist such problems as incomplete regulatory capital deductions, some unqualified debt capital instruments and loose treatment of equity investment. The new definition of capital will not only require commercial banks to face actual higher capital adequacy requirements, but also reduce their optional capital when replenishing capital, thus making the banks under the capital supervision push the pressure of replenishing capital to the capital market. Meanwhile, the greater supply will bring down the stock price, which will to some extent also increase the regulatory coordination requirements of the CBRC and the China Securities Regulatory Commission (CSRC). On the other hand, higher standards of debt capital instruments will also increase the cost of capital replenishment from exogenous financing channels. *The Central Bank's Spokesperson's Press Conference on Expanding the Pilot Securitization of Credit Assets*, released on August 28, 2013, can count as an attempt for regulators to increase the capital replenishment mechanism and encourage the innovation of financial instruments.

Considering that there are few innovative financial instruments in China's banking sector and that Common Equity Tier 1 capital, Tier 1 capital and total capital converge, the flexible use of innovative financial instruments to supplement Additional Tier 1 capital and Tier 2 capital will be an important means to meet the new regulatory capital requirements. In addition, the capital replenishment mechanism through exogenous financing channels can relieve the pressure of capital in the short term, but in the long run, a new capital replenishment mechanism must be established through endogenous capital accumulation to enhance profitability and strengthen risk and cost management. Rushing to control the risks of banks with excessively high capital adequacy may cause banks to have insufficient time to implement long-term planning, and fail to effectively improve the capital structure and change the profit-making model, which is not conducive for banks to the establishment of long-term sustainable endogenous capital replenishment mechanism. More likely, banks will be forced to opt for capital markets, ultimately passing costs on to investors and consumers.

40.3.2 Objectively Assessing the Impact of Regulatory Indicators System Adjustments

Based on relevant requirements in the rules, it can be seen that in the formulation process of China's implementation version, the local adaptability is carefully considered, with the requirements for risk weights and indicator figures being more stringent than Basel III, and the measurement approaches for some risk capital simplified.

China's implementation standards raise the eligibility figures of such indicators as Common Equity Tier 1 capital adequacy ratios and leverage ratios, but most banks still use the foundation internal ratings-based (F-IRB) approach or the standardized approach for credit risk, and the information disclosure requirements in Pillar 3 concerning the innovative business such as asset securitization, and derivatives, are not perfect yet. In short, on the one hand, China's implementation version can better adapt to the current situation of the banking risk management; because the banking sector has not formally launched the business of asset securitization, there are few derivatives, and the market is not developed, so the current standards can meet the regulatory requirements. On the other hand, with the continuous development of the derivatives market, including the improvement in the technical level of banks, more banks will adopt the Advanced Measurement Approach to save capital in the future and the types of risk business will also increase. Therefore, when assessing the effect of the regulatory indicators system, regulators should take into account the differences in the market structure and market development stage during the specific implementation, and constantly improve and revise the regulatory standards to adapt to the future banking development.

40.3.3 Putting the Awareness of Risk Management into the Banking Business Activities and Continuously Improving the Banking Risk Management Capability

Implementing Basel III, especially the internal ratings-based approach, will change the current risk management system of China's banking in terms of different levels and dimensions such as the risk management, policy process, measurement models, and data IT. In particular, implementing Basel III will enable Chinese banks to shift from the qualitative and expert-oriented risk management mode to the combination of qualitative and quantitative modes and at the same time correspondingly brings about a huge shift from the credit process and business system to the specific operation mode. During the shift, it is necessary to reserve a certain run-in time, as well as time for data accumulation and system improvement. To effectively enhance the banking risk management level must not only start from the technical means of risk management, and, more importantly, involve putting the awareness of risk management into banking operational activities, building risk management system and culture, and improving the internal governance structure and organization process as well as helping the banks with the quantitative management of all kinds of risks, thus laying a sound foundation for implementing overall risk management.

Chapter 41
How to Address the Gray Rhino Risk of Local Government Debt

41.1 The Current Situation of Local Government Debt

By the end of 2016, the outstanding local government debt in China stood at 15.32 trillion yuan, with the debt ratio of 80.5%, down 8.7% from 2015. In addition, the upper limit for local government debt, approved at the Fifth Session of the 12th National People's Congress for 2017, is 18.82 trillion yuan, and the outstanding debt as of the end of June is 15.86 trillion yuan, within the official limit, but the potential risks of China's local government debt should not be ignored.

In early January 2017, the Ministry of Finance sent letters to local governments of Inner Mongolia Autonomous Region, Henan Province and Chongqing Municipality, requesting a serious investigation into the malpractices of some counties and cities in securing financing, a move ever made by the Ministry of Finance for the first time. On July 12, the Ministry of Finance announced the results of investigating the malpractices or illegal borrowing of the People's Government of Huangshi, Hubei Province in this regard, including punishments for several responsible persons. Later at the National Financial Work Conference held from July 14 to 15th, it was clearly proposed that local debt be strictly controlled. On July 17, *People's Daily* published an article entitled "Effective Prevention of Financial Risks," which first put forward guarding against "gray rhinos." At the press conference held by the State Council Information Office on July 27, the concept of "gray rhinos," was clarified, including local government debt. At the executive meeting of the State Council held the following day, how to defuse local government debt risks and curb implicit debt increments became an important issue.

Why is China's local government debt problem so prominent? Exploring its causes is an important prerequisite for effectively preventing this "gray rhino."

Source: www.toutiao.com, dated August 1, 2017.

S. Ba, *The New Cycle and New Finance in China*,
https://doi.org/10.1007/978-981-16-8209-4_41

41.2 The Causes of Local Government Debt

The causes of excess local government debt in China are complex with its specific historical background. It mainly stems from fiscal and taxation system, government assessment system and macroeconomic policy.

41.2.1 A High Degree of Mismatch Between Administrative and Fiscal Powers Among Governments at All Levels After the Revenue-Sharing System Reform

Since the implementation of the revenue-sharing system in 1994, the proportion of local finance in the total national fiscal revenue has been declining, resulting in local governments not having sufficient financial resources to exercise their powers and fulfill their responsibilities, a serious imbalance in local fiscal revenues and expenditures, and thus worsening local financial situation. The old *Budget Law* stipulates that the local budgets at various levels shall be compiled according to the principles of keeping expenditures within the limits of revenues and maintaining a balance between revenues and expenditures, and shall not contain deficit; the local governments must not issue local government bonds, except as otherwise prescribed by laws or the state council. This makes expanding extra budgetary revenues and borrowing become the main ways for local governments to ease the revenue and expenditure contradiction, leading to a build-up of local government debt. Although this provision was revised after the implementation of the new *Budget Law* in 2015 to clarify the entities and ways of securing financing, malpractices by local governments still occur from time to time.

41.2.2 Improper View on Political Achievements

The enthusiasm of some local officials for vanity projects is another important reason for the excess local government debt. The current assessment mode of local government based on economic performance in China determines that local officials often seek promotion or seek to climb the career ladder through regional economic development achievements, and the best way to boost economic growth is to increase investments. Given limited budget funds, borrowing to invest has become an important way for local governments. Driven by the system of evaluating political achievements based on the GDP growth, local governments secure financing regardless of their solvency and debt structure, resulting in a rising scale of local debts.

41.2.3 *Unsound Local Financial System*

The unsound local financial system, mainly reflected in decentralized management, lack of management and duplicate or overlapping management, is also responsible for the growing scale of local government debt. Lack of a unified debt management mechanism and duplicate or overlapping management make it difficult to collect debt information statistics, control debt, improve debt capital efficiency and supervise debt, resulting in unclear balance, unclear rights and responsibilities, and the loss of control of the scale of the debts.

41.3 In the Long Run, the Ways to Forestall and Defuse Local Government Debt Risk

To resolve local government debt, we must take a long-term view, which means that we must establish a long-term management mechanism for local government debt, including a sound early warning mechanism for government debt risk, a sound constraint mechanism for local government debt and a strict accountability system. Only by implementing effective management of local government debt in an all-dimensional and whole-process way, can we strive to address both the symptoms and the root causes of local government debt.

41.3.1 *Establishing an Early Warning Mechanism for Government Debt Risk*

The early warning mechanism for government debt risk is the premise of preventing local financial risk. First of all, a standardized and adequate information disclosure system of local government debt shall be established. Local governments shall not only regularly report to the higher governments and local people's congresses, but also make the information public through the news media. Secondly, a system of early warning indicators for local government debt risk shall be established as soon as possible. These indicators shall mainly include the local fiscal self-sufficiency rate, the proportion of available local fiscal resources, the degree of debt dependence, the debt-bearing ratio, the debt-servicing ratio, the ratio of internal and external debts, the proportion of the amount of borrowing new debt to repay the existing amount in total debt and so on. Also, a reasonable debt safety line and risk indicators control range shall be set up, and local fiscal risk signals shall be scientifically categorized, so that local governments can understand and fully grasp the government debt risk profile in a timely manner, and take prompt measures to forestall, control and defuse debt risks.

41.3.2 Strengthening the Constraint Mechanism for Local Government Debt

The establishment of local government debt constraint mechanism is one of the important means to strengthen the management of local government debt. In order to ensure the repayment of principal and interest on schedule, local financial departments at all levels shall establish financial sinking funds to be used for servicing various local government debts through such channels as annual budget arrangement, adjustment of fiscal balance and transfer of a certain proportion of the revenue from debt investment projects, which not only helps eliminate the disadvantages of the local finance insufficiently implementing the local budget due to the sudden rapid increase in the annual debt expenditure but also helps ensure a stable source of funds for financial debt repayment and strictly curb the growth of new fiscal debts.

41.3.3 Strengthening Local Government Debt Accountability System, and Reducing the Negative Effects of Soft Budget Constraints

Implementing the accountability system for local government debt is a strong guarantee for reducing the local government debt risk. At the National Financial Work Conference, it was proposed that local party committees and governments at all levels should establish a proper view about political achievements, strictly control the local government debt increments, and be held accountable for serious breaches of duty for life.“ The governments at all levels shall conduct financing in rigid accordance with the normative policies which have been rolled out on government investment funds, public–private partnership (PPP), and government purchase of services, and hold accountable those who borrow money in violation of laws and regulations.

References

1. Ba Shusong. How Should Local Government Debt Be Resolved [J]. Southwest Finance, 2011–10.
2. Ba Shusong, Niu Bokun, Yu Yafang. Ba Shusong: Where will the Money Come from in 2015?[J], Real Estate Industry in China, 2015–01.
3. Li Honghan. On Supervision of Local Government Debt in China under the New Budget Law[J]. Financial Supervision, 2016–07.
4. He Jinjin, Li Miaoxian, Lu Zhengwei. On the State Council Information Office of PRC Press Conference: *the* Office of *the Central Leading Group on Financial and Economic Affairs* Explains “Grey Rhino” in Detail[R]. Industrial Securities, 2017.
5. Zeng Gang. The Current Situation and Countermeasures of Local Government Debt [J]. Modern Bankers, 2017–07.

Chapter 42
How Supervision Drives the Transformation of Bank Outsourcing Business

In a general sense, bank outsourcing business refers to a business model in which commercial banks entrust their funds to other professional asset management institutions for investment management, but so far, regulators have not rolled out corresponding management measures specifically for outsourcing business in their regulatory documents, except that the 2017 new version of 1104 Off-Site Reporting System, released at the end of 2016, defines the outsourcing of wealth management (including purchasing asset management products and conducting outsourcing investment through agreement), and that the *Guiding Opinions of the China Banking Regulatory Commission on Risk Prevention and Control of the Banking Sector (No. 6 [2017])*, issued in April 2017, stipulate that "banking financial institutions shall prudently carry out outsourcing investment business, strictly examine entrusted institutions, manage their name lists, and clarify such requirements as a cap on the outsourcing investment and the proportion of entrusted assets to a single trustee." From the perspective of the trend, under the guidance of the basic tone of deleveraging policy, the increasingly tightening supervision is putting bank outsourcing business under the actual pressure of transformation.

42.1 With Strengthened Supervision, the Scale of Bank Outsourcing Business Tends to Decline

42.1.1 Supervision Over Bank Outsourcing Business Has Been Significantly Strengthened

Against the backdrop of accelerating financial deleveraging, regulators have recently unveiled new regulations for outsourcing investment successively, aiming to reduce

Source: www.toutiao.com, dated October 15, 2017.

S. Ba, *The New Cycle and New Finance in China*,
https://doi.org/10.1007/978-981-16-8209-4_42

the investment leverage of commercial banks. In mid-March 2017, the China Securities Regulatory Commission (CSRC) proposed that customized entrusted funds should adopt closed operation (or open operation on a regular basis), initiating fund and other modes, and that if the entrusted funds are not customized, the proportion of a single holder should not exceed 50%. In early April, the CBRC announced the *Notice on Measures Addressing Regulatory Arbitrage, Idle Funds Arbitrage and Related Entity Arbitrage within the Banking Sector (No.46)*, saying that the phenomena that non-bank institutions take advantage of entrusted funds to further increase their leverage, duration and risk fall into the category of financial idle funds arbitrage, about which banking institutions need to conduct self-examination. In addition, the Notice requires banks to outline the scale of their entrusted wealth management funds and active and non-active management and the structure of transactions. In May, the China Banking Wealth Management Registration and Depository Center (WM Center) issued the *Notice on Further Regulating the Penetrating Registration of Wealth Management Products*, requiring that the penetrating registration of product information should follow the principle of stratification, including the asset management plans and outsourcing through agreements as well as the underlying information. In the case of multilayered nesting, the underlying asset and liability information should be included according to the penetrating registration principle.

42.1.2 The Decline of Bank Outsourcing Investment Scale Has a Direct Impact on Both the Stock and Bond Markets

At present, it is not easy to find systematic statistical data on the scale of bank outsourcing investment, and there are differences in the estimations in the market. Roughly estimated based on the currently collected data and the data the four large banks have exchanged (there may be some discrepancy between the estimated and the actual data), at the peak of the scale in 2016 the four large banks' outsourcing investment scale is 2.5 trillion–3 trillion yuan, with the scale of the Industrial and Commercial Bank of China (ICBC) exceeding 1 trillion yuan, the scale of China Construction Bank standing at 700 billion–800 billion yuan, the scale of the other two large banks being roughly 300 billion yuan, and the whole banking outsourcing investment scale being 5 trillion–6 trillion yuan; if the insurance companies as well as finance companies affiliated to central and state-owned enterprises are included, the data may be greater.

Affected by the new regulatory requirements, the whole banking outsourcing scale declined in 2017, and some banks in the market began to repurchase the entrusted. As can be seen from Table 42.1, in the first half year of 2017, the wealth management products of all financial institutions in the banking sector declined, including not only small- and medium-sized banks more dependent on asset management business, but also large state-owned banks and national joint-stock banks. According to statistical

Table 42.1 Balance of wealth management products in different types of banking financial institutions

	Unit: trillion yuan						
Month	Large state-owned banks	National joint-stock banks	City commercial banks	Foreign banks	Rural financial institutions	Other institutions	Total monthly balance
Jan	9.69	13.02	4.50	0.37	1.71	1.01	30.31
Feb	9.66	12.59	4.44	0.37	1.72	1.05	29.84
March	9.29	12.40	4.43	0.36	1.68	0.99	29.15
April	9.88	12.80	4.53	0.38	1.69	1.01	30.29
May	9.61	12.37	4.45	0.38	1.67	0.98	29.45
June	9.27	11.80	4.39	0.37	1.62	0.93	29.38

Source China Banking Wealth Management Market Report (first half of 2017)

data, since the beginning of 2017, the balance of wealth management products at the end of the month has dropped from 30.31 trillion yuan at the beginning of the year to 29.38 trillion yuan in June. Research shows that the proportion of entrusted investment in wealth management products is at about 1:3, excluding a small amount of entrusted investment of proprietary funds. Roughly estimated from the wealth management scale, the scale of the wealth management funds invested through outsourcing dropped from 10 trillion yuan to 9.7 trillion yuan, showing a falling trend, which indicates that financial institutions under the guidance of regulatory policies began to adjust their measures.

At the same time, repurchasing the entrusted has also exerted a lot of influence on the stock and bond markets. From the perspective of asset structure, most of the wealth management funds are invested in credit bonds, rate bonds, money funds and other types of assets, among which equity accounts for little, as shown in Fig. 42.1. This is especially true for outsourcing investment, with more than 90% channeled into investment in credit bonds, rate bonds, money funds and other types of assets, and the proportion of equity being not more than 10%. Therefore, visually, the decline in outsourcing has a greater impact on the bond market than on the stock market.

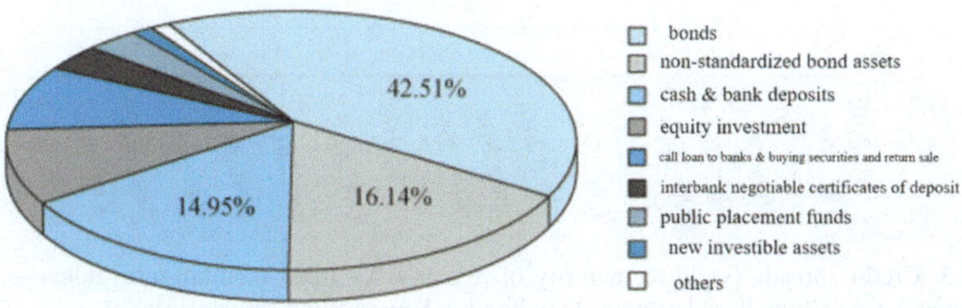

Fig. 42.1 Asset allocation of wealth management products. *Source* China Banking Wealth Management Market Report (first half of 2017)

Specifically, for credit bonds, outsourcing contraction may push funds back into banks' balance sheets, while the implementation of the regulatory penetrating principle will gradually reduce banks' risk appetite, and the demand for low-level credit bonds may fall. As can be seen from Figs. 42.2, 42.3 and 42.4, credit spreads have been declining since the end of 2014, with narrowed arbitrage space, which was at a low peak from the second half of 2016 to the first half of 2017 and recovered, but not by much in the second half of 2017.

Fig. 42.2 Yield to maturity of 3-year treasury bonds. *Source* Wind Information

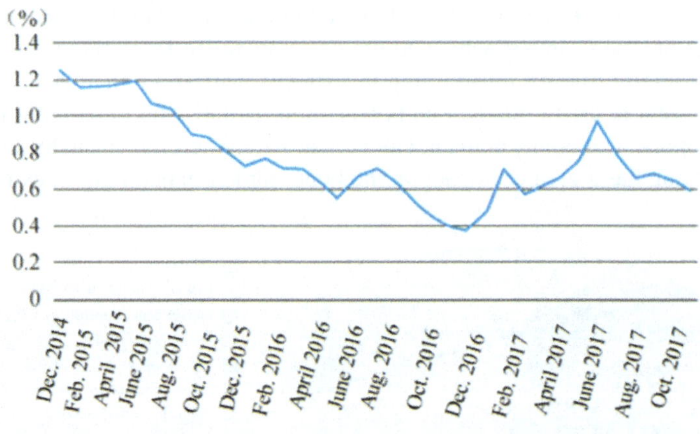

Fig. 42.3 Credit spreads (yield to maturity of 3-year AA+ rated medium-term notes—yield to maturity of 3-year China Development Bank bonds). *Source* Wind Information

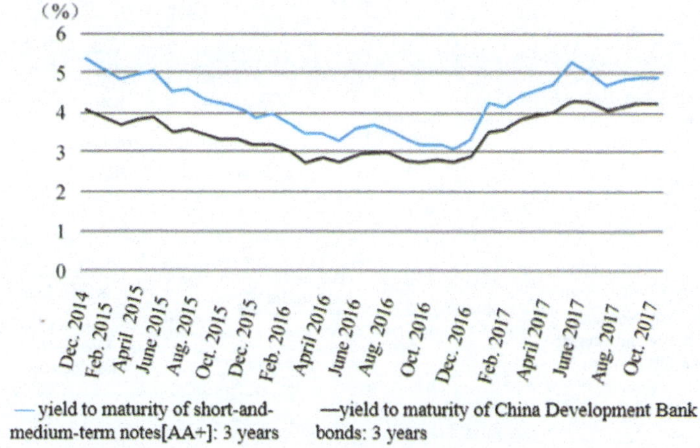

Fig. 42.4 Changes in arbitrage space. *Source* Wind Information

42.2 The Past and Present of Bank Outsourcing Business

Speaking of the history of outsourcing business, we should start from the shadow banking business of commercial banks. From the perspective of the development process, unlike the commonly known shadow banking business system in developed markets, the scale of shadow banking business in China started rapidly after the 2008 financial crisis. Objective market demands, circumvention of regulation and the existence of arbitrage space are the main driving forces for the development of shadow banking business. Generally speaking, shadow banks try to achieve business innovation by bypassing such on-balance sheet business models as traditional deposit and lending business, and employing other on-and-off-balance sheet items, and achieve credit expansion through cooperation with non-bank financial institutions. The resulting capital chains constantly increase leverage, which with improper risk management may push up financial risks without being fully identified. The development of shadow banking in China is always in the game between financial innovation and financial supervision.

Outsourcing business is an active area of shadow banking business in commercial banks. From the statistical analysis, its scale was relatively small until 2014 and the second half of 2015 might be a turning point, for under the influence of the abnormal stock market volatility at the time, investment channels for bank wealth management products were constrained. However, the bank wealth management scale continued to grow with limited investment channels, which promoted the growth of bank outsourcing business, most notably in small and medium-sized banks (see Fig. 42.5). Evaluated from the objective data, the dependence of commercial banks on outsourcing investment business is related to their assets and liabilities structure, especially their own investment capability. Small- and medium-sized banks with strong liabilities and weak assets operating within a certain region are more likely to

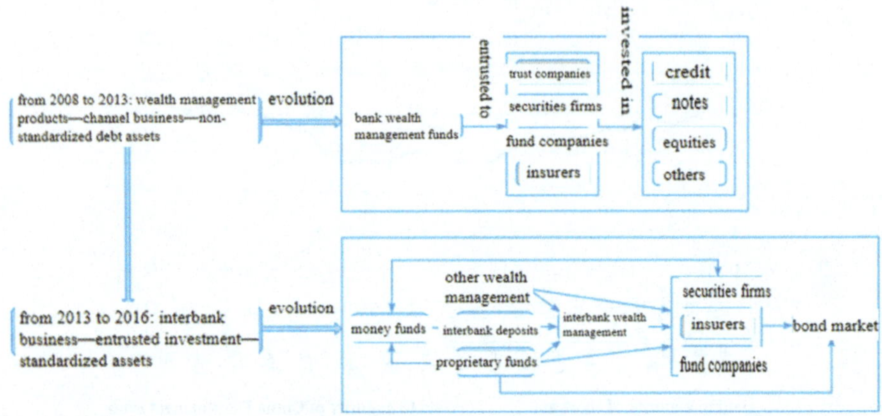

Fig. 42.5 Evolution of shadow banking modes

generate the demand for outsourcing investment. In the context of narrowing spreads of traditional credit business, small- and medium-sized banks are forced to expand new sources of business, and the asset management business, especially outsourcing business, naturally attracts their attention.

From the perspective of capital flow, the entrusted funds of a bank may come from its proprietary department, asset management department and interbank department, and the management ways and means for the entrusted funds also vary according to the different institutions, business lines and departments. In general, outsourcing investment should first meet the relevant regulations and regulatory requirements of the CBRC on banking investment, such as restrictions on investment types and leverage ratio. Secondly, it should meet the regulatory requirements the designated managers are subject to. For example, if a bank entrusts funds to the securities companies for management, then the investment should be subject to the regulatory requirements the China Securities Regulatory Commission (CSRC) impose on asset management business of the securities companies. After meeting the requirements of outside regulations, a bank shall carry out outsourcing business in accordance with the internal management measures. Firstly, elements such as the scale, market and variety of outsourcing investment, risk–return requirements and product structure shall be determined according to the business development needs and risk appetites of the bank. Then entrusted managers shall be selected through qualitative and quantitative indicators, including team members, historical performance, risk and control indicators. After the implementation of outsourcing business, tracking management about the entrusted managers shall be continuously conducted, including their performance assessments, communications with them and their dynamic management.

When choosing the entrusted managers, commercial banks within the industry have many financial institutions to choose from. Take private placement funds managers as an example. According to the latest G06 statement, it is in line with the future regulatory requirements for banks to entrust private placement funds

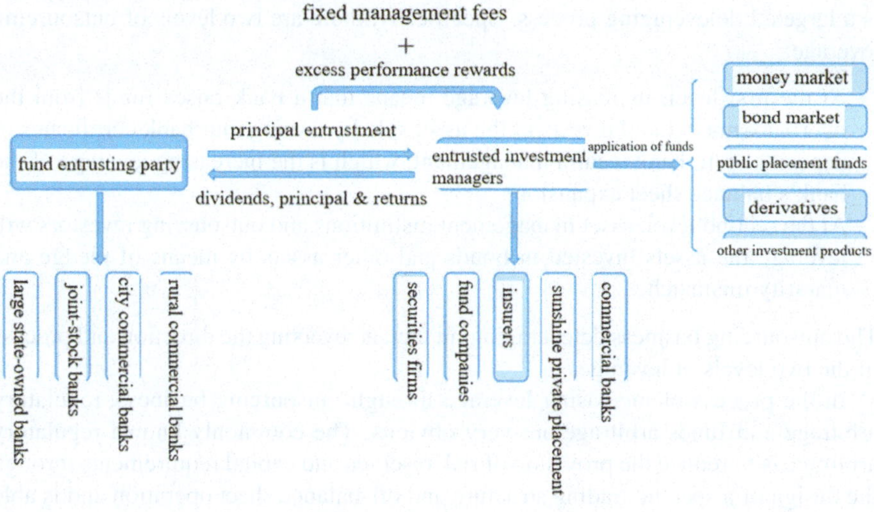

Fig. 42.6 Outsourcing investment modes

filing with the Asset Management Association of China with asset management at the wealth management level. Compared with traditional managers, private placement funds have more flexible and diversified investment strategies and can provide some customized services for bank outsourcing investment. However, some banks conduct illegal highly leveraged investments through private placement funds, which magnifies their risks. In the future, with the reshaping of the regulatory rules for the asset management industry, bank outsourcing business and the investment business of private placement funds will be more standardized. The pattern of outsourcing investment is shown in Fig. 42.6.

42.3 Why the New Regulations Target Bank Outsourcing Business

Analyzed from the current business models, the general bank outsourcing investment business, usually means that because the cost of funds obtained by banks from the market is relatively low, and in the market there are relatively high-yielding investment targets, banks obtain arbitrage opportunities through outsourcing investment business, and that with improper control of risk in the arbitrage process, among others, maturity mismatch and increasing leverage may increase financial risks. Therefore, regulators recently issued a series of new regulations to reduce the outsourcing scale and the investment leverage of commercial banks. The nesting of multilevel products and the lengthening of industrial chains are the focus of the regulatory policies, which is a targeted deleveraging process. Specifically, there are two levels of outsourcing leverage:

> At the first level, increasing leverage means that a bank raises funds from the interbank market and invests in the asset side by issuing interbank certificates of deposit or interbank wealth management, which is the increasing leverage of the bank's balance sheet expansion.
> At the second level, asset management institutions and outsourcing investors will leverage the assets invested in bonds and other assets by means of pledge and maturity mismatch.

The outsourcing business deleveraging, in fact, is reversing the direction and process of the two levels of leverage.

In the process of increasing leverage through outsourcing business, regulatory arbitrage and funds arbitrage are very obvious. The commonly known regulatory arbitrage is to reduce the provision of risk reserves and capital requirements through the design of a specific trading structure and off-balance sheet operation and is able to break through industry restrictions, regional restrictions, and restrictions of credit investment and scale through channel businesses.

Why are the nesting of multilevel products and the lengthening of industrial chain the focus of strengthening supervision on outsourcing business? At the micro-individual level of the market, there are mainly two issues: the first is clients' adaptability to risk, namely whether the products with the right risk are sold to suitable clients, or whether the high-risk assets are sold to clients with low risk-bearing capacity through the structural arrangements; the second is the compliance of the final asset investment, namely the product aspect penetrates into the underlying asset to identify whether the final asset class conforms to the regulation of asset management and whether its risk has been properly assessed.

From the perspective of the whole financial system, domestic financing costs in China are still relatively high compared with historical levels. One of the reasons for the rise in financing costs is the complexity of financing channels. In recent years, various types of financial institutions in China have entered a period of rapid development, and the asset scale of the financial industry has expanded rapidly. The problem caused by the increasingly complex trading structure of the financial industry is that in the process of capital flow, the chain from virtual to real is obviously prolonged, and the financing cost of the real sector will also rise after the capital experiences more links and institutions' revenue sharing. The essence of financial deleveraging is to dismantle this elongated link and promote the transparency of the whole trading process. However, due to the overlapping of financial leverage and real sector leverage, if the process of financial deleveraging is too drastic, the pressure on corporate financing will intensify accordingly. Under the current dual objectives of stabilizing economic growth and containing risks, deleveraging policies need to achieve a balance between reducing existing leverage and alleviating corporate financing pressures.

42.4 Under the Guidance of Strengthened Supervision, Bank Outsourcing Business Presents a New Development Trend

42.4.1 With the Deepening of Financial Deleveraging, the Growth of Outsourcing Business Will Return to a Reasonable Level

From the perspective of market environment, with the gradual deepening of financial deleveraging, outsourcing business will return to a reasonable level. The essence of financial deleveraging is to shorten the arbitrage link in the financing chain and reduce financial risks. In the first half of 2017, in terms of supervision, the central bank included off-balance sheet wealth management in the macroprudential assessment (MPA) in 2017 and officially announced that inter-bank deposits will be included in the MPA in 2018 through the China monetary policy report. The CBRC has launched a strong regulatory campaign against the problems of "Three Arbitrages," "Three Violations" and "Four Improprieties" and actively rectified financial irregularities. These regulatory moves will spur outsourcing business to rational growth.

42.4.2 Improve Dynamic Management of Entrusted Institutions and Shift from Channel to Problem-Solving Type

Although the growth of outsourcing business has slowed down to some extent recently, in the long run, after strengthening risk supervision, there is still room for standardized development of outsourcing business. Different financial institutions have different core competitiveness, and the standardization of outsourcing business driven by rigorous supervision will promote the shuffling of managers and reshape the format of banking asset management. On the one hand, in order to maximize the returns under the effective risk control, banks shall select entrusted managers more strictly, take into account the investment strategies and management expertise of different institutions, set different investment upper limits for them, and define their investment authority. In addition, the investment performance, compliance with internal control, risk management and other aspects of entrusted institutions shall be periodically assessed. It is also necessary to periodically reexamine their qualifications, dynamically adjust their access, retain the fittest, and dynamically adjust the capital injection amount of banks' wealth management. On the other hand, outsourcing business will be upgraded from the originally simple channel business to one of the complementary advantages. Small- and medium-sized banks need the help of securities firms and fund companies in asset allocation; that is, they shall adopt problem-solving-type asset allocation solutions, not just channel-type asset allocation solutions. Complementing the advantages, and strengthening the asset allocation capability, outsourcing investment promises to bring market differentiation, with the focus of the market shifting from the channel-type asset allocation to multistrategy cross-sector asset allocation and asset trading ability.

42.4.3 Actively Explore Ways to Establish an Off-Balance Sheet Management System

In terms of corporate governance, actively exploring the establishment of off-balance sheet management system is one of the effective measures to prevent the risk of outsourcing investment. At present, there are still problems such as maturity mismatch, customer mismatch and credit risk accumulation and rise with outsourcing investment, which urgently need standardized and systematic management. The traditional balance sheet management system of banks fails to fully reflect the operation characteristics of financial innovative products and businesses, so it cannot effectively manage non-credit businesses, and the existing off-balance sheet business management system is not fully applicable to the management of non-credit businesses such as outsourcing investment. Therefore, we should actively explore the establishment of off-balance sheet management system, and promote the standardized development of outsourcing investment on the basis of strengthening the risk management ability.

References

1. Ba Shusong. There Is Still Room for Outsourcing Business, Which Should Be Upgraded from Channel Type to Problem Solving Type [R]. 2017 China Banking Industry Asset Management Summit Forum.
2. Ba Shusong, Zhu Hong. China's Economy Is a New Form of Volatility, Not a New Cycle [J]. *Foreign Exchange*, 2017-17.
3. China Banking Wealth Management Registration & Depository Center. China Banking Wealth Management Market Report (first half of 2017) [R]. 2017.
4. Wang Zhe, Zhang Ming, Liu Shida. From "Channel" to "Interbank"—Evolution Process, Potential Risks and Development Direction of China's Shadow Banking System [J]. *International Economic Review*, 2017-04.

Chapter 43
Global Systemically Important Banks: Emphasis on Higher Loss Absorbency

43.1 Introduction

Global systemically important financial institutions (G-SIFIs) are institutions with global characteristics, assuming critical functions in the financial markets. And their distress or failure would cause significant dislocation to the global economy and the financial system and even systemic risks. Among G-SIFIs, global systemically important banks are regarded as the stabilizers of the global banking industry. During the 2008 international financial crisis, some large and complex financial institutions in Europe and the United States fell into a business crisis or even collapsed, which spread to other financial institutions, and evolved into systemic risks. Some public authorities were left with no option but to bail them out using taxpayers' funds, thus inducing the social discontent and raising extensive concern of different countries over the issue of supervising G-SIFIs. How to address the too-big-to-fail (TBTF) issue, reduce moral hazards posed by financial institutions and guard against financial systemic risks has become a hot and thorny issue in the financial regulatory reforms in the past five years since the outbreak of the crisis.

After the crisis, the international community actively promoted policy research on the regulation of systemically important financial institutions. In July 2011, the Financial Stability Board (FSB) and the Basel Committee on Banking Supervision (hereinafter referred to as "the Basel Committee"), respectively, issued the two consultative documents on *Effective Resolution of Systemically Important Financial Institutions* and on *Global Systemically Important Banks: Assessment Methodology and the Additional Loss Absorbency Requirement*, setting out a methodology comprising quantitative and qualitative indicators for assessing global systemic importance of commercial banks. In July 2013, the Basel Committee revised the assessment methodology for G-SIBs, while the International Association of Insurance Supervisors also published the assessment methodology and policy measures for

Wang Jingyi, Liu Xiaoyi, and Zheng Ming participated in the drafting and discussion of this paper, which appeared in China's Banking Industry in 2016 (6).

S. Ba, *The New Cycle and New Finance in China*,
https://doi.org/10.1007/978-981-16-8209-4_43

global systemically important insurance institutions. In November 2014, the Financial Stability Board (FSB) issued policy proposals consisting of a set of principles and a detailed term sheet on the adequacy of loss-absorbing capacity of G-SIBs, proposing that national regulators should retain a substantial capital buffer for a G-SIB, holding equity and unsecured debt equivalent to 16–20% of its risk-weighted assets (RWA). Regulators see the provision as a solution in ending the so-called too-big-to-fail problem for large banks, an important step toward preventing bailouts of large banks and avoiding taxpayers' support of bank failures.

43.2 An Overview of the Literature

After the outbreak of the financial crisis in 2008, global regulators attached great importance to the supervision of systemically important financial institutions and issued a series of policies aimed at establishing a regulatory framework more suitable for these institutions. Among them, the most troubling issue for the regulators is how to rectify and improve the regulatory philosophy of "too big to fail". Stern and Feldman (2004), scholars of the Federal Reserve, point out that the disorderly failure of some financial institutions, because of their size and systemic interconnectedness, would pose material risks to the wider financial system and economic activity. Because of such fears, policymakers in many countries, developed and less developed, have to protect uninsured creditors of the banks from the losses they otherwise would face. These banks have assumed the title of "too big to fail" (TBTF). Ba Shusong (2012) points out that the too-big-to-fail problem is derived from two aspects. One is that the institution is vital to the macro-economy, and the other is that the government or central bank rescues it. In particular, a government bailout for the banks and other financial institutions can foster the perceived expectation of government support, that is, the expectation that, having bailed out troubled banks once, governments would do so again, which led to soft budget constraints and eventually evolved into the too-big-to-fail problem. William Dudley (2013) points out that the problem has caused people to underestimate risks in the financial system, and formulate a set of bad incentive measures and that the risks might become higher in the future, if they could not be completely resolved. Wang Zhaoxing (2013) believes that "too big to fail" means that systemic importance of a financial institution determines that if it is allowed to fail, it will cause a serious systemic crisis. Therefore, the government will choose to bail it out rather than allow it to fail.

In response to the crisis, the Basel Committee has adopted a large number of regulatory policy measures on G-SIBs. However, given that their business models have generally placed greater emphasis on trading and global activities related to capital markets, which are particularly susceptible to increasing risk coverage within the capital framework, these policy measures are significant but are not sufficient to address all the negative externalities posed by G-SIBs. The issue needs to be addressed through a multi-pronged approach. Therefore, on the basis of existing policy measures, the Basel Committee should further identify, assess and group

G-SIBs, requiring corresponding loss absorbency for G-SIBs according to their different levels of global systemic importance, and thereby reducing the likelihood of their failing. Bongini and Nieri (2015) argue that there are two methods to identify systemically important banks. The academia usually uses the market-based measurement approach, while regulators prefer the indicator-based measurement approach. Among them, expected shortfall (ES) method is used to measure systemic risk, and Shapley value method is used to effectively measure systematic importance of financial institutions. The market-based measurement approach, commonly adopted by the academia, measures systemic risk by selecting relevant market data such as stock price, bond price and CDS, while regulators identify systemically important banks through a series of indicators. Currently, scholars at home and abroad conduct little comparative study of the two kinds of measurement approaches. Castro and Ferrari (2014) develop a statistical test based on the measure proposed by Adrian and Brunnermeier (2011) to test for systematic importance of a sample of 26 large European banks and conclude that under the measurement approach based on market data, very few banks can be ranked as SIBs. Agarwal and Taffler (2008), and Bauer and Agarwal (2014) compare the predictions about bank bankruptcy under the two approaches and believe that the market-based measurement approach is superior to the indicator-based measurement approach, but there are no unified conclusions on the selection and acquisition channels of data. The Basel Committee subsequently issued a revised measurement approach, but has not properly regulated the applicable scope of market data.

Based on the above relevant researches on systemically important banks, it is not difficult to find that currently in academia there is insufficient research on systemic risks generated by systemically important banks, including the definition, contagion and characteristics of risks. Most scholars still mainly refer to relevant research methods of systemic risks in the general sense to analyze systemically important banks. As a special kind of bank, systemically important banks are different from other banks mainly due to their systemic importance, which determines that they will play a central role in the financial system and have a strong influence on both financial stability and the real economy. Therefore, systemically important banks should be moderately developed and strictly regulated because their own attributes are most likely to occasion systemic risk. The theoretical study of systemically important banks should focus on their characteristics, how the risks they face accumulate, spread and evolve into systemic risks, and how they should be regulated effectively.

43.3 Assessment Methodology for and Identification of G-SIBs

The Basel Committee has developed an assessment methodology to identify G-SIBs, which is an indicator-based measurement approach. Since the methodology aims to identify G-SIBs that will be subject to higher loss absorbency requirements, the Basel

Committee is of the view that the three indicators of size, interconnectedness and cross-jurisdictional activity are insufficient to capture all aspects of G-SIBs, so the indicators that measure the degree of global activity and complexity are added.

The selected indicators reflect the different aspects of what generates negative externalities of G-SIBs and also explain what makes them critical for the stability of the financial system. The advantages of the multiple indicator-based measurement approaches are that it encompasses many dimensions of systemic importance, highlights the impact of an individual financial institution on the financial system and other financial institutions, better reflects the degree of interconnectedness among financial institutions, and better enables the identification of systemically important banks. It is simpler and more robust than currently available model-based measurement approaches and methodologies that rely on many assumptions and a small set of indicators.

The assessment methodology comprising both quantitative and qualitative indicators assesses global systemic importance of commercial banks based on twelve indicators for five drivers of systemic importance of global (cross-jurisdictional) activity, size, interconnectedness, substitutability and complexity. The methodology gives an equal weight of 20% to each of the five categories of systemic importance. With the exception of the size category, multiple indicators in each of the categories have been identified, with each indicator equally weighted within a category. (That is, where there are two indicators in a category, each indicator is given a 10% overall weight; where there are three, the indicators are each weighted 6.67%, i.e., 20/3.) Among them, cross-jurisdictional activity measures the importance of a bank's activities outside its home (headquarter) jurisdiction and captures its global footprint and provision of financial services; size refers to the total exposures of a bank; interconnectedness measures how financial distress at one institution can materially raise the likelihood of distress at other institutions; substitutability means after a bank's failure to what extent other financial institutions can provide the same service; complexity refers to how complex a bank is in its organizational structure, business models and structural aspects. Each of the five categories has an equal weight of 20% (see Table 43.1).

The assessment methodology provides a basic framework for periodically reviewing the G-SIB status of a given institution. That is, banks have incentives to change their risk profile and business models in ways that reduce their systemic spillover effects. The Basel Committee is not proposing to develop a fixed list of G-SIBs, which cannot be changed. Banks can migrate in and out of G-SIB status over time depending on their business conditions. For example, as emerging market countries continue to become more prominent in the global economy, the number of banks from these countries to be identified as G-SIBs might increase. There should be more transparency to both the designated institutions and the markets about the criteria used to identify G-SIBs, thus gradually reducing the impact of systematic risks on the global economy and maintaining long-term global financial stability.

The Basel Committee groups G-SIBs into different categories (buckets) through the bucketing approach (allocating G-SIBs to each bucket based on the systemic importance score produced by the assessment methodology), with each bucket being

Table 43.1 Indicator-based measurement approach for G-SIBs

Category (and weighting)	Individual indicator	Indicator weighting (%)
1. Global (Cross-jurisdictional) activity (20%)	Cross-jurisdictional claims	10
	Cross-jurisdictional liabilities	10
2. Size (20%)	Total exposures as defined for use in the Basel III leverage ratio	20
3. Interconnectedness (20%)	Intra-financial system assets	6.67
	Intra-financial system liabilities	6.67
	Wholesale funding ratio	6.67
4. Substitutability (20%)	Assets under custody	6.67
	Payments cleared and settled through payment systems	6.67
	Values of underwritten transactions in debt and equity markets	6.67
5. Complexity (20%)	OTC derivatives notional value	6.67
	Level 3 assets	6.67
	Held for trading and available for sale value	6.67%

Source Official website of the Bank for International Settlements (BIS)

Table 43.2 Grouping by global systemic importance and corresponding additional capital requirements[1]

Bucketing	Allocation across buckets (basis points, bps)	Higher loss absorbency requirement (%)
Bucket 5	530 ~ 629	3.5
Bucket 4	430 ~ 529	2.5
Bucket 3	330 ~ 429	2.0
Bucket 2	230 ~ 329	1.5
Bucket 1	130 ~ 229	1.0

Source FSB, Updated Global Systemically Important Banks Cluster, dated November 2014

subject to a different requirement for additional loss absorbency. Initially, there will be five buckets (see Table 43.2), with capital requirements ranging from 1 to 3½ percent of risk-weighted assets, to be met by common equity Tier 1 capital. That is, the magnitude of additional loss absorbency for the lowest Bucket 1 will be at least 1% of risk-weighted assets, with Bucket 2 1.5%, Bucket 3 2%, Bucket 4 2.5% and a currently empty top bucket (Bucket 5) 3.5%. In November 2014, the FSB and

[1] The cut-off scores and bucket thresholds in this figure are calculated based on end-2011 data provided by all sample banks.

Table 43.3 List of G-SIBs

Country of head office of G-SIBs	Bank (selected time)
China (3)	Bank of China (2011), Industrial & Commercial Bank of China (2013), Agricultural Bank of China (2014)
United States (8)	JP Morgan Chase (2011), Citigroup (2011), Bank of America (2011), Wells Fargo (2011), Goldman Sachs (2011), Morgan Stanley (2011), Bank of New York Mellon (2011), State Street (2011)
UK (4)	Hongkong and Shanghai Banking Corp. (2011), Barclays Bank (2011), Royal Bank of Scotland (2011), Standard Chartered Bank (2012)
Italy (1)	Unicredit Group (2011)
Spain (2)	Santander (2011), Banco Bilbao Vizcaya Argentaria (2012)
Switzerland (2)	Credit Suisse (2011), Union Bank of Switzerland (2011)
Sweden (1)	Nordea (2011)
Japan (3)	Mitsubishi UFJ Financial Group (2011), Mizuho Financial Group (2011), Sumitomo Mitsui Financial Group (2011)
Netherlands (1)	Internationale Nederlanden Group (ING Bank) (2011)
France (4)	*BNP Paribas* (2011), Banque Populaire CdE (2011), Group Crédit Agricole (2011), Société Générale (2011)
Germany (1)	Deutsche Bank (2011)

Source FSB, Updated Global Systemically Important Banks Cluster, dated November 2014

the Basel Committee published an updated list of G-SIFIs, comprising a total of 30 banks with one new bank, Agricultural Bank of China, being added (see Table 43.3).

43.4 Total Loss-Absorbing Capacity (TLAC)

In October 2014, the Financial Stability Board (FSB) issued a policy proposal consisting of a series of principles on loss-absorbing and recapitalization capacity of G-SIBs and a term sheet on total loss-absorbing capacity (TLAC) to enhance loss-absorbing capacity of G-SIBs, proposing that national regulatory authorities should retain substantial capital buffers for a G-SIB, holding equity and unsecured debt equivalent to 16% to 20% of its risk-weighted assets (RWA). Regulators see the proposal as a means for ending the so-called too-big-to-fail problem, a key step toward preventing bailouts of large banks and avoiding taxpayers' support of bank failures. Under the proposal, 30 G-SIBs must be subject to a minimum external TLAC requirement of 16–20% of risk-weighted assets. And their minimum TLAC must be at least twice the quantum of capital required to meet the Basel III leverage ratio (i.e., 6% where the Basel III leverage ratio is set at 3%). The FSB will work with the Basel Committee to carry out a market survey, a quantitative impact study (QIS) and macro- and microeconomic impact assessment about the proposal.

43.4.1 Minimum External TLAC Requirement

G-SIBs will be required to meet a new requirement for minimum external total loss-absorbing capacity alongside the minimum regulatory capital requirements. The TLAC standard is designed to ensure that if a G-SIB fails during a crisis it has sufficient loss-absorbing and recapitalization capacity available in resolution, and avoid exposing taxpayers (i.e., public funds) to loss in order to bail failing banks out, thus without posing global financial panic or putting financial stability at risk.

Regulated Institutions

The minimum TLAC requirement will apply to each resolution entity within each G-SIB, which may be a parent company, or an operating subsidiary, or an intermediate or ultimate holding company. The minimum TLAC requirement for each resolution entity will be set in relation to the consolidated balance sheet of each resolution group and all its direct or indirect subsidiaries. In addition, considering that the emerging market economies have insufficient depth of the capital market, and funding difficulties, and that higher regulatory standards may generate a certain degree of negative effects on the real economy funding, the FSB specifically set the transitional periods for G-SIBs that are headquartered in emerging market economies, but the lengths of the transitional periods are not specified in the consultative document.

Regulatory Standards

The FSB has set a new regulatory standard in terms of minimum TLAC and minimum leverage ratio for G-SIBs, comprising the elements of Pillar 1 and Pillar 2.

The Pillar 1 Common Minimum TLAC Requirement

In the minimum external TLAC requirement for G-SIBs, the first pillar components are determined by quantitative impact study and cost–benefit analysis. Pillar 1 requires G-SIBs to maintain a sizeable capital buffer, holding capital equivalent to 16–20% of risk-weighted assets. For G-SIBs with the 1% capital surcharge requirement, they are required to hold at least 19.5–23.5% of risk-weighted assets, and for G-SIBs with the 2.5% capital surcharge requirement, they are required to hold at least 21–25% of risk-weighted assets. Besides, the minimum TLAC of these G-SIBs must be at least twice the quantum of capital required to meet the Basel III leverage ratio (i.e., 6% where the Basel III leverage ratio is set at 3%).

Pillar 2 TLAC Requirement

The calibration and composition of Pillar 2 TLAC requirements should be jointly determined by the Crisis Management Groups and the Resolvability Assessment Process. The basic principles of Pillar 2 requirement are to ensure the effectiveness of the loss-absorbing capacity of G-SIBs and to minimize the impact of systemic risks on financial stability.

Regulatory Objectives

Alongside the minimum external TLAC requirement, the FSB requires that a G-SIB should meet a minimum TLAC requirement of at least 16% of its risk-weighted assets as from January 2019 and at least 18% as from January 2022. And the FSB stipulates that a G-SIB's minimum TLAC must be at least 6% of the Basel III leverage ratio denominator as from January 2019 and at least 6.75% as from January 2022.

Consistency with the Basel III Capital Requirements

TLAC Pillar 1 requirement and the Basel III Pillar 1 regulatory capital requirements have the following two relationships. On the one hand, minimum TLAC is an additional requirement to minimum regulatory capital requirements set out in the Basel III framework, a higher requirement aimed at G-SIBs. Capital that counts toward satisfying minimum regulatory capital requirements may also count toward satisfying the minimum TLAC requirement. The second is its relationship with the capital buffer. Capital buffers are used to absorb losses in going-concern operations and are therefore outside the minimum TLAC requirement. Only Common Equity Tier 1 (CET1) in excess of that required to satisfy the minimum TLAC requirement may count toward regulatory capital buffers.

Specifically, the minimum TLAC requirement shall include 8% of the minimum regulatory capital requirements set out in the Basel III framework, but shall not include the Basel III capital buffers and capital surcharge requirements for G-SIBs, because the capital is assumed to be used before G-SIBs enter resolution. The requirement that TLAC be at least 16% ~ 20% of the consolidated risk-weighted assets has covered the Basel III minimum regulatory capital requirements, but does not include the capital buffer requirement. Calculated according to the method, if the capital conservation buffer is calibrated at 2.5% (reserve capital is calibrated at 2.5%, capital surcharge for systemically important institutions at 1% ~ 3.5% and countercyclical capital at 0), the total loss-absorbing capacity of G-SIBs of Category 1 shall reach

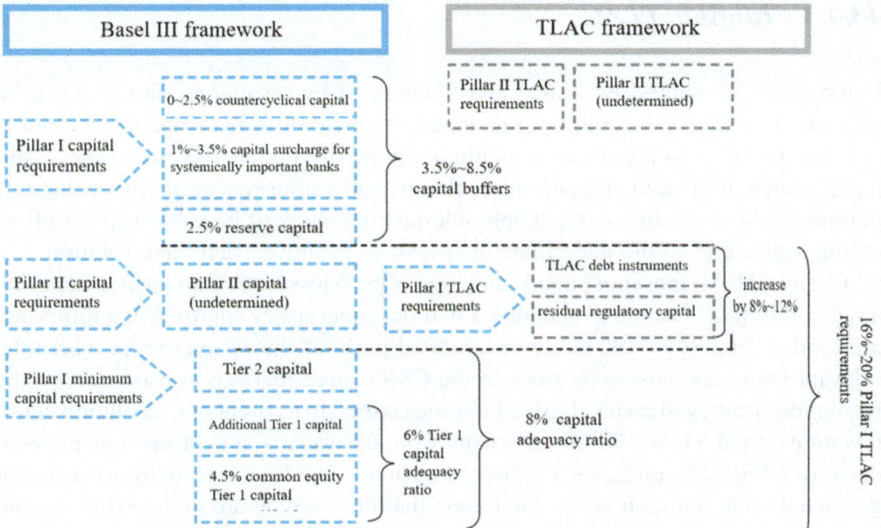

Fig. 43.1 Relationship between TLAC and Basel III regulatory capital

19.5% ~ 23.5% of risk-weighted assets on a consolidated basis, and the total loss-absorbing capacity of G-SIBs of Category 4 shall reach 21% ~ 25%. If regulators require a countercyclical buffer, the above ranges will be raised by 0–2.5%, according to national circumstances (see Fig. 43.1).

43.4.2 Internal TLAC Requirements

The objective of internal TLAC is to ensure the appropriate distribution of loss-absorbing capacity within material subgroups or subsidiaries of a G-SIB. The term sheet requires that material subgroups meet a minimum eligible internal TLAC requirement to enable them to first use internal loss-absorbing capital write-offs in the face of significant losses and recapitalization to avoid a systemic shock to G-SIBs.

Internal TLAC that comprises regulatory capital instruments must comply with the relevant provisions of Basel III. Each material subsidiary must maintain 75–90%internal TLAC—the range is determined by the actual data derived from the QIS in the external minimum TLAC. To avoid "double gearing," the relevant authority of a G-SIB should issue and maintain as much external TLAC as the sum of internal TLAC to cover material risks on its own balance sheet. However, external TLAC may usually be lower to ensure internal stability.

43.4.3 Eligible TLAC

External TLAC should be issued and maintained by resolution entities, must be unsecured and have a minimum remaining maturity of at least one year. Eligible external TLAC must absorb losses without giving rise to material risk of successful legal challenge or valid compensation claims; and authorities must ensure that this is transparent to creditors. TLAC-eligible instruments will be subject to set off or netting rights that would undermine their loss-absorbing capacity in resolution.

Eligible TLAC must not include and must absorb losses prior to: insured deposits; any liability that is callable on demand without supervisory approval; liabilities that are funded directly by the issuer or a related party of the issuer, except where the relevant home and host authorities in the CMG agree that it is consistent with the resolution strategy to count eligible liabilities issued to a parent of a resolution entity toward external TLAC; liabilities arising from derivatives or debt instruments with derivative-linked features, such as structured notes; liabilities arising from other than through a contract, such as tax liabilities; liabilities which are preferred to normal senior unsecured creditors under the relevant solvency law; any other liabilities that, under the laws governing the issuing entity, cannot be effectively written down or converted into equity by the relevant resolution authority.

The core features of TLAC-eligible instruments are that eligible TLAC must absorb losses prior to liabilities excluded from TLAC in insolvency or in resolution, which requires TLAC-eligible instruments to be subordinated to a list of excluded liabilities. The subordination requirement may be achieved in three means: contractual subordination, (i.e., eligible instruments must be contractually subordinated to excluded liabilities on the balance sheet of the resolution entity), statutory subordination, (namely, eligible instruments must be junior in the statutory creditor hierarchy to excluded liabilities on the balance sheet of the resolution entity) and structural subordination. Some large banking groups adopt the organizational structure of non-operating holding companies. There are basically no operating activities at the group level, but they mainly carry out specific businesses through their subsidiaries. These holding companies typically do not have any excluded liabilities on its balance sheet. And their senior liabilities will take precedence over the common liabilities of their operating subsidiaries to absorb losses, so such debt instruments do not need to be contractually or statutorily required and are inherently subordinated.

In addition, considering that when a G-SIB enters resolution, its equity capital is likely to have run out, and that loss-absorbing procedures for high-priority debt instruments, such as non-insured deposits, are very complex, to help ensure that a failed G-SIB has sufficient capital for absorbing losses in resolution, the FSB proposes that the sum of TLAC instruments in the form of debt liabilities and other TLAC-eligible instruments that are not eligible as regulatory capital, should be equal to or greater than 33% of their Pillar 1 TLAC or minimum TLAC requirements.

43.5 Assessment and Impact of Higher Loss-Absorbing Capacity

The quality of capital in the global banking system was poor at the onset of the crisis, and the base level and quality of capital were severely eroded as the crisis escalated. Deficiencies in the regulatory capital management of the existing financial regulatory system have threatened the stability of the financial system. After the crisis, regulators realized that the quality of capital was as important as the quantity. Therefore, in order to improve the quality of capital and enhance the loss-absorbing capacity of banks' capital instruments, the Basel Committee revised the definition of regulatory capital and put forward more stringent capital requirements, which are mainly reflected in the changes in capital components at all levels and the unification of regulatory capital adjustments.

43.5.1 The Basel III Capital Components

In general, Basel III has a stronger definition of Tier 1 capital, with Tier 2 capital simplified and Tier 3 capital removed. A comparison of the capital components under Basel III and Basel II is shown as follows in Table 43.4:

Table 43.4 A comparison of the capital components under Basel III and Basel II

Capital components under Basel II	Capital components under Basel III
Tier 1 capital	Tier 1 capital
Paid-in capital/common shares	Common shares
Stock surplus(share premium)	
Retained earnings	
Surplus reserve	Other going-concern capital
Minority interest	Not included in Tier 1 capital
Innovative capital instruments(a limit of 15% at maximum)	Not included in Tier 1 capital
Tier 2 capital	Tier 2 capital
General reserve	Simplified Tier 2 capital, with only one set of eligibility criteria and with other subcategories to be removed
Hybrid debt capital instruments	
Subordinated debt	
Tier 3 capital (market risk exposures)	Tier 3 capital (removed)

Source FSB website, dated November 2014

Change in Tier 1 Capital

After the definition of Tier 1 capital is revised, its predominant forms must be common shares and retained earnings. And common shares must meet a set of eligibility criteria before inclusion in Tier 1 capital. Minority interest will not receive recognition in Common Equity Tier 1 capital. Some innovative capital instruments, such as dividend increments, which will constantly erode the quality of Tier 1 capital, will be phased out. In addition to common shares, capital that meets certain criteria may be included in other going-concern capital.

Changes in Tier 2 Capital and Tier 3 Capital

Tier 2 capital will be simplified, and there exists only one set of eligibility criteria for Tier 2 capital, while other subcategories will be removed. The Basel Committee has set a minimum standard for Tier 2 capital and removed the limit that Tier 2 capital cannot exceed Tier 1 capital. The removal of Tier 3 capital will ensure the quality of capital to cover market risks.

43.5.2 Assessment of Loss-Absorbing Capacity of Capital Instruments

From the perspective of protecting the interests of depositors and enhancing the security of the banking system, the core function of bank capital is to absorb losses. The financial crisis has shown that overly complex capital structures are flawed in the following three ways. First, they have limited loss-absorbing capacity. Although commercial banks have high nominal capital adequacy ratios, a significant proportion is debt capital instruments that, because they can only take losses under certain circumstances and to a certain extent, are far from enough for the huge losses incurred during the crisis. Second, the ceiling of debt capital instruments included in the regulatory capital is constrained by the size of common stock, so when common stock is used to reverse the loss, the number of debt capital instruments included in the regulatory capital declined proportionally, causing a bigger fall in the capital adequacy ratio, limiting the banking credit supply ability and magnifying the negative impact on the real economy. Third, due to the differences in legal frameworks, regulatory provisions, accounting and tax policies, the transparency and comparability of regulatory capital instruments around the world have declined, which to some extent is not conducive to fair competition.

The Basel Committee mainly judges the loss-absorbing capacity of capital instruments from three aspects: first, whether the capital instruments help banks to preserve economic resources to meet the maturing debts during the economic recession; second, whether the capital instruments have the relevant mechanism to eliminate the investor's claim right to the bank; third, whether capital instruments can help to avoid the insolvency of bank balance sheets. Whether a capital instrument can absorb losses under the going-concern condition is an important basis for judging the quality of regulatory capital, so the Basel Committee requires banks to be more loss-absorbing.

First, banks are required to produce recovery and resolution plans; that is, how to rely on the financial institutions themselves to solve problems in the event of a crisis without resorting to taxpayer support. The current proposals are bail-in debt and contingent capital arrangements. Bail-in debt means that under certain conditions, the bonds issued by banks can be directly converted into equity (capital). Contingent capital means that a set of trigger conditions are assumed where contingent capital can be fully converted into common equity when the conditions arise. Contingent capital must meet all the eligibility requirements for Tier 2 capital.

Second, cross-border resolution arrangements. As for G-SIBs, the regulatory authorities of different countries should consult with each other and work out resolution plans in case crises break out in systemically important banks.

Third, peer reviews will be conducted to promote more information transparency of systemically important banks. Mainly led by a number of international organizations, mutual peer reviews of systemically important banks will be undertaken to play the role of peer supervision and promote financial stability. Peer reviews, which have been conducted by the UK's Financial Services Authority (FSA) and the International Monetary Fund, are mostly off-the-spot. The peer review information mainly comes from questionnaires, with the self-appraisals of regulatory authorities, and the inspections conducted by the internal and external agencies of the Basel Committee serving as auxiliary sources.

43.5.3 Consequences of Failing to Meet Capital Surcharge Requirements

If a G-SIB does not meet higher loss-absorbing requirements, it will be required to agree to a capital recovery plan to return to a compliant regulatory framework. It will be subject to dividend limits, as well as other arrangements and requirements imposed by the management, until it completes the plan and reverts to specified requirements. If a G-SIB is promoted from a lower tier to a higher one, the bank will be subject to a higher loss-absorbing requirement, thus requiring the bank to meet the new capital requirement within 12 months. After the grace period, if the bank fails to meet higher loss-absorbing requirements, it will be required to retain capital to expand its capital reserves.

43.6 Policy Recommendations

With economic globalization, the gradual deepening of financial integration and the continuous rise in China's comprehensive strength, China's banking industry has achieved rapid developments, with its constantly improving degree of internationalization, its significantly strengthened comprehensive strength and global service capability, its experiences in successfully dealing with the impact of the international financial crisis, and its greatly elevated ranking in the global banking industry. Based on the characteristics of systemically important financial institutions, the Financial Stability Board (FSB) develops and implements the assessment criteria, and assesses and classifies systemically important institutions globally on an annual basis. According to the reports released in each November of 2011, 2012, 2013 and 2014, the Bank of China was listed as a G-SIB for four consecutive years; Industrial and Commercial Bank of China was listed as a G-SIB in November 2013, and Agricultural Bank of China was also listed as a G-SIB in November 2014. With the improvement of domestic financial environment and the development of financial institutions, more and more financial institutions will become global systemically important financial institutions in the future. Therefore, the selection of these financial institutions is both an opportunity and a challenge for the development of domestic financial industry.

43.6.1 Assessment on Impact of Higher Loss-Absorbing Capacity on China's Banking Sector

On the one hand, the status of G-SIBs is an important symbol of large transnational banking groups. The involvement of international supervision will help promote the China's banking sector to consciously comply with the international standards.

On the other hand, being selected as G-SIBs also brings new challenges to China's banking sector. First, stricter regulatory standards. G-SIBs will face higher regulatory requirements in terms of capital surcharge, liquidity and so on. Although the international regulatory standards on additional liquidity and large risk exposure are currently under study, and the relevant domestic regulatory policies are still being formulated, it is expected that the timing of meeting the standards will precede the international transitional arrangement. Second, increase in the difficulty and cost of information disclosure. G-SIBs will face tougher cross-border regulatory requirements, including regular international joint regulatory meetings, measurement and evaluation of global systemic importance and other specific measurements. Third, stringent requirements for innovative capital instruments. For the poor capital quality and limited loss-absorbing capacity exposed in the crisis, the Basel Committee has imposed strict restrictions on the role of new capital instruments in meeting G-SIBs' capital surcharge requirements, and from the perspective of continuous loss-absorbing capacity, proposed that the capital surcharge requirements should be met with Common Equity Tier 1 capital and that regulatory authorities should consider using high trigger contingent capital to meet the domestic portion of capital surcharge requirements higher than international standards. At present, domestic banks have relatively limited channels to implement exogenous capital replenishment, and capital instruments innovation mechanism and supporting policies are still to be improved, which poses greater challenges to China's banking sector in adapting to international regulatory requirements.

43.6.2 Push Forward the Priorities of Implementing the Regulatory Reforms of G-SIBs

The first is for domestic regulators to adopt prudential regulatory measures suitable for the development of domestic financial institutions, improve laws and regulations and raise the regulatory requirements for domestic financial institutions in terms of capital management, information disclosure, liquidity management, crisis management, etc., coupled with the new standards of international regulatory requirements.

The second is to strengthen internal governance of financial institutions, and for their senior management and risk management committees to continuously evaluate and improve their governance framework, constantly optimize their assets and liabilities structure, and their operation models, gain deep insight into market environment, regulatory requirements, and risk profile, grasp their risk appetites and business strategies, strengthen their ability to cope with risks, form their own characteristics in the competition, and resist external risks through prudent operations, innovative development and diversified financing, while assuming the social responsibility corresponding to their status.

Thirdly, compared with similar international institutions, Chinese commercial banks are faced with the problems of lack of a diversified capital structure, simple business models and narrow and limited capital replenishment channels. From the perspective of prudential regulation, capital instruments with lower TLAC may lead to their frequent triggering and, if TLAC is set too high, the banks will have to bear higher costs. Therefore, in the long run, domestic banks must change their business growth model, broaden their financing channels, gradually establish a capital replenishment mechanism dominated by internal capital accumulation, and support the steady and sustainable growth of the real economy so as to continuously meet the new regulatory standards.

References

1. Federal Reserve Board. Notice of Proposed Rule Making. "Total Loss-Absorbing Capacity, Long-Term Debt, and Clean Holding Company Requirements for Systemically Important

U.S. Bank Holding Companies and Intermediate Holding Companies of Systemically Important Foreign Banking Organizations; Regulatory Capital Deduction for Investments in Certain Unsecured Debt of Systemically Important U.S. Bank Holding Companies [Z]. October 28, 2015.
2. Financial Stability Board. Adequacy of loss-absorbing capacity of global systemically important banks in resolution [R]. Financial Stability Board Consultative Document, November 10, 2014.
3. Kupiec, P. Is Dodd Frank Orderly Liquidation Authority Necessary to Fix Too-Big-to-Fail? [R]. AEI Economic Policy Working Paper No. 2015–09.
4. Federal Deposit Insurance Corporation and Bank of England. "Resolving Globally Active, Systemically Important, Financial Institutions [R]. December 10, 2014.
5. Calomiris, C. and R. Herring. How to design a contingent convertible debt requirement that helps solve our too-big-to-fail problem [J]. *Journal of Applied Corporate Finance*, 2013, vol. 25, No. 2, pp. 21-44

Chapter 44
On Financial Regulatory System Reforms from the Perspective of Financial Structure

Abnormal fluctuations in China's stock market in 2015 have drawn attention to the issue of financial supervision, and the flaws in the financial regulatory regime are considered as one of the important causes for the stock market volatility. After in-depth reflections, theorists and practitioners have called for accelerating the reform of the financial regulatory system, and the government decision-making departments have also included the reform of the financial regulatory system in the outline of the national "13th Five-Year Plan". However, they are divided about which model to refer to and how to promote the current reform of China's financial regulatory system. From the perspective of financial structure, China needs to learn from the development trend of global financial structure and financial supervision after the financial crisis and choose the financial regulatory model suitable for China according to the development stage and risk structure characteristics of its financial structure.

44.1 Financial Structure Determines the System and Structure of Financial Supervision

According to Goldsmith, financial structure refers to the relative size of financial instruments and financial institutions; a country's financial structure comprises the form, nature and relative size of various financial instruments and financial institutions, and constantly evolves over time. The evolution of financial structure will produce different financial risk structures, and risk control is the top task of financial supervision, which requires corresponding financial regulatory model to adapt to it. From the perspective of the laws of financial development in overseas markets, the financial regulatory model tailored to the adjustments of financial structure can usually effectively control financial risks and avoid financial crises. However, the

Shen Changzheng participated in the drafting and discussion of this article, which was published in *Contemporary Finance and Economics*, Issue 9, 2016.

S. Ba, *The New Cycle and New Finance in China*,
https://doi.org/10.1007/978-981-16-8209-4_44

regulatory model that does not adapt to the adjustments of financial structure is often inefficient, restricting financial development and innovation, or even triggering a financial crisis. After the onset of the financial crisis, the original financial regulatory system and structure are often faced with reform or even restructuring, so it can be said that financial structure determines the system and structure of financial supervision. For example, before the 1929 stock market crash in the USA, American securities market, with a history of more than 100 years, had played a huge role in financing military expenditures during the American civil war and later the construction of railroads and the development of manufacturing industry. However, the securities market was unregulated at that time, and the phenomena of market speculation and manipulation were rampant, with the development of the stock market accompanied by frequent stock market panic. From 1893 to 1929, there were seven stock market crashes in the United States, among which the 1929 stock market crash triggered the Great Depression of American economy. To save the American economy, the Roosevelt administration, which came to power in 1933, pushed forward the New Deal, including a series of reforms for financial cleanup. The most prominent were the promulgation of *Glass-Steagall Act* in 1933 and the *Securities Exchange Act* in 1934. The former separates businesses of investment banks and commercial banks while strengthening the financial regulatory status of the Federal Reserve Board, whereas the latter mainly regulates securities trading, and at the same time creates the Securities and Exchange Commission (SEC).

44.2 The Global Financial Structure Trend Has not Changed After the Outbreak of the Financial Crisis

From the perspective of corporate financing, financial structure can be divided into two types: bank-based and financial-market-based; from the perspective of the business of financial institutions, financial system can be divided into two types: separate operation and mixed operation. Before the 2008 global financial crisis, especially after the 1997 Asian financial crisis, the model of crony capitalism, which was bank-based and ignored the market allocation capacity of resources, was widely criticized, while the Anglo-Saxon financial model, with financial markets as the core and emphasizing the market allocation capacity of resources, has become a model or target model of reforming the financial system in many countries. At the same time, with the development of financial markets and financial globalization, traditional commercial banks face not only challenges posed by financial disintermediation, but also competitive pressures from mixed operations in financial institutions abroad. Many countries gradually relax restrictions on separate financial operations and gradually achieve mixed financial operations, so the trend of the global financial system before the financial crisis was toward mixed operations. After the outbreak of the financial crisis, some scholars expressed concern over mutual transmission and positive feedback of financial risks between the financial market and financial institutions during the subprime mortgage crisis and the European sovereign debt crisis, and asserted that the outbreak and continuation of the subprime mortgage crisis might become the turning point of the development of the market-based financial model. However, during the seven years after the onset of the financial crisis, the trend of the global financial system tilting in favour of the financial market and mixed financial operations has not changed, whether based on the analysis of financial regulatory policies or the observation of the changing trend of the financial structure itself.

44.2.1 Analyze the Changing Trend of the Global Financial Structure from the Perspective of Financial Regulatory Policies

Before the financial crisis, America and Britain were models of financial-market-based structures and mixed operations. Although the contagion of risk between financial markets and financial institutions played a role in triggering the subprime mortgage crisis, from the perspective of financial reform policies, Britain and America did not restrict the development of financial markets after the financial crisis. Instead, America and Britain took this kind of development trend seriously, and improved the safety of the financial system under the premise of continuing to ensure efficiency and competitiveness in the financial industry by enhancing systemic risk prevention and the risk separation between financial market and commercial banks (such as the Volcker Rule in the USA and ring-fencing rule proposed by the Vickers Report in UK), transforming high-risk financial market (the over-the-counter derivatives market requires concentrated liquidation) and so on.

Before the financial crisis, Germany implemented the universal or full-service banking model, which enabled banks to operate commercial banking, investment banking, insurance and other businesses and to occupy a dominant position in the national economy. After the financial crisis, in October 2012 the European Union announced the Liikanen Report, putting forward suggestions about the structural reform of the EU banking, and requiring that large commercial banks should put trading assets likely to affect the financial stability (including proprietary and market-making trading) into independent legal entity, and that if a bank's trading assets surpass 15–25% of its total assets, or the scale of its trading assets is more than 100 billion euros, it should be forcibly quarantined. The Liikanen Report calls on establishing an effective firewall between the two legal entities to ensure that deposit-taking banks are not exposed to the risk contagion of trading entities and that the low-cost deposit funds with implicit government subsidies are no longer used to support high-risk trading operations. Although the Liikanen Report does not make clear the specific structure of the firewall, the separation between legal entities of trading banks and those legal entities of other banking business including deposit business means that the trend of Germany carrying out mixed operations through universal banks may face challenges, and the financial holding model may be a more realistic choice.

From the perspective of Japan's financial development history and post-crisis financial reform measures, Japan will maintain the mixed operation model of financial holding group and further improve financial supervision to enhance the global competitiveness of Japan's financial market. After World War II, Japan was once famous as the most important developed country to imitate the United States' separate financial regulatory model. However, at the end of the twentieth century, Japan changed from following the United States to adopting mixed operation ahead of the United States. Japan shifted from separate operation to mixed operation mainly through two ways: one is targeting the holding companies as objectives of mutual infiltration of different financial businesses, and making laws to allow financial holding companies to use different establishing forms from general companies in order to reduce the inconvenience to their market access, taxation, and procedures and thus reduce the cost of their establishment; the other is restructuring the original financial regulatory system to provide organizational and institutional guarantees for strengthening the regulation over financial holding companies. During this financial crisis, although Japan's economy has declined to some extent, its financial system has been less impacted, with limited losses, and its risks are controllable. Therefore, from the perspective of Japan's financial regulatory reform policies, Japan has no tendency to carry out a significant reform in the current financial regulatory system. However, Japan hopes to make its financial market more open, transparent and efficient through the financial reforms focusing on enhancing the competitiveness of Japan's financial market and improving financial supervision, and to become one of the most globally important and appealing international financial hubs after the subprime mortgage crisis.

44.2.2 Observe the Global Financial Structure Changing Trend in Terms of Financial Structure Indicators

The securitization ratio[1] is an important indicator to measure the development degree of a country's securities market. During the financial crisis, due to rapid volatility of the global financial market, whether it is a financial-market-based country, as typified by the UK and the United States, or a bank-based country, as represented by Germany and Japan, or an emerging market country, as represented by China and South Korea, the securitization ratio dropped sharply from 2007 to 2008 (see Fig. 44.1). After the financial crisis, as the financial market gradually stabilized.

[1] The securitization ratio refers to the ratio of the total market value of various securities of a country to the country's GDP. In actual calculations, the total market value of securities is usually represented by the total market value of stocks + the total market value of bonds + the total market value of mutual funds, etc. For convenience, this article replaces the total market value of securities with the total market value of listed companies.

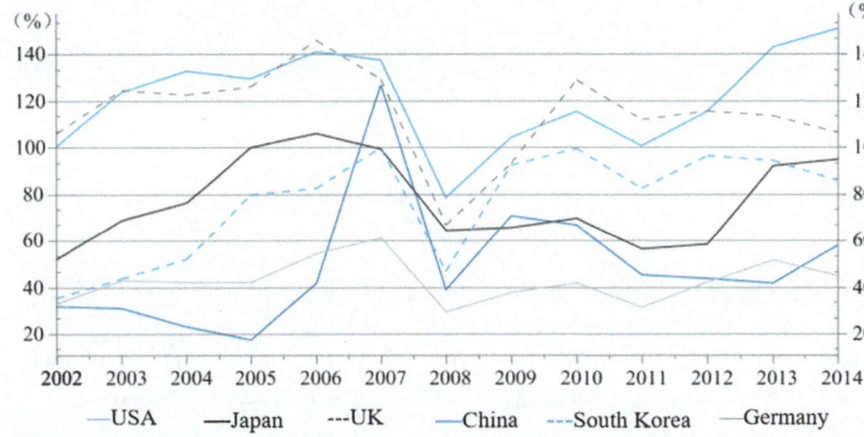

Fig. 44.1 Proportion of total market values of listed companies in the world's major countries to GDP from 2002 to 2014

The securitization ratio in the world's major countries has recovered steadily. Among them, the United States returned to the level before the financial crisis in 2014, and Japan, South Korea and the United Kingdom returned to levels close to that before the financial crisis. Although there is a certain gap in the securitization ratios between before and after the crisis in China and Germany, the tendency of the global financial system tilting in favor of financial markets has not changed on the whole.

In order to more comprehensively measure the relative importance of capital markets and bank intermediaries in the financial system before and after the financial crisis, the author creates the indicator "total market value of listed companies and domestic credit provided by the banking sector" to observe the development of the financial structure in major countries worldwide before and after the financial crisis (see Fig. 44.2). Like the securitization ratio indicator, during the financial crisis, both the total market value of listed companies in various countries and the domestic credit provided by the banking sector fell sharply, which shows that the role of the banking sector became more prominent during the crisis due to the failure of the financial market. After the financial crisis, as the financial market gradually stabilized, with the exception of China and South Korea, the ratio of the total market value of listed companies to the domestic credit provided by the banking sector in other countries has gradually picked up, indicating that whether it is a traditional financial-market-based country or a bank-based country, after the financial crisis, the tendency of the financial structure continuing to tilt in favor of the financial market remains unchanged; while in emerging market countries such as China and South Korea, after the financial crisis, economic stimulus policies are more dependent on the banking system, so the role of banking intermediaries in the financial system is actually being further strengthened.

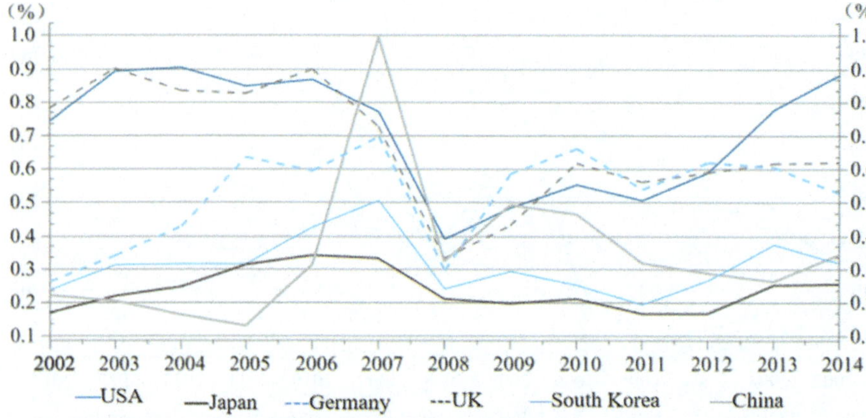

Fig. 44.2 Proportion of total market values of listed companies in the world's major countries to domestic credit provided by the banking sector from 2002 to 2014

44.2.3 On the Development Trend of the Global Financial Structure from the Change in American Financial Structure

Since the global financial crisis originated from the subprime mortgage crisis in the United States, and American financial market is the most developed in the world, and its financial system is also the object to be learned from and imitated by major countries in the world, the changing trend of the financial structure in the United States is bound to have an important impact on the change in the global financial structure. By observing the changes in the proportion of assets of all kinds of financial structures in the United States and in the direct financing structure of American enterprises, we find that the financial structure in the United States did not change dramatically before and after the financial crisis. The changes in the proportion of assets of various financial institutions in the United States reflect the history of the transformation of American financial structure. From 1970 to 2014, in terms of the changing trend of the proportion of the assets of the three major types of financial institutions, although during the financial crisis, the three major types of financial institutions had some fluctuations in asset structure (the proportion of the assets of both depository institutions and insurance institutions slightly rebounded, and the proportion of the assets of all investment institutions somewhat reduced), after the financial crisis, the proportions of assets in the three major types of financial institutions stayed very stable (Fig. 44.3).

The United States is a typical financial-market-based country. Direct financing instruments such as stocks, corporate bonds and asset-backed bonds are the main means of corporate financing. Observing the changes in the direct financing structure of American enterprises can help intuitively analyze the changes in American financial structure before and after the financial crisis (see Fig. 44.4). Before the

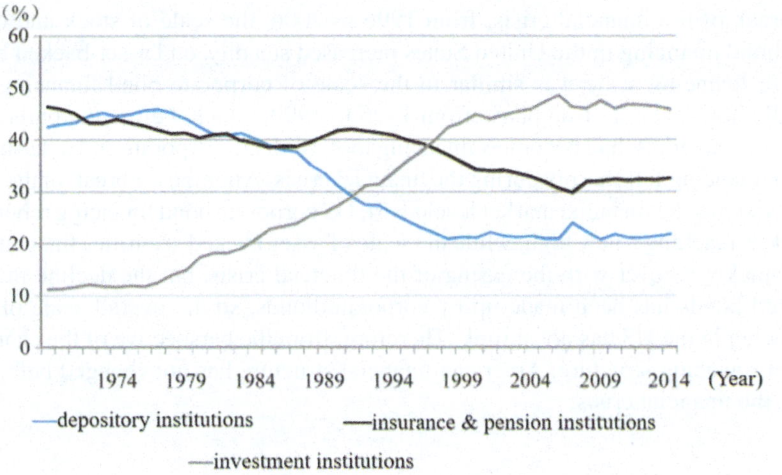

Fig. 44.3 Proportion of assets of the three types of financial institutions[2] in the United States from 1970 to 2014. *Source* http://www.federalreserve.gov/ the flow of funds accounts

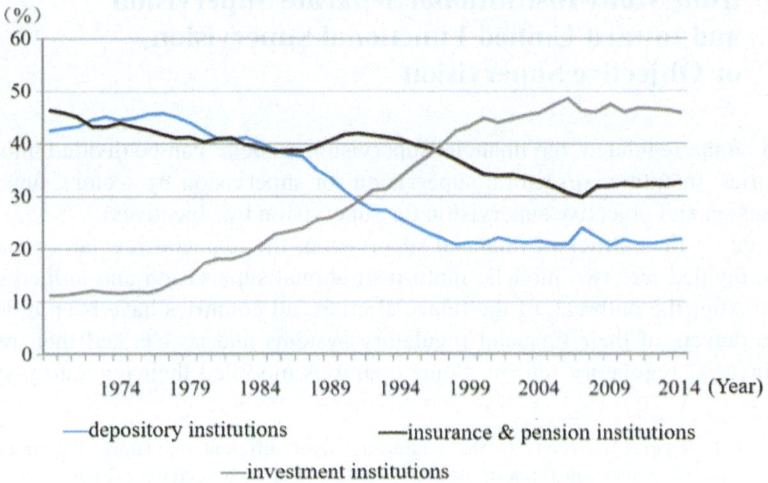

Fig. 44.4 Trends in direct financing structure of American enterprises from 1970 to 2014

[2] The three major types of financial institutions in this article refer to depository institutions, including commercial banks, savings/thrift institutions and credit unions; insurance and pension institutions, including property insurance companies, life insurance companies, private and public pension funds; and investment institutions, mainly including money market mutual funds, mutual funds, closed-end exchange-traded funds, government-sponsored enterprises (GSE), institutions or GSE-backed mortgage capital pools, issuers of asset-backed securities, finance companies, real estate investment trusts, security brokers, financing companies, holding companies and sponsored enterprises.

outbreak of the financial crisis, from 1996 to 2006, the scale of stock and corporate bond financing in the United States increased steadily, and asset-backed bonds, whose financing scale was similar to the scale of corporate bond financing, rose rapidly after their start-up phase from 1996 to 1999, which, before the outbreak of the financial crisis, had become a financing tool. Both US corporate and asset-backed bond financing fell sharply during the financial crisis. After the outbreak of the financial crisis, as the financial market leveled off, US corporate bond financing rebounded quickly, reaching a new high, while the scale of asset-backed securities financing did not quickly recover with the easing of the financial crisis, but the decline in asset-backed bonds has been made up by corporate bonds, so the overall scale of bond financing in the US has not shrunk. Therefore, from the perspective of the change in direct financing structure, American financial structure has not changed before and after the financial crisis.

44.3 After the Financial Crisis, Global Financial Supervision Has Shown a Trend Away from Multi-Institutional Separate Supervision and toward Unified Functional Supervision or Objective Supervision

Based on the regulated, the financial supervision models[3] can be divided into three categories: institutional/sectoral supervision (or supervision by sector), functional supervision and objective supervision (or supervision by objectives).

Based on the entities of financial supervision, the financial regulatory models[4] can be divided into two models: multi-institutional supervision and unified supervision. After the outbreak of the financial crisis, all countries have been reflecting on the defects of their financial regulatory systems and accelerated their respective financial regulatory reform. Some countries modified their regulatory system

[3] Institutional supervision refers to the establishment of different regulatory departments for different types of financial institutions, and the jurisdiction of each regulatory department is determined according to the nature of the regulated financial institutions. Functional supervision refers to designing the supervision model according to the basic functions of financial institutions, so businesses with similar or identical functions are subject to the same supervision, and different types of financial institutions engaged in the same financial business are supervised by the same regulator. Objective supervision refers to designing a regulatory structure according to the regulatory objectives, so that systematic regulation, prudential regulation and business regulation can achieve their respective objectives.

[4] Multi-institutional supervision model means that different financial institutions, financial products and financial industries are supervised by special regulatory agencies respectively. There is no subordination relationship between the regulatory agencies in terms of organizational structure, and they exercise their regulatory powers and fulfill their regulatory obligations within the scope authorized by the law; other regulatory agencies shall not overstep their regulatory powers. Unified supervision means that one or two regulators are responsible for the supervision of all financial institutions, which can be divided into single supervision model or twin-peak supervision model.

based on the original financial regulatory mechanism, while some countries reorganized their original financial regulatory framework. Although after reform, there exist diverse global financial regulatory models, from the perspective of financial regulatory reform policies, global financial supervision after the financial crisis showed a certain trend of convergence. This trend is that the financial supervision models of various countries gradually develop from institutional supervision to functional supervision and objective supervision, while the financial regulatory systems gradually change from multi-institutional supervision to unified supervision, with their central banks' financial regulatory responsibilities re-granted or expanded.

44.3.1 After the Financial Crisis, the US Financial Regulatory System Has Taken a Further Step toward Unified Functional Supervision

Before the financial crisis, the United States implemented the "two-tier multi-institutional" separate supervision model: multi-institutional supervision at the federal level, while two-tier supervision at the federal and state levels. American separate supervision model originated from the *Glass-Steagall Act* passed in 1933, which distinguishes between the financial market and financial institutions as specific sectors; banking, securities and insurance are independent of each other, and under the supervision of independent regulators. The *Financial Services Modernization Act* of 1999 repealed the barriers between commercial banking and investment banking and allowed for the creation of financial services holding companies or bank holding companies which could engage in any kind of financial activity, including entering into the areas of business of insurance companies and securities firms, which was a symbol of America's shift from separate operations to mixed operations. The Act also prescribes the principles of functional supervision without completely abolishing separate regulatory system laid down in the *Glass-Steagall Act* of 1933 or establishing regulatory structure reflecting functional regulation. Therefore, the financial regulatory system, established based on separate operation model, is difficult to adapt to the demands of the development of mixed financial operations, with problems of overlapping or duplicate regulation and the absence of regulation, eventually resulting in the outbreak of the subprime crisis due to neglect of regulation of systemic risk and the absence of regulation of OTC derivatives market.

After the outbreak of the financial crisis the United States began to reflect on the disadvantages of its financial regulatory system and actively implement reforms, with the top tasks to reform the financial regulatory framework, strengthen the regulatory models of attaching equal importance to institutional supervision and market regulation and modify the original financial regulatory framework from the following three aspects: establishing the Financial Stability Oversight Council (FSOC) to strengthen the cooperation among regulators, expanding the regulatory powers of the Federal Reserve and strengthening its central role in the financial regulatory system, merging the consumer financial protection functions previously performed by seven departments and establishing the independent Consumer Financial Protection Bureau within the Federal Reserve System. The Consumer Financial Protection Bureau, with the exclusive regulatory authority, have powers like mandatory takeover, and compulsory enforcement, to regulate various banks and non-bank financial institutions, requiring them to offer consumers transparent, fair and reasonable financial products, without misleading financial fraud, and strengthening the supervision over the financial intermediaries and the protection of investors. Although the financial regulatory reform did not fundamentally change the US multi-institutional supervision and institutional supervision models, the reform measures such as establishing the Financial Stability Oversight Council, expanding the scope of Fed's financial supervision and merging the consumer protection functions, has made the US financial regulatory system step further toward unified functional supervision model.

44.3.2 *After the Financial Crisis, the UK Established a Quasi-Twin-Peak Model Led by the Central Bank Based on Objective Supervision*

Before the financial crisis, the UK financial system was under the supervision and management of three parties: the UK Treasury was responsible for establishing the regulatory framework and financial legislation; the Financial Services Authority regulated the financial system as a whole; the Bank of England was in charge of monetary policies. The financial crisis exposed flaws in the UK's "tripartite systems". First, the UK Treasury, which designed and enacted the UK's financial regulatory framework and legislation, was not granted responsibility for dealing with crises. Second, the Bank of England lacked the tools necessary to maintain the stability of the financial system. Third, the Financial Services Authority lacked the ability to identify, judge and deal with systemic risks.

After the financial crisis, the UK drew lessons from the failure of financial supervision and actively promoted the financial regulatory reforms, shifting from the tripartite regulatory system by the Bank of England, the UK Treasury, and the Financial Services Authority (FSA) to a quasi-twin-peak regulatory system by the Bank of England and the UK Treasury, and establishing a new financial regulatory framework, with the Bank of England as the core, the Financial Policy Committee (FPC) leading, and the Prudential Regulation Authority (PRA) and the Financial Conduct Authority (FCA) assuming their respective responsibilities (see Fig. 44.5). The new regulatory system took effect on April 1, 2013. Its main contents are as follows. First, the Financial Policy Committee (FPC) is put under the court of Directors of the Bank of England, given powerful macroprudential management tools. The FPC has four main functions: (1) to identify and monitor systemic risks and maintain the stability of the UK financial system; (2) to publish a Financial Stability Report twice a year, identifying key threats to the stability of the UK financial system; (3) to direct the PRA

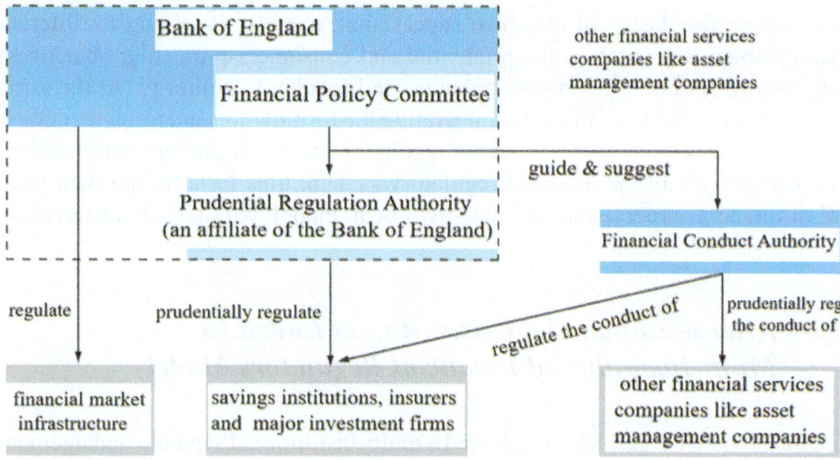

Fig. 44.5 Current UK financial regulatory framework

and the FCA to take corresponding measures on the regulated community to achieve the purpose of macroprudential management; (4) to make recommendations to the Bank of England, the UK Treasury, the PRA, the FCA or other regulators. Second, the PRA is incorporated within the Bank of England to strengthen the central bank's supervision function. The PRA is responsible for the examination and prudential supervision and regulation of the business of deposit-taking institutions (including banks, building societies and credit unions), insurers and specified investment firms, with the overall goal to promote the healthy and smooth operations of the regulated institutions, namely, to ensure that the businesses of regulated institutions do not produce or reduce their negative effects on the stability of the UK financial system. Third, the Financial Conduct Authority (FCA) is established to strengthen the protection of financial consumers and the supervision of the conduct of market entities. The FCA is an independent regulator, funded entirely by the firms it regulates, accountable to the UK Treasury and the Parliament, but guided and advised by the Bank of England in business. The FCA's primary responsibility is to formulate the codes of conduct and relevant regulations related to retail and wholesale markets pursuant to the Act and guide their conduct of market. The performance of FCA shall be consistent with its strategic and operational objectives. Among them, the strategic objective is to ensure the smooth and healthy operation of the financial market and other markets providing regulated financial services; and the operational objectives include the following three aspects: first, client protection, that is, securing an appropriate degree of protection for consumers; second, safeguarding the soundness of the financial system, that is, protecting and enhancing the stable development of the UK financial system; third, promoting competition, that is, promoting effective competition in the banking industry in the interests of consumers.

The reformed UK financial regulatory model is neither a single one, nor a multi-institutional one based on the concept of institutional or functional supervision, but more based on the theory of objective supervision, namely, according to different regulatory objectives (such as the prudential and consumers-protecting objectives) setting up corresponding regulatory agencies and regulatory authority. At the same time, the reformed Bank of England, integrating the formulation and implementation of monetary policy, and macroprudential regulation and microprudential regulation, plays a central role in the financial regulatory system, thus forming the twin-peak model of financial supervision, or quasi-twin-peak model, with UK characteristics.

44.3.3 After the Financial Crisis, Russia Ended Its Multi-Institutional Financial Regulatory Model

Before the financial crisis, Russia adopted a multi-institutional separate management mode, that is, the central bank was mainly responsible for the supervision and regulation of the credit market, the Financial Market Authority was mainly responsible for the supervision of the capital market, and the Ministry of Finance also assumed some financial supervision responsibilities. It was difficult to form a unified financial policy and effective financial supervision in the multi-institutional supervision model. Meanwhile, the central bank and the Ministry of Finance were independent of each other on the surface, but in fact, the central bank was mostly subject to the Ministry of Finance, which was likely to cause conflicts. In particular, when the global financial crisis broke out in 2008, due to the impact of global deleveraging and liquidity crunch, a large amount of funds were withdrawn from the Russian market, which severely impacted the Russian financial system and exposed the problems with Russian financial supervision. After the financial crisis, Russia actively promoted the reform in financial supervision and regulation. In July 2013, Russia promulgated *Amending the Russian Federal Act on Transferring the Functions of the Supervision and Regulation of Financial Market to the Central Bank of the Russian Federation (Bank of Russia)*, ending the multi-institutional financial management mode, with the Bank of Russia (the central bank) regulating the financial system.

After the reform, the Russian central bank will take over the Federal Financial Market Authority to regulate business activities of all financial institutions such as securities dealers, insurance companies, small financial organizations, exchange investments and pension funds. At the same time, the central bank will partly take over the Ministry of Finance and other government departments in formulating financial market regulatory standards, and participate in drafting related laws and regulations. The establishment of a unified mega-regulator of financial market in Russia is conducive to improving the stability and supervision efficiency of the operation of the financial market and eliminating the duplicate or overlapping functions and conflicting policies of various federal legal institutions. At the same time, the reform of the Russian financial regulatory system has established the authoritative position of the central bank of Russia in the financial market, which conforms to the trend of the international financial regulatory reform of strengthening the financial stability and financial supervision functions of the central bank. It not only helps improve the competitiveness of the financial system, but also can effectively prevent financial systemic risks.

In addition to the United States, the UK and Russia, before the financial crisis, Australia established the twin-peak model based on objective supervision as early as in 1998. In 2001, Japan established a unified financial regulatory system with the Financial Services Agency as the core, so although before the financial crisis the financial systems in both Australia and Japan were very complex, implementing financial mixed operation and having highly developed financial market, thanks to the appropriate financial regulatory systems, during the financial crisis the financial systems in the two countries ran into relatively limited impact, and after the financial crisis the economies in the two countries were the first to get rid of the financial crisis.

44.4 Referential Significance for the Reform of China's Financial Regulatory System

Banks are still the main players in China's financial structure, which play a major role in social financing. In 2015, RMB loans accounted for 73.1% of total social financing, while corporate bond financing and non-financial corporate equity financing accounted for only 24%. From the perspective of financial institutions' business, China still implements a separate operation system, with regulatory authorities imposing strict business restrictions on banks, securities, insurers and other institutions, and various types of financial institutions' businesses being separated and independent of each other. In recent years, with the development of financial market reform and financial innovation, the role and status of financial market in China's financial system are strengthening, the boundaries of financial institutions are blurring, financial markets and financial institutions are more closely related, and China's financial structure has showed the same trend of tilting in favor of the financial markets and financial mixed business. At present, China still adopts the multi-institutional institutional regulatory model, and the current financial regulatory system can no longer adapt to the development of financial structure. The problems of overlapping regulation and lack of regulation are very prominent, and so is the problem of insufficient systemic risk prevention and insufficient protection for financial consumers. At present, China urgently needs to accelerate China's financial regulatory reforms by learning from the experience of foreign countries in this regard.

In terms of specific schemes, there are many models to refer to, among which the UK financial regulatory model attracts more attention, in which the responsibilities of financial institutions are redefined and divided according to the principles of objective supervision. A complete financial regulatory system needs to achieve at least three objectives: macro-and-microprudential regulation and financial client protection. And after the financial crisis, the UK regulatory framework designates the Bank of England to undertake the macro-and-microprudential regulatory responsibilities and brings the consumer financial protection as well as the conduct of financial institutions under the supervision of the relatively independent Financial Conduct Authority, which in form is accountable to the Parliament via the Ministry of Finance, but accepts the guidance of the Bank of England in business. The Consumer Financial Protection Bureau was established in the United States, given the power to formulate and enforce consumer financial protection rules to prevent any harm to financial consumers for the sake of the stability of financial institutions. However, the Financial Stability Oversight Council (FSOC) has veto power over the rules made by the Consumer Financial Protection Bureau. Based on the experience of the UK and the US, it is proposed that a special Financial Policy Committee be set up within the People's Bank of China to take charge of macroprudential regulation, focusing on guarding against financial systemic risks. The Financial Prudential Supervision Committee and Financial Conduct Supervision Committee will be brought within the People's Bank of China; the former is mainly responsible for microprudential regulation of financial institutions to ensure their compliance with the requirements of sound operation, while the latter is mainly responsible for overseeing financial conducts to ensure their compliance. The Consumer Financial Protection Bureau will be set up outside of the People's Bank of China, focusing on formulating and implementing rules for consumer financial protection and checking and balancing the supervision of financial institutions in some measure.

At the same time, it is also necessary to strengthen the financial regulatory coordination and establish a sound communication and coordination mechanism among different financial regulators.

Compared with multi-institutional separate supervision, the communication and coordination between different regulatory agencies under the unified objective regulatory model are equally important. If the supervision coordination under the multi-institutional separate supervision model is mainly to prevent regulatory arbitrage and lack of regulation, while the supervision coordination under the unified objective supervision model emphasizes more on the sharing of regulatory information and the prevention of overlapping regulation, so as to reduce the burden of the regulated. The UK's *Financial Services Act* has devoted a lot to formulating rules about regulatory coordination mechanism, which has referential significance for the reform of China's financial regulatory system. Firstly, the coordination mechanism among the Financial Prudential Supervision Committee, the Financial Conduct Supervision Committee and the Consumer Financial Protection Bureau shall be established, and the statutory coordination responsibilities and corresponding working procedures shall be clarified. The second is to establish a coordination mechanism between the Financial Policy Committee (FPC) and the Financial Prudential Supervision Committee (FPSC), and a coordination mechanism between the Financial Conduct Supervision Committee (FCSC) and the Consumer Financial Protection Bureau (CFPB), with the emphasis on two-way communication about macroprudential policies; if necessary, the FPC has the power to give FPSC and FCSC binding directives and quasi-binding advice of obeying or explaining and retain veto power to policies by

CFPB with reference to the experience of the United States. Finally, it is necessary to establish a coordination mechanism between the People's Bank of China and the Financial Prudential Supervision Committee and the Financial Conduct Supervision Committee. The regulatory coordination between the People's Bank of China and the Financial Prudential Supervision Committee is mainly reflected in information sharing. The Financial Prudential Supervision Committee needs to provide the People's Bank with information on the risk status of financial institutions, so as to analyze the overall risks of the financial sector. The regulatory coordination with the Financial Conduct Supervision Committee is mainly reflected in the regulatory coordination of systemically important financial institutions and the financial market infrastructure.

References

1. Ba Shusong, Shen Changzheng. The Trend of International Financial Regulatory Reform and Policy Options of China's Financial Regulatory Reform[J]. *Southwest Finance*, 2013–08.
2. Ba Shusong. What does the Stock Market Volatility Have to Do with the Financial Regulatory System? [N]. *The First Finance and Economics*, 2015–09.
3. Wang Zhaoxing. Structural Reform: The Middle Way of Separate and Financial Mixed Operations [J] *China Finance*, 2014–23.
4. Research Group of Census and Statistics Department of Jinan Branch of People's Bank of China. Comparative Study on the Reform of International Financial Regulatory System and Its Enlightenment to China [J]. *Financial Development Review*, 2012–09.
5. Chen Yulu, Ma Yong. The Change in Financial Organization Form and the Options of Financial Regulatory System: A Global Perspective and Comparative Analysis [J]. *Monetary and Financial Review*, 2008–06.
6. Huang Zhiqiang. A New Framework for the UK Financial Regulatory Reform and Its Enlightenment [J]. *International Journal of Financial Studies*, 2012–05.
7. Wu Xiaoxiong. The Foundation of and Frontier Research on Financial Risk Management [J]. *Journal of Southwest Jiaotong University (Social Science edition)*, 2009–02.

Chapter 45
An Objective Assessment of the Current "Shadow Banking System" from the Perspective of Financial Structure Evolution

Recently, with bank wealth management products becoming a hot topic in China, shadow banking system has become a concept of common concern. In fact, the definition, connotation and significance of shadow banking system given by the international financial circle are closely linked with the economic and financial structures, different stages of financial development and financial regulatory environments of various economies.

45.1 Connotations and Features of Shadow Banking System

Paul Allen McCulley, managing director of the Pacific Investment Management Company (PIMCO), was the first to put forward the concept of shadow banking system in 2007. Currently, the international financial regulatory organizations have generally agreed upon the concept. According to "Shadow Banking: Scoping the Issues", a research report by the Financial Stability Board (FSB) in April 2011, shadow banking system refers to "the system of credit intermediation that involves entities and activities outside the regular banking system, and may pose systemic risks as well as regulatory arbitrage concerns". Shadow banking entities have the potential to pose systemic risks mainly from four factors: maturity mismatch, liquidity transformation, credit transformation and high-leverage ratio.

Although FSB has defined "shadow banking system" and described its features clearly, the structures of the shadow banking system are varied due to the variety of financial structures, different development stages of financial markets and financial regulatory environments of various countries. The shadow banking system of the United States mainly includes the credit intermediation systems, such as investment funds like money market funds, and investment banks, conducted through risk diversification and leverage enlargement centering on securitization, whereas the shadow

This article appeared in the China Economic Times, dated March 29, 2013.

S. Ba, *The New Cycle and New Finance in China*,
https://doi.org/10.1007/978-981-16-8209-4_45

banking system in Europe mainly includes investment funds like hedge funds, and securitization transactions. Few similar institutions like those holding a dominant position in the shadow banking system in developed European countries and the United States are found in China's present financial system.

People in the financial circle have made a multi-dimensional study of the shadow banking system from different perspectives to correspond to the present Chinese financial market, which generally includes four scopes: the narrowest scope, which only involves bank wealth management business and trust companies; the narrow scope, which involves bank wealth management business and such non-bank financial institutions as trust companies, finance companies, auto financing companies, financial leasing companies and consumer finance companies; the wide scope, which involves the narrow scope, interbank business and such off-balance sheet business as entrusted loans, as well as such non-bank financial institutions as financing guarantee companies, microcredit companies and pawnshops; the widest scope, which includes the wide scope and private lending. This article selects for discussion the narrow scope that draws the most attention and is currently the most prevalent, namely the non-bank financial institutions such as bank wealth management business and trust companies, the so-called shadow banking system in China.

45.2 Shadow Banking System in China is Different in Nature from Shadow Banking System in Europe and the United States

Based on the above-mentioned definition and feature descriptions, and in line with the performance of the shadow banking system in the international financial crisis, scoping the shadow banking system should mainly include the following three aspects. First, whether the shadow banking system is brought into the regular financial regulatory system. Before the financial crisis, the shadow banking system in the United States and Europe, such as the hedge fund, had not been monitored to the full, and propelled by such financial innovations as repurchase agreements (repos) and asset securitization, such institutions had constantly expanded their balance sheets to realize their low-cost and high-risk operations. Second, whether the shadow banking system is characterized by maturity mismatch and high-leverage operation, and thereby may cause high firm-specific risks. During the financial crisis, the shadow banking liabilities in the United States and Europe were focused on short-term wholesale funding, such as the interbank lending and commercial papers, but investments were made in protracted and poorly liquid assets such as assets-backed securities, thus bringing about a serious maturity mismatch. Before the crisis, the balance sheets of the major US investment banks had expanded drastically, even with the average leverage scoring a 40-fold increase or so and, during the crisis, the ferocious deleveraging effect also quickened the substantial slump in the asset prices. And third, whether the shadow banking system is interconnected and contagious, and thereby may make the advent of systemic risks possible. Before the crisis, the shadow banking system had correlated with the commercial banking system by means of business contacts and equity investment in Europe and the United States, spreading the crisis-incurred risks quickly from the shadow banking system to the traditional commercial banking system and thus bringing about systemic risks. According to the above-stated three aspects, although the driving force behind the emergence of the shadow banking system in China is basically aimed at the regulatory arbitrage and is also characterized by liquidity transformation and credit risks, and although some risk control links should be strengthened, the shadow banking system has been brought under the regular regulatory system on the whole and is not typically characterized by the high leverage and the maturity mismatch that may trigger systemic risks and, meanwhile, its size and risks have not yet produced any huge impact on systemic risks.

Firstly, the shadow banking system is still being financially monitored in China. At present, the bank wealth management products fall within the statistical requirements enforced now by regulatory authorities, the performance of the wealth management products issued by commercial banks should be submitted to regulatory authorities at regular intervals, and the particulars of the wealth management products should also be submitted to the central bank to bring into the scope of the aggregate social financing. The *Interim Measures on Management of Personal Wealth Management Services with Commercial Banks* promulgated in 2005 and the *Measures on Management of Sales of Wealth Management Products of Commercial Banks* implemented in 2012 are the regulatory frameworks for bank wealth management services. Regulatory authorities have also exercised rigorous management over trust companies; including access management and capital regulation (The *Measures on Management of Net Capital of Trust Companies* demands that the trust companies' ratio of net capital to risk capital should surpass 100%). Constrained by such rules and regulations as the *Measures on Management of Finance Companies of Enterprise Groups*, the *Provisional Measures on the Assessment of Indicators Monitoring Risks of Finance Companies of Enterprise Groups*, the *Measures for the Implementation of Administrative Approvals for Non-Bank Financial Institutions*, the *Measures on Management of Auto Financing Companies* and the *Pilot Measures on Management of Consumer Finance Companies*, regulatory authorities, with reference to the regulatory requirements over commercial banks, have set up a complete set of prudential regulatory systems over related non-banking financial institutions.

Secondly, the shadow banking system in China is not characterized by marked high leverage and mammoth maturity mismatch. Capital pool for regular bank wealth management products should be administered independently and relevant information should be disclosed fully to match every sum of funds with corresponding assets and to enable each earnings to cover the risks on the whole (According to Wind Information, the anticipated annual rate of return on banks' present 3-month wealth management products is around 4.6%, being lower than the short-term 6-month loan interest rate of 5.6%, and within the same 6-month period, the rates of return on national debts and central bank bills are about 2.7% and 2.9% respectively; according to ShengBo, an American-funded security trader, only less than 10% of the wealth management products yield an interest rate higher than 5%). Hence, risks of wealth management products should be basically close to those of similar investment products issued under publicly-offered funds within the regular regulatory system. In terms of the project assets for which the wealth management funds make way, the time limit for over 90% of the assets is generally within 5 years, and the degree of maturity mismatch is equivalent to that of traditional commercial banking. For trust companies, currently trust companies in China should neither operate on borrowings nor give loans to banks, thus having no conditions for leverage-based operation. Meanwhile, the trust funds are being operated in a seal-off way, demanding a consistency in investment duration and project duration. Therefore, high leverage and maturity mismatch are not the features of the trust funds.

Thirdly, the shadow banking system in China does not yet have the potential to pose systemic risks. First, in terms of size, the current overall size of trust companies in China is small. According to the data released by China Trustee Association, as of September 2012, the size of wealth management in banking financial institutions is RMB6.73 trillion, and 66 trust companies' total assets amount to RMB6.32 trillion, accounting for 5.2% of the total. By contrast, the asset size of finance companies, leasing companies, auto financing companies and consumer finance companies is smaller, with a total of no more than RMB3 trillion, and with good asset quality as well as adequate capital and provisions. Second, in terms of the use of funds, about 40% of the wealth management products are invested in bonds and money market instruments, 20% in deposits, 20% in project financing assets, and only 10% in equity assets and other assets, all with a good overall credit. Of the trust assets, 40% are invested in loans, with long-term equity investments, trading financial assets investments, saleable and hold-to-maturity investments, depository institutions and other assets accounting for 10% respectively. In terms of investment orientation, industrial and commercial enterprises and basic industries each account for 25%, and real estate and financial institutions account for 10% respectively, so the safety of capital utilization is guaranteed to some extent. At the same time, in order to control the excessive growth of real estate trust business, regulatory authorities also issued a series of regulations. Thirdly, in terms of risk contagion, given the possible risk contagion between trust companies and banks, regulatory authorities in early 2011 issued the *Notice on Further Regulating the Trust-Bank Wealth Management Cooperation Business*, clarifying the risk attribution of the cooperative business between banks and trust companies, and requiring commercial banks to strictly implement the provisions on transferring off-balance sheet assets of the cooperative business into the balance sheet to control the risk contagion between the banking system and trust companies. And the borrowing by other finance companies through commercial banks accounts for less than 1% of the total loan size of commercial banks, so the chances of large-scale risk contagion are slim.

In conclusion, based on different financial structures and related functional characteristics, the shadow banking system in China fundamentally differs from that in Europe and the United States (as shown in Table 45.1), with the obvious differences occurring in the regulatory status quo, size, degree of leverage, maturity mismatch conditions, and correlation, and the risk characteristics are also different in nature.

Table 45.1 A Comparison of the shadow banking system in China and in Europe and the United States

Items	China's shadow banking system	Shadow banking systems in Europe and the United States
Regulatory position	Basically within the regulatory system	Lack of effective oversight and regulation
Size	Around 13% of banks' total assets	Equivalent to the size of traditional commercial banks
Degree of leverage	There is basically no debt management	The leverage is about 40 times
Maturity mismatch conditions	Rely on retail financing, equivalent to the maturity mismatch of traditional commercial banks	Under the effect of repurchase agreements (repos) and asset securitization, rely on short-term wholesale financing and the maturity mismatch is serious
Correlation	Basically separated from the business risks of traditional commercial banks	Highly correlated with the risks of traditional commercial banks through equity investment and business contracts
Risk characteristics	Unclear business positioning and legal risk, and the moral risk behind rigid payment	Due to high correlation and contagion, it is easy to trigger systemic risk
Functions assumed	Provide direct financing and meet financing needs of the real economy	Being divorced from the real economy and focused on risk diversification and leverage enlargement to achieve the self-realization of the price bubble of financial instruments
Regulatory objectives	Improving financial structure and promoting the transformation of economic structure while forestalling systemic risks	Draw lessons from the financial crisis and guard against systemic risks

More importantly, unlike the shadow banking system in European and American financial markets, which copies the core functions of commercial banks and expands rapidly in order to avoid regulation, the shadow banking system in China, to a large extent, assumes the functions of providing direct financing and meeting the financing needs of the real economy.

45.3 The Role of China's Shadow Banking System in Improving Financing Structure and Promoting Economic Transformation

In the context of financial development stage and financial structure evolution, in China's current financial regulatory system, the so-called shadow banking system is more one of the manifestations in the process of the financial structure development and diversified financing.

The main driving force of China's shadow banking system at the present stage stems from the market choice when the financing demands of the real economy are limited by specific conditions. From a specific perspective, bank wealth management business in essence is a trial of interest rate liberalization, with the yield of wealth management products closer to a certain extent to the market price of risk-less capital, and on the whole being at the same level of the inter-bank offered rate (IBOR) (e.g., on January 6, 2013, the 7-day IBOR is 3.6%, and over the same-month period the annual yield of wealth management products is about 4.13%, well lower than the private financing interest rate at the same period; according to the data released by the Wenzhou Finance Office, the comprehensive interest rate of private financing in Wenzhou reached 26.2% during the same period). After the completion of interest rate liberalization, when banks can take deposits through independent pricing, wealth management products may gradually shrink and other forms of financial innovation may occur. Therefore, the current shadow banking system in China is more a specific manifestation in the process of financing diversification and interest rate liberalization against the background of financial structure change.

The significance of the shadow banking system in China in the current environment lies in correcting financial repression and improving the efficiency of the financial system. At present, 20% of wealth management products and 40% of trust products are invested in the real economy, which meets a large number of capital needs in the real economy and facilitates the transfer of social savings into effective social investments. The proportion of indirect financing in China's financial system is always too high, which not only makes the financial systemic risks accumulate in the banking sector, but also limits the efficiency of financial allocation of resources. The existence of the shadow banking system in China such as bank wealth management, trust and finance companies provides important investment instruments for residents as well as more financing channels for the enterprises, giving full play to commercial banks' professional investment management capability and guiding the social capital into reasonable fields for the capital to achieve a more market-based allocation in a more market-based chain of capital operation.

45.4 Phase Out the Shadow Banking System and Implement Differentiated Supervision from the Perspective of Preventing Systemic Risks

Reviewing the development course of China's financial sector since the reform and opening-up, the non-traditional financial innovations, which were distinguished by many different terms, like "extracorporeal circulation of capital" before the term "shadow banking system" was borrowed from abroad, are not recent occurrences and seem to be attributed more negative connotations with the emergence of the term. From the trend of the financial structure, the concept of "shadow banking system" should be phased out, and better be deemed as innovations of non-traditional financing markets and non-bank credit intermediaries, whose risk features and functions and efficiency should be classified and discussed and over which different regulatory policies should be implemented to maximize their role in improving financial structure as well as guarding against systemic risks.

Firstly, the shadow banking system is essentially a kind of financial innovation. In the context of the current financial structure liberalization and diversified social financing, the concept of the shadow banking system should not be simply copied, and these financial innovations should be regulated and guided more from the perspective of serving the real economy and promoting the sound development of non-traditional banking businesses. The shadow banking system is a special kind of financial innovation from a specific point of view, with the basic characteristics of financial innovations. At present, it may take the form of bank wealth management, and in a new market environment, may take another form of financial innovation. However, not all financial innovations outside the regular financial system and non-traditional banking businesses should be included in the category of the shadow banking system that may pose systemic risks. Financial innovations that will not cause systemic risks should be actively encouraged and pushed forward from the perspective of adjusting the social financing structure.

Secondly, the financial innovations of non-traditional banking businesses should be differentiated and subdivided, over which differentiated supervision should be implemented according to different risk characteristics. Although financial innovations have played a positive role in improving the allocation of financial resources and financial efficiency, it does not follow that we should leave them alone. Instead, we should also pay sufficient attention to the risks they may bring about, especially regional and systemic risks. All the non-traditional banking businesses should not be generalized, and they should be properly distinguished according to such factors as institutional entities and risk characteristics of financial innovations, and be implemented targeted differentiated supervision. First of all, the rationality and function of financial innovations should be objectively judged. For example, in China's financial structure with the banking system holding a dominant position, it is inevitable to choose banks as the carrier of financial innovation and financial liberalization. In the current process of financial liberalization and social financing diversification, the risks of the financial instruments serving as a trial run should be properly monitored while encouraging their healthy development. Second, different financial innovative instruments should be classified according to their characteristics, such factors as whether they have the function of credit creation, whether they have the characteristics of high leverage and mammoth maturity mismatch that may cause firm-specific risks, and whether they have the potential to pose systemic risks. Last, it is necessary to implement targeted differentiated supervision over them. Take wealth management products for example. Special importance should be attached to such hidden risks as internal risk accumulation in the banking system due to improper business positioning, the liquidity risk attributable to unclear classification of financial asset pool, the moral risk brought about by rigid payment, indistinct legal relationship, and unclear valuation links and such regulatory measures as information disclosure and investors' education should be strengthened.

Thirdly, the oversight and regulation of non-traditional banking businesses should also follow a certain counter-cyclical pattern to prevent the financing crunch which may be brought about by the campaign-style clean-up from wreaking havoc on the real economy. The financial innovations of China's non-traditional banking businesses are characterized by a significant regulatory counter-cyclical effect. When the direction of macro-control changes or the real economy is too tight, financial innovations other than traditional banking businesses tend to develop rapidly, for example, the rapid development of wealth management products in 2011 under the pressure of tighter monetary policies and the assessment of the average daily loan-to-deposit ratio. Therefore, the regulation and strengthened supervision beyond these non-traditional banking businesses should also follow a certain counter-cyclical pattern. In the process of financing diversification, particularly when there is capital shortage in the real economy and when the monetary policy transmission has not gone into effect, if the financing activities outside the non-traditional financial services are subject to campaign-style clean-up, and lending cannot expand accordingly due to various constraints, the financing crunch brought about by severe clean-up of these financing channels other than loans may significantly impact the real economy, and may pose new risks. Currently, there exist some wealth management products which may use asset pool in violation of relevant provisions, and the normal operations of the products in the short term depend on investors' confidence in the products and their continuous issuance. Mandatory restrictions imposed on the products may make the products operating normally suddenly face the risk of capital chain rupture. Therefore, for the potential risks posed by the irregularities, a feasible approach is mitigation in a "soft landing" manner by stepping up regulation of the asset pool.

The manufacturer's authorised representative in the EU is Springer Nature Customer Service Centre GmbH, Europaplatz 3, 69115 Heidelberg, Germany. If you have any concerns regarding our products, please contact ProductSafety@springernature.com

Printed and bound by CPI Group (UK) Ltd, Croydon, CR0 4YY
30/09/2026
02225330-0014